Criminal

Pearson
Education

We work with leading authors to develop the
strongest educational materials in law,
bringing cutting-edge thinking and best learning
practice to a global market.

Under a range of well-known imprints, including
Longman, we craft high quality print and
electronic publications which help readers
to understand and apply their content,
whether studying or at work.

To find out about the complete range of our
publishing please visit us on the World Wide Web at:
www.pearsoneduc.com

Criminal Law

Third Edition

Catherine Elliott
and Frances Quinn

An imprint of **Pearson Education**

Harlow, England · London · New York · Reading, Massachusetts · San Francisco
Toronto · Don Mills, Ontario · Sydney · Tokyo · Singapore · Hong Kong · Seoul
Taipei · Cape Town · Madrid · Mexico City · Amsterdam · Munich · Paris · Milan

Pearson Education Limited
Edinburgh Gate
Harlow
Essex CM20 2JE
England

and Associated Companies throughout the world

Visit us on the World Wide Web at:
www.pearsoneduc.com

_____

First published 1996
Second edition 1998
Third edition 2000

ISBN 0–582–42352–X   PPR

British Library Cataloguing-in-Publication Data

A catalogue record of this book is available from the British Library

Typeset by 35 in 10.5/12 pt Baskerville
Printed in Great Britain by Henry Ling Ltd.,
at the Dorset Press, Dorchester, Dorset

Contents

Preface

This book is designed to provide a clear explanation of criminal law. As well as setting out the law itself, we look at the principles behind it and discuss some of the issues and debates arising from it. The criminal law is frequently the subject of heated public debate, and we hope that the material here will allow you to enter into this debate and develop your own views as to how the law should progress.

One of our priorities in writing this book has been to explain the material clearly, so that it is easy to understand, without lowering the quality of the content. Too often, law is avoided as a difficult subject, when the real difficulty is the vocabulary and style of legal textbooks. For that reason, we have aimed to use 'plain English' as far as possible, and explain the more complex legal terminology where it arises. In addition, chapters are structured so that material is in a systematic order for the purposes of both learning and revision, and clear subheadings make specific points easy to locate.

Although we hope that many readers will use this book to satisfy a general interest in the law, we recognize that the majority will be those who have to sit an examination on the subject. Therefore, each chapter features typical examination questions, with detailed guidance on answering them, using the material in the book. This is obviously useful at revision time, but we recommend that when first reading the book, you take the opportunity offered by the questions sections to think through the material that you have just read and look at it from different angles. This will help you to both understand and remember it. You will also find a section at the end of the book which gives useful general advice on answering examination questions on criminal law.

This book is part of a series produced by the authors. The other books in the series are *The English Legal System*, *Contract Law* and *Tort Law*.

We have endeavoured to state the law as at 1 January 2000.

Acknowledgements

We are indebted to the following examination boards for permission to reproduce questions which have appeared in their examination papers.

The Associated Examining Board (*AEB*)

Edexcel (*London*)

Northern Examinations and Assessment Board (*NEAB*)

Oxford Cambridge and RSA Examinations (responsible for examinations previously conducted by OCSEB, UCLES and UODLE) (*Oxford*)

The examination boards are not responsible for the suggested answers to the questions. Full responsibility for these is accepted by the authors.

Companion Web Site

A COMPANION WEB SITE ACCOMPANIES *CRIMINAL LAW*, 3RD EDITION BY ELLIOTT AND QUINN

Visit the *Criminal Law* Companion Web Site at *http://www.booksites.net/ elliottquinn* to find valuable teaching and learning material including:

- Updates for this text
- Links to useful web sites
- Links to articles and resources
- A syllabus manager that will build and host a course web page
- Downloadable supplementary material

Table of cases

Table of statutes

Criminal liability is imposed on conduct felt to be against the general interests of society. Obviously if millions of people have to live together, their lives will be more pleasant and peaceful if some measures are taken to prevent people from killing or physically attacking others, walking into their houses and taking things away, or smashing up someone else's car. Most of us would agree that these types of behaviour are anti-social, and we want them to be controlled. But there is not always agreement on what kinds of conduct should be considered criminal. Smoking in public places is considered anti-social by many, along with eating smelly fast food on public transport, or wearing too much perfume or aftershave. Smoking can even harm others who passively inhale the smoke. Yet none of these constitute a crime, and very few people would wish them to be. On the other hand, there are types of behaviour which may affect nobody but the people involved – smoking cannabis and failing to wear a seat belt are examples – which are nevertheless criminal acts.

The types of conduct which are considered criminal vary from society to society. In our own system, for example, homosexuality was once a crime, while, until 1991, it was not a crime for a man to rape his wife. As general attitudes change over time, so do attitudes to the kinds of behaviour we label as criminal. And at any stage in a society, there will be some kinds of behaviour about which there is dispute – at the moment, for example, smoking cannabis is a crime and some people argue that it should not be, while abortion (within certain rules) is not a crime, and some believe it should be. It is important therefore to realize that there is no absolute definition of criminal behaviour – 'criminal' is no more than a label attached to different types of behaviour at different times in different societies.

How much crime is there?

Official statistics on crime are published annually in the UK, and provide two main kinds of information: the number of crimes committed, as a whole and by type of crime; and certain characteristics, such as age and sex, of convicted offenders. The figures tend to be reported in the media under headlines such as 'Violent crime up 10 per cent', or 'Burglaries reduced by 25 per cent'. However, since the 1960s, increasing doubt has been shed on this interpretation of official statistics. We now know that when official figures say that, for example, burglaries are down by 25 per cent, it does not necessarily mean that there have been 25 per cent fewer burglaries than the year before. This is because these statistics do not measure the crime that has taken place, but the crimes that have been officially recorded, and they may be two very different things. The reason for this is that before a crime can be recorded, a series of processes must occur: a person (the victim, the police, or someone else) must be aware that it has happened; if the police have not discovered it, someone must report it; and the police must accept that the law has been broken. Each stage has implications as to whether the incident appears in the official statistics or not.

Awareness of crime

While in the case of crimes such as burglary or theft it will be clear to the victim that a crime has been committed, many offences do not have an obvious victim. For example, tax evasion victimizes the whole community, because if dishonest people avoid paying their fair share, the rest of us have to pay more, but we are not likely to be aware of it happening. Unless the police, or other enforcement agencies, discover such crimes, nobody but the criminals will know that they have taken place.

Whether the police discover a crime depends heavily on where police officers are actually placed. Areas where police believe that crime is likely to occur are allocated higher policing levels, so crime is more likely to be discovered there, and presumably less likely to be discovered in areas not seen as likely to produce crime. Styles of policing may also play a part in this, as the sociologists Lea and Young point out in their book *What is to be Done About Law and Order?* In suburban and country areas, policing is more likely to be what Lea and Young describe as 'consensual', with officers seeing themselves as supporting the community in upholding the law. In cities, they see themselves as controlling the community, and preventing it from breaking the law. Lea and Young suggest that people are more likely to be stopped and searched in the second type of area, and thus more likely to be discovered if they do commit crime.

Reporting crime

Numerous studies have shown that the majority of crimes which take place are not reported to the police. Victimization surveys ask respondents whether they have been the victim of crime over the previous year, whether they have reported it, and whether it was recorded by the police. The best known is the Home Office British Crime Survey, which takes place every couple of years. It regularly reveals a huge number of crimes which have not been reported to the police. The 1998 survey uncovered almost 16.5 million crimes, four times the official figure of 4.6 million. In addition, rates of reporting varied widely between different types of offence. Clearly this throws doubt on the official picture of which types of crime are committed most frequently; not only are the numbers wrong, but also the proportions.

What influences the decision to report? According to the British Crime Survey, the main reasons for not reporting are that the victim saw the offence as trivial, and/or believed that the police would not be able to do anything about it. People also tend to report crimes where there is an obvious advantage to them in doing so – 98 per cent of car thefts are reported, presumably because that is necessary in order to make an insurance claim. Other factors which the survey has highlighted are that some crimes are regarded as personal matters, to be sorted out between the individuals; victims may want to protect the offender, particularly in crimes such as child abuse or domestic violence; and victims may be too embarrassed to report to police, especially where the offence is of a sexual nature.

Kinsey, Lea and Young in *Losing the Fight Against Crime* provide additional reasons why crime may go unreported, and therefore unrecorded in official statistics. They argue that inner-city communities have little faith in the police, and this expresses itself in two ways: residents believe the police are biased against them, and they also fear reprisals from criminals, against which the police will not be able to protect them. Another victimization study, the Merseyside Crime Survey, has shown that the higher the crime in an area, the lower the willingness to report.

However, even victimization studies probably underestimate the true amount of crime committed. They can only record certain types of crime – those with an obvious victim. They therefore do not include drugs offences, prostitution, tax, corporate or white-collar crime. Sexual offences are also likely to be underreported; although victims may be more likely to report these in the confidentiality of such surveys than they are to go to the police, many will still be too embarrassed to admit to them, especially as there may seem to be no practical point in doing so.

Victimization surveys also rely on victims' memories, and their ability to define an act as a crime. Minor criminal acts may be forgotten, not regarded as serious enough to record, or not seen as crime.

Recording crime

Even where a crime is reported to (or discovered by) the police, it will not necessarily end up being recorded by them. Sociologists have suggested that whether the police perceive an individual's behaviour as a crime may depend on how they label the offender. An American study by

Chambliss looked at two teenage groups, one working-class (known as the 'roughnecks') and one middle-class (the 'saints'). Despite the fact that the 'saints' committed more, and more serious, delinquent acts, they did not conform to the police image of young criminals, and were able to present their activities as harmless pranks. Whilst they were questioned, they were never charged, and therefore their activities were not recorded as crimes.

The proportions of different types of crime recorded in official statistics may be distorted by the fact that some acts potentially fall within the definitions of more than one crime – different types of assault, for example. Which crime is recorded may depend on police discretion. In addition, different forces may have different attitudes to types of crime, reflecting the priorities of their senior officers. If the result is that forces concentrate resources on some crimes at the expense of others, this may make it appear that certain crimes are rising by comparison with others, when in fact they may simply be more likely to be detected.

White-collar and corporate crime

White-collar crime is the name given to criminal activities performed by those in fairly high-status occupations, during the course of their work – fraud is the obvious example. Corporate crime is that committed by companies. Fraud also tends to be the area most associated with corporate crime, but sociologists such as Steven Box have argued that deaths and injuries caused by companies to employees or customers also often amount to crimes.

Neither white-collar nor corporate crimes are adequately reflected in official statistics, for two main reasons. First, there is low awareness of the fact that they have been committed. Many such offences victimize the community as a whole, or large groups of consumers. Where a company breaks safety legislation and an employee dies or is injured as a result, the situation is often viewed as accidental, so although the company may be sued for compensation, criminal charges are rarely brought. In cases of bribery and corruption, both parties may benefit, and both are liable to prosecution, so neither is likely to report the offence.

Secondly, these crimes are frequently investigated not by the police, but by regulatory authorities such as the Health and Safety Executive, who, as a matter of policy, rely on persuasion rather than prosecution; the number of companies who need 'persuading' to stop breaking the law is not recorded in the criminal statistics.

Statistics and conclusions

These weaknesses of official statistics make them unreliable not only as a picture of current crime rates, but for the purposes of comparison

– which is a problem, given the huge media attention paid to such comparisons, and its influence on policy. For example, rape figures have risen since the early 1980s, but the figures themselves cannot show whether this means more rapes are being committed, or more are being reported, perhaps as a result of more sensitive police treatment of victims. In addition, methods of gathering and/or categorizing statistics may vary over time. Consequently, it is difficult to draw reliable conclusions from either apparent increases or decreases in the crime rate. A rise, for example, in the official crime statistics is usually seen as bad news. Yet it may not reflect more crimes committed, but more crimes reported, which may in turn be a result of higher public confidence in the police, and/or less tolerance by victims and others of crimes such as marital rape, child abuse or domestic violence.

Similar problems can be seen in the picture painted by the official statistics of offenders. They suggest that most crime is committed by young, working-class males, and that black people are more heavily represented than might be expected from the proportion of the population that they make up. Many important theories of criminology have been based on these findings, with experts accepting that working-class men are the main offenders, and then setting out to explain what it was about these men that made them likely to commit crime.

However, in recent years, other criminologists, known as 'labelling theorists', have questioned these assumptions, asking whether it is in fact the case that some sections of society appear more frequently in the crime figures because they are more likely to be convicted, and not because they commit more crime. As we have seen, the offenders who appear in official statistics are likely to be a small proportion of actual offenders, given the amount of crime which is not reported or recorded. As Chambliss's research shows, some groups are more likely to appear in official statistics because of who they are, not what they have done. If young, working-class men are most likely to be stopped by police, or to have their activities defined as criminal, it is not surprising that this is reflected in the official statistics. Lea and Young have suggested that the police may also be more likely to stop and question black people, with the same result.

It has been argued that police behaviour to these two groups reflects the fact that they actually do commit more crime, but even if this is the case, it ignores the fact that in concentrating on some groups, the behaviour of others is not recorded, and so the balance presented in statistics is distorted. In other words, the targeted groups may commit more crime – but not as much more as statistics suggest.

The same applies to the absence of white-collar and corporate crime in official statistics. Box's study of these areas suggests that if the true picture of criminal activity were revealed, the assumption that crime is a working-class activity would soon be overturned.

A further problem with official statistics is that they aim to present a picture of crime as a whole, which may ignore the reality of crime statistics for some groups or geographical areas. For example, the Islington Crime Survey found that residents of that borough had much higher than average chances of being a victim of certain serious crimes. Women were 40 per cent more likely to suffer non-sexual assault and rates of sexual assault were 14 times the national average. This was even though women were five times more likely than men to avoid going out alone after dark, and six times more likely to avoid going out alone. Burglary in the borough was five times the national average. Clearly this suggests that the national average rates underestimate the effects of crime in such areas, and by implication, overestimate its effects in other districts.

Similarly, the British Crime Survey reveals that many apparently separate instances of crime may involve the same victims over and over again; this is known as repeat victimization. Regarding burglary, for example, the 1998 British Crime Survey found that 12.7 per cent of households suffering burglaries had done so twice in the year, and 6.8 per cent had been burgled three or more times. High-crime areas may not contain more victims, but a similar number to other places, who are victimized more often. Again, this is not reflected in the official statistics, but since these figures are used to help make decisions on policy and allocation of resources, such variations are important.

It seems clear that official statistics are not – and should not be regarded as – reliable, at least not in the role they are designed to perform. They may be very revealing about the assumptions used in defining crime, by police and others, but as a picture of how much crime is committed and by whom, they are seriously flawed.

1 Elements of a crime

A person cannot usually be found guilty of a criminal offence unless two elements are present: an *actus reus*, Latin for guilty act; and *mens rea*, Latin for guilty mind. Both these terms actually refer to more than just moral guilt, and each has a very specific meaning, which varies according to the crime, but the important thing to remember is that to be guilty of an offence, an accused must not only have behaved in a particular way, but must also usually have had a particular mental attitude to that behaviour. The exception to this rule is a small group of offences known as crimes of strict liability, which are discussed in the next chapter.

The definition of a particular crime, either in statute or under common law, will contain the required *actus reus* and *mens rea* for the offence. The prosecution has to prove both of these elements so that the magistrates or judge and jury are satisfied beyond all reasonable doubt of their existence. If this is not done, the person will be acquitted, as in English law all persons are presumed innocent until proven guilty – **Woolmington v DPP** (1935).

ACTUS REUS

An *actus reus* can consist of more than just an act; it comprises all the elements of the offence other than the state of mind of the defendant. Depending on the offence, this may include the circumstances in which it was committed, and/or the consequences of what was done. For example, the crime of rape requires unlawful sexual intercourse by a man with a person without their consent. The lack of consent is a surrounding circumstance which exists independently of the accused's act.

Similarly, the same act may be part of the *actus reus* of different crimes, depending on its consequences. Stabbing someone, for example, may form the *actus reus* of murder if the victim dies, or of causing grievous bodily harm (GBH) if the victim survives; the accused's behaviour is the same in both cases, but the consequences of it dictate whether the *actus reus* of murder or GBH has been committed.

7

▶ Conduct must be voluntary

If the accused is to be found guilty of a crime, his or her behaviour in committing the *actus reus* must have been voluntary. Behaviour will usually only be considered involuntary where the accused was not in control of his or her own body (when the defence of insanity or automatism may be available) or where there is extremely strong pressure from someone else, such as a threat that the accused will be killed if he or she does not commit a particular offence (when the defence of duress may be available).

In a much criticized decision of **R** *v* **Larsonneur** (1933), a Frenchwoman was arrested as an illegal immigrant by the authorities in Ireland, and brought back to the UK in custody where she was charged with being an alien illegally in the UK and convicted. This is not what most of us would describe as acting voluntarily, but it apparently fitted the courts' definition at the time. It is probably stricter than a decision would be today, but it is important to realize that the courts do define 'involuntary' quite narrowly at times.

▶ Types of *actus reus*

Crimes can be divided into four types, depending on the nature of their *actus reus*.

Action crimes

The *actus reus* here is simply an act, the consequences of that act being immaterial. For example, perjury is committed whenever someone makes a statement which they do not believe to be true, while on oath. Whether or not that statement makes a difference to the trial is not important to whether the offence of perjury has been committed.

State of affairs crimes

Here the *actus reus* consists of circumstances, and sometimes consequences, but no acts – they are 'being' rather than 'doing' offences. The offence committed in **R** *v* **Larsonneur** is an example of this, where the *actus reus* consisted of being a foreigner who had not been given permission to come to Britain and was found in the country.

Result crimes

The *actus reus* of these is distinguished by the fact that the accused's behaviour must produce a particular result – the most obvious being murder, where the accused's act must cause the death of a human being.

Result crimes raise the issue of causation: the result must be proved to have been caused by the defendant's act. If the result is caused by an intervening act or event, which was completely unconnected with the defendant's act and which could not have been foreseen, the defendant will not be liable. Where the result is caused by a combination of the defendant's act and the intervening act, and the defendant's act remains a substantial cause, then he or she will still be liable (see p. 41).

Omissions

Criminal liability is rarely imposed for true omissions at common law, though there are situations where a non-lawyer would consider that there had been an omission but in law it will be treated as an act and liability will be imposed. There are also situations where the accused has a duty to act, and in these cases there may be liability for a true omission.

Act or omission?

It must first be decided whether in law you are dealing with an act or an omission. There are three situations where this question arises: continuing acts, supervening faults, and euthanasia.

Continuing acts The concept of a continuing act was used in **Fagan** *v* **Metropolitan Police Commissioner** (1969) to allow what seemed to be an omission to be treated as an act. The defendant was told by a police officer to park his car close to the kerb; he obeyed the order, but in doing so he accidentally drove his car on to the constable's foot. The constable shouted, 'Get off, you are on my foot.' The defendant replied, 'Fuck you, you can wait', and turned off the ignition. Convicted of assaulting the constable in the execution of his duty, the defendant appealed on the grounds that at the time he committed the act of driving on to the officer's foot, he lacked *mens rea*, and though he had *mens rea* when he refused to remove the car, this was an omission, and the *actus reus* required an act. The appeal was dismissed, on the basis that driving on to the officer's foot and staying there was one single continuous act, rather than an act followed by an omission. So long as the defendant had the *mens rea* at some point during that continuing act, he was liable.

The same principle was held to apply in **Kaitamaki** (1985). The accused was charged with rape, and his defence was that at the time when he penetrated the woman, he had thought she was consenting. However, he did not withdraw when he realized that she was not consenting. The court held that the *actus reus* of rape was a continuing act, and so when Kaitamaki realized that his victim did not consent (and therefore formed the necessary *mens rea*) the *actus reus* was still in progress.

Supervening fault A person who is aware that he or she has done something which has endangered another's life or property, and does nothing to prevent the relevant harm occurring, may be criminally liable, with the original act being treated as the *actus reus* of the crime. The significance of this principle is that it can impose liability on defendants who do not have *mens rea* when they commit the original act, but do have it at the point when they fail to act to prevent the harm they have caused.

This was the case in **R** *v* **Miller** (1983). The defendant was squatting in a building. He lay on a mattress, lit a cigarette and fell asleep. Some time later, he woke up to find the mattress on fire. Making no attempt to put the fire out, he simply moved into the next room and went back to sleep. The house caught fire leading to £800 worth of damage. Miller was convicted of arson. As the fire was his fault, the court was prepared to treat the *actus reus* of the offence as being his original act of dropping the cigarette.

Euthanasia Euthanasia is the name given to the practice of helping severely ill people to die, either at their request, or by taking the decision that life support should be withdrawn when the person is no longer capable of making that decision. In some countries euthanasia is legal but, in this country, intentionally causing someone's death can constitute murder, even if carried out for the most compassionate reasons. However, in the light of the case of **Airedale National Health Service Trust** *v* **Bland** (1993), liability will only be imposed in such cases for a positive act, and that the courts will sometimes say there was a mere omission when strictly speaking there would appear to have been an act, in order to avoid imposing criminal liability. The case concerned Anthony Bland, who had been seriously injured in the Hillsborough football stadium disaster when only seventeen. As a result he suffered irreversible brain damage, leaving him in a persistent vegetative state, with no hope of recovery or improvement, though he was not actually brain-dead. His family and the health trust responsible for his medical treatment wanted to turn off his life support machine, but in order to ensure that this did not make them liable for murder, they went to the High Court to seek a declaration that if they did this they would not be committing any criminal offence or civil wrong.

The declaration was granted by the High Court, and upheld by the House of Lords. Since the House was acting in its civil capacity, strictly speaking the case will not be binding on the criminal courts, but it will be highly persuasive. Part of the decision stated that turning off the life support system should be viewed as an omission, rather than an act. Lord Goff said:

> I agree that the doctor's conduct in discontinuing life support can properly be categorized as an omission. It is true that it may be difficult to describe what the doctor actually does as an omission, for example where he takes some positive step to bring the life support to an end. But discontinuation of life support is, for present

purposes, no different from not initiating life support in the first place. In each case, the doctor is simply allowing his patient to die in the sense that he is desisting from taking a step which might, in certain circumstances, prevent his patient from dying as a result of his pre-existing condition: and as a matter of general principle an omission such as this will not be unlawful unless it constitutes a breach of duty to the patient.

In this case, it was pointed out that there was no breach of duty, because it was no longer in Anthony Bland's interests to continue treatment as there was no hope of recovery.

Offences capable of being committed by omission

Where the conduct in question is genuinely an omission, and not one of the categories just discussed, the next question is whether the particular offence can, in law, be committed by omission. The rules here are contained in both statute and common law with regard to the particular offences – for example murder and manslaughter can be committed by omission, but assault cannot (**Fagan** *v* **Metropolitan Police Commissioner**, above).

An example of the offence of murder being committed by an omission is **R** *v* **Gibbins and Proctor** (1918). In that case, a man and a woman were living together with the man's daughter. They failed to give the child food and she died. The judge directed that they were guilty of murder if they withheld food with intent to cause her grievous bodily harm, as a result of which she died. Their conviction was upheld by the Court of Appeal.

A duty to act

Where the offence is capable in law of being committed by an omission, it can only be committed by a person who was under a duty to act (in other words, a duty not to commit that omission). This is because English law places no general duty on people to help each other out, or save each other from harm; such a duty will only be imposed where there is a relationship between two people, and the closer the relationship the more likely it is that they will owe a duty to act, and be liable if they fail to do so.

An obvious example of a relationship giving rise to a duty to act is that of parents to their children, but a duty to act can also be imposed where there is no blood relationship. In **Gibbins and Proctor** (above), the House of Lords held that by living with a man and receiving money from him for food a woman assumed a duty towards the man's child.

A contract may give rise to a duty to people who are not party to the contract, but are likely to be injured by failure to perform it. In **R** *v* **Pittwood** (1902) a gatekeeper of a railway crossing opened the gate to let a car through, and then forgot to shut it when he went off to lunch. As a result, a haycart crossed the line while a train was approaching, and was hit, causing the driver's death. The gatekeeper was convicted of manslaughter.

A duty to act may also be imposed where someone voluntarily accepts responsibility for another. In **R** *v* **Stone and Dobinson** (1977), Stone's sister, Fanny, lived with him and his girlfriend, Dobinson. Fanny was mentally ill, and became very anxious about putting on weight. She stopped eating properly and became bed bound. Realizing that she was ill, the defendants had made halfhearted and unsuccessful attempts to get medical help and after several weeks she died. The couple's efforts were found to have been inadequate. The Court of Appeal said that they had accepted responsibility for Fanny as her carers, and that once she became bed bound the appellants were, in the circumstances, obliged either to summon help or else to care for her themselves. As they had done neither they were both found to be liable for manslaughter.

It will depend on the facts of each case whether the court is prepared to conclude that the relationship is sufficiently close to justify criminal liability for a failure to act to protect a victim. This approach has been heavily criticized by some academics, who argue that the moral basis of the law is undermined by a situation which allows people to ignore a drowning child whom they could have easily saved, and incur no criminal liability so long as they are strangers. In some countries, legislation has created special offences which impose liability on those who fail to take steps which could be taken without any personal risk to themselves in order to save another from death or serious personal injury. The offence created is not necessarily a homicide offence, but it is an acknowledgement by the criminal law that the individual should have taken action in these circumstances. The photographers involved in the death of Princess Diana may be prosecuted for such an offence in France.

Termination of the duty

The duty to act will terminate when the special relationship ends, so a parent, for example, probably stops having a duty to act once the child is grown up.

● ● ● ● ● ● ● ● ● ● ● ●

MENS REA

Mens rea is the latin for 'guilty mind' and traditionally refers, to the state of mind of the person committing the crime. The required *mens rea* varies depending on the offence, but there are four main states of mind which separately or together can constitute the necessary *mens rea* of a criminal offence: intention, Cunningham recklessness, Caldwell recklessness, and negligence.

When discussing *mens rea*, we often refer to the difference between subjective and objective tests. Put simply, a subjective test involves looking at what the actual defendant was thinking (or in practice, what the magistrates or jury believe the defendant was thinking), whereas an objective test considers what a reasonable person would have thought in the defendant's position.

▶ Intention

Intention is a subjective concept: a court is concerned purely with what the particular defendant was intending at the time of the offence, and not what a reasonable person would have intended in the same circumstances.

To help comprehension of the legal meaning of intention, the concept can be divided into two: direct intention and oblique intention. Where the consequence of an intention is actually desired, it is called direct intent – where, for example, Ann shoots at Ben because Ann wants to kill Ben. However a jury is also entitled to find intention where a defendant did not desire a result, but it is a virtually certain consequence of the act, and the accused realizes this and goes ahead anyway. This is called oblique intent. An example might be where Ann throws a rock at Ben through a closed window, hoping to hit Ben on the head with it. Ann may not actively want the window to smash, but knows that it will happen. Therefore, when Ann throws the rock Ann intends to break the window as well as to hit Ben. It should be noted that Lord Steyn suggested obiter, in the House of Lords judgment of **R** *v* **Woollin**, that 'intention' did not necessarily have precisely the same meaning in every context in the criminal law. He suggested that for some offences nothing less than purpose (direct intention) would be sufficient. He gave a possible example as the case of **Steane** which concerned the offence of assisting the enemy with intent to do so. Steane had given a broadcast for the Nazis in order to save his family from being sent to concentration camps. The accused did not desire to help the Nazis and was found to be not guilty of the offence.

The developments in the law on intention have come about as a result of murder cases, and so we discuss intention more fully in Chapter 3.

▶ Recklessness

In everyday language, recklessness means taking an unjustified risk. However, its legal definition is not quite the same as its ordinary English meaning and careful direction as to its meaning in law has to be given to the jury. Two different types of recklessness exist which are named after the cases in which they were defined: **R** *v* **Cunningham** (1957) and **MPC** *v* **Caldwell** (1982).

Cunningham recklessness

In the past **R** *v* **Cunningham** was the leading authority on recklessness. The defendant in the case broke a gas meter to steal the money in it, and the gas seeped out into the house next door. Cunningham's prospective mother-in-law was sleeping there, and became so ill that her life was endangered; consequently, Cunningham was charged under s. 23 of the Offences Against the Person Act 1861 with 'maliciously administering a noxious thing so as to endanger life'.

The Court of Appeal said that 'maliciously' meant intentionally or recklessly. They defined recklessness as foreseeing that the kind of harm that in fact occurred might occur, and going ahead anyway. This is called a subjective test: the accused must actually have had the required foresight. Cunningham would therefore have been reckless if he realized there was a risk of the gas escaping and endangering someone, and went ahead anyway. His conviction was in fact quashed because of a misdirection at the trial.

Caldwell recklessness

The case of **MPC** *v* **Caldwell** created a new and much wider test for recklessness. Caldwell was an ex-employee of a hotel and nursed a grudge against its owner. He started a fire at the hotel, which caused some damage and was charged with arson. This offence is defined in the Criminal Damage Act 1971 as requiring either recklessness or intention.

On the facts, there was no intention and, on the issue of recklessness, Lord Diplock stated that the definition of recklessness in **Cunningham** was too narrow for the Criminal Damage Act 1971. For that Act, he said, recklessness should not only include the **Cunningham** meaning, but also go further. He said that a person is reckless as to whether any property would be destroyed or damaged if:

(1) he does an act which in fact creates an obvious risk that property would be destroyed or damaged and
(2) when he does the act he either has not given any thought to the possibility of there being any such risk or has recognized that there was some risk involved and has nonetheless gone on to do it.

Thus there are actually two potential ways that **Caldwell** recklessness can be proved. The first way is very similar to the old **Cunningham** test: 'he does an act which in fact creates . . . a risk . . . and . . . has recognized that there was some risk'. The second way is the important extension to the meaning of recklessness: 'he does an act which in fact creates . . . an obvious risk . . . and . . . he has not given any thought to the possibility of there being any such risk'.

The first limb of this definition is essentially a subjective test, because it requires the defendant actually to see the risk – we will call this limb the 'advertent' limb as the defendant adverts to the risk; he or she sees the risk.

The second limb is more difficult to categorize. It has often been claimed to be an objective test, because the defendant does not actually have to see the risk, so long as the risk was so obvious that a reasonable person would have seen it. For this reason, **Caldwell** recklessness as a whole is often described as an objective standard, because although its first limb is subjective, it is much easier for the prosecution to prove the second limb – it is more difficult to prove what was actually going through defendants' minds at any particular time than it is to prove what reasonable people would consider should have been going through their minds. However, the label 'objective' was criticized by the House of Lords in **R** *v* **Reid** (1990), on the basis that even for the second limb, the actual state of mind of the particular defendant is still relevant, since the defendant is required to have given no thought to the risk. We will therefore call this the 'inadvertent' limb, because essentially it means that the defendant failed to advert to the risk; he or she failed to think about the risk.

In **R** *v* **Lawrence** (1982), decided immediately after **Caldwell**, the House of Lords looked at the meaning of recklessness in the context of the old offence of reckless driving, and held that the **Caldwell** test of reckless-ness applied to this offence. They reformulated the test slightly in their judgment, so that the phrase 'obvious risk' became 'obvious and serious risk'. The test also had to be adapted to take into account the fact that the type of risk would inevitably be different for this different offence. There-fore instead of talking about a risk that 'property would be destroyed or damaged', they spoke of a risk of 'injury to the person or of substantial damage to property'.

The **Caldwell** test has been further adapted and analysed by the more recent House of Lords case of **R** *v* **Reid** (1990). Reid had been driving his car along a busy road near Hyde Park in London. He tried to overtake a car on the inside lane, but the inside lane narrowed to accommodate a taxi-drivers' hut. Reid's car hit the hut, and spun off into the oncoming traffic. Reid's passenger was killed and he was charged with the old offence of causing death by reckless driving. The jury were directed in accordance with the **Caldwell**/**Lawrence** test, and he was convicted. An appeal against this conviction eventually reached the House of Lords; it was rejected, but the House made several helpful points in relation to the **Caldwell** test. They made it clear that while Lord Diplock had given a model direction in **Caldwell** (as amended by **Lawrence**) it was no longer necessary to use his exact words, for it could be adapted to fit the particu-lar offence. Courts were free to move away from his words altogether if it would assist the jury to understand the meaning of the test.

Following Lord Goff's comments in **Reid**, it appears that when Lord Diplock spoke of the risk being 'obvious', the risk only needed to be obvious in relation to the inadvertent limb, and it need not be proved in relation to the advertent limb. The logic for this conclusion is that if the defendant actually personally saw the risk then it does not really matter whether a reasonable person would have seen it: the defendant is at fault for seeing the risk and going ahead anyway. On the other hand, both limbs of the test require that the risk must be serious.

Taking into account these points of clarification, Lord Diplock's model direction could be redrafted as follows:

> A person will be reckless if (1) he or she does an act which in fact creates a serious risk that property would be destroyed or damaged and (2) either (a) when he or she does the act he or she has not given any thought to the possibility of there being any such risk, and the risk was in fact obvious; or (b) has recognized that there was some risk of that kind involved and has nonetheless gone on to do it.

To whom must the risk be obvious?

In the light of Lord Goff's speech in **Reid**, we have seen that the issue of the risk being obvious is only relevant to the inadvertent limb of the test. The case of **Elliott** *v* **C (a minor)** (1983) made it clear that where it had to be proved that the risk was obvious, it only had to be shown that the risk was obvious to a reasonable person, not to the actual defendant. The facts of the case show that this rule can operate extremely harshly, punishing defendants who might not be capable of realizing the risk, no matter how hard they thought about it. The defendant was a fourteen-year-old girl, who was in a remedial class at school. Playing with matches and white spirit, she set fire to a neighbour's shed, which was destroyed. The magistrates found that she gave no thought to the risk of damage, but even if she had, she would not have been capable of appreciating it. Consequently she was acquitted of recklessly destroying the shed. The Divisional Court allowed an appeal by the prosecution, on the grounds that the **Caldwell** test was purely objective, and the fact that the girl was not capable of appreciating the risk was irrelevant to the issue of recklessness. When the court in **Caldwell** had talked about an obvious risk, it had meant obvious to a hypothetical reasonable person, and not obvious to the particular defendant if he or she had thought about it.

An attempt was made to moderate the harshness of the inadvertent test of recklessness in **R** *v* **R** (1991), a case in which marital rape was first recognized as a crime. Counsel for the accused unsuccessfully argued that in deciding what was obvious to the reasonable person, that reasonable person should be assumed to have the permanent, relevant characteristics of the accused. This method is used by the courts to moderate the objective test for the partial defence of provocation (see p. 54). The Court of Appeal held that there was no reason for bringing such an approach into the **Caldwell** test.

However, in **R** *v* **Reid** (1990) the harsh approach to this issue taken in these two cases was softened slightly. The House of Lords recognized that sometimes the issue of capacity could be relevant, but their examples were limited to situations where there was a sudden loss of capacity, such as a heart attack while driving. More recently in **R v Coles** (1994), a case involving arson committed by a youth of an allegedly low mental capacity, the Court of Appeal followed **Elliott** strictly. It stated that the only relevant capacity was that of the average person.

The *Caldwell* lacuna

The idea behind the test developed in **Caldwell** was to broaden the concept of recklessness, so that people who it was felt were morally at fault could not escape liability because it was impossible to prove their actual state of mind. Unfortunately, it appears that the test has left a loophole, or lacuna, through which equally blameworthy conduct can escape liability. **Caldwell** recklessness imposes liability on those who either realize there is a risk and take it anyway, or who fail to see a risk that, by the standards of ordinary people, they ought to have seen. But what about the defendant who does consider whether there is a risk, but wrongly concludes that there is not? An example might be where a person is driving a car and wants to overtake a lorry. In approaching a bend, the car driver considers whether there is a risk involved in overtaking on this stretch of the road, and wrongly decides that there is not. In fact there is a risk and an accident is caused. In theory, the car driver in this situation would appear to fall outside Lord Diplock's two limbs of recklessness, yet most people would agree that the driver was at least as much at fault as a person who fell within the inadvertent recklessness limb by failing even to consider a risk.

The question of the **Caldwell** lacuna was raised in the case of **Chief Constable of Avon and Somerset Constabulary v Shimmen** (1986). The defendant had been learning martial arts, and wanted to show off his new skills to his friends. He boasted that he could kick at a shop window, but exercise such control as just to miss breaking the glass. He was wrong; the glass shattered and he was charged with criminal damage. At his trial he argued that he fell within the lacuna and therefore lacked the relevant *mens rea* of **Caldwell** recklessness for the offence; he claimed to have thought about whether there was a risk and to have mistakenly concluded there was none, so that when he acted he did not think he was taking a risk. The court did not believe his version of the facts; it felt he was aware that there was a slight risk of breaking the window, and knowingly took that risk, putting him within the advertent limb of **Caldwell** recklessness. This meant that the court did not have to decide whether or not the lacuna actually existed.

The issue was eventually tackled by the House of Lords in **R v Reid**. The House of Lords recognized that the lacuna did in fact exist, but they said that it was narrower than some academics had originally suggested. It was held that people would only fall within the lacuna if they thought about whether there was a risk and, due to a *bona fide* mistake (meaning a genuine, honest mistake), decided there was none; in such cases they would not be considered reckless. If they thought about whether there was a risk, and decided on the basis of a grossly negligent mistake that there was none, then they would still be reckless for the purposes of **Caldwell**. The logical conclusion seems to be, though the House of Lords did not specifically state this, that this last scenario actually creates a third limb of **Caldwell** recklessness.

The defendant in **R** *v* **Merrick** (1995) fraudulently obtained the permission of a householder to remove electrical equipment from his house. In doing so he exposed a live cable for six minutes which he then buried under rubble and cemented over. In his appeal to the Court of Appeal against a conviction for criminal damage being reckless as to the endangering of life (discussed at p. 164), he argued that he fell within the lacuna. The Court of Appeal rejected this argument because he had actually thought about the risk, seen the risk and gone ahead and taken that risk. The fact that he thought he would rapidly be able to bring an end to the risk (within six minutes) was not sufficient. The court drew a distinction between steps directed at preventing the risk arising and steps directed at remedying it after it had arisen. Only the former would be sufficient.

Which type of recklessness?

Caldwell did not overrule the old **Cunningham** reckless test; both tests still exist, but apply to different offences. The problem is knowing which offences require which type of recklessness; while in some offences this is well known, there are others where the requirement is still unclear.

Offences requiring *Caldwell* recklessness

There are only a few illustrations of offences to which **Caldwell** currently applies. It is still the *mens rea* for criminal damage, which was the offence in **Caldwell** itself. In **Data Protection Registrar** *v* **Amnesty International** (1995) **Caldwell** recklessness was applied to the statutory offence of recklessly disclosing personal data (s. 5, Data Protection Act 1984). Amnesty International was found guilty of this offence when it had exchanged mailing lists containing 20,000 names and addresses with another charity.

In **Lawrence**, it was applied to reckless driving, but this offence has since been repealed and replaced by the offence of dangerous driving. In **R** *v* **Seymour** (1983) it was used for the common law offence of reckless manslaughter, but the more recent House of Lords case of **R** *v* **Adomako** (1994) means this offence no longer exists (see p. 81).

It is not at all clear to which other offences **Caldwell** recklessness applies. In **Seymour**, Watkins LJ stated that 'The **Lawrence** direction on recklessness is comprehensive and of general application to all offences . . .' unless otherwise specified by Parliament, and this was approved by the Privy Council in **Kong Cheuk Kwan** *v* **R** (1985). These cases were at one time taken to mean that the **Caldwell** test should be used for most statutory offences containing the word 'reckless'. However, the strength of both of these authorities has been greatly damaged by the dicta in **R** v **Adomako**, which specifically overruled much of the law in **Seymour**. Even before this, in **Reid** the House of Lords appeared to take a more restrictive view of the role of **Caldwell** recklessness, merely stating that it would probably be the appropriate test where the defendant had chosen to undertake some dangerous activity such as driving, because he or she was choosing to take the risk of subsequent liability. Nowhere in the discussion did they provide support for the idea that it should be the usual test for statutory offences. Instead they suggested that 'words such as reckless or recklessly, which can be used in a number of different contexts, may not necessarily be expected to bear the same meaning in all statutory provisions in which they are found'.

Offences requiring **Cunningham** recklessness

Again, it is unclear precisely when the **Cunningham** form of recklessness applies. The courts have decided that it must be used in the following three situations, though there are many other offences to which it could also apply.

- Where the terms of the offence use the word maliciously, as in **Cunningham** which concerned maliciously administering a noxious substance so as to endanger life.
- Non-fatal offences against the person. The word 'malicious' appears in the definition of some of the non-fatal offences in the Offences Against the Person Act 1861, and as we have seen, 'malice' means either intention or **Cunningham** recklessness. In **R** v **Spratt** (1991), this interpretation has been held to apply to all the assault offences, even if the word 'malicious' does not appear in the definition.
- Rape and indecent assault: The Sexual Offences Act 1976 was passed specifically to give statutory effect to the decision in **DPP** v **Morgan** (1976) that an honest but unreasonable belief in the victim's consent means the *mens rea* for rape is not fulfilled. Therefore **Caldwell** recklessness, which was only established in 1982 and which would impose liability in such a situation, cannot apply (**R** v **Satnam** (1984)).

Problems with recklessness

Two tests

Having two different tests for the same word causes confusion and is unnecessary. As the law currently stands concern has been expressed that the higher **Cunningham** standard is applied to rape and the lower **Caldwell** standard is applied to criminal damage. This means that property is better protected than people.

Lower threshold for liability

The adoption of **Caldwell** recklessness means that a *mens rea* generally considered less morally blameworthy than **Cunningham** recklessness is being applied to some serious offences.

Lord Diplock argued that there were three good reasons for extending the test for recklessness. First, a defendant may be reckless in the ordinary sense of the word, meaning careless, regardless or heedless of the possible consequences, even though the risk of harm had not crossed his or her mind. Secondly, a tribunal of fact cannot be expected to rule confidently on whether the accused's state of mind has crossed 'the narrow dividing line' between being aware of risk and not troubling to consider it. Thirdly, the latter state of mind was no less blameworthy than the former.

Overlap with negligence

The **Caldwell** test has blurred the distinction between recklessness and negligence. Before **Caldwell**, there was an obvious difference: recklessness meant knowingly taking a risk; negligence traditionally meant unknowingly taking a risk of which you should have been aware. **Caldwell** clearly comes very close to negligence.

The approach to capacity

The **Elliott** approach to capacity has been viewed as extremely harsh. L.H. Leigh, Professor of Criminal Law at the London School of Economics, has argued that the approach in **Elliott** is not the interpretation of the **Caldwell** test that Lord Diplock himself would have had in mind when giving his model direction. To support this argument Professor Leigh has pointed out that the issue of capacity was not relevant to the facts of **Caldwell** so it was not at the forefront of Lord Diplock's mind when he gave the direction. But in an earlier judgment of his, **R** *v* **Sheppard** (1981), he had acknowledged the relevance of capacity where capacity was in issue. Parents were convicted of causing cruelty to their child by wilful neglect, contrary to s. 1 of the Children and Young Persons Act 1933. In considering the word 'wilful', Lord Diplock drew a distinction between advertent and inadvertent states of mind and in the former situation he clearly thought the issue of capacity was relevant as he says that parents would be excused from liability if, owing to lack of intelligence, they are genuinely unaware that their child's health may be in danger.

The lacuna

The case of **R** *v* **Merrick** has been criticized as unrealistic. In practice, replacing electrical equipment often creates a temporary danger which cannot be avoided, yet technically each time in criminal law the electrician is reckless.

Problems for juries
The **Caldwell/Lawrence** formula is notorious for being difficult for juries to understand.

Suggestions for reform

The Law Commission
The Law Commission's draft Criminal Liability (Mental Element) Bill provides a redefinition of *mens rea* generally, and defines recklessness in subjective terms, in accordance with **Cunningham** rather than **Caldwell** recklessness. However, in 1996 when reviewing the law on manslaughter, the Law Commission confronted the issue of liability for consequences that are neither intended nor knowingly risked. It concluded that there are good grounds for criminalizing the inadvertent causing of death where the risk of death or serious injury is obviously foreseeable and where the defendant has the capacity to advert to the risk.

*Reversion to **Cunningham** alone*
Smith and Hogan argue that a distinction should be made between someone who knowingly takes a risk, and someone who simply gives no thought to the fact that there might be a risk. They may both be blameworthy, but not, in Smith and Hogan's opinion, equally so. They recommend reverting to the stricter **Cunningham** definition for recklessness.

Including characteristics of the defendant
If the purpose of **Caldwell** is to ensure that people do not get away with giving no thought to a risk of which they should have been aware, a fairer test of what constitutes an obvious and serious risk might be 'in the circumstances, should the defendant (given such characteristics as age, or any mental incapability) have realized there was a risk?' This would ensure that blameworthy thoughtlessness would incur liability, but would exclude the unfairness of cases like **Elliott**.

▶ Negligence

Negligence is a concept that is most often found in civil law, but it does have some relevance to criminal law as well. It is traditionally an objective test, which asks whether the defendant has gone below the standards to be expected of a reasonable person. Traditionally, the standard of the reasonable person for the purposes of criminal negligence takes no account of the defendant's actual characteristics: in **McCrone** *v* **Riding** (1938), which concerned a charge of careless driving, it was held that the accused's driving could be considered careless if he had failed to come up to the standard of a reasonably experienced driver, even though he was himself a learner driver.

True crimes of negligence are rare in criminal law, though there are some statutory offences of negligence, particularly those concerned with motoring. More commonly, an offence of strict liability (where no *mens rea* is required) may allow the accused to use the defence of having acted with all due diligence; in other words, of not being negligent.

There is one important common law crime where negligence is the *mens rea*: gross negligence manslaughter. Because this is a very serious offence the courts are not just looking for negligence but for gross negligence. We will consider the concept of gross negligence in much more detail when we look at this offence at p. 80. However, at this point it is worth noting that in the House of Lords judgment in **R** *v* **Adomako** (1994), gross negligence seems to be not simply a more severe form of negligence, but may also cover subjective as well as objective criteria.

Problems with negligence

Professor Hall, a criminal law academic, has suggested that it is difficult to accept negligence as amounting to a moral fault. He states that being insensitive to the rights of others is not necessarily morally blameworthy – in the case of car accidents caused by negligence for example, Professor Hall suggests that 'a dull mind, slow reactions, awkwardness and other ethically irrelevant factors' may be to blame.

On the other hand, Professor Williams (1961) points out that punishing negligence may encourage people to think about risks before they act, but he says that this justification cannot be taken too far; he feels negligence should incur liability only in exceptional cases.

▶ Transferred malice

If Ann shoots at Ben, intending to kill him, but happens to miss, and shoots and kills Chris instead, Ann will be liable for the murder of Chris. This is because of the principle known as transferred malice. Under this principle, if Ann has the *mens rea* of a particular crime and does the *actus reus* of the crime, Ann is guilty of the crime even though the *actus reus* may differ in some way from that intended. The *mens rea* is simply transferred to the new *actus reus*. Either intention or recklessness can be so transferred.

As a result the defendant will be liable for the same crime even if the victim is not the intended victim. In **Latimer** (1886), the defendant aimed a blow at someone with his belt. The belt recoiled off that person and hit the victim, who was severely injured. The court held that Latimer was liable for maliciously wounding the unexpected victim. His intention to wound the person he aimed at was transferred to the person actually injured.

Where the accused would have had a defence if the crime committed had been completed against the intended victim, that defence is also transferred. So if Ann shot at Ben in self-defence and hit and killed Chris instead, Ann would be able to rely on the defence if charged with Chris's murder.

In **Attorney-General's Reference (No. 3 of 1994)** the defendant stabbed his girlfriend who was to his knowledge between 22 and 24 weeks pregnant with their child. The girlfriend underwent an operation on a cut in the wall of her uterus but it was not realized at the time that the stabbing had damaged the foetus's abdomen. She subsequently gave birth prematurely to a baby girl who later died from the complications of a premature birth. Before the child's death the defendant was charged with the offence of wounding his girlfriend with intent to cause her grievous bodily harm to which he pleaded guilty. After the child died, he was in addition charged with murdering the child. At the close of the prosecution case the judge upheld a defence submission that the facts could not give rise to a conviction for murder or manslaughter and accordingly directed the jury to acquit. The Attorney-General referred the case to the Court of Appeal for a ruling to clarify the law in the field. The Court of Appeal considered the foetus to be an integral part of the mother until its birth. Thus any intention to injure the foetus prior to its birth was treated as an intention to injure the mother. If on birth the baby subsequently died, an intention to injure the baby could be found by applying the doctrine of transferred malice. This approach was rejected by the House of Lords. It held that the foetus was not an integral part of the mother, but a unique organism. The principle of transferred malice could not therefore be applied, and the direction was criticized as being of 'no sound intellectual basis'.

▶ Mens rea and motive

It is essential to realize that *mens rea* has nothing to do with motive. To illustrate this, take the example of a man who suffocates his wife with a pillow, intending to kill her because she is afflicted with a terminal disease which causes her terrible and constant pain. Many people would say that this man's motive is not a bad one – in fact many people would reject the label 'murder' for what he has done. But there is no doubt that he has the necessary *mens rea* for murder, because he intends to kill his wife, even if he does not want to do so. He may not have a guilty mind in the everyday sense, but he does have *mens rea*. Motive may be relevant when the decision is made on whether or not to prosecute, or later for sentencing, but it makes no difference with regard to legal liability.

▶ Proof of *mens rea*

Under s. 8 of the Criminal Justice Act 1967, where the definition of an offence requires the prosecution to prove that the accused intended or foresaw something, the question of whether that is proved is one for the court or jury to decide on the basis of all the evidence. The fact that a consequence is proved to be the natural and probable result of the accused's actions does not mean that it is proved that he or she intended or foresaw such a result; the jury or the court must decide.

▶ Problems with the law on *mens rea*

Lack of clarity

The terminology used has become very unclear and uncertain. On the one hand the boundaries between gross negligence and recklessness have become blurred; on the other hand, one term – **Caldwell** recklessness – covers two significantly different mental states.

Older terms are even less clear, and the same word may be defined differently in different offences. For example, 'malice' means one thing in relation to murder, another in relation to the Malicious Damage Act, and yet another in relation to libel.

Mens rea and morality

Problems arise because in practice the courts stretch the law in order to convict those whose conduct they see as blameworthy, while acquitting those whose behaviour they feel does not deserve the strongest censure. For example, the offence of murder requires a finding of intention to kill or to cause serious injury. The courts want to convict terrorists of murder when they kill, yet do they have the requisite *mens rea*? If you plant a bomb but give a warning, do you intend to kill or to cause serious injury? Assuming a fair warning, could death or serious injury be seen as a virtually certain consequence of your acts? What if a terrorist bomber gives a warning that would normally allow sufficient time to evacuate the relevant premises, but owing to the negligence of the police, the evacuation fails to take place quickly enough and people are killed? The courts are likely to be reluctant to allow this to reduce the terrorist's liability, yet it is hard to see how this terrorist could be said to intend deaths or

serious injury to occur – in fact the giving of a warning might suggest the
opposite. The courts are equally reluctant to impose liability for murder
where it is difficult to find real moral guilt, even though technically this
should be irrelevant. The problem is linked to the fact that murder carries a mandatory life sentence, which prevents the judge from taking
degrees of moral guilt into account in sentencing (see p. 54).

The academic Alan Norrie has written an exciting article on this subject called *After Woollin*. He argues that the attempt of the law to separate
the question of *mens rea* from broader issues of motive and morality is
artificial and not possible in practice. He points to the fact that the jury
are merely 'entitled to find' indirect intention and that for some offences
(illustrated by **Steane**) only direct intention will suffice. In his view through
this flexibility the courts want to allow themselves the freedom to acquit
in morally appropriate cases. Such moral judgments on the basis of the
defendant's motive are traditionally excluded from decisions on *mens rea*.

George Fletcher (*Rethinking the Criminal Law* (1978)) has noted how
historically there has been a development of the law from terms with a
moral content such as 'malice' to the identification of 'specific mental
states of intending and knowing'. Fletcher observes that:

> Descriptive theorists seek to minimise the normative content of the
> criminal law in order to render it, in their view, precise and free
> from the passions of subjective moral judgement .... [Such a
> concern] may impel courts and theorists towards value free rules
> and concepts; the reality of judgement, blame and punishment
> generates the contrary pressure and insures that the quest for a
> value free science of law cannot succeed.

Making a judgment on someone that he is a 'murderer' and that he
should have a life sentence are both moral judgments. Judges are con-
stantly making judgments on right and wrong and what should happen
to wrongdoers. But they have to render these judgments in specialist
legal terms using concepts such as 'intention' and 'foresight'. These terms
are different from everyday terms of moral judgment, but they are used
to address moral issues. Norrie argues:

> ... as a result of this, lawyers end up investing 'nominally descriptive
> terms with moral force'. Thus terms like 'intent', 'state of mind' and
> 'mental state' which appear to be descriptive are used to refer to
> issues that require normative judgement.

In Norrie's view the desire to exclude 'subjective moral judgement' really
results from the desire in the past to safeguard a criminal code based on
the protection of a particular social order. He considers that:

> ... if one examines the historical development of the criminal law,
> one finds that a legal code designed to establish an order based on

private property and individual right was legitimated by reference to the dangers of subjective anarchy. This argument was the ideological window-dressing justifying the profound institutional changes taking place.

Thus, he considers that the apparently impartial language used to describe *mens rea* is actually very partial and unfair to many. The law is based upon the supposed characteristics of the average person, stressing the free will of the individual. It ignores the 'substantive moral differences that exist between individuals as they are located across different social classes and according to other relevant divisions such as culture and gender'.

One way to avoid this tension between the legal rules and the moral reality is to develop the defences that are available. Defences such as duress (discussed at p. 270) explicitly allow moral issues to enter into the legal debate through questions of proportionality. Defendants in situations such as **Steane** should be able to avoid liability through the use of a defence such as duress rather than an inconsistent application of the law on *mens rea*.

▶ Coincidence of *actus reus* and *mens rea*

The *mens rea* of an offence must be present at the time the *actus reus* is committed. So if, for example, Ann intends to kill Ben on Friday night, but for some reason fails to do so, then quite accidentally runs Ben over on Saturday morning, Ann will not be liable for Ben's murder. However, there are two ways in which the courts have introduced flexibility into this area: continuing acts, which are described above, and the interpretation of a continuous series of acts as a single transaction. An example of the latter occurred in **Thabo Meli** *v* **R** (1954). The defendants had attempted to kill their victim by beating him over the head, then threw what they assumed was a dead body over a cliff. The victim did die, but from the fall and exposure, and not from the beating. Thus there was an argument that at the time of the *actus reus* the defendant no longer had the *mens rea*. The Privy Council held that throwing him over the cliff was part of one series of acts following through a preconceived plan of action and therefore could not be seen as separate acts at all, but as a single transaction. The defendants had the required *mens rea* when that transaction began, and therefore *mens rea* and *actus reus* had coincided.

ANSWERING QUESTIONS

1 Critically analyse the situations where a person can be liable in criminal law for an omission to act.

This is not a difficult question – the circumstances in which criminal liability will be imposed for true omissions are clearly explained above. You should also include the situations in which liability is imposed for conduct which would in everyday language be described as an omission, but which in law is an act, and vice versa. Remember that you are asked to analyse the law critically so it is not good enough simply to provide a description, you should also evaluate the law by pointing out its strengths and weaknesses. For example, you could look at the issue of the drowning child and whether the law is adequate in this situation and you could also consider the approach taken by the courts to Tony Bland's case.

2 **The term 'recklessness' plays a crucial role in determining criminal liability yet its meaning still appears uncertain. Critically assess the meaning of the term 'reckless' in criminal law.** *Oxford*
Most of the material discussed under the heading recklessness is relevant here. You might start by explaining why recklessness 'plays a crucial role in determining criminal liability'. To do so you could point out that most offences require proof of *mens rea*. In proving *mens rea* a distinction often has to be drawn between recklessness and intention because the more serious offences often require intention only, conviction for which would impose a higher sentence. For lesser offences recklessness is usually sufficient and a lighter sentence would be imposed.

The rest of your essay could be structured in much the same order as the relevant section of this book. In looking at the meaning of the term 'recklessness' you would have to discuss both **Cunningham** recklessness and **Caldwell** recklessness. As you are asked to 'critically assess' a mere description of the two tests will not be sufficient – you will need, in addition, to look at issues raised under the headings 'problems with recklessness' and 'suggestions for reform'.

2 Strict liability

There are a small number of crimes which can be committed without any *mens rea*, or without *mens rea* regarding at least one aspect of the *actus reus*. These offences are known as strict liability crimes, and most of them have been created by statute, though public nuisance and blasphemous libel are examples of common law strict liability offences.

A classic example of the application of strict liability is **Prince** (1874). The accused was charged under s. 55 of the Offences Against the Person Act 1861, which stated that 'Whosoever shall unlawfully take or cause to be taken any unmarried girl, being under the age of sixteen years, out of the possession and against the will of her father or mother . . . shall be guilty of a misdemeanour . . .' The girl, Annie Phillips, was actually thirteen, but she looked at least sixteen. The jury found that there was reasonable evidence that she had told Prince, before the abduction, that she was eighteen, and that he genuinely believed her, and given her appearance it was reasonable for him to do so. However, the court held that the statute could be interpreted as allowing strict liability – the girl was under sixteen, and Prince had taken her out of the possession of her parents, against their will, and that was all that the Act required. The fact that he did not know she was under sixteen was irrelevant as no *mens rea* for the offence was required.

A recent case where **Prince** was applied is **B** *v* **DPP** (1998). A 15-year-old boy had sat next to a 13-year-old girl and asked her to give him a shiner. The trial judge observed that '[t]his, in the language of today's gilded youth, apparently means, not a black eye, but an act of oral sex'. The boy was charged with committing an act of gross indecency on a child under the age of 14. This is a strict liability offence and it was ruled by the both the trial judge and the appeal court that no defence was available that the boy believed the girl to be over 14.

▶ Which crimes are crimes of strict liability?

Unfortunately, statutes are not always so obliging as to state 'this is a strict liability offence'. Occasionally the wording of an Act does make this clear, but otherwise the courts are left to decide for themselves. The principles on which this decision is made were considered in **Gammon (Hong Kong) Ltd** *v* **A-G** (1985). The defendants were involved in building works in Hong Kong. Part of a building they were constructing fell down, and it was found that the collapse had occurred because the builders had failed to follow the original plans exactly. The Hong Kong building regulations prohibited deviating in any substantial way from such plans, and the defendants were charged with breaching the regulations, an offence punishable with a fine of up to $250,000 or three years' imprisonment. On appeal they argued that they were not liable because they had not known that the changes they made were substantial ones. However, the Privy Council held that the relevant regulations created offences of strict liability, and the convictions were upheld.

Explaining the principles on which they had based the decision, Lord Scarman confirmed that there is always a presumption of law that *mens rea* is required before a person can be held guilty of a criminal offence, but that there were factors which could, on their own or combined, displace this presumption. In general, there are four such factors which the courts use to decide whether a crime is one of strict liability.

The crime is a regulatory offence

A regulatory offence is one in which no real moral issue is involved, and usually (though not always) one for which the maximum penalty is small – the mass of rules surrounding the sale of food are examples. In **Gammon** it was stated that the presumption against strict liability was less strong for regulatory offences than for truly criminal offences.

This distinction between true crimes and regulatory offences had previously been made in the case of **Sweet** *v* **Parsley** (1970). Ms Sweet, a teacher, took a sublease of a farmhouse outside Oxford. She rented the house to tenants, and rarely spent any time there. Unknown to her, the tenants were smoking cannabis on the premises. When they were caught, she was found guilty of being concerned in the management of premises which were being used for the purpose of smoking cannabis, contrary to the Dangerous Drugs Act 1965 (now replaced by the Misuse of Drugs Act 1971).

Ms Sweet appealed, on the grounds that she knew nothing about what the tenants were doing, and could not reasonably have been expected to have known. Lord Reid acknowledged that strict liability was appropriate for regulatory offences, or 'quasi-crimes' – offences which are not criminal 'in any real sense', and are merely acts prohibited in the public interest. But, he said, the kind of crime to which a real social stigma is attached should usually require proof of *mens rea*; in the case of such offences it was not in the public interest that an innocent person should be prevented from proving that innocence in the interests of making it easier for guilty people to be convicted.

Since their Lordships regarded the offence under consideration as being a 'true crime' – the stigma had, for example, caused Ms Sweet to lose her job – they held that it was not a strict liability offence, and since Ms Sweet did not have the necessary *mens rea*, her conviction was overturned.

Unfortunately the courts have never laid down a list of those offences which they will consider to be regulatory offences rather than 'true crimes'. Those generally considered to be regulatory offences are the kind created by the rules on hygiene and measurement standards within the food and drink industry, and regulations designed to stop industry polluting the environment, but there are clearly some types of offences which will be more difficult to categorize.

The statute deals with an issue of social concern

According to **Gammon**, where a statute is concerned with an issue of social concern (such as public safety), and the creation of strict liability will promote the purpose of the statute by encouraging potential offenders to take extra precautions against committing the prohibited act, the presumption against strict liability can be rebutted. This category is obviously subject to the distinctions drawn by Lord Reid in **Sweet** *v* **Parsley** – the laws against murder and rape are to protect the public, but this type of true crime would not attract strict liability.

The types of offences that do fall into this category cover behaviour which could involve danger to the public, but which would not usually carry the same kind of stigma as a crime such as murder or even theft. The breach of the building regulations committed in **Gammon** is an example, as are offences relating to serious pollution of the environment. In **R** *v* **Blake** (1996) the defendant was accused of making broadcasts on a pirate radio station and was convicted of using wireless telegraphy equipment without a licence, contrary to s. 1(1) of the Wireless Telegraphy Act 1949. His conviction was upheld by the Court of Appeal which stated that this offence was one of strict liability. This conclusion was reached as the offence had been created in the interest of public safety, given the interference with the operation of the emergency services that could result from unauthorized broadcasting.

These crimes overlap with regulatory offences in subject area, but unlike regulatory offences, may carry severe maximum penalties. Despite such higher penalties, strict liability is seen to be a necessary provision given the need to promote very high standards of care in areas of possible danger.

The wording of the Act

Gammon states that the presumption that *mens rea* is required for a criminal offence can be rebutted if the words of a statute suggest that strict liability is intended. At present it is not always clear whether a particular form of words will be interpreted as creating an offence of strict liability. However, some words have been interpreted fairly consistently, including the following.

'Cause'

In **Alphacell** *v* **Woodward** (1972) the defendants were a company accused of causing polluted matter to enter a river. They were using equipment designed to prevent any overflow into the river, but when the mechanism became clogged by leaves the pollution was able to escape. There was no evidence that the defendants had been negligent, or even knew that the pollution was leaking out. The House of Lords stated that where statutes create an offence of causing something to happen, the courts should adopt a common-sense approach – if reasonable people would say that the defendant has caused something to happen, regardless of whether he or she knew he or she was doing so, then no *mens rea* is required. Their Lordships held that in the normal meaning of the word, the company had 'caused' the pollution to enter the water, and their conviction was upheld.

'Possession'

There are many offences which are defined as 'being in possession of a prohibited item', the obvious example being drugs. They are frequently treated as strict liability offences.

'Knowingly'

Clearly use of this word tells the courts that *mens rea* is required, and tends to be used where Parliament wants to underline the fact that the presumption should be applied.

The smallness of the penalty

Strict liability is most often imposed for offences which carry a relatively small maximum penalty, and it appears that the higher the maximum penalty, the less likely it is that the courts will impose strict liability. However, the existence of severe penalties for an offence does not guarantee that strict liability will not be imposed. In **Gammon** Lord Scarman held that where regulations were put in place to protect public safety, it was quite appropriate to impose strict liability, despite potentially severe penalties.

Relevance of the four factors

Obviously these four factors overlap to a certain extent – regulatory offences usually do have small penalties, for example. And in **Alphacell** *v* **Woodward**, the House of Lords gave their decision the dual justification of applying the common-sense meaning of the term 'cause', and recognizing that pollution was an issue of social concern.

It is important to note that all these categories are guidelines rather than clear rules. The courts are not always consistent in their application of strict liability, and social policy plays an important part in the decisions. During the 1960s, there was intense social concern about what appeared to be a widespread drug problem, and the courts imposed strict liability for many drugs offences. Ten years later, pollution of the environment had become one of the main topics of concern, hence the justification of the decision in **Alphacell** *v* **Woodward**. Today, there appears to be a general move away from strict liability, and some newer statutes imposing apparent strict liability contain a limited form of defence, by which an accused can escape conviction by proving that he or she took all reasonable precautions to prevent the offence being committed. However, the courts could begin to move back towards strict liability if it seemed that an area of social concern might require it.

▶ The effect of mistake

Where strict liability applies, an accused cannot use the defence of mistake, even if the mistake was reasonable.

▶ Arguments in favour of strict liability

Promotion of care

By promoting high standards of care, strict liability, it is argued, protects the public from dangerous practices. Social scientist Barbara Wootton has defended strict liability on this basis, suggesting that if the objective of criminal law is to prevent socially damaging activities, it would be absurd to turn a blind eye to those who cause the harm due to carelessness, negligence or even an accident.

Deterrent value

Strict liability is said to provide a strong deterrent, which is considered especially important given the way in which regulatory offences tend to be dealt with. Many of them are handled not by the police and the Crown Prosecution Service (CPS), but by special Government bodies, such as the Health and Safety Inspectorate which checks that safety rules are observed in workplaces. These bodies tend to work by putting pressure on offenders to put right any breaches, with prosecution, or even threats of it, very much a last resort. It is suggested that strict liability allows enforcement agencies to strengthen their bargaining position, since potential offenders know that if a prosecution is brought, there is a very good chance of conviction.

Easier enforcement

Strict liability makes enforcing offences easier; in **Gammon** the Privy Council suggested that if the prosecution had to prove *mens rea* in even the smallest regulatory offence, the administration of justice might very quickly come to a complete standstill.

Difficulty of proving *mens rea*

In many strict liability offences, *mens rea* would be very difficult to prove, and without strict liability, guilty people might escape conviction. Obvious examples are those involving large corporations, where it may be difficult to prove that someone knew what was happening.

No threat to liberty

In many strict liability cases, the defendant is a business and the penalty is a fine, so individual liberty is not generally under threat. Even the fines are often small.

Profit from risk

Where an offence is concerned with business, those who commit it may well be saving themselves money, and thereby making extra profit by doing so – by, for example, saving the time that would be spent on observing safety regulations. If a person creates a risk and makes a profit by doing so, he or she ought to be liable if that risk causes or could cause harm, even if that was not the intention.

▶ Arguments against strict liability

Injustice

Strict liability is criticized as unjust on a variety of different grounds. First, that it is not in the interests of justice that someone who has taken reasonable care, and could not possibly have avoided committing an offence, should be punished by the criminal law. This goes against the principle that the criminal law punishes fault.

Secondly, the argument that strict liability should be enforced because *mens rea* would be too difficult to prove is morally doubtful. The prosecution often find it difficult to prove *mens rea* on a rape charge, for example, but is that a reason for making rape a crime of strict liability? Although many strict liability offences are clearly far lesser crimes than these, some do impose severe penalties, as **Gammon** illustrates, and it may not be in the interests of justice if strict liability is imposed in these areas just because *mens rea* would make things too difficult for the prosecution. It is inconsistent with justice to convict someone who is not guilty, in the normal sense of the word, just because the penalty imposed will be small.

Even where penalties are small, in many cases conviction is a punishment in itself. Sentencing may be tailored to take account of mitigating factors, but that is little comfort to the reputable butcher who unknowingly sells bad meat, when the case is reported in local papers and customers go elsewhere. However slight the punishment, in practice there is some stigma attached to a criminal conviction (even though it may be less than that for a 'true crime') which should not be attached to a person who has taken all reasonable care.

In addition, as Smith and Hogan point out, in the case of a jury trial, strict liability takes crucial questions of fact away from juries, and allows them to be considered solely by the judge for the purposes of sentencing. In a magistrates' court, it removes those questions from the requirement of proof beyond reasonable doubt, and allows them to be decided according to the less strict principles which guide decisions on sentencing.

Strict liability also delegates a good deal of power to the discretion of the enforcement agency. Where strict liability makes it almost certain that a prosecution will lead to a conviction, the decision on whether or not to prosecute becomes critical, and there are few controls over those who make this decision.

Ineffective

It is debatable whether strict liability actually works. For a start, the deterrent value of strict liability may be overestimated. For the kinds of offences to which strict liability is usually applied, the important deterrent factor may not be the chances of being convicted, but the chances of being caught and charged. In the food and drinks business particularly, just being charged with an offence brings unwelcome publicity, and even if the company is not convicted, they are likely to see a fall in sales as customers apply the 'no smoke without fire' principle. The problem is that in many cases the chances of being caught and prosecuted are not high. In the first place, enforcement agencies frequently lack the resources to monitor the huge number of potential offenders – the Factory Inspectorate in 1980 had 900 inspectors who were responsible for reporting on at least 600,000 different workplaces. Even where offenders are caught, it appears that the usual response of enforcement agencies is a warning letter. The most serious or persistent offenders may be threatened with prosecution if they do not put matters right, but only a minority are actually prosecuted. Providing more resources for the enforcement agencies and bringing more prosecutions might have a stronger deterrent effect than imposing strict liability on the minority who are prosecuted.

In other areas too, it is the chance of getting caught which may be the strongest deterrent – if people think they are unlikely to get caught speeding, for example, the fact that strict liability will be imposed if they do is not much of a deterrent.

In fact in some areas, rather than ensuring a higher standard of care, strict liability may have quite the opposite effect: knowing that it is possible to be convicted of an offence regardless of having taken every reasonable precaution may reduce the incentive to take such precautions, rather than increase it.

As Professor Hall points out, the fact that strict liability is usually imposed only where the possible penalty is small means that unscrupulous companies can simply regard the criminal law as 'a nominal tax on illegal enterprise'. In areas of industry where the need to maintain a good reputation is not so strong as it is in food or drugs, for example, it may be cheaper to keep paying the fines than to change bad working practices, and therefore very little deterrent value can be seen. In these areas it might be more efficient, as Professor Hall says, 'to put real teeth in the law' by developing offences with more severe penalties, even if that means losing the expediency of strict liability.

Justifying strict liability in the interests of protecting the public can be seen as taking a sledgehammer to crack a nut. It is certainly true, for example, that bad meat causes food poisoning just the same whether or not the butcher knew it was bad, and that the public needs protection from butchers who sell bad meat. But while we might want to make sure of punishment for butchers who knowingly sell bad meat, and probably those who take no, or not enough, care to check the condition of their meat, how is the public protected by punishing a butcher who took all possible care (by using a normally reputable supplier for example) and could not possibly have avoided committing the offence?

The fact that it is not always possible to recognize crimes of strict liability before the courts have made a decision clearly further weakens any deterrent effect.

Little administrative advantage

It is also open to debate whether strict liability really does contribute much to administrative expediency. Cases still have to be detected and brought to court, and in some cases selected elements of the *mens rea* still have to be proved. And although strict liability may make conviction easier, it leaves the problem of sentencing. This cannot be done fairly without taking the degree of negligence into account, so evidence of the accused's state of mind must be available. Given all this it is difficult to see how much time and manpower is actually saved.

Inconsistent application

The fact that whether or not strict liability will be imposed rests on the imprecise science of statutory interpretation means that there are discrepancies in both the offences to which it is applied, and what it actually means. The changes in the types of cases to which strict liability is applied over the years reflect social policy – the courts come down harder on areas which are causing social concern at a particular time. While this may be justified in the interests of society, it does little for certainty and the principle that like cases should be treated alike.

The courts are also inconsistent in their justifications for imposing or not imposing strict liability. In **Lim Chin Aik** *v* **R** (1963), the defendant was charged with remaining in Singapore despite a prohibition order against him. Lord Evershed stated that the subject matter of a statute was not sufficient grounds for inferring that strict liability was intended; it was also important to consider whether imposing strict liability would help to enforce the regulations, and it could only do this if there were some precautions the potential offender could take to prevent committing the offence. 'Unless this is so, there is no reason in penalizing him and it cannot be inferred that the legislature imposed strict liability merely in order to find a luckless victim.'

In the case of **Lim Chin Aik**, the precaution to be taken would have been finding out whether there was a prohibition order against him, but Lord Evershed further explained that people could only be expected to take 'sensible' and 'practicable' precautions: Lim Chin Aik was not expected to 'make continuous enquiry to see whether an order had been made against him'.

Presumably then, our hypothetical butcher should only be expected to take reasonable and practicable precautions against selling bad meat, and not, for example, have to employ scientific analysts to test every pork chop. Yet just such extreme precautions appear to have been expected in **Smedleys** *v* **Breed** (1974). The defendants were convicted under the Food and Drugs Act 1955, after a very small caterpillar was found in one of three million tins of peas. Despite the fact that even individual inspection of each pea would probably not have prevented the offence being committed, Lord Hailsham defended the imposition of strict liability on the grounds that 'To construe the Food and Drugs Act 1955 in a sense less strict than that which I have adopted would make a serious inroad on the legislation for consumer protection.' Clearly the subject areas of these cases are very different, but the contrast between them does give some indication of the shaky ground on which strict liability can rest – if the

House of Lords had followed the reasoning of **Lim Chin Aik**, Smedleys would not have been liable, since they had taken all reasonable and practical precautions.

Better alternatives are available

There are alternatives to strict liability which would be less unjust and more effective in preventing harm, such as better inspection of business premises and the imposition of liability for negligence (see below).

▶ Reform

The Law Commission's draft Bill

The Law Commission's draft Criminal Liability (Mental Element) Bill of 1978 requires that Parliament should specifically state if it is creating an offence of strict liability. Where this is not done the courts should assume *mens rea* is required. The practice of allowing the courts to decide when strict liability should be applied, under cover of the fiction that they are interpreting parliamentary intention, is not helpful, leading to a mass of litigation, with many of the cases irreconcilable with each other – as with **Lim Chin Aik** and **Smedley** *v* **Breed**, above. If legislators knew that the courts would always assume *mens rea* unless specifically told not to, they would be more likely to adopt the habit of stating whether the offence was strict or not.

Restriction to public danger offences

Strict liability could perhaps be more easily justified if the tighter liability were balanced by real danger to the public in the offence – the case of **Gammon** can be justified on this ground.

Liability for negligence

Smith and Hogan suggest that strict liability should be replaced by liability for negligence. This would catch defendants who were simply thoughtless or inefficient, as well as those who deliberately broke the law, but would not punish people who were genuinely blameless.

Defence of all due care

In Australia a defence of all due care is available. Where a crime would otherwise impose strict liability, the defendant can avoid conviction by proving that he or she took all due care to avoid committing the offence.

Extending strict liability

Baroness Wootton advocates imposing strict liability for all crimes, so that *mens rea* would only be relevant for sentencing purposes.

• •

ANSWERING QUESTIONS

Strict liability tends to arise in essay rather than problem questions, because the offences to which it applies tend not to be included in course syllabuses. Given the large amount of theoretical discussion for and against strict liability, it should not be difficult to discuss critically, and is therefore a good choice for essay questions.

1 **Is the imposition of strict liability ever justifiable in criminal law?** *Oxford*
Avoid the natural temptation of using this question simply as a trigger for writing everything you know on the subject without applying that material to the specific question asked. Obviously you will want to learn off a lot of material before the exam, and it will probably help to follow the structure of this book when you do this, so that for this chapter, for example, you might learn the lists of arguments for and against strict liability. That material will provide the basis for answering many differently worded questions on strict liability, but in the exam, you must angle that material to the actual question being asked. In this question, the key words are 'imposition' and 'justifiable' and these and their synonyms should be used at several points in the essay to show that you are answering the particular question asked. You could start by stating where strict liability is currently imposed, before discussing whether such impositions are justified – in this part you can describe the kind of offences to which strict liability applies, giving examples from case law. You should, however, devote the bulk of your essay to discussing when the imposition of strict liability is justified, if ever in your opinion, and when not, using the arguments for and against it to back up your points.

2 **It is often asserted that there should be no criminal liability without proof of fault.**
(a) Explain what might be meant by fault in this context. *(10 marks)*
(b) Consider how far criminal liability *does* and *should* depend upon fault.
(15 marks) AEB, 1993
This is a slightly more difficult question, but one for which it should be possible to get good marks if you plan your answer carefully. As well as strict liability discussed in this chapter, the question also raises issues discussed in the previous chapter on 'Elements of a crime'. A good answer to part (a) could include such issues as an explanation of *actus reus* (including causation and voluntariness), and *mens rea* and the absence of defences (such as insanity and duress) as a marker of fault. Part (b) could look at strict liability offences, state of affairs

offences, the thin skull rule (discussed in Chapter 3), the **Miller** case, the different degrees of *mens rea*, and the limits on defences.

3 'If the object of the criminal law is to prevent the occurrence of socially damaging actions, it would be absurd to turn a blind eye to those which were due to carelessness, negligence, or even accident.' (B. Wootton, *Crime and the Criminal Law*.) Discuss. *NEAB*

Again this question spans both this and the previous chapter. A possible starting point to this topic is that normally *mens rea* needs to be proved before criminal liability will be imposed. Once you have studied defences you might also bring in issues of automatism and statutory authority, discussed later in the book. 'Carelessness' and 'negligence' mean much the same thing – traditionally that a person has fallen below a recognized standard of care. In criminal law we have seen that this is occasionally considered to be sufficient to satisfy the criteria of *mens rea*. The most significant example of this is gross negligence manslaughter, which will be studied in more detail in the chapter on involuntary manslaughter. Apart from these rare exceptions, unlike civil liability, negligence/carelessness is not generally sufficient to impose criminal liability.

As regards accidents, again, persons will not usually be criminally liable because they will lack *mens rea*. However the inadvertent limb of *Caldwell* recklessness could be considered to allow *mens rea* to be imposed in such situations, and you could discuss **Elliott** on this point. Liability for accidents might also be imposed for strict liability offences provided the person does not fall within a defence.

You could then consider how far criminal law in general is used to prevent the occurrence of socially damaging actions. You might be able to think of examples of criminal offences which you do not feel prevent such an occurrence, such as the offences that have been created by the Criminal Justice and Public Order Act 1994 to prevent the holding of 'raves'.

Consideration could be given as to how far the current imposition of criminal liability for careless, negligent and accidental conduct prevents the occurrence of socially damaging actions and whether an extension of such liability would do so. You could consider whether any such advantages gained would be outweighed by the disadvantages and in this field some of the advantages and disadvantages of strict liability in general would be helpful.

3 Murder

Offences against the person fall into two main categories: fatal (unlawful homicide) and non-fatal offences. Homicide means the killing of a human being, and in some circumstances it may be lawful – for example, in self-defence, or during a military operation in war time. We are concerned here with unlawful homicides.

▶ The common elements of homicide offences

To be liable for any homicide offence the defendant must cause the death of a human being. We will look at each of these three elements in turn which hereafter will be referred to as the common elements.

A human being

For the purposes of the homicide offences, a person is a human being when capable of having an existence independent of a mother. Killing an unborn child (a foetus) can still be unlawful, but would be covered by a different category of crime such as child destruction. In **Attorney-General's Reference (No. 3 of 1994)** where a man stabbed his pregnant girlfriend, the Court of Appeal stated that there was no requirement that the person who died had to be a person in being when the act causing the death was perpetrated. Thus, if a man injured a foetus and the baby was then born alive but subsequently died from the injuries the concept of a 'human being' would be satisfied for the purposes of a homicide offence. This aspect of the Court of Appeal judgment was approved by the House of Lords.

Death

There is no single legal definition of 'death'. In the past, absence of a heartbeat, pulse or breathing meant that a person could safely be pronounced dead, but medical advances mean that a person may now be kept on a life support machine for many years. As a result, the courts have had to consider whether such a person is alive or dead and, if dead, at what point death can be said to have occurred. In **R** *v* **Malcherek and Steel** (1981) the court appeared to favour the approach that death occurs when the victim is brain-dead, but this did not form part of the *ratio decidendi* of the decision. Because there is no fixed legal definition of 'death', the point at which a person dies will be a question of fact for the court to decide in each case.

Causation

The prosecution must prove that the death was caused by the defendant's act. In many cases this will be obvious: for example, where the defendant shoots or stabs someone, and the victim dies immediately of the wounds. Difficulties may arise where there is more than one cause of death. This might be the act or omission of a third party which occurs after the defendant's act, and before the death, or some characteristic of the victim which means that the victim dies of the injury when a fitter person would have survived. Defendants can only be held responsible for a death where their acts are both a 'factual' and a 'legal' cause of the victim's death.

Factual causation

In order to establish factual causation, the prosecution must prove two things:

- That *but for* the conduct of the accused the victim would not have died as and when they did.

   The defendant will not be liable for the death if the victim would have died at the same time regardless of the defendant's act (or omission): in **White** (1910), the defendant gave his mother poison, but before it had a chance to take effect, she died of a heart attack which was not caused by the poison. He was not liable for her death.
- That the original injury arising from the defendant's conduct was *more than a minimal cause* of the victim's death.

   This is known as the *de minimis* rule, and it refers to the fact that when we say a person kills someone, what we actually mean is that they make the person's death occur earlier than it otherwise would, since we are all dying anyway. The acceleration of death caused by the defendant's conduct must be more than merely trivial; pricking the thumb of a woman bleeding to death would hasten her death, for example, but not enough to be the real cause of it.

Legal causation

Even if factual causation is established, the judge must direct the jury as to whether the defendant's acts are sufficient to amount in law to a cause of the victim's death. Legal causation can be proven in any one of the following three ways or by a combination of them:

The original injury was an operative and significant cause of death Under this criterion the prosecution must show that at the time of the victim's death, the original wound or injuries inflicted by the defendant were still an 'operative and substantial' cause of that death. In **R** *v* **Smith** (1959), a soldier was stabbed in a barrack-room brawl. He was dropped twice as he was being taken to the medical officer, and then there was a long delay before he was seen by a doctor, as the doctor mistakenly thought that his case was not urgent. When he did eventually receive treatment it was inappropriate for the injuries he was suffering from and harmful. Nonetheless the court took the view that these intervening factors had not broken the chain of causation so that the original wound was still an operative cause and the accused was liable for murder.

The same principle was followed in **R** *v* **Malcherek and Steel** (1981). The victims of two separate attacks had been kept on life support machines; these were switched off when tests showed that they were brain-dead. The two defendants argued that when the hospital switched off the machines the chain of causation was broken, thereby relieving the defendants of liability for murder. The court rejected this argument on the grounds that the original injuries were still an operative cause of their victims' deaths.

In **R** *v* **Cheshire** (1991), a dispute developed in a fish and chip shop, ending with the defendant shooting his victim in the leg and stomach, and seriously wounding him. The victim was taken to hospital, where his injuries were operated on, and he was placed in intensive care. As a result of negligent treatment by the medical staff, he developed complications affecting his breathing, and eventually died. His leg and stomach wounds were no longer life-threatening at the time of his death. The court stated that the critical question for the jury to answer was 'Has the Crown proved that the injuries inflicted by the defendant were a significant cause of death?' Negligent medical treatment could only break the chain of causation if it was so independent of the accused's acts, and such a powerful cause of death in itself, that the contribution made by the defendant's conduct was insignificant. This means that medical treatment can only break the chain of causation in the most extraordinary cases; incompetent or even grossly abnormal treatment will not suffice if the original injury is still an operative cause of death.

An example of such an extraordinary case might be **R** *v* **Jordan** (1956). The defendant was convicted of murder after stabbing the victim, but the conviction was quashed by the Court of Criminal Appeal when it heard new evidence that, at the time of the death, the original wound had almost healed, and the victim's death was brought on by the hospital giving him a drug to which he was known to be allergic – treatment that was described as 'palpably wrong'. It was held that the wound was no longer an operative cause of death. **Jordan** was described in the later case of **R** *v* **Smith** as a very particular case dependent upon its exact facts, and in **Malcherek** as an exceptional case, and is therefore unlikely to be used as a precedent. It seems that the law still requires very extraordinary circumstances for medical treatment to break the chain of causation.

It was pointed out in **R** *v* **Mellor** (1996) that the burden of proof is on the prosecution, so the defence do not have to prove that there was, for example, medical negligence in order to avoid liability. In that case the accused attacked a 71-year-old man breaking his ribs and facial bones. The victim died two weeks later of broncho-pneumonia, which would probably not have been fatal if, on the day of his death, he had been given oxygen. This failure may have constituted medical negligence. Certain passages in the judge's summing-up implied that there was a burden on the defence to prove medical negligence. Citing with approval the vital question on causation laid down in **Cheshire**, it was accepted that the jury had been misdirected. Nevertheless the conviction was upheld as the evidence against the appellant was overwhelming so that a correctly directed jury would have convicted.

The intervening act was reasonably foreseeable An intervening act which is reasonably foreseeable will not break the chain of legal causation. For example, if the defendant knocks the victim unconscious, and leaves him or her lying on a beach, it is reasonably foreseeable that when the tide comes in, the victim will drown, and the defendant will have caused that death. However, the defendant would not be liable for homicide if the victim was left unconscious on the seashore and run over by a car careering out of control off a nearby road as this could not have been foreseen. In **R** *v* **Pagett** (1983), the defendant was attempting to escape being captured by armed police, and used his girlfriend as a human shield. He shot at the police, and his girlfriend was killed by shots fired at him in self-defence by the policemen. The defendant was found liable for the girl's death as it was reasonably foreseeable that the police would shoot back and hit her in response to his shots. This is despite the fact that the police appear to have been negligent, as the mother of the girl subsequently succeeded in a claim for negligence in respect of the police operation in which her daughter was killed.

In cases involving medical treatment, only grossly abnormal treatment will be treated as not reasonably foreseeable, according to **Cheshire**. Treatment falling within the 'normal' band of incompetence will be regarded as foreseeable.

A defendant will avoid liability if a victim responds to their conduct in a way that is so daft that it could not have been foreseen. This issue arose in **R** *v* **Corbett** (1996) when a mentally handicapped man had been drinking heavily all day with the defendant. An argument ensued and the defendant started to hit and head-butt the victim who ran away. The victim fell into a gutter and was struck and killed by a car. At Corbett's trial for manslaughter the judge directed that he was the cause of the victim's death if the victim's conduct of running away was within the range of foreseeable responses to the defendant's behaviour. An appeal against this direction was rejected.

In **R v Dear** (1996) the Court of Appeal suggested that if the defendant's conduct was still an operative and significant cause of the death, the defendant would in law be the cause of that death, regardless of whether or not any intervening factors were foreseeable. The accused's daughter told him that she had been sexually assaulted. On hearing this allegation the accused stabbed the alleged abuser repeatedly with a knife. The victim died two days later. On appeal against his conviction for murder the appellant argued that he was not the cause of the death. He contended that the deceased had committed suicide either by reopening his wounds or, the wounds having reopened themselves, by failing to seek medical attention and the suicide broke the chain of causation. The appeal was dismissed as the injuries inflicted on the deceased were an operative and significant cause of the death. In such a case as this it was not necessary to consider the degree of fault in the victim or to consider how foreseeable the victim's conduct was. This approach has been criticized on the basis that it ignores previous authorities which state that the chain of causation is broken if the victim's conduct was so daft that it could not have been foreseen. It may be that this case will be distinguished from those authorities on the basis that the operative and substantive test had been satisfied on the facts of the case, and not in the earlier authorities; or it may be that **R v Dear** will not be followed.

The 'thin skull' test Where the intervening cause is some existing weakness of the victim, the defendant must take the victim as he or she finds him. Known as the 'thin skull' rule, this means that if, for example, a defendant hits a person over the head with the kind of blow which would not usually kill, but the victim has an unusually thin skull which makes the blow fatal, the defendant will be liable for the subsequent death. The principle has been extended to mental conditions and beliefs, as well as physical characteristics. In **R v Blaue** (1975), the victim of a stabbing was a Jehovah's Witness, a church which, among other things, forbids its members to have blood transfusions. As a result of her refusal to accept a transfusion, the victim died of her wounds. The Court of Appeal rejected the defendant's argument that her refusal broke the chain of causation, on the ground that the accused had to take his victim as he found her.

Failure to prove causation

If the prosecution fail to prove both factual and legal causation of the death, the defendant will escape liability for murder (or any other unlawful homicide), on the ground that the original injury was not in law the cause of death. However, the defendant may still be liable for the original act, for example under a charge for a non-fatal offence against the person.

MURDER

There are three types of unlawful homicide: murder, voluntary manslaughter and involuntary manslaughter. The degree of seriousness applied to each offence is essentially a reflection of the defendant's state of mind with regard to the killing. Murder is the most serious category of unlawful homicide, and is designed to apply to those killings which society regards as most abhorrent.

▶ Definition

The offence of murder is not defined in any statute. It is committed under common law where a person causes the death of a human being, with malice aforethought. Thus the *actus reus* comprises the common elements of all homicide offences discussed above, and the *mens rea* is malice aforethought. Murder carries a mandatory sentence of life imprisonment.

▶ *Mens rea*

The *mens rea* for murder is defined as malice aforethought, which has come to mean either an intention to kill or an intention to cause grievous bodily harm. 'Grievous' simply means 'really serious' – **DPP** *v* **Smith** (1961). When directing a jury, the judge can sometimes miss out the word 'really' and simply talk about the requirement that the defendant intended 'serious bodily harm'. In **R** *v* **Janjua and Choudury** (1998) a young man was stabbed to death with the five-and-a-half inch blade of a knife. The trial judge merely referred to a requirement that the defendants needed to have intended 'serious bodily harm' in order to be liable for murder. They were convicted and appealed on the basis of a misdirection because the word 'really' had been omitted. The Court of Appeal dismissed the appeal stating that, given the nature of the weapon and the injuries caused, the use of the word 'really' in this case was not required. It was a matter for the trial judges in the light of the factual situations with which they were confronted to decide whether or not to use the word 'really' before the word 'serious'.

The term malice aforethought is actually deceptive: the defendant's motives need not be malicious, and are in fact irrelevant; deliberate euthanasia prompted by motives of compassion satisfies the *mens rea* requirement just as well as shooting someone because you hate them. Nor, despite the word 'aforethought', is premeditation a necessary requirement; so long as the required intention is there, it is perfectly possible for a murder to be committed on the spur of the moment. For these reasons, the *mens rea* of murder is best thought of as intention to kill or cause grievous bodily harm. In Chapter 1 it was observed that there are actually two types of intention, direct and oblique, both of which are sufficient for the purposes of the criminal law.

Intention is purely subjective

The test of what the defendant foresaw and intended is always a subjective one, based on what the jury believes the defendant actually foresaw and intended, and not what he or she should have foreseen or intended, or what anyone else might have foreseen or intended in the same situation.

In **DPP** *v* **Smith** (1961), a police officer tried to stop a car that had been involved in a robbery, by clinging to its bonnet as the car drove off, and was killed. The defendant said he did not want to kill the police officer; he had simply wanted to get away. The House of Lords appeared to say that a person intended death or grievous bodily harm if a reasonable person would have foreseen that death or grievous bodily harm would result from the act of the defendant, even if the defendant did not actually foresee this. However, this objective test was considered bad law and s. 8 of the Criminal Justice Act 1967 was passed to change it. This provides that a person is not to be regarded as having intended or foreseen the natural and probable consequences of an act simply because they were natural and probable, although this may be evidence from which the jury may infer that it was intended. The crucial issue is what the defendant actually foresaw and intended, not what he or she *should* have foreseen or intended.

Direct intent

Direct intent corresponds with the everyday definition of intention, and applies where the accused actually wants the result that occurs, and sets out to achieve it. An obvious example of direct intention to kill would be deliberately pointing a gun at someone you want to kill and shooting them.

Oblique intent

Oblique or indirect intention is less straightforward. It applies where the accused did not desire a particular result but in acting as he or she did, realized that it might occur. For example, a mother wishes to frighten her children and so starts a fire in the house. She does not want to kill her children, but she realizes that there is a risk that they may die as a result of the fire. The courts are now quite clear that oblique intention can be sufficient for murder: people can intend deaths that they do not necessarily want. But in a line of important cases, they have tried to specify the necessary degree of foresight required in order to provide evidence of intention.

In **R *v* Moloney** (1985) the defendant was a soldier who was on leave at the time of the incident that gave rise to his prosecution. He was staying with his mother and stepfather, with whom he was apparently on very good terms. The family held a dinner party, during which the appellant and his stepfather drank rather a lot of alcohol. They stayed up after everyone else had left or gone to bed; shortly after 4.00 a.m. a shot was fired and the appellant was heard to say, 'I have shot my father.'

The court was told that Moloney and his stepfather had had a contest to see who could load his gun and be ready to fire first. Moloney had been quicker, and stood pointing the gun at his stepfather, who teased him that he would not dare to fire a live bullet; at that point Moloney, by his own admission, pulled the trigger. In evidence he said, 'I never conceived that what I was doing might cause injury to anybody. It was just a lark.' Clearly he did not want to kill his stepfather, but could he be said to have intended to do so? Lord Bridge pointed out that it was quite possible to intend a result which you do not actually want. He gave the example of a man who, in an attempt to escape pursuit, boards a plane to Manchester. Even though he may have no desire to go to Manchester – he may even hate the place for some reason – that is clearly where he intends to go.

Foresight is merely evidence of intent

Moloney established that a person can have intention where they did not want the result but merely foresaw it, yet the courts are not saying that foresight is intention. Foresight is merely evidence from which intention can be found.

Before **Moloney**, in the case of **Hyam *v* DPP** (1975), it had looked as though foresight was actually intention, though the judgment in that case was not very clear. The defendant, Pearl Hyam, put blazing newspaper through the letterbox of the house of a Mrs Booth, who was going on holiday with Pearl Hyam's boyfriend; Mrs Booth's two children were killed in the fire. On the facts it appeared that Pearl Hyam did not want to kill the two children; she wanted to set fire to the house and to frighten Mrs Booth. The court held that she must have foreseen that death or grievous bodily harm were highly likely to result from her conduct, and that this was sufficient *mens rea* for murder. In **Moloney**, the House of Lords held that **Hyam** had been wrongly decided, and that nothing less than intention to kill or cause grievous bodily harm would constitute malice aforethought: merely foreseeing the victim's death as probable was not intent, though it could be evidence of it.

Lord Bridge suggested that juries might be asked to consider two questions: was death or really serious injury a 'natural consequence' of the defendant's act, and did the defendant foresee that one or the other was a natural consequence of their act? If the answer was 'yes' the jury might infer from this evidence that the death was intended.

This guidance for juries in turn proved to be problematic. In **R** *v* **Hancock and Shankland** (1986), the defendants were striking miners who knew that a taxi, carrying men breaking the strike to work, would pass along a particular road. They waited on a bridge above it, and dropped a concrete block which hit the taxi as it passed underneath, killing the driver. At their trial the judge had given the direction suggested by Lord Bridge in **Moloney** and they were convicted of murder. On appeal, the House of Lords held that this had been incorrect, and a verdict of manslaughter was substituted. Their Lordships agreed with Lord Bridge that conviction for murder could result only from proof of intention, and that foresight of consequences was not in itself intention; but they were concerned that the question of whether the death was a 'natural consequence' of the defendants' act might suggest to juries that they need not consider the degree of probability. The fact that there might be a ten-million-to-one chance that death would result from the defendants' act might still mean that death was a natural consequence of it, in the sense that it had happened without any interference, but, with this degree of likelihood, there would seem to be little evidence of intention.

Lord Scarman suggested that the jury should be directed that: '. . . the greater the probability of a consequence, the more likely it is that the consequence was foreseen and that if that consequence was foreseen the greater the probability is that that consequence was also intended . . . But juries also need to be reminded that the decision is theirs to be reached upon a consideration of all the evidence.'

Thus if a person stabs another in the chest, it is highly likely this will lead to death or grievous bodily harm, and since most people would be well aware of that, it is likely that they would foresee death or serious injury when they acted. If they did foresee this then that is evidence of intent, from which a jury might conclude that the death was intended. But if you cut someone's finger, that person could die as a result – from blood poisoning for example – but since this is highly unlikely, the chances are that you would not have foreseen that they might die when you cut the finger, and your lack of foresight would be evidence that you did not intend the death.

The concept was further clarified in **R** *v* **Nedrick** (1986). The defendant had a grudge against a woman, and poured paraffin through the letterbox of her house and set it alight. The woman's child died in the fire. Lord Lane CJ said:

Where the charge is murder and in the rare cases where the simple direction is not enough, the jury should be directed that they are not entitled to infer the necessary intention unless they feel sure that death or serious bodily harm was a virtual certainty (barring some unforeseen intervention) as a result of the defendant's actions and that the defendant appreciated that such was the case.

Where a man realizes that it is for all practical purposes inevitable that his actions will result in death or serious harm, the inference may be irresistible that he intended that result, however little he may have desired or wished it to happen . . . The decision is one for the jury to be reached on a consideration of all the evidence.

In other words, Lord Scarman considered that even if death or grievous bodily harm is not the defendant's aim or wish, the jury may infer intent if they decide that death or grievous bodily harm were virtually certain to result from what the defendant did, and the defendant foresaw that that was the case. Such foresight was still only evidence from which they might infer intent, and not intent itself, although it would be difficult not to infer intent where the defendant foresaw that death or grievous bodily harm was practically inevitable as a result of his or her acts.

The virtual certainty test in **Nedrick** became the key test on indirect intention. Then confusion was thrown into this area of the law by the Court of Appeal judgment in **R** *v* **Woollin** in 1996. Having given various explanations for his three-month-old son's injuries in the ambulance and in the first two police interviews, Woollin eventually admitted that he had 'lost his cool' when his son had choked on his food. He had picked him up, shaken him and thrown him across the room with considerable force towards a pram standing next to a wall about five feet away. He stated that he had not intended or thought that he would kill the child and had not wanted the child to die. The judge directed the jury that it was open to them to convict Woollin of murder if satisfied that he was aware there was a 'substantial risk' he would cause serious injury. On appeal the defence argued that the judge had misdirected the jury by using the term 'a substantial risk' which was the test for recklessness and failing to use the phrase 'virtual certainty' derived from **Nedrick** for oblique intention. The appeal was rejected by the Court of Appeal which held that in directing a jury a judge was obliged to use the phrase 'virtual certainty' if the only evidence of intent was the actions of the accused constituting the *actus reus* of the offence and their consequences on the victim. Where other evidence was available, the judge was neither obliged to use that phrase, nor a phrase that meant the same thing. The Court of Appeal felt that otherwise the jury function as laid down in s. 8 of the Criminal Justice Act 1967 would be undermined. This section (discussed on p. 24) states:

> A court or jury in determining whether a person had committed an offence,
> (a) shall not be bound in law to infer that he intended or foresaw a result of his actions by reason only of its being a natural and probable consequence of those actions; but
> (b) shall decide whether he did intend or foresee that result by reference to all the evidence, drawing such inferences from the evidence as appear proper in the circumstances.

Thus Parliament had recognized in that provision that a court or jury could infer that a defendant intended a result of their actions by reason of its being a natural and probable result of those actions. In deciding whether the defendant intended the natural and probable result of their actions, s. 8 stated that the court or jury was to take into account all the evidence, drawing such inferences as appeared proper. Section 8 contained no restrictive provision about the result being a 'virtual certainty'. The facts of **Woollin** fell within the category of cases where there was more evidence of intention than purely the conduct of the defendant constituting the *actus reus* of the offence and the result of the conduct, for in addition there was the conduct of the defendant in the first two interviews and his description of events to the ambulance controller.

A further appeal was made to the House of Lords. This ruled that the Court of Appeal and the trial judge had been mistaken. It said that the **Nedrick** direction was always required in the context of indirect intention. Otherwise there would be no clear distinction between intention and recklessness as both would be concerned simply with the foresight of a risk. The **Nedrick** direction distinguishes the two concepts by stating that intention will only exist when the risk is foreseen as a virtual certainty. Accordingly, a conviction for manslaughter was substituted.

Thus the **Nedrick** 'virtual certainty' direction was approved, though two amendments were made to it. Firstly, the original **Nedrick** direction told the jury that 'they are not entitled to *infer* the necessary intention, unless they feel sure that death or serious bodily harm was a virtual certainty'. The House of Lords substituted the word 'find' for the word 'infer'. This change was to deal with the criticism that the jury were told in the past that they could 'infer' intention from the existence of the foresight and this suggested that intention was something different from the foresight itself, but did not specify what it was. But the difficulties are not completely resolved by the change from 'infer' to 'find' as the jury are still only 'entitled' to make this finding, and it is still a question of evidence for the jury – it is not clear when this finding should be made. It might be more logical to oblige a jury to conclude that there is intention where a person foresaw a result as a virtual certainty.

The second amendment was that the majority of the House of Lords felt that the first sentence of the second paragraph of Lord Lane's statement in **Nedrick** quoted above ('Where a man realises . . . .') did not form part of the model direction. So the jury will not normally be pressurized into finding intention by being told that a finding of intention 'may be irresistible'. Thus the model direction now reads as follows:

> Where the charge is murder and in the rare cases where the simple direction is not enough, the jury should be directed that they are not entitled to find the necessary intention unless they feel sure that death or serious bodily harm was a virtual certainty (barring some unforeseen intervention) as a result of the defendant's actions and that the defendant appreciated that such was the case. The decision is one for the jury to be reached on a consideration of all the evidence.

▶ Criticism

Definition of death

The lack of a precise definition of death creates uncertainty in the law, but the courts are reluctant to clarify the issue because it is such an emotive subject. In many other comparable jurisdictions, legislation has been passed to provide a definition of death, with most countries accepting that for legal purposes death occurs when the brain stem is dead and the victim's brain cannot function spontaneously. However, when the Criminal Law Revision Committee considered the issue in 1980, it concluded that statute should not intervene.

The year and a day rule

For centuries, in order for a defendant to be liable for a homicide offence, the victim had to die within 366 days of the last act (or omission) done to the victim by the defendant. The rule traditionally acted as a rather primitive test of causation; if the victim survived for longer than a year and a day, it could be reasonably assumed that death was caused by something other than the defendant's act. In **R** *v* **Dyson** (1908), a father physically abused his baby daughter Lily on 13 November 1906 and then again on 29 December 1907. She died on 5 March 1908. On appeal, Dyson's conviction for murder was quashed, because the judge had wrongly directed at the original trial that he could be convicted even if she had died solely as a result of the first assault. This was incorrect because that act had taken place over a year and a day before her death.

Over the years this rule had attracted considerable criticism. Advances in medical science – particularly life support technology – mean that victims can be kept alive for longer than a year and a day, even though the original injuries remain the actual cause of death. The Law Reform (Year and a Day Rule) Act 1996 has therefore abolished the old common law rule.

In order to prevent oppressive prosecutions, proceedings for a fatal offence require the consent of the Attorney-General if the victim dies over three years after the infliction of an injury which is alleged to have caused the death, or the accused has previously been convicted of an offence for the original injury.

Intention to cause grievous bodily harm

Murder is the most serious homicide offence and associated in the public's mind with deliberate killing, yet defendants may be convicted of it without intending to kill, or even foreseeing that death was a possible result of their acts, if they intended to cause grievous bodily harm. The rule has been questioned by several judges, notably in **Hyam**, but it was confirmed by the House of Lords in **Moloney**.

There has been a lengthy campaign to reduce the forms of malice aforethought to one, the intent to kill, on the grounds that the term murder should be reserved for the most blameworthy type of behaviour. A House of Lords Select Committee recommended replacing intent to cause grievous bodily harm with intent to cause serious personal harm, being aware that death may result from that harm. This is contained in the draft Criminal Code. 'Being aware' would imply subjective knowledge; it would not be sufficient that a reasonable person would have known if the accused did not.

Problems with intention

The criminal law as laid down in **Moloney** and subsequent cases does not define intent, it only gives guidelines on how a jury might tell when it is present; so the same facts might equally produce a conviction or acquittal depending on the make-up of the jury. As Smith and Hogan point out, this effectively means that juries will end up calling awareness of the probable consequences 'intention' if they think the circumstances of the case demand a conviction, and find that the same degree of foresight does not amount to intention where they feel an acquittal is appropriate.

Smith and Hogan also argue that the requirement that the consequences should actually be virtually certain is illogical, since the person who wrongly thinks that death is likely to result is as morally guilty as the one who is correct in his assumption. If you point a gun at someone with the intention of killing him, that intention is not lessened by the fact that unknown to you he is wearing a bulletproof vest.

Euthanasia

For a discussion of the issues surrounding euthanasia see p. 292.

▶ **Proposals for reform**

Foresight of harm to equal intention

The Law Commission has stated that 'it is in the interests of clarity and the consistent application of criminal law to define intention'. In common with a House of Lords Select Committee, it recommends that foresight of a virtual certainty should amount to intention. This would mean that foresight would again be part of the substantive law, not merely part of the evidence. At present, a person who kills foreseeing death or grievous bodily harm as virtually certain *may* be a murderer; under the reformed scheme such a person *would* be a murderer. The House of Lords judgment in **Woollin** only goes halfway to achieving this reform, as the jury are still only 'entitled' to find intention and the matter is still a question of evidence. Lord Bridge in **R** *v* **Moloney** had not wanted to treat foresight as intention in law because he was anxious to draw a distinction between intention and recklessness. Thus foresight amounted to recklessness in law, while foresight was only evidence of intention. But this problem is now avoided by drawing the distinction between the two forms of *mens rea* on the basis that only foresight of a virtual certainty will suffice for intention, while a lesser degree of foresight will suffice for recklessness.

'Conditional' intent

This concept is put forward by Smith and Hogan. To explain it, they use the example of a person who throws a stone at someone who is behind a closed window; the thrower's aim may be to hit the person inside, and they may have no desire to break the window, yet they know that the window will be broken if the stone is to hit its target. In other words, a result may be said to be conditionally intended where it was not the actor's purpose, but was a condition of achieving that purpose. Smith and Hogan suggest that a consequence should only be considered to have been intended if it was either the defendant's purpose, or a result which he or she knew or believed had to take place if that purpose was to be achieved. As they point out, anything less certain than this represents a difficult boundary between intention and recklessness.

Mens rea to include recklessness

It could be argued that there are some reckless killings which ought to be classified as murder, since they show such an enormous disregard for human life that they are morally equivalent to intentional killings. The example above of terrorists who plant bombs, but in some cases escape liability for murder because a warning was given, might be included in this category, as may the owners of companies who flout health and safety laws in the pursuit of profit, sometimes causing the most horrific deaths. In one such case, a factory owner was warned several times by the Health and Safety Executive (HSE) that a plastic-shredding machine should be fenced while it was in operation, but because the machine worked faster unfenced, the warnings were ignored, with the result that an employee was dragged into the machine and killed. In such cases, the individuals are rarely prosecuted at all, because the HSE prefers a persuasive approach, but when they are, as in this case, it is for manslaughter, because intention is difficult to prove in a company situation. Yet this degree of carelessness with human life is surely as morally blameworthy as pointing a gun at someone.

Lord Goff has recommended the adoption in English law of the Scottish definition of murder, which goes beyond intention to kill and labels as murder a killing which displays 'such wicked recklessness as to imply a disposition depraved enough to be regardless of the consequences'. However, this definition can be criticized as being vague, and likely to present problems for juries.

A system of classifications

An offence of second degree murder, where the accused does not fit into the legal definition of intention, but was aware of the risk of death, might be one way to include a higher proportion of terrorist and corporate crimes in the definition of murder.

Abolish distinctions between murder and manslaughter

It has been suggested that the present distinction between murder and manslaughter should be abolished, creating a single offence of homicide, or unlawful killing. The offence would be the same, regardless of the accused's state of mind and the circumstances, but these would be taken into account in order to determine the appropriate level of punishment. One criticism of this suggestion is that it would take important elements of the decision out of the hands of the jury, and the standard of proof beyond reasonable doubt, and give them to the judge, who would decide them on the basis of the less strict criteria used in sentencing.

Abolish the mandatory life sentence

The mandatory life sentence for murder means that once convicted of the offence, defendants face the same penalty whether they are savage

and cold-blooded killers or terrorists, people who have helped a terminally ill relative to die on compassionate grounds, people like Moloney,
more foolish than evil – or anywhere in between. This inflexibility prevents the court from taking into account motive or circumstances, both
of which may make an enormous difference to the way in which society
would view the individual offence – and after all, in dealing with murder
victims, the courts are supposed to be registering society's disapproval.
This issue has been highlighted in cases where women have killed their
abusive partners. A House of Lords Select Committee that reported in
1989 has recommended that the mandatory sentence of life imprisonment for murder be abolished, and the sentence left at the discretion of
the court. This change would probably have to be combined with either
a system of classification, or the abolition of separate offences of manslaughter and murder, in order to allow the jury to give its verdict on the
seriousness of the offence.

• •
ANSWERING QUESTIONS

1 Simon wants to kill his girlfriend Polly and in order to do so, puts rat
poison in her coffee. This would normally only be sufficient to make an
ordinary person sick, but Polly is unusually sensitive to rat poison. She is
taken to hospital where the doctor diagnoses her illness as appendicitis. She
is kept in hospital and dies a few days later from poisoning. Discuss Simon's
liability for Polly's death.
Note that you are only asked to discuss Simon's liability, so you are not
concerned with any possible liability of the doctors. The starting point in
looking at Simon's liability is the offence of murder. Work your way through
the elements of liability in the same order discussed in this chapter. Look first
at the *actus reus*. Quite a lot of your time will be spent on discussing the issue
of causation. Two factors might have broken the chain of causation – the
abnormal sensitivity of Polly to the poison and the doctor's misdiagnosis – and
you need to apply the tests of both factual and legal causation. As far as the
doctor's misdiagnosis is concerned, relevant cases include **Cheshire** and **Smith**.
You need to consider whether the original acts of Simon are still an operative
cause of Polly's death, and whether the misdiagnosis falls into the 'normal band
of competence' and was therefore reasonably foreseeable. Polly's abnormal
sensitivity to rat poison is covered by **Blaue** and the 'thin skull' test.
   Some students get confused and think that if one person, such as the
doctor, is the cause of death nobody else (such as Simon) can be, but this is
not the case: more than one person can be the cause of death.
   If the chain of causation has been broken (unlikely) Simon could not be
liable for any other homicide offence, but he could be liable for a non-fatal
offence. You then need to consider the *mens rea* of murder: we know that
Simon intended to kill, which if it can be proved is sufficient *mens rea*. Simon's

knowledge, or lack of it, concerning Polly's sensitivity to rat poison will be important evidence from which the jury may infer intent. Cite the relevant authorities such as **Moloney, Nedrick** and **Woollin** to support your argument.

2 Critically evaluate the *mens rea* of murder.

Your introduction should define the *mens rea* of murder, pointing out that it is a subjective test, covers both intention to kill and to cause grievous bodily harm, and includes both direct and indirect intention. On indirect intention cases such as **Moloney, Hancock and Shankland, Nedrick,** and the latest case of **R** *v* **Woollin** should be looked at in detail. Then go through the criticism that applies to the current law on *mens rea* and some of the proposed reforms (see p. 53). Your conclusion might highlight the fact that *mens rea* is the factor that makes murder our most serious offence, and that it is therefore important that problems with it should be ironed out.

Make sure you stick to answering the question: you are asked only about the *mens rea* of murder, so you cannot discuss the *actus reus* of the offence. Nothing will be gained by analysing the law on, for example, causation. As the *mens rea* of murder is intention no marks would be gained either for discussing **Caldwell** and **Cunningham**, which are both concerned with recklessness. Avoid making the classic error of stating that the offence of murder is defined in s. 1 of the Homicide Act 1957. It is not. Murder is a common law offence and is therefore not defined in a statute.

4 Voluntary manslaughter

Most unlawful homicides which are not classified as murder are manslaughter. There are two kinds of manslaughter: voluntary, which is considered here; and involuntary, which will form the subject of the next chapter. The basic difference between these two types of manslaughter is that for voluntary manslaughter the *mens rea* for murder exists, whereas for involuntary manslaughter it does not.

Voluntary manslaughter occurs where the accused has the necessary *actus reus* and *mens rea* for murder, but there are mitigating circumstances which allow a partial defence, and so reduce liability to that of manslaughter (we call this a partial defence to distinguish it from other defences which remove liability completely). It is not therefore possible to charge someone with voluntary manslaughter; they will be charged with murder, and must then put their defence during the trial.

The three partial defences available are provocation, diminished responsibility, and suicide pacts, which are defined in ss. 2, 3 and 4 of the Homicide Act 1957. Successful pleading of one of the three means that on conviction the sentence is at the discretion of the judge, and can be anything from life imprisonment to an absolute discharge, depending on the circumstances of the case; unlike murder, which carries a mandatory sentence of life imprisonment.

PROVOCATION

Section 3 of the Homicide Act 1957 provides:

> Where on a charge of murder there is evidence on which the jury can find that the person charged was provoked (whether by things done or by things said or by both together) to lose his self-control, the question whether the provocation was enough to make a reasonable man do as he did shall be left to be determined by the jury; and in determining that question the jury shall take into account everything both done and said according to the effect which, in their opinion, it would have on a reasonable man.

Three elements have to be proved: provocative conduct; that the provocation made the defendant lose their self-control; and that a reasonable person would have been so provoked. It was emphasized by the Court of Appeal in **R v Baille** (1995) that these issues are to be decided by the jury. So the question of provocation should usually be left to the jury rather than the judge deciding that as a matter of law provocation did not exist. In that case the defendant had shot and killed a man who sold drugs to his three sons. He opposed their drug use and had been thrown into a rage when he heard that the drug dealer had put pressure on one of his sons to buy more drugs than the son wanted. While there were factors which weighed against a finding of provocation the matter should still have been left to the jury.

▶ Provocative conduct

Since the Homicide Act 1957, provocation may be 'by things done or by things said or by both together', so words alone may suffice. The provocative act need not be illegal or even wrongful: in **Doughty** (1986), it was held that the persistent crying of a baby could amount to provocation.

Mere circumstances cannot constitute provocation, so a novelist discovering that his or her manuscript has been eaten by a dog, or a farmer finding a crop ruined by flooding, would not have a defence if they consequently lost control and struck out and killed the nearest person.

The provocative acts need not have been directed at the defendant. In **R v Pearson** (1992), two brothers killed their violent, tyrannical father with a sledgehammer. It was held that the father's violent treatment of the younger brother, during the eight years when his older brother was away from home, was relevant to the older boy's defence, especially as he had returned home to protect his brother.

The old case of **Duffy** (1949) had ruled that the provocation had to be something 'done by the dead man to the accused', but the 1957 Act removes this requirement. In **R v Davies** (1975), it was held that the acts of the lover of Davies's wife could be taken into account as provoking Davies to kill his wife.

The fact that the provocation was induced by the defendant in the first place does not necessarily prevent the defence being made out. In **R v Johnson** (1989), Johnson and a friend, R, had been drinking at a night club. Johnson threatened violence towards R's female friend and to R himself, and a struggle developed between Johnson and R. Johnson was carrying a flick knife, and stabbed R, killing him. He was convicted of murder and appealed on the ground that the judge should have directed the jury on provocation. His appeal was allowed and a conviction for manslaughter was substituted.

However, in such cases the provocation of the defendant must be extreme by comparison with the defendant's original act. The defendant in **Edwards** *v* **R** (1973) tried to blackmail his victim, who attacked him with a knife. A fight ensued, during which Edwards grabbed the knife and fatally stabbed his attacker. The Privy Council held that the defendant could only rely on provocation as a defence if the victim's reaction to the blackmail had been extreme, compared to the blackmail itself. In this case they felt that it was, but said there could be cases where provocation should not be left to the jury because it was self-induced.

A defendant who is provoked as the result of a mistake of fact is entitled to be treated as if the facts were as that defendant mistakenly supposed them to be. In **R** *v* **Brown** (1972), the defendant, a soldier, struck his victim with a sword and killed him, because he wrongly, but apparently reasonably, supposed that his victim was a member of a gang attacking him. His defence of provocation was successful.

▶ Loss of self-control

This is a subjective test; did the defendant actually lose their self-control? The loss of self-control must be due to a loss of temper and the case of **R** *v* **Cocker** (1989) shows that this can produce harsh results. The accused suffocated his wife, who was suffering from a painful terminal illness, and had repeatedly begged him to end her life. The judge withdrew the issue of provocation from the jury, who then felt they had no alternative but to convict of murder, but wrote a letter of protest to the judge, stating that they felt the decision they had been forced to make was unfair. The Court of Appeal held that the judge had acted correctly: loss of self-control meant loss of temper and the appellant on these facts had not lost his temper but merely succumbed to his wife's requests.

An important but controversial qualification was laid down in **R** *v* **Duffy** (1949): namely that the loss of self-control must be 'sudden and temporary'. This was unlikely to be the case if the murder was committed for revenge, since 'the conscious formation of a desire for revenge means that a person has had time to think'. This principle was further developed in **R** *v* **Ibrams** (1981), where it was held that the existence of a 'cooling-off period' between the act of provocation and the killing was evidence that the loss of self-control was not 'sudden and temporary'. The defendants and a young woman had been severely bullied by a man called Monk, over a period up to and including Sunday 7 October, and had tried and failed to obtain effective police protection. On Wednesday 10 October, they discussed the fact that Monk was likely to terrorize them again on Sunday 14 October, and made a plan. On Sunday, they would get Monk drunk, and encourage him to take to his bed. The woman would leave a signal for the defendants, who would then enter and attack him, with the aim of breaking his arms and legs. All this they did, with the result that Monk was in fact killed. The appellants were convicted of murder and appealed on the ground that the judge had wrongly withdrawn the defence of provocation from the jury. The appeal was rejected; although it was possible that provocation might extend over a long period of time, it must culminate in a sudden explosion of temper, which did not seem to be apparent in the carefully planned killing.

The requirement for a 'sudden and temporary' loss of control, with the implication against a 'cooling-off period' as raised in **Ibrams**, has been controversial because it is said to discriminate against women, an issue discussed in more detail below. Recent cases have given a more generous interpretation of the time factor. In **R** *v* **Thornton** (1992) Sara Thornton had at one point declared her intention of killing her husband, who had for years been beating her. Later, after a fresh provocation, she went to the kitchen, took and sharpened a carving knife and returned to another room where she stabbed him. The original trial judge considered that despite the time lapse the issue of provocation should be left to the jury; nevertheless the jury convicted Sara Thornton of murder. At her appeal the Court of Appeal confirmed that the issue of whether or not there had been a sudden and temporary loss of self-control was one for the jury.

A striking example of the courts being lenient where there has been a time lapse is **R** *v* **Pearson** (1992). The Court of Appeal considered there was evidence of provocation even though the two defendants had armed themselves in advance with a sledgehammer, and had sufficient self-control to act together in the killing. It should be remembered though that the existence of a cooling-off period is not a matter of law, but a piece of evidence which the jury may use to decide whether at the time of the killing the defendant was deprived of self-control. This was emphasized in the case of Ahluwalia.

In considering the provocation, a court can take into account the cumulative provocation that has taken place over a long period of time before the last provocative act. This point was made in a recent case relating to battered women: **R** *v* **Humphrey** (1995). Emma Humphrey's parents divorced when she was very young and she was brought up by her mother and stepfather, who were both alcoholics. She developed anti-social behaviour, frequently attempting suicide, usually by slashing her wrists, and she had to receive psychiatric treatment. When she was sixteen she became a prostitute and moved in with a man who was both her boyfriend and her pimp. He had previous convictions for violence and mentally, physically and sexually abused her. Later that year he brought another woman friend to live in the house as well. One evening Emma met up with her boyfriend, his son and two friends in a pub. He told these people that they would be 'all right for a gang-bang' that night. When Emma and her boyfriend returned to the house, he removed his clothes apart from his shirt and she feared that he was going to rape her. Taking two knives she cut her wrists but he taunted her that she had not made a very good job of it, at which point she stabbed him. She was convicted of murder but ten years later in 1995 the Court of Appeal allowed her appeal because of misdirections at her original trial on the law of provocation, and substituted a verdict of manslaughter, thus allowing her immediate release.

The Court of Appeal criticized the judge's direction to the jury to consider only the deceased's taunts about her wrist-slashing in deciding whether she had been provoked and whether her reaction was reasonable. They said that the whole history of their relationship was relevant: his violence, his taking in another girl, the reference to a 'gang-bang' and his undressing to his shirt should all have been treated as part of the provocative conduct, not simply as background to the taunt. Thus the jury can look at the period of cumulative provocation and not just the immediately preceding provocative conduct.

▶ The 'reasonable person' test

For the defence to succeed, it must be proved that not only would a reasonable person have been provoked, but that such provocation would have made a reasonable person act as the defendant did – in other words, that the response was not out of all proportion to the provocation.

The House of Lords stated in **R** *v* **Acott** (1997) that where, on a charge of murder, there is evidence on which the jury can find that the person charged was provoked to lose their self-control, the question whether the provocation was enough to make a reasonable person do as they did must be left to be determined by the jury. If there is only a speculative possibility of provocation the issue should not be left to the jury. Acott's mother was found dead after having consumed a substantial quantity of alcohol and after having received multiple injuries. At the accused's trial for her murder, his defence was that his mother's injuries had been the result of an accidental fall and his unskilled attempts to resuscitate her. During cross-examination it was submitted by the prosecution that the accused had killed her having lost his temper because of the cumulative effect of an argument, her heavy drinking bouts, being treated as if he was still a child and the humiliation of having to ask her for money as he was unemployed. The judge did not direct the jury as to a possible defence of provocation and Acott was convicted of murder. His appeal was dismissed by the Court of Appeal and the House of Lords. The House stated that as there was no specific evidence of provocation, but merely speculation, the judge was right not to direct the jury on the issue of provocation.

A whole string of cases have dealt with the question of who is the reasonable person in the context of the objective test of provocation.

It was laid down in **Camplin** that this was a matter of fact for the jury to decide: the judge could not direct that, for example, fists might be answered with fists, but never with a deadly weapon **(Duffy)**. It was pointed out in **Philips** (1968) that in deciding whether the response was appropriate, the jury would have to bear in mind that the response took place when self-control was already lost.

Before the Homicide Act 1957, judges frequently took it upon themselves to tell juries what could be expected from the reasonable person, taking no account of the defendant's actual characteristics. This approach led to the notorious case of **Bedder** *v* **DPP** (1954). The defendant, an eighteen-year-old who was sexually impotent, had tried, unsuccessfully, to have intercourse with a prostitute. She taunted him and kicked him in the genitals, and he responded by stabbing her, as a result of which she died. The trial judge directed that the jury should not have to work out what the effects of the woman's provocation might be on a man who suffered from impotence, but should apply them to a reasonable man, who, by virtue of the fact that he was a reasonable man, could not be impotent! As the reasonable man would probably be fairly indifferent to taunts about being sexually impotent when he knew that he was not, it is not surprising that the jury rejected his defence of provocation.

This approach was upheld by the House of Lords but a more rational approach was subsequently taken in **DPP** *v* **Camplin** (1978) and **Bedder** *v* **DPP** is now bad law. In **DPP** *v* **Camplin**, the House of Lords defined the 'reasonable man' as a person with the power of self-control to be expected from an ordinary person of the defendant's age and sex, and sharing any other permanent characteristics of the defendant that the jury believed affected the gravity of the provocation to him. Camplin was a 15-year-old boy. At the time of the offence he had been drinking, and claimed that he had been homosexually assaulted by his victim and that afterwards the man had laughed at him. Camplin lost control, hit his victim over the head with a chapatti pan and killed him. The court said that the question the jury should ask themselves was whether the provocation offered would have caused a reasonable boy of Camplin's age to act as he did.

In **R** *v* **Roberts** (1990), a 23-year-old man, who suffered from substantial deafness and impaired speech, killed someone as the result of taunts about this condition. It was held that the judge had rightly directed that the hypothetical reasonable man had those characteristics.

The case of **R** *v* **Dryden** (1995) arose from a planning dispute. The appellant had built a bungalow without the necessary planning permission. There followed a long-running battle with the local planning authority during which the defendant stated that he would shoot the planning officer if he tried to demolish the property. On 20 June 1991 a local planning officer arrived at the bungalow and informed the appellant that it was about to be demolished. The appellant went into his property, picked up a gun and shot the planning officer dead. He was convicted of murder and appealed on the basis that, in relation to the defence of provocation, the trial judge had failed to put forward the appellant's obsessive personality as a characteristic that should be attributed to the reasonable person. The Court of Appeal accepted that this characteristic should have been left to the jury as it was a significant and permanent characteristic that marked him out from the run of mankind. Despite this, the appeal was rejected as on the facts there was no sudden and temporary loss of self-control.

In **Ahluwalia** the court raised the possibility that 'battered woman's syndrome', a kind of post-traumatic stress disorder, might constitute a relevant characteristic. This has now been confirmed by the Court of Appeal in the case of **R** *v* **Thornton** (1995) and failure to take this evidence into account was the principal ground for ordering a retrial.

In the case of Emma Humphrey, a psychiatric report considered at the original trial said that she was immature and attention-seeking. The judge had told the jury to exclude these characteristics when applying the test of the reasonable person, but the Court of Appeal said that the trial judge was wrong to have done so.

Excluded characteristics

Certain characteristics will not be taken into account for reasons of public policy. In particular, **Camplin** showed that a defendant's unusually quick temper will not be relevant, since the reasonable person is assumed to possess the degree of self-control to be expected of a reasonable person. Such exceptional irritability or bad temper will be irrelevant whether it is simply a peculiarity of the defendant's character, or a result of his or her culture or some other specific factor. Because of this, in **Roberts**, psychiatric evidence that immature, prelingually deaf people are subject to irrational explosions of violence was excluded on the grounds that exceptional excitability, whatever the origin, could not be taken into account.

Relevant characteristics must be long-term and do not, therefore, include temporary states of mind such as depression. The fact that a person is drunk at the time of committing the offence will not be accepted as a relevant characteristic (**Camplin** and **Newell**).

The House of Lords considered the issue of excluded characteristics in **R** *v* **Morhall** (1995). The defendant was addicted to glue sniffing and after a long session of sniffing glue he was taunted by the deceased about his addiction. A fight ensued and he stabbed and killed the man. At his trial he argued that he fell within the defence of provocation; this was rejected at first instance and by the Court of Appeal, but his appeal was allowed by the House of Lords. Lord Goff gave the leading judgment of the House and said that the characteristic of being addicted to glue sniffing should have been taken into account when applying the objective test. Just because a characteristic was discreditable did not mean that it had to be ignored. Thus, being a paedophile was a characteristic that could be considered in applying the test. In Lord Goff's view, the term 'reasonable person' was misleading as it suggested that the person must have acted in a 'reasonable manner' whereas what was really meant was that the defendant must have had the self-control of an 'ordinary person'. He also considered that the term 'characteristic' could be misleading as circumstances might also need to be taken into account, such as the defendant's history or the general circumstances at the relevant time. On the other hand, he confirmed that while being an addict could be taken into account, the fact of actually being intoxicated could not. He said that despite dicta in some other cases, this exclusion was not because intoxication was only a temporary state, but was part of the general common law rule that intoxication does not of itself excuse a man from committing a criminal offence.

In **R** *v* **Newell** (1980) the Court of Appeal considered which characteristics of the defendant, apart from age and sex, could be taken into account when applying the objective test. Newell was a chronic alcoholic; his girlfriend, who had been living with him for some time, had left him and he was very depressed about that. He and a friend got drunk, and the friend made unpleasant remarks about the ex-girlfriend. These words caused Newell immediately to lose his self-control, and he violently attacked his friend with an ashtray, eventually killing him. The court held that Newell's alcoholism was not a relevant characteristic to be taken into account, because the provocation was not related to his alcoholism but to his girlfriend. To be a 'relevant' characteristic there must be some connection between the characteristic and the provocation – so, for example, in the case of **Bedder**, the fact that he was impotent could have been taken into account in assessing the effects of taunts about his impotence, but would not have been relevant if he had killed his victim because she had mocked his stupidity, his religion or his lack of skill on the football field.

This approach was further developed by the Privy Council in **Luc Thiet Thuan** *v* **R** (1996). The appellant had been charged with the murder of his former girlfriend in Hong Kong. The law on the issue was the same as in England. At his trial he alleged that he had gone to her flat to collect some money that she owed him. While he was there she had compared him unfavourably with her new boyfriend, taunting him about his sexual inadequacy. He lost his self-control and killed her. Medical experts testified that following a fall the accused suffered from brain damage which could make it difficult for him to control his impulses. When directing the jury on the issue of provocation, the trial judge made no reference to the defendant's brain damage. The defendant's appeal to the Court of Appeal in Hong Kong was rejected. He made a further appeal to the Privy Council on the basis that the jury should have been directed at his trial to consider whether a reasonable person having his characteristics (including his brain damage) would have reacted as he did. The Privy Council rejected the appeal. It was felt that if evidence of 'purely mental peculiarities' was admitted as part of the objective test of provocation, it would blur the distinction between provocation and diminished responsibility. They quoted and adopted a statement made by Professor Ashworth back in 1976 that:

> The proper distinction . . . is that individual peculiarities which bear on the gravity of the provocation should be taken into account, whereas individual peculiarities bearing on the accused's level of self-control should not.

Thus the court is drawing a distinction between what have been described as 'control characteristics' and 'response characteristics'. Control characteristics are those which merely have an effect on the defendant's ability to control themself and, according to the majority view in **Luc Thiet Thuan**, these characteristics cannot be taken into account for the objective test of provocation. Response characteristics are those which are the subject of the provocation and can be taken into account. On the facts of **Luc Thiet Thuan** the court was faced with a control characteristic and it was therefore right to ignore it when considering the response of a reasonable person. If on the other hand the former girlfriend had taunted the defendant about his brain damage, this would have become a response characteristic and could have been taken into account.

If this case were to be followed it would throw into doubt much of the progress made with the defence of provocation in such cases as **Ahluwalia**; **Dryden** (1995); **Humphreys** and **Thornton (No. 2)** (1996). A Privy Council judgment is not binding on domestic courts, but merely a persuasive authority. A forceful dissenting judgment was given in **Luc Thiet Thuan** by Lord Steyn and in the first Court of Appeal cases to consider the implications of the Privy Council ruling it is this dissenting judgment which has been preferred. In **R** *v* **Parker** (1997) the defendant had been charged with the murder of his neighbour. In support of his defence of provocation, he sought to adduce evidence that he was a chronic alcoholic with damage to the left temporal lobe of his brain which rendered him more susceptible to provocation. Following the Privy Council decision in **Luc Thiet Thuan** (1996), the trial judge ruled that this evidence was inadmissible. An appeal was allowed and a retrial ordered as the Court of Appeal stated that it was bound by its own previous decisions rather than those of the Privy Council.

This approach was again taken by the Court of Appeal in **R** *v* **Smith (Morgan James)** (1999). The defendant had been charged with murder, and had raised the defence of provocation. He adduced medical evidence that he had been suffering from severe depression which made him more likely to be disinhibited, and thus reduced his power of self-control. The trial judge directed the jury that this was relevant for the subjective but not the objective test. The Court of Appeal ruled that the depressive state could be taken into account as a characteristic of a reasonable person for the purposes of the objective test. The jury had therefore been misdirected and the appeal was allowed. Leave to appeal to the House of Lords was granted and an important judgment on this issue is expected.

▶ Criticism and reform

Discrimination against women

A significant campaign in support of women who kill their partners after having being battered has developed in the light of the cases of Kiranjit Ahluwalia and Sara Thornton. The campaign was given new impetus in 1995, when the television programme 'Brookside' featured a storyline about a battered wife who killed her husband, highlighting the deficiencies of provocation as a defence, and provoking much newspaper coverage of the issue.

Campaigners have suggested that the requirement for 'a sudden and temporary loss of self-control' discriminates against women. In their view the lashing out in a moment of temper is a male way of reacting, and takes no account of the fact that women, partly because they lack physical strength, may react to gross provocation quite differently, yet lose self-control just as powerfully. This is supported by American research which has developed the theory of the 'battered woman syndrome'. As Sara Thornton's counsel, Lord Gifford, put it at her original appeal in 1992, 'the slow burning emotion of a woman at the end of her tether . . . may be a loss of self-control in just the same way as a sudden rage'. Helena Kennedy QC describes the classic female reaction to provocation as 'a snapping in slow motion, the final surrender of frayed elastic'. A former Lord Chief Justice, Lord Lane, has suggested that 'sometimes there is not a time for cooling down but a time for realizing what happened and heating up'.

The much publicized cases of **Thornton** and **Ahluwalia** both involved women killing husbands who had subjected them to extreme violence – for over ten years in Kiranjit Ahluwalia's case – and in both there appeared to be evidence of a cooling-off period. In Sara Thornton's original trial the prosecution stressed that she had deliberately gone into the kitchen and sharpened the knife she used to kill her husband; Kiranjit Ahluwalia waited for her husband to fall asleep before attacking him. At their original trials, the prosecution claimed that this meant there had been no sudden and temporary loss of self-control, and both were convicted of murder.

The courts do appear to have gone some way to appease their critics. Ahluwalia's final appeal was eventually granted on the grounds of diminished responsibility but it was pointed out that just because there had been a time gap between the last provocative act and the lashing out, this did not automatically rule out provocation because they could have lost control at the last minute. In Thornton's appeal in 1995 it was recognized that the concept of 'battered woman's syndrome' could be taken into account when deciding whether there had been a sudden and temporary loss of control. Another woman who had killed the partner who abused her for years, Emma Humphrey, successfully won an appeal against conviction for murder, and in her case the court accepted that the cumulative effects of years of abuse were relevant to provocation.

For some, these developments are feared as providing battered women with 'a licence to kill'. This ignores the fact that the successful raising of the defence results not in an acquittal but in conviction for manslaughter, allowing the judge to choose any sentence from life imprisonment to an absolute discharge. If the defendant really did lose control – whether suddenly or cumulatively – she is not held to be comparable to one who murders in cold blood, and her punishment can be suited to her actual guilt. While few would argue that men who beat up their wives deserve to be killed, the law should recognize that, as the former MP Lord Ashley has put it, 'many people cannot regain normal self-control after brutality'.

Many consider that the recent developments in the case law do not go far enough to prevent discrimination against women. Lord Ashley has tried – so far without success – to get the law changed to remove the need for a sudden loss of self-control – which actually comes not from statute but from Lord Devlin in the case of **Duffy**. In Australia, both case law and legislation stipulate that the provocative conduct of the deceased is relevant whether or not it occurred immediately before the killing and the act causing death does not have to be done suddenly.

Campaigners on behalf of battered women who kill their abusive partners have proposed that there should be a new defence of self-preservation available to defendants both female and male, which would reduce their liability from murder to manslaughter. It has been pointed out by Lord Hailsham, interviewed on 'Newsnight' in 1995, that such a defence would have considerable similarities to the current defence of self-defence. While this is true, self-defence, like provocation, can also be seen as a male-orientated defence; its requirement that the defendant respond to an imminent threat is similar to the rules for provocation against a cooling-off period, and ignores the imbalances in strength between men and women – most battered women who fought back during an attack would simply risk a more serious beating. Self-defence is also a complete defence and would lead to an acquittal, whereas self-preservation would only be a partial defence, allowing society to mark its disapproval of killing, but also to take the circumstances into account – so avoiding the 'licence to kill' argument. The adoption of the new defence of self-preservation, which takes into account the way women react, would be a better option than tinkering with defences such as provocation (and self-defence) which are designed for men. That is not to say that provocation should be applied only to men and self-preservation to women – all defences must be applicable to both sexes in relevant cases – but simply that the law should take into account the fact that women and men do behave and react differently in some situations, and a law designed largely by men for men is inadequate and unfair.

Difficulties for the jury

The questions put before a jury on the issue of provocation can be difficult to answer. For example, in **R** *v* **Raven** (1982), the 22-year-old defendant had a mental age of nine, and had lived in squats for about three years of his life. The jury were directed to consider the reasonable man as having lived the same type of life as Raven with his retarded development and mental age.

However, it is difficult to see how this problem can be avoided. Without some form of 'reasonable person' test, every little insult which might cause a loss of temper could be raised as provocation. Equally, a reasonable person test which did not require jurors to take into account the characteristics of the accused would result in, for example, teenagers being expected to exhibit adult standards of behaviour, or the injustice seen in **Bedder** *v* **DPP**.

DIMINISHED RESPONSIBILITY

Section 2 of the Homicide Act 1957 states:

> Where a person kills or is party to the killing of another, he shall not be convicted of murder if he was suffering from such abnormality of mind (whether arising from a condition of arrested or retarded development of mind or any inherent causes or induced by disease or injury) as substantially impaired his mental responsibility for his acts and omissions in doing or being a party to the killing.

This defence was introduced because of problems with the very narrow definition of insanity under the M'Naghten Rules (see p. 243), and has been given quite a broad interpretation.

▶ 'Abnormality of mind'

An abnormality of mind is a state of mind which a reasonable person would consider abnormal, and it covers all aspects of the mind's activities, rather than just the brain. In **R** *v* **Byrne** (1960), the defendant strangled a young woman in a YWCA hostel, and afterwards mutilated her body. He claimed that, since childhood, he had suffered from perverted sexual desires which created almost irresistible impulses; on the day in question, he said his acts were driven by one of these impulses. The trial judge directed that this was irrelevant to the defence, but that direction was held to be incorrect by the Court of Appeal. The defence covered all the activities of the mind, including not only the capacity to make rational judgments, but also 'the ability to exercise willpower to control physical acts in accordance with that rational judgement'. Byrne's conviction for murder was quashed.

The abnormality of mind does not have to be connected with madness. In **R** *v* **Seers** (1985), the defendant stabbed his estranged wife, and claimed diminished responsibility on the grounds of his chronic reactive depression. The trial judge directed that for the defence to be successful, the accused had to be bordering on the insane, but on appeal this was held to be a misdirection.

The required abnormality of mind has been held to cover severe shock or depression, especially in cases of 'mercy killing', and pre-menstrual syndrome. In 1997 in **R** *v* **Hobson** the Court of Appeal accepted that 'battered woman's syndrome' was a mental disease and could cause an abnormality of mind.

▶ Causes of the abnormality

The abnormality must arise from one of the following: a condition of arrested or retarded development of mind; any inherent cause; or disease or injury.

This excludes drink or drugs, but in **Tandy** (1988) it was held to include a disease caused by long-term alcoholism or drug-taking. Tandy was an alcoholic, and claimed diminished responsibility on the strength of this. Could a craving for drink or drugs be sufficient in itself to produce an abnormality of mind? The Court of Appeal decided that it could, but where this was submitted, jurors had to decide whether the first drink of the day was taken voluntarily, or involuntarily as a result of the accused's alcoholism; only in the latter case could the defence be available.

In **R** *v* **Gittens** (1984), the courts considered the position of an abnormality of mind caused partly by the person being drunk, and partly by inherent causes. The defendant suffered from depression, and had been in hospital. During a visit home, he argued with his wife, and ended up beating her to death; he then raped and killed his stepdaughter. At the time of the killings, he had been drinking alcohol and was also taking drugs for his depression. It was held that the jury had to decide whether the inherent cause – Gittens's depression – would have caused him to act as he did if he had not drunk alcohol or taken the drugs.

In **Di Duca** (1959), it was argued that the transient effect of drink on the brain is an injury, but the court doubted whether this could be held to be the case.

▌ Effect of the abnormality of mind

The abnormality of mind must be such that it substantially impairs the defendant's mental responsibility for his or her acts or omissions with regard to the killing. This impairment of control need not be complete, but it must be considerable. In **Byrne**, for example, there was evidence that the impulses from which the defendant suffered were not absolutely irresistible, but were extremely difficult to control. In that case this was considered sufficient, but this will always be a matter of fact for the jury to decide.

▌ Burden of proof

The defence must prove diminished responsibility on a balance of probabilities, calling evidence from at least two medical experts.

▌ Criticism and reform

Prosecution's right to argue insanity in response

In some cases, once diminished responsibility is put forward as a defence, the prosecution may respond by arguing that the defendant is legally insane, leading to a situation where the prosecution is trying to get the defendant acquitted (by reason of insanity) while the defendant is arguing that he or she should be found guilty of manslaughter. The reason behind this apparently bizarre situation is that acquittal from a murder charge on the grounds of insanity inevitably leads to committal to a mental institution for an indeterminate length of time, which the prosecution may consider desirable if it feels the defendant is dangerous.

Use of the defence for policy reasons

In cases of 'mercy killing', the prosecution sometimes accepts a plea of diminished responsibility even though the evidence for it is scanty; psychiatrists are often prepared to provide helpful diagnoses in these cases. By reducing the defendant's conviction to manslaughter, this allows the court to take into account the defendant's motivation when sentencing, and to treat a deserving case sympathetically. While this may be the best option given the current state of the law, it is often a misuse of the defence, and a better solution would be to abolish the mandatory life sentence for murder.

By contrast, it appears the defence may also be wrongfully refused on policy grounds. In **R *v* Sutcliffe** (1981) – the trial of the 'Yorkshire Ripper' – both the defence and prosecution wanted the trial to proceed on the basis of diminished responsibility, and were backed by well-respected psychiatric experts. But the judge refused and Sutcliffe was eventually convicted of murder. Since Sutcliffe has spent his sentence in solitary confinement in a mental hospital, it looks as though the lawyers and psychiatrists were right, but as Helena Kennedy QC has pointed out, it appears that public policy demanded that a man accused of such a notorious string of crimes should, if guilty, bear the label of murderer.

It has been suggested that qualified defences should be created to take account of the sort of mitigating circumstances involved in cases of mercy killing. While this does have considerable problems of its own, it might be preferable to the current bending of the rules to fit circumstances for which they were never designed.

Diminished responsibility unclear

The Butler Committee on mentally abnormal offenders suggested that the meaning of the phrase 'diminished responsibility' was unclear, since it is not a medical fact relating to the accused. They also thought it was difficult to measure the impairment of such responsibility.

The Committee proposed that a person should not be convicted of murder 'if there is medical or other evidence that they were suffering from a form of mental disorder as defined in s. 4 of the Mental Health Act 1959 and if, in the opinion of the jury, the mental disorder was such as to be an extenuating circumstance which ought to reduce the offence to manslaughter'.

The result would be that the phrase 'mental disorder' would replace the phrase 'abnormality of mind', and would also be the name of the defence. According to s. 1(2) of the Mental Health Act 1983 (repeating s. 4(1) of the 1959 Act), 'mental disorder' means 'mental illness, arrested or incomplete development of mind, psychopathic disorder and any other disorder or disability of mind'. The phrase 'any other disorder or disability of mind' is extremely wide, and does not require that the disorder or disability arise from disease, injury or inherent causes.

The Criminal Law Revision Committee agreed with the sense of the proposals but were not happy with the words used. In place of the last part of the Butler formula they preferred the words: '. . . the mental disorder was such as to be a substantial enough reason to reduce the offence to manslaughter'.

The Butler Committee did not intend the rewording of the defence to make substantial changes to its effect in practice. However, removing the requirement that the abnormality must arise from 'a condition of arrested or retarded development of mind or any inherent causes or induced by disease or injury' could well increase the range of disorders falling within the section. Psychiatrists might be more willing to put forward temporary disorders of mind that they would not formerly have felt to be relevant, and prosecutors and judges might be more willing to accept these.

On the other hand such a change might involve expert witnesses taking on part of the role that rightfully belongs to the jury. At present, psychiatrists may give their opinion as to whether the defendant's mental responsibility was 'substantially impaired' as part of medical evidence, leaving it to the jury to decide whether such impairment was sufficient to reduce the defendant's mental responsibility in law. Asking psychiatrists to state whether a mental disorder was a substantial enough reason to reduce the offence to manslaughter would clearly involve trespassing on the jury's function.

Abolition of the mandatory life sentence for murder

This would make a formal defence of diminished responsibility unnecessary, because the circumstances and state of mind of the defendant could be taken into account for sentencing. However, as stated in the section on murder, this would remove an important aspect of the decision from the jury.

Change to burden of proof

Under the draft Criminal Code, the burden of proof would be on the prosecution.

SUICIDE PACTS

Section 4 of the Homicide Act 1957 states that:

> It shall be manslaughter and shall not be murder for a person acting in pursuance of a suicide pact between him and another to kill the other or be party to the other being killed by a third person.

Suicide was once a crime. This is no longer the case, but when that offence was abolished, the crime of aiding and abetting suicide remained, on the grounds that helping someone to take their own life might well be done with an ulterior motive – by a beneficiary of the deceased's will, for example. Where someone dies due to acts of another and that person intended to cause the death, he or she could be liable for murder.

Where the person can show that the death was a suicide and was part of a pact in which that person too intended to die, liability will be reduced to manslaughter. It is for the defence to prove this, on a balance of probabilities.

ANSWERING QUESTIONS

1 How far is provocation a defence to a crime? Do you think the defence should be extended? *Oxford*

This is a fairly straightforward question to answer. Note that it breaks neatly into two halves; you would be well advised to break up your answer in the same way, with the first half looking at what the law is and the second half looking at the criticism.

As always, angle your material to fit the question. The first half asks how far provocation is a defence, so emphasize its limitations, such as that it is only available to murder and is merely a partial defence. You might make the point here that many consider the defence not to be fully available to women, and state why.

In the second half do not just list your learnt criticisms, but use those criticisms to argue whether or not the law needs extending. One of your arguments might be that because at the moment battered women who kill their violent partners often fall outside the defence it should be extended so that it includes such women. Alternatively, you might argue as we do, that rather than extending the defence of provocation, a new defence of self-preservation should be created to deal with this problem.

2 Ann had been married for twenty years. She had been brutally treated by her husband on many occasions. She was very depressed but was both shy and proud so had not sought help for her problems. One day her husband came home drunk and started shouting and hitting her. She was very frightened and thought that he was going to kill her. In fact he fell asleep and while he was sleeping she decided to kill him. She took some petrol from the garden shed, poured it over his body and burned him alive. Afterwards, when the police found her he was already dead and she said that she was very sorry but that she could not take any more. Discuss her criminal liability.

You need to look at murder first of all. Ann appears to have both the *actus reus* and the *mens rea* – we are specifically told that she wants to kill him. You could then consider whether she has a partial defence to murder. The most relevant defence would be provocation, and in particular you will need to look at the question of the cooling-off period as there is a time gap between her husband's last provocative act and her actions to kill him. In applying the second objective test for provocation her characteristics of being shy, proud and depressed could all be taken into account, according to the principles laid down in **Camplin**, provided **Luc Thiet Thuan** is not followed.

Diminished responsibility could also be considered but its chances of success will depend on the degree of her depression.

Involuntary manslaughter

Involuntary manslaughter is the name given to an unlawful homicide where the *actus reus* of murder has taken place, but without the *mens rea* for that offence. This area of the law has undergone significant case law development in recent years, leaving a considerable amount of uncertainty. It appears that now there are two kinds of involuntary manslaughter under common law: manslaughter by an unlawful and dangerous act (sometimes known as constructive manslaughter), and gross negligence manslaughter.

MANSLAUGHTER BY AN UNLAWFUL AND DANGEROUS ACT

▶ *Actus reus*

The prosecution must prove that the common elements of a homicide offence exist, but unlike other unlawful homicides death must be caused by an act; an omission is not sufficient. In **R** *v* **Lowe** (1973), the accused committed the offence of neglecting his child so as to cause unnecessary suffering or injury to health (s. 1(1), Children and Young Persons Act 1933). This neglect caused the child's death. The Court of Appeal held that, for the purposes of constructive manslaughter, there should be a difference between omission and commission, and that neglecting to do something should not be grounds for constructive manslaughter, even if the omission is deliberate.

An unlawful and dangerous act

The act which causes the death must be a criminal offence; unlawfulness in the sense of a tort (a civil wrong), or a breach of contract would not be sufficient. At one time it was thought that an act could be considered unlawful for this purpose if it was a tort, but the case of **Franklin** (1883) established that this was incorrect. The defendant was on the West Pier at Brighton. He picked up a large box from a refreshment stall and threw it into the sea. The box hit someone who was swimming underneath and caused their death. The prosecution argued that throwing the box into

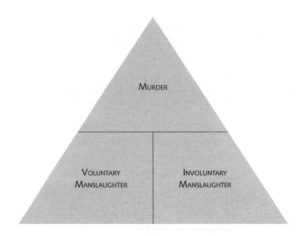

Fig. 1. The Homicide Offences

the sea comprised the tort of trespass to the stall keeper's property and was therefore an unlawful act making the defendant liable for manslaughter. However, the trial judge concluded that a mere tort was not sufficient to give rise to liability for constructive manslaughter; the unlawful act had to be a crime. The accused was in fact convicted of gross negligence manslaughter.

The courts have on occasions taken a fairly flexible approach to identifying the relevant crime for these purposes. In **R** *v* **Cato** (1976), two drug addicts injected each other several times during the night with heroin. Each man made up his preferred mixture of the powder and water, loaded the syringe and then passed it to his friend to perform the injection. By the morning, they were both extremely ill and Cato's friend died. Cato himself survived and was charged with the manslaughter of his friend. The court accepted that what he had done to his friend was not an offence under the Misuse of Drugs Act 1971 or the Offences against the Person Act 1861. Nevertheless, it held that there was an unlawful act, which could be described as injecting the deceased with a mixture of heroin and water which at the time of the injection, and for the purposes of the injection, he had unlawfully taken into his possession. While the act of injecting itself was not an offence it was so closely associated with the offence of possession that this was treated as sufficient to be part of the *actus reus* of manslaughter by an unlawful and dangerous act.

This can be contrasted with the case of **R** *v* **Dalby** (1982) which also concerned two drug addicts who took drugs together. As in **Cato**, one of the drug users died and the other one was charged with his manslaughter. In this case the drug supplied had been obtained legally by Dalby on prescription. As a result, the Court of Appeal found that there was no unlawful act; Dalby's appeal was allowed and his conviction for manslaughter quashed.

More recently in **R** *v* **Kennedy** (1999) the victim had asked the defendant for something to make him sleep. The defendant had prepared a syringe filled with heroin and passed it to the victim. The victim had paid the defendant, injected himself and left immediately. He was dead within an hour. The defendant was convicted of manslaughter and appealed. He relied on **R** *v* **Dalby** to support his argument that he had not committed an unlawful act that caused the death of the victim. The Court of Appeal held that as the defendant prepared the syringe and handed it over for immediate use by the deceased, he had committed the unlawful act of assisting or encouraging the deceased to inject himself. In other words, it considered that the self injection by the deceased was unlawful and the defendant was an accomplice to this offence (liability of accomplices is discussed in Chapter 11). It distinguished the case of **Dalby** because in that case the defendant had simply supplied the drug and left it entirely up to the recipient whether or not to use it. By contrast, Kennedy had supplied the drug in a made up syringe for immediate injection which connoted an element of encouragement to inject. In the former case, there was no question of the defendant being guilty of manslaughter. In the latter, it was a question of fact for the jury whether the defendant's actions caused the death. The appeal was dismissed. There is a fundamental problem with this judgment that no offence is actually committed where a person injects themselves with a drug. Under the law of accomplices an offence by the main offender is required before an accomplice can be liable. There is an offence of possession, but the mere possession of this drug did not cause the death, the injecting caused the death. This case could potentially make many drug dealers liable for the death of the drug users that they supply, provided an element of encouragement to use the drug can be found.

The act must be dangerous

In **R** *v* **Church** (1966) the Court of Appeal held that an act could be considered dangerous if there was an objective risk of some harm resulting from it. The accused and a woman went to his van to have sexual intercourse, but he was unable to satisfy her and she became angry and slapped his face. During the ensuing fight, the woman was knocked unconscious. Thinking she was dead, the accused panicked, dragged her out of the van and dumped her in a nearby river. In fact she was alive at the time, but then drowned in the river.

The Court of Appeal said that an act was dangerous if it was such as: 'all sober and reasonable people would inevitably recognize must subject the other person to, at least, the risk of some harm resulting therefrom, albeit not serious harm'. As this is a purely objective test, it did not matter that the accused himself did not realize that there was a risk of harm from throwing the woman in the river (because he thought she was already dead), as sober and reasonable people would have realized there was such a risk. Though there had been a misdirection on unlawful and dangerous act manslaughter by the court of first instance, the conviction for gross negligence manslaughter was upheld.

In **R** *v* **Dawson** (1985) the judge stated that when applying the objective test laid down in **Church**, 'sober and reasonable people' could be assumed to have the same knowledge as the actual defendant and no more. The defendants had attempted to rob a garage, wearing masks and carrying an imitation firearm and a pickaxe handle. Their plan went wrong when the 60-year-old garage attendant pressed an alarm button, and the robbers fled. Unfortunately the attendant had a severe heart condition, and shortly after the police arrived he died of a heart attack. The robbers were found and charged with his manslaughter, but the conviction was quashed on the grounds that they did not know about their victim's weak heart, and therefore their unlawful act was not dangerous within the meaning of **Church**.

Dawson was distinguished in **R** *v* **Watson** (1989), where the accused burgled the house of a frail 87-year-old man, who died of a heart attack as a result. The courts held that the accused's unlawful act became a dangerous one for the purposes of the **Church** test as soon as the old man's frailty and old age would have been obvious to a reasonable observer; at that point the unlawful act was one which a reasonable person would recognize as likely to carry some risk of harm. The result of **Watson** is that where there are peculiarities of the victim which make an act dangerous when it might otherwise not be (such as the old man's frailty), they will only be treated as dangerous for the purpose of the *actus reus* of constructive manslaughter if they would have been apparent to a reasonable observer. In the event Watson's conviction was quashed because it was not proved that the shock of the burglary caused the heart attack and the old man's death.

In order to be considered 'dangerous' in this context, the unlawful act must be sufficient to cause actual physical injury. Emotional or mental shock are not enough on their own, though they will be relevant if they cause physical injury – by bringing on a heart attack, for example.

In **R** *v* **Ball** (1989), it was confirmed that whether an act was dangerous or not should be decided on a reasonable person's assessment of the facts, and not on what the defendant knew. Therefore a defendant who makes an unreasonable mistake is not entitled to be judged on the facts as he or she believes them to be. Ball had argued with some neighbours, who then came over to his house. Ball owned a gun, and frequently kept live and blank cartridges together in a pocket of his overall. He testified that he had been frightened by the arrival of the neighbours, and, intending to scare them, had grabbed a handful of cartridges from his pocket, and, thinking one was a blank cartridge, loaded it into the gun. In fact the cartridge was a live one, and just as one of the neighbours was climbing over a wall, he shot and killed her. He was acquitted of murder but convicted of manslaughter by an unlawful and dangerous act.

Causation

The unlawful and dangerous act must cause the death – as **Watson** shows, the fact that the accused has done an unlawful and dangerous act and someone concerned in the events has died is not enough without a proven causal link. On the other hand, in **R** *v* **Kennedy** (1999) (discussed at p. 77) the Court of Appeal did not consider the fact that the victim injected himself to amount to an intervening act that broke the chain of causation between the defendant supplying the drug and the victim's death.

The target of the act

The unlawful and dangerous act need not be aimed at the victim, nor even at a person. In **R** *v* **Mitchell** (1983) the accused took part in a fight, and someone who was not involved in the fight was knocked over and died as a result. Mitchell was found guilty of manslaughter under the doctrine of transferred malice.

It had been thought from dicta in **Dalby** that the act had to be aimed at someone: the drug addicts in that case had injected themselves and it appeared that this meant that the acts of the defendant were not aimed at the victim, as opposed to **Cato**, where they injected each other and the defendant was found liable for manslaughter. In fact, in **R** *v* **Goodfellow** (1986) the Court of Appeal said that the dicta in **Dalby** did not mean that the unlawful act had to be aimed at somebody, it simply meant that the unlawful act had to cause the death. Goodfellow lived in a council house from which he wanted to move, but he felt there was no hope of the council rehousing him if the usual procedures were followed. He therefore set fire to the house, trying to make the fire look like the result of a petrol bomb so that the council would be forced to rehouse him and his family on the basis that they were homeless. His wife, another woman and his child were all killed in the fire. Goodfellow argued that he was not guilty of manslaughter because his act of setting the house on fire was aimed at the house, not the deceased. The court rejected this argument, stating that his acts did not need to be aimed at someone, and that the dicta in **Dalby** merely meant that the chain of causation must not be broken. This interpretation is supported by the recent judgment of the Court of Appeal in **R** *v* **Kennedy** (1999) discussed at p. 77.

▶ Mens rea

The *mens rea* of unlawful and dangerous act manslaughter is simply that of the crime constituting the unlawful act, which may be intention or recklessness depending on the definition of the particular offence.

In **R** *v* **Lamb** (1967), the accused pointed a gun at his friend, as a joke and with no intention of harming him. As far as the accused knew, there were two bullets in the chambers of the gun, but neither was in the chamber opposite the barrel. He then pulled the trigger, which caused the barrel to rotate, putting a bullet opposite the firing pin. The gun went off and the friend was killed. The unlawful act in this case would have been assault and/or battery. The *mens rea* is intention or **Cunningham** recklessness in hitting the victim (battery) or in making the victim frightened that they were about to be hit (assault). As the accused viewed the whole incident as a joke, and did not know how a revolver worked, he neither intended nor saw the risk of hitting or frightening his victim. He therefore lacked the *mens rea* for either offence, and so did not have the *mens rea* of unlawful and dangerous act manslaughter either.

▶ Criticism

Liability for omissions

The distinction between acts and omissions may be reasonable when applied to an omission which is simply negligent, but it is difficult to find grounds for excluding liability where an accused deliberately omits to do something and thereby causes death, and where that omission is clearly morally wrong.

Mens rea

The *mens rea* is very easy to satisfy, which can be seen as anomalous given the seriousness of the offence. The Law Commission (1996) has commented on unlawful and dangerous act manslaughter:

> [W]e consider that it is wrong in principle for the law to hold a person responsible for causing a result that he did not intend or foresee, and which would not even have been foreseeable by a reasonable person observing his conduct. Unlawful act manslaughter is therefore, we believe, unprincipled because it requires only that a foreseeable risk of causing some harm should have been inherent in the accused's conduct, whereas he is actually convicted of causing death, and also to some extent punished for doing so.

GROSS NEGLIGENCE MANSLAUGHTER

In civil law, an individual who fails to take the care a reasonable person would exercise in any given situation is described as negligent. Clearly there are degrees of negligence – if it is negligent for a nurse to leave a very sick patient alone for ten minutes, for example, it will be even more negligent to leave that patient alone for an hour. Negligence which is so severe as to deserve punishment under the criminal law is sometimes described as gross negligence and if it leads to death can give rise to liability for gross negligence manslaughter.

Until the summer of 1993 it was generally accepted that two forms of involuntary manslaughter existed: constructive manslaughter, described above, and **Caldwell** reckless manslaughter. However, that stance had to be reconsidered in the light of the House of Lords decision in **R *v* Adomako** (1994) approving most of the Court of Appeal's judgment on the case in **R *v* Prentice** (1992). Lord Mackay LC gave the leading judgment in **R *v* Adomako**, with which all the other Law Lords agreed. He stated that **Caldwell** reckless manslaughter does not exist but that instead there is gross negligence manslaughter.

At the Court of Appeal level, several appeals had been heard together as they raised the same legal issues; one concerned Drs Prentice and Sulman, a second concerned Mr Adomako, and the third, Mr Holloway. Prentice and Sulman had injected a 16-year-old leukaemia patient in the base of her spine, unaware that the substance injected should have been administered intravenously, and that injecting it into the spine made it a virtual certainty that the patient would die. She did in fact die shortly afterwards. Adomako was an anaesthetist whose patient had died from lack of oxygen when the tube inserted into their mouth became detached from the ventilator; Adomako had not realized quickly enough why his patient was turning blue. Holloway was an electrician who had accidentally wired up a customer's mains supply to the kitchen sink, causing the death by electrocution of a man who touched the sink. All were convicted at first instance of manslaughter.

The appeals by Sulman, Prentice and Holloway were allowed by the Court of Appeal, but not that of Adomako. He, therefore, was the only one to appeal to the House of Lords, which is why the Court of Appeal judgment is known as **R *v* Prentice** and the House of Lords judgment as **R *v* Adomako**. Adomako's appeal was dismissed and Lord McKay gave the following analysis of the law:

> ... in my opinion the ordinary principles of the law of negligence apply to ascertain whether or not the defendant has been in breach of a duty of care towards the victim who has died. If such breach of duty is established the next question is whether that breach of duty should be characterised as gross negligence and therefore as a crime. This will depend on the seriousness of the breach of duty committed by the defendant in all the circumstances in which the defendant was placed when it occurred. The jury will have to consider whether the extent to which the defendant's conduct departed from the proper standard of care incumbent upon him,

involving as it must have done a risk of death to the patient, was such that it should be judged criminal.

This was found to be the key statement of the law by the Court of Appeal in **R** *v* **Watts** (1998). In that case the appellant's daughter was born severely handicapped. An operation was performed to assist the child with her breathing, and a tube was placed in her throat and held in place with tape. When the child was 14 months old she was admitted to hospital for a few days. Her mother spent the last night before the child was due to be discharged at the hospital. The following morning she took a suitcase to her car and was away from her child's bedside for three and a half minutes. When the mother returned the breathing tube was out of her child's neck and she was still and grey. She shouted for help but very shortly thereafter the child died. The mother was charged with murder, with the prosecution alleging that she had removed the tube before she had gone to the car. She was convicted of manslaughter and appealed against her conviction on the grounds that the judge's direction on manslaughter was inadequate as it had indirectly referred to the possibility of a conviction for gross negligence manslaughter, but had failed to mention the ingredients of this offence.

The Court of Appeal allowed the appeal. It ruled that where gross negligence manslaughter might have been committed, the trial judge had to direct the jury in accordance with the passage from **Adomako** cited above. He had failed to do this, and therefore the conviction was quashed. Thus, in order for liability for gross negligence manslaughter to arise there must be the common ingredients of all homicide offences, plus a risk of death, a duty of care, breach of that duty, and gross negligence as regards that breach. These criteria all fall into the *actus reus* of the offence, apart from gross negligence, which is part of the *mens rea*.

▶ Actus reus

The common elements of homicide offences need to be proved and are discussed at p. 40.

A 'duty' of care

It is not exactly clear when a duty of care exists for the purpose of this offence. Soon after the decision in **Adomako** three differing interpretations were given for the potential meaning of a 'duty'. First, the Law Commission suggested, rather unhelpfully, that the concept of a duty in this offence may have no meaning at all. Secondly, a very narrow interpretation was put forward that a duty may arise where there is a professional relationship between the defendant and their client, such as between doctors and their patients or electricians and their customers. This interpretation was suggested following the Court of Appeal judgment, but is unlikely to be favoured in the light of dicta in the House of Lords. Thirdly, a very broad meaning was given for the term 'duty' by the leading criminal law academic, J.C. Smith (1996), who wrote: 'Where a negligent act is alleged, the existence of a duty of care is unlikely to cause a problem; everyone must be under a duty not to do acts imperilling the lives of others, in the absence of circumstances of justification or excuse.' If this third meaning is adopted, then the requirement of a duty would in effect have no significance as it will exist wherever the defendant has caused a death.

However, it is submitted that none of these interpretations is correct. Unfortunately, following conflicting and ambiguous judgments of the Court of Appeal the exact meaning of a duty in this context is uncertain. After the House of Lords' judgment of **R** *v* **Adomako** the authors thought that a duty in this context had exactly the same meaning as it has in the civil law of negligence. Lord Mackay had stated in **Adomako** itself: '. . . in my opinion the ordinary principles of the law of negligence apply to ascertain whether or not the defendant has been in breach of a duty of care towards the victim who has died'. Given that the phrase 'a duty of care' has a very precise meaning within the civil law of negligence, if the House of Lords did not intend this meaning, one would expect them specifically to say so; since they did not do this, it seems reasonable to assume it is exactly the meaning they intended. It is only when deciding whether or not there has been a breach of that duty that a different criterion would need to be imposed under criminal law from that in civil law. The classic statement of where a duty of care is owed in negligence is provided by Lord Atkin in **Donoghue** *v* **Stevenson** (1932), where he laid down what has been called the 'neighbour principle':

> You must take reasonable care to avoid acts or omissions which you can reasonably foresee would be likely to injure your neighbour. Who then, in law, is my neighbour? The answer seems to be – persons who are so closely and directly affected by my act that I ought reasonably to have them in contemplation as being so affected when I am directing my mind to the acts or omissions which are called in question.

This would suggest that where a death occurs, the crucial test when deciding whether or not a duty is owed under the law of negligence – and also in relation to gross negligence manslaughter – is reasonable foresight that the plaintiff would be injured. In addition, following **Caparo Industries plc** *v* **Dickman** (1990), account will sometimes be taken of issues of public policy and whether the imposition of a duty would be just and reasonable. This was precisely the approach which was taken by the trial judge in **R** *v* **Singh** (1999), and the trial judge's approach was expressly approved by the Court of Appeal. The issue as to whether there was a duty of care was treated as a question of law to be determined by the judge rather than the jury which seems an appropriate approach as this is a technical area of civil law.

However, the judgment of the Court of Appeal in **R** *v* **Khan and Khan** (1998) appeared to take a different approach. This judgment referred to cases where a duty will be imposed in the context of omissions that were discussed at p. 9. The judgment is confused: it may be saying that the relevant duty required for all gross negligence manslaughter cases is that required generally for omissions. Alternatively, it may be drawing a distinction between cases of gross negligence manslaughter by omission and gross negligence manslaughter by an act. In the former, a duty would have the general meaning given in the context of omissions, in the latter a duty would have the meaning given in the civil law of negligence. In support of this is the fact that the Court of Appeal in **R** *v* **Khan and Khan** treated **R** *v* **Adomako** as a case of manslaughter by an act as it stated: 'In **R** *v* **Adomako** (1995) . . . the Defendant was an anaesthetist whose *act* paralysed a patient when a tube became disconnected from a ventilator and the patient subsequently died.' This interpretation is also supported by the fact that the dicta in **R** *v* **Adomako** makes no reference to the cases on general liability for omissions. However, such an approach seems highly unsatisfactory and it is unnecessary to have two different meanings in the same offence for the single concept of a duty. As the Court of Appeal in **R** *v* **Singh** (which itself was concerned with an omission) made no reference to **R** *v* **Khan and Khan** and took a different approach, it is to be hoped that this case will not be followed. A possible future solution would be for the courts to apply the tort test for a duty of care in the context of determining liability for omissions generally.

Breach of the duty of care

The defendant's conduct must have gone below the standard of care expected of a reasonable and sober person.

▶ Mens rea

Gross negligence

The *mens rea* of the offence is gross negligence. Traditionally, negligence has been an objective criterion, in which a person is judged by the standards of reasonable and sober people. Lord Mackay in **Adomako** stated that he was not prepared to give a detailed definition of gross negligence, and simply gave the key statement quoted at p. 81.

He also quoted with approval a well-known statement on the issue made by Lord Hewart CJ in **R** *v* **Bateman** (1925):

> in order to establish criminal liability the facts must be such that, in the opinion of the jury, the negligence of the accused went beyond a mere matter of compensation between subjects and showed such disregard for the life and safety of others as to amount to a crime against the State and conduct deserving punishment.

Lord Mackay does not provide a more detailed definition of gross negligence, as he is concerned that a jury would find such a definition incomprehensible. This appears to be his main reason for rejecting the **Caldwell** model direction for juries in this context. To achieve this goal of simplification for the jury, the House of Lords might have been wiser to follow their own advice in **R** *v* **Reid** that judges need not use the exact words of the Diplock direction, but could adapt them for the particular case. But the implications of not providing a definition go beyond merely making the law simpler for the jury. Without a definition that could have limited the scope of gross negligence, the term could potentially be given a very broad meaning by a jury, much broader than the previous test of **Caldwell** recklessness. If the House of Lords guidance was strictly followed then a jury could simply have been told that a person's conduct was grossly negligent if they thought it was sufficiently negligent to justify criminal liability. There would therefore have been no fixed limits on what gross negligence could mean, the only limiting factor being the potentially unreliable and certainly inconsistent contribution of the jury's common sense.

In fact in **R** *v* **Singh** (1999), while claiming to be applying **R** *v* **Adomako**, the trial judge gave the jury more detailed directions than those suggested by the House of Lords. The case arose when a tenant in a lodging house was killed by carbon monoxide poisoning from a gas heater in the building. The trial judge directed the jury to ask themselves:

> . . . was the neglience which caused the death gross negligence? The question posed is having regard to the risk of death involved was the conduct of the defendants so bad in all the circumstances as to amount in your judgement to a criminal act or omission? The circusmtances must be such that a reasonably prudent person would have foreseen a serious and obvious risk not merely of injury, even serious injury, but of death. If you find such circumstances in the case of the defendant whom you are considering, you must decide whether what he did or failed to do was so bad that it was criminal. That of course means that the degree of neglience was very high. Those are the issues which you have to decide.

The Court of Appeal approved this direction. Traditionally negligence has been viewed as an objective test. Immediately following the judgment of **R** *v* **Adomako** it appeared that in the future gross negligence could cover both objective and subjective criteria. As no detailed definition of gross negligence was going to be given to the jury, there was no reason why the jury might not choose of their own volition to take into account the actual state of mind of the defendant rather than the state of mind that a reasonable person would have had in the circumstances. This was certainly the view of the Court of Appeal – whose approach was fully endorsed by the House of Lords. Lord Taylor CJ stated in the Court of Appeal:

> without purporting to give an exhaustive definition, we consider proof of any of the following states of mind in the defendant may properly lead a jury to make a finding of gross negligence:
> (a) indifference to an obvious risk of injury to health;
> (b) actual foresight of the risk coupled with a determination nevertheless to run it;
> (c) an appreciation of the risk coupled with an intention to avoid it but also coupled with such a high degree of negligence in the attempted avoidance as the jury consider justifies conviction;
> (d) inattention or failure to advert to a serious risk which goes beyond mere inadvertence in respect of an obvious and important matter which the defendant's duty demanded he should address.

Both (b) and (c) are concerned with subjective criteria. Thus gross negligence appeared to resemble **Caldwell** recklessness in covering both objective and subjective states of mind. **R** *v* **Singh**, seems to be an attempt by the Court of Appeal to put an end to such a development and is likely to be successful. It favours the traditional objective meaning.

But a previous judgment of the Court of Appeal appeared to have favoured a subjective interpretation of gross negligence. A recent illustration of a finding of gross negligence is **R** *v* **Litchfield** (1998). A boat's engine had failed and it had crashed into rocks off the Cornish coast killing three members of the crew. The appellant was owner and master of the boat and was prosecuted for gross negligence manslaughter. He had steered an unsafe course that was too close to a dangerous shore and he had sailed in a way that meant he had to rely on the vessel's engines when he knew they might fail through fuel contamination. A jury found that his behaviour amounted to gross negligence, and he was liable for gross negligence manslaughter. His conviction was upheld by the Court of Appeal which seemed to rely on a subjective form of *mens rea* as it said it was for the jury to decide whether a highly experienced sailor like the appellant 'must have appreciated the risk he was taking' in using contaminated fuel. The Court of Appeal also made it clear that as it was for the jury to decide not merely the facts but also the point at which a breach of duty became the offence of manslaughter, and there would need to be compelling grounds before it would be proper for the Court of Appeal to say that the jury had set the standard impermissibly high. It is likely that the purely objective test laid down in **R** *v* **Singh** is likely to be favoured. In any case an objective criteria is indirectly introduced through the concept of a duty if this is given its civil law meaning.

While it is submitted that Adomako did not expressly take an objective approach to negligence, such an interpretation would make sense of one aspect of the **Adomako** judgment: Lord Mackay made a point of emphasizing that there had to be a risk of death in order for a person to be liable for gross negligence manslaughter. He seemed to feel that this requirement imposed a significant restriction on liability. Yet logically, if a person has died then there clearly was a risk of death so this in itself would be very easy to prove. By requiring that there be an 'obvious and serious risk of death' liability is limited.

▶ Criticism

The rebirth of gross negligence manslaughter by the House of Lords was both unexpected and heavily criticized. By mixing concepts of civil law with the criminal law, maintaining liability for manslaughter for an objective form of *mens rea*, and potentially broadening liability, its reincarnation in its **Adomako** form has added to the confusion in this field of law.

The Court of Appeal in **R** *v* **Prentice** gave several reasons for preferring gross negligence manslaughter over **Caldwell** reckless manslaughter. They argued that the **Caldwell** recklessness test was not satisfactory for situations in which a duty was owed. Their reasoning was that the 'obvious risk' of Lord Diplock's formulation in **Caldwell** meant obvious to 'the ordinary prudent individual'. But while most people know what can happen when you strike a match or drive the wrong way down a one-way street, an expert (such as an electrician or a doctor) who undertakes a task within his or her particular field would be expected to be aware of certain risks of which the 'ordinary prudent individual' might well know nothing. The reinsertion of the concept of an 'obvious' risk by the Court of Appeal in **R** *v* **Singh** means that this benefit has not been attained.

The **Caldwell** test for recklessness implies that the defendant actually created the risk, but in cases involving doctors, for example, the doctor might not have created the risk, but might still be reasonably expected to be aware of it and deal with it competently.

The Court of Appeal was also concerned that **Caldwell** reckless manslaughter left a significant gap in the law because of the lacuna. However, this concern seemed to ignore the House of Lords' judgment in **R** *v* **Reid**, where the scope of the lacuna was narrowed to where a person made an honest and reasonable mistake that there was no risk. Such a person would not be **Caldwell** reckless, but it is unlikely that he or she would be found grossly negligent either.

The approach taken in **R** *v* **Bateman** (1925) can also be criticized. It is absurd to simply ask the jury to decide whether the negligence goes beyond a mere matter of compensation between parties. The negligence may go beyond that while still falling far short of what is required for manslaughter. The question should not be whether the negligence is bad enough to give rise to criminal liability, but whether it is bad enough to give rise to liability for the very serious offence of manslaughter.

The reintroduction of gross negligence has brought with it the concept of a 'duty' to the law of involuntary manslaughter, which is regrettable. In the first place, no purpose is served by unnecessarily complicating this area of law by reference to civil law concepts. This occurs in other areas of criminal law, in particular in relation to issues of ownership in property offences, where it has caused considerable problems. It may nevertheless be necessary in that area of the law, due to the nature of the offences, but there is no such need for importing civil law concepts into the law of manslaughter.

Secondly, in many factual situations, the concept of a duty merely duplicates issues concerning how far the risk should have been foreseen, which would often have to be considered anyway when deciding whether or not there was gross negligence. The issue of foresight would be better dealt with under the sole heading of *mens rea*, rather than making it also part of the *actus reus* of the offence by imposing the need for a duty. This overlap merely serves to complicate the law.

Thirdly, if the defendant actually does foresee the risk of harm to the defendant, it should not matter whether a reasonable person would have foreseen it. A duty of care in negligence law is defined in objective terms as a result of the objective principle which applies to many areas of civil law – that external appearances matter more than the particular defendant's state of mind. However, such a criterion is wholly inappropriate to a criminal law offence – particularly of the gravity of manslaughter – where the defendant's subjective state of mind should be a key issue for deciding culpability and degrees of culpability.

• •

SUBJECTIVE RECKLESS MANSLAUGHTER?

The rather unexpected judgment in **Adomako** has produced considerable uncertainty as to the current forms of involuntary manslaughter. Before **Adomako**, the cases of **R** *v* **Seymour** (1983) and **Kong Cheuk Kwan** (1985) suggested that there was an offence of **Caldwell** reckless manslaughter. In **Seymour** (1983) the accused had argued with his girlfriend, and afterwards ran into her car with his lorry. She got out of the car, and he drove at her, crushing her between the car and the lorry. She died of her injuries. Seymour maintained that he had not seen her, and was merely trying to free his lorry from her vehicle. He was convicted of manslaughter and on

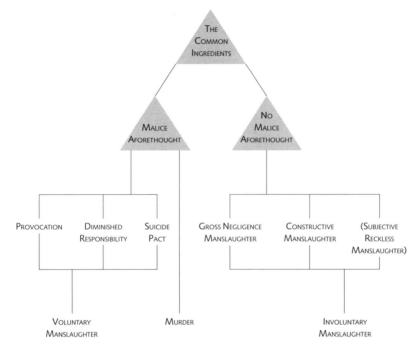

Fig. 2. The Structure of the Homicide Offences

appeal Lord Roskill approved the application of **Caldwell** recklessness as the relevant form of *mens rea.*

The subsequent case of **Kong Cheuk Kwan** (1985) was an appeal from the Hong Kong Court of Appeal to the Privy Council. It concerned a collision at sea on a clear sunny day of two hydrofoils, carrying passengers from Hong Kong to Macau. Two passengers died in the collision. The appellant was at the helm and in command of one of the vessels, and was convicted of manslaughter. Lord Roskill quashed his conviction on the grounds that the judge should have directed the jury on the basis of the **Caldwell/Lawrence** test for recklessness.

Because **Caldwell** recklessness is so broad and includes objective criteria, it was thought that there was no longer any need to have gross negligence manslaughter because this would completely overlap with **Caldwell** reckless manslaughter. However, **R** *v* **Seymour** was overruled by **R** *v* **Adomako** and **Kong Cheuk Kwan** was criticized, so it appears that **Caldwell** reckless manslaughter does not now exist.

Professor J.C. Smith has suggested that alongside gross negligence manslaughter there should also be a subjective reckless manslaughter, because there would otherwise be a gap in the law. A person would avoid liability if they caused a death having seen a risk that their conduct would cause this, despite the fact that the risk was not serious and obvious (unless they fell within constructive manslaughter). This conclusion seems to have been reached on the basis that gross negligence was a purely objective *mens rea*. Lord Mackay does not himself appear to consider that it would be desirable to have any further type of involuntary manslaughter in existence beyond constructive manslaughter and gross negligence manslaughter. He considers that any exceptions to the general test of gross negligence would give rise to 'unnecessary complexity'.

One of the first Court of Appeal judgments to consider manslaughter following the **Adomako** ruling does not support the idea of subjective reckless manslaughter. In **R** *v* **Khan and Khan** (1998) the victim was a 15-year-old prostitute. The two defendants had supplied her with heroin in a flat. She consumed the drug by snorting it through her nose and eating it. It was probably the first time she had taken the drug, but the quantity she consumed was twice the amount likely to be taken by an experienced drug user. She began to cough and splutter and then went into a coma. The defendants left and when they returned the following day they found her dead. If the girl had received medical attention at any stage before she died she would probably have survived. The trial judge left the case to the jury on the basis of 'manslaughter by omission'. The defendants were convicted of manslaughter and appealed. The Court of Appeal ruled that there was no separate offence of manslaughter by omission and stated that there were only two forms of involuntary manslaughter: unlawful and dangerous act manslaughter and gross negligence manslaughter. A retrial was ordered.

However, the later Court of Appeal judgment of **R** *v* **Singh** restricts gross negligence manslaughter to an objective meaning. If this approach is followed then there will, as J.C. Smith suggests, be a gap in the law unless a subjective reckless manslaughter exists.

CAUSING DEATH BY DANGEROUS DRIVING

This offence is contained in s. 1 of the Road Traffic Act 1988, which provides: 'A person who causes the death of another person by driving a mechanically propelled vehicle dangerously on a road or other public place is guilty of an offence.' The maximum sentence for the offence has been increased from five years to ten, in response to public concern over deaths being caused by joyriders driving dangerously.

No *mens rea* as regards the death needs to be proved for this offence. The prosecution merely have to prove that the defendant drove dangerously in a public place, and that this caused the death of the victim.

The primary issue will be whether the driving was dangerous. Section 2A provides that a person was driving dangerously if:

(a) the way he drives falls far below what would be expected of a competent and careful driver, and

(b) it would be obvious to a competent and careful driver that driving in that way would be dangerous.

Subsection (2) states that ' "dangerous" refers to danger either of injury to any person or of serious damage to property'.

In deciding whether the defendant's driving was dangerous, the courts will take account of the condition that the vehicle was in (including the way it was loaded) and any circumstances of which the defendant was aware. Apart from this final point, the issue is purely objective.

In **R** *v* **Skelton** (1995) the Court of Appeal upheld a conviction for causing death by dangerous driving. The appellant was a lorry driver who had taken his lorry on to a motorway despite being warned by another driver that his air pressure gauges were low. The effect of such a condition is for the handbrake system to be activated and expert evidence at his trial said that a competent driver would have been aware of this. When his handbrake activated, his lorry was left blocking the nearside lane and the victim drove his own lorry into the back of it and died.

The importance of the word 'obvious' in s. 2A(b) was emphasized by the Court of Appeal in **R** *v* **Roberts and George** (1997). George had driven a truck owned and operated by his employer, Roberts. A rear wheel became detached from the truck and hit another vehicle, killing the driver. The prosecution case was that the truck was in a dangerous condition because of lack of proper maintenance which should have been obvious to both men. The defence case was that the design of the wheel was inherently dangerous and the wheel could come off without there being any indication that anything was wrong. In accordance with Robert's instructions, George undertook a visual inspection of the wheels every day and physically checked the wheel nuts every week. They were both convicted but their appeals were allowed because the jury had been misdirected on the law. The Court of Appeal stated that, in determining liability for the offence, the jury had to decide whether the loose wheel bolt was obvious. Something was obvious to a driver if it could be 'seen or realized at first glance'. More might be expected of a professional driver than an ordinary motorist. Where a driver was an employee it would be important to consider the instructions given by the employer. Generally speaking it would be wrong to expect him to do more than he was instructed to do, provided that the instructions were apparently reasonable.

The focus was on the state of the driver rather than the state of the vehicle in **R** *v* **Marison** (1996). Marison was a diabetic who, while driving his car, veered on to the wrong side of the road and collided head-on with an oncoming vehicle, killing its driver. During the previous six months Marison had suffered several hypoglycaemic episodes (for an explanation of this term see p. 244) some of which involved losing consciousness without warning, and one of which had already led to a car accident. The trial judge ruled that the risk that he might have a hypoglycaemic attack while driving was obvious and fell within s. 2A. His conviction was upheld on appeal.

•••

CAUSING DEATH BY CARELESS DRIVING UNDER THE INFLUENCE OF DRINK OR DRUGS

The Road Traffic Act 1988 s. 3A contains a new offence, inserted in 1991, of causing death by careless driving under the influence of drink or drugs. The section provides:

> (1) If a person causes the death of another person by driving a mechanically propelled vehicle on a road or other public place without due care and attention, or without reasonable consideration for other persons using the road or place, and—
> (a) he is, at the time when he is driving, unfit to drive through drink or drugs, or
> (b) he has consumed so much alcohol that the proportion of it in his breath, blood or urine at that time exceeds the prescribed limit, or
> (c) he is, within 18 hours after that time, required to provide a specimen in pursuance of section 7 of this Act, but without reasonable excuse fails to provide it, he is guilty of an offence.

Essentially the section is laying down an objective negligence test, which requires simply that the defendant's driving has fallen below the reasonable standard of care, and drink or drugs were involved. In **R *v* Millington** (1995) the defendant had killed a pedestrian while driving after drinking six vodkas and two pints of beer, taking the defendant to nearly twice the legal limit. In upholding his conviction, the Court of Appeal stated that the issue of drink was relevant to the question of whether he had been careless as well as to whether he was under the influence of drink and drugs.

▶ Criticism

Deaths caused by vehicles

The Road Traffic Act 1991 amended the Road Traffic Act 1988 to replace the previous offence of causing death by reckless driving – with which such cases as **R *v* Reid** and **R *v* Lawrence** (1982) were concerned. The original statutory offence was created because juries were reluctant to convict a driver who caused death on a charge of manslaughter. Their attitude was often 'there but for the grace of God, go I'. However, evidence suggested that jurors continued to be reluctant to convict when the offence was defined as causing death by reckless driving. A joint report in 1988 for the Department of Transport and the Home Office concluded that part of the problem was that the test of recklessness still contained elements of subjectivity, and juries became reluctant to convict wherever they were asked to move on from the question of the standard of driving and consider the mental state of the defendant. The high rate of acquittals then led to reluctance to prosecute the offence at all, which meant that the law was simply not doing its job.

Even now that the law has been changed to focus on the standard of driving, there are over 4,000 deaths on the road each year, yet at most a few hundred prosecutions are brought under this section. Rather like accidents at work, accidents on the road seem to be seen as a risk we all have to take, even though a great many of them are not caused by chance or fate, but by human action, and the risk is often one of serious injury or death. Perhaps if the Government, the police and the media made as much fuss about these as they do about the much less serious risk of street crime, the situation would change.

In the light of these problems, some have suggested that the offence of causing death by dangerous driving should be abolished altogether, and such drivers should simply be charged with dangerous driving, which has a maximum sentence of two years. Since in practice people convicted of causing death by dangerous driving rarely get a sentence of more than two years, this may be a practical solution to the problem.

▶ Reform of involuntary manslaughter

Abolish gross negligence manslaughter

A leading criminal law academic, Glanville Williams, has argued that neither negligence, even if gross, nor **Caldwell** recklessness is a sufficient base for a crime as serious as manslaughter. He feels that the *mens rea* for involuntary manslaughter should be intention to cause serious harm, or recklessness as to whether death or serious personal harm will be caused (recklessness being defined to mean subjective, **Cunningham** recklessness).

Williams argues that making subjective recklessness the minimum fault requirement would protect people from being charged with such a serious offence merely because their behaviour was inadequate. New, less serious offences could be created to deal with acts of gross but not deliberate negligence which caused death or injury and appeared to deserve punishment, though Williams believes that most such cases are already adequately covered by existing legislation, particularly the law on safety at work. In such circumstances, he suggests, vindictive punishment should be avoided.

However, these ideas can be criticized on the ground that abandoning gross negligence manslaughter in favour of what are really regulatory offences, usually punished only by fines, is an open invitation to companies to neglect safety standards, in an area where prosecution is already rare, and punishment, by the standards of large companies, very slight. While the kind of unthinking oversight that Williams is referring to might appear weak grounds for such a serious charge, gross negligence also covers states of mind that might be argued to be very much more blameworthy, yet still fall outside **Cunningham** recklessness.

▶ The Law Commission proposals

In its report *Legislating the Criminal Code: Involuntary Manslaughter* (1996), the Law Commission heavily criticized the existing common law. It proposes that constructive manslaughter and gross negligence manslaughter should be abolished and replaced by three new offences:

* reckless killing
* killing by gross carelessness
* corporate killing.

Reckless killing

This offence would be committed if:

(1) a person by his or her conduct causes the death of another;
(2) he or she is aware of a risk that his or her conduct will cause death or serious injury; and
(3) it is unreasonable for him or her to take that risk, having regard to the circumstances as he or she believes them to be.

Thus, recklessness is restricted to its subjective meaning. The offence would be punishable with life imprisonment.

Killing by gross carelessness

This offence would be committed where:

(1) a person by his or her conduct causes the death of another;
(2) a risk that his or her conduct will cause death or serious injury would be obvious to a reasonable person in his or her position;
(3) he or she is capable of appreciating that risk at the material time; and
(4) either
  (a) his or her conduct falls far below what can reasonably be expected of him or her in the circumstances, or

(b) he or she intends by his or her conduct to cause some injury, or is aware of, and unreasonably takes, the risk that it may do so and the conduct causing (or intended to cause) the injury constitutes an offence.

The offence may be committed in two ways – (4)(a) and (4)(b). The former relies on a fault similar to that of dangerousness in road traffic offences and aims to avoid the circularity of the test in **Adomako**, though it does still leave the jury with a very considerable discretion. The latter is a narrower version of unlawful and dangerous act manslaughter and its inclusion has been criticized. The report envisages a likely maximum sentence of ten years' imprisonment.

Corporate killing

This crime could only be committed by a corporation. The framework of the offence is the same as that of killing by gross carelessness. The prosecution would have to prove that the death was caused by failings in the organization of the company's activities such as to amount to neglecting the health and safety of its employees or those affected by its actions. The fault element, as for the gross carelessness offence, would be that the company's conduct fell far below what could be expected. There would be no requirement to prove that the risk was obvious or that the company was capable of appreciating it. The offence would be punishable by a fine, or an order to rectify the company procedures that led to the death. The Government has announced that it intends to pass legislation to introduce this offence.

• •
ANSWERING QUESTIONS

When tackling a problem question concerned with homicide offences, a logical approach is to start by considering liability for murder. If the defendant has both the *actus reus* and *mens rea* of murder, then consider whether they have a complete defence or a partial defence. If they have the *actus reus* of murder but not the *mens rea*, then you can look at whether they could be liable for involuntary manslaughter. If they lack the *actus reus* of murder, then they can only be liable for a non-fatal offence.

1 **Anna had become wholly obsessed with the idea that it was wrong to exploit animals for any purpose. She had been ridiculed for her views for many years during which, she now felt, she had campaigned without success, and she had recently become very depressed. She was convinced that the whole system of exploitation was underpinned by finance from the banks. Consequently, she decided to stage a dramatic robbery at her local bank. She went to the bank armed with a shotgun and forced Erica, the**

manager, to come out of her office to listen to her speech about animal exploitation. During the speech, a bank customer shouted, 'She is just one of those stupid animal rights idiots.' Hearing this, Anna moved in the customer's direction with the shotgun raised but Erica obstructed her and in the struggle that followed Erica was shot and killed. Anna then rushed outside and got into a taxi which was just about to drive off with a passenger. Sitting in the back seat, she held the gun to the passenger's head and told Ben, the taxi driver, not to stop for any reason. Ben drove through red traffic lights at a road junction and collided with a cyclist, Christine. Christine later died from her injuries.

(a) Discuss Anna's criminal liability for the death of Erica. *(15 marks)*

(b) Discuss Ben's criminal liability for the death of Christine. *(15 marks)*

(c) If Anna and Ben were tried for offences of unlawful homicide, explain which courts would deal with them, including any appeals which might be made. *(5 marks)*

(d) Anna's problems were associated partly with a desire to bring a particular cause to the attention of the public. Explain and discuss the approach of English law to support for, and protection of, freedom to do so. *(15 marks) AEB, 1994*

Part (a): the most serious offence that Anna might be liable for is murder. On the question of *actus reus*, it is not clear whether she pulled the trigger so causation may be an issue, though particularly in the light of **Pagett** causation is likely to be satisfied. Because we do not know whether Anna pulled the trigger, the issue of *mens rea* will be particularly problematic and reference to cases considering foresight of consequences should be made, such as **Moloney** and **Nedrick**. If Anna has the *mens rea* of murder then she may be able to raise a defence of provocation or diminished responsibility. Words alone are now sufficient to be provocation, though whether the defence could be relied on, if **Luc Thiet Thuan** is not followed, will partly depend on the words used by the customer, taking into account the years of ridicule suffered by Anna. A possible defence of diminished responsibility would be based on Anna's obsessive beliefs and her depression.

If Anna lacks the *mens rea* of murder, then she may be liable for involuntary manslaughter, probably unlawful and dangerous act manslaughter. Using the shotgun to threaten people was clearly an unlawful act which was dangerous. To all the offences insanity (discussed at p. 241) would be a possible defence, but this is unlikely to succeed as there is no evidence that she did not know what she was doing or that it was legally wrong.

Part (b): Ben will only be liable for Christine's murder if he had both the *actus reus* and *mens rea* of murder. Proof of the *mens rea* will be particularly difficult. There is no suggestion that he wanted to kill Christine so he did not have direct intention. The only possibility would be to show that he had indirect intention. In the light of **Nedrick** it would have to be shown that death or grievous bodily harm was a virtual certain consequence of his acts and that he foresaw it as such. This would then be very strong evidence from which the jury could infer intention.

A more likely charge is involuntary manslaughter. You would need to look at whether he satisfies the elements of gross negligence manslaughter. He is likely to be found to owe a duty to Christine, a fellow road user, but a jury might not be prepared to find that he has been so negligent as to justify criminal liability – the test for gross negligence. Alternatively, he may be liable for unlawful and dangerous act manslaughter. Going through red lights is a criminal offence but there may be problems if **Dalby** is followed as could it be said that his acts were directed at someone? Brief consideration could be given to subjective reckless manslaughter, whose very existence is uncertain.

If the elements of murder are found he will not be able to rely on the defence of duress in the light of the decision of **R** v **Howe**. The defence of duress by threats might be available to manslaughter. You could also consider public and private defences. A discussion of these issues can be found in Chapter 13.

Part (c): this raises issues that you will come across when studying the English legal system in general. Relevant material can be found in the authors' book on the subject. You would need to give an explanation of the process of a criminal case through the courts. Note that this is a serious indictable offence and would therefore ultimately be tried in the Crown Court. It would never be tried in the magistrates' court. Also make sure you do not confuse your civil courts with the criminal courts, for example the county court is not relevant at all as that is a purely civil court. The main route of appeal would be to the Criminal Division of the Court of Appeal and then to the House of Lords. Be careful not to spend too long on this part of the question as it was only allocated 5 marks compared with 15 marks for the other parts.

Part (d): again, this part of the question does not fall within the syllabus of a typical criminal law course, but enters the realms of a course on the English legal system. You need to place the particular factual situation within a broader framework of the general approach of the law to the bringing of causes to the attention of the general public. A possible starting point would be to consider the notion of 'residual freedoms', that is to say that people are free to do what they want provided there is no specific law restraining that freedom. Examples are freedom of speech, freedom of association and freedom of the person. You could look at the European Convention of Human Rights, the Labour Government's proposals to assimilate this convention into domestic law and the arguments surrounding the introduction of a Bill of Rights.

2 **A, who is on bad terms with his neighbour B, hurls a petrol bomb through B's living room window intending to destroy the house, but also being aware that the occupants of the house are highly likely to be severely injured. Mrs B and her baby are badly cut by flying glass but manage to escape from the ensuing fire. Both Mrs B and the baby are taken to hospital where doctors recommend blood transfusions. Mrs B refuses a transfusion because she is afraid of contracting the AIDS virus. She lapses into a coma and dies shortly afterwards. The baby is to receive a blood transfusion but C,**

a hospital technician, mistakenly identifies the baby's blood group. As a result, the baby receives incompatible blood and dies. Consider the liability of A for the deaths of Mrs B and the baby. *Oxford*

As you are asked to consider the criminal liability of A for the deaths you should restrict yourself to looking at liability for homicide offences – a discussion of criminal damage, arson and non-fatal offences would be irrelevant because of this limitation. You should also not look at the liability of the hospital technician because you are asked only about the liability of A. You need to consider the death of each victim in turn as they raise slightly different factual issues.

On the issue of A's liability for a homicide offence, your starting point should again be murder. Causation needs to be looked at in depth with particular emphasis on the leading case of **Cheshire** and the blood transfusion case of **Blaue**.

As regards the *mens rea* of murder, A does not seem to have direct intention; the question will be whether he has indirect intention. We are told that he foresees severe injury as highly likely. You will have to consider whether this satisfies the **Nedrick/Woollin** criteria, and if it does this foresight will provide very strong evidence of intention, though it is not itself intention.

If A is found to have the *actus reus* and *mens rea* of murder you could consider quickly whether he might have a partial defence. On the facts we are given there is no basis for any such defence, though more facts might have revealed that he had been provoked by the neighbours or that he suffered diminished responsibility.

As we cannot say for certain that a jury would conclude that there was intention to cause grievous bodily harm you should consider in slightly less detail the issue of involuntary manslaughter. Unlawful and dangerous act manslaughter would be particularly relevant to these facts.

3 Whilst having a drink in a pub with his wife, Nina, Mark was subjected to a lot of rude comments from a very noisy and drunken group of women sitting nearby. Jane was particularly persistent in making sexual suggestions and, eventually, Nina went across to the group and threw a pint of beer over Jane. Mark and Nina then left.

Later that evening, Nina found herself in the toilets of a nightclub at the same time as Jane and called her a 'squint-eyed slut'. (Jane was, in fact, rather sensitive about the appearance of her eyes.) She immediately produced a small knife from her bag and stabbed Nina twice. One of the stab wounds pierced Nina's lung and she died a few days later.

Nina's death brought about a significant personality change in Mark. He found it difficult to concentrate, drank heavily and was treated for depression by his doctor. He worked in the service department of a garage and had been responsible for carrying out repairs on a car which had subsequently crashed into a bus shelter, resulting in injuries to a number of people in the queue and the death of a passer-by, Ian, from a heart attack. When examined, the car's steering was found to be seriously defective but, though the fault must have been present before the service, the service record made no mention of it.

When questioned, Mark was able only to say that he had felt 'very down' when he serviced the car, did not really know what he was doing at the time and had no recollection of it now.

(a) Discuss Jane's liability for the murder of Nina. *(15 marks)*

(b) Discuss Mark's liablity for the manslaughter of Ian. *(15 marks)*

(c) Explain what assistance may be available to Jane and Mark to help them to pay for legal advice and representation. *(10 marks)*

(d) Discuss the aims pursued by the courts in the sentencing of offenders and indicate how they might be applied to Mark, were he to be convicted of manslaughter. *(10 marks) AEB, 1996*

Part (a): this question raised no significant issues about the *actus reus* of murder and therefore this should have been dealt with concisely. More time should have been spent at looking at whether Jane had the *mens rea* of murder. Having considered and applied cases such as **Moloney** and **Nedrick** you should have considered the defence of intoxication which is discussed in Chapter 13. There is a possibility that a jury would find that the elements of murder existed. You could have then considered whether Jane would have had any defence (other than intoxication) to murder. The defence to consider in the most detail was the partial defence of provocation. You needed to consider the concept of cumulative provocation discussed in **R** v **Humphrey** and the attitude a court might take to alcohol consumption in the light of cases such as **R** v **Morhall**.

Part (b): there was no evidence that Mark intended to cause death or serious injury to anyone. In answering this question you should therefore concentrate on involuntary manslaughter rather than voluntary manslaughter. Thus, despite the reference to depression, you could not discuss diminished responsibility. Mark's conduct amounted to an omission and so there does not appear to be an unlawful act for the purposes of unlawful and dangerous act manslaughter. Having explained this, you need to concentrate on gross negligence manslaughter as defined by **Adomako**. Mark was clearly under a duty and his omission had created a risk of death. Ultimately it would be for the jury to decide whether Mark's conduct was sufficiently negligent to justify criminal liability. You also need to discuss the issue of causation, for while there was clearly factual causation there would only be legal causation if **Blaue** was strictly applied. The defences of insanity and, more briefly, non-insane automatism need to be looked at. These are discussed in Chapter 13.

For a discussion of the legal issues raised in parts (c) and (d), please see the authors' book, *English Legal System*.

4 Alice and Ben have been married for ten years, during five of which Ben has been addicted to heroin. In consequence, Alice has had to endure unpredictable behaviour from Ben, including verbal and physical abuse to herself and their children, unexplained absences, lack of money and loss of her possessions to Ben for the purchase of drugs. During the last two years,

Alice has increasingly resorted to drink and her own behaviour has become unpredictable. In particular, she has become anxious, depressed and short-tempered, and has engaged in casual prostitution to supplement their income. In turn, this behaviour has led to further abuse from Ben and to two fights between them in which Alice suffered quite serious injuries.

Two days ago, Alice returned from seeing a 'client' and immediately drank half a bottle of whisky in front of Ben, whom she accused of being no use to her in any way at all. Ben punched her, called her a drunken whore and said that he would 'finish the job properly' after he had injected a dose of heroin. He then went off upstairs whilst Alice pushed the television set off its stand, broke a mirror and poured whisky over the furniture as well as drinking more of it. She then went into the kitchen and made and drank a cup of coffee.

About ten minutes after the incident with Ben, she armed herself with a knife and went upstairs. There, she found Ben unconscious and surmised that he had taken an excessively large or pure dose of heroin. She went back downstairs and paced around in an agitated manner, throwing pictures and other objects around the room from time to time until about an hour had gone by. She then telephoned for an ambulance. However, when the ambulance arrived, the medical emergency team failed to revive Ben and a doctor pronounced him dead.

(a) Explain the elements of the offence of murder and, ignoring Alice's anxiety and depression and Ben's behaviour towards her, apply them to determine whether Alice could be guilty of murdering Ben. *(10 marks)*

(b) Considering, especially, Alice's anxiety and depression and Ben's behaviour towards her, explain the elements of any defence(s) which Alice may raise to seek to reduce the crime to manslaughter and apply them to determine whether she would be successful in doing so. *(10 marks)*

(c) Explain the elements of unlawful act manslaughter and gross negligence manslaughter and consider whether, if a murder charge were to fail, Alice would be guilty of either. *(10 marks)*

(d) Alice might have difficulty in being able to pay for legal advice and representation. Explain what statutory provision is made to assist accused persons in her position. *(10 marks)*

(e) In answering parts (a)–(c) above, you have discussed rules of law concerning the offences of murder and manslaughter and related defences. Select either the offences or the defences and consider what criticisms may be made of the rules and what improvements might be suggested. *(10 marks)* AEB, 1997

(a) You only needed to consider whether Alice satisfied all the elements of murder. Looking first at the *actus reus* of murder, on the facts we are concerned with an omission as Alice initially failed to call for medical assistance. While Alice did carry out various acts, such as going upstairs with a knife, it is only her initial failure to summon medical advice that could have caused the death. The law on omissions is discussed at p. 9. Murder is an offence that can potentially be committed by omission, and an example of this is **R v Gibbins and Proctor** (1918). She is likely to be found to have owed a duty to act as Ben was her husband and you would need to refer to cases concerning duties between close family members. The question of causation needs to be looked at in detail but on the available facts it is impossible to conclude definitely whether or not she would be found to have been the cause of Ben's death. It may be that he would have died even if the medical assistance had been summoned immediately and that medical workers would not have even been able to delay his death, in which case Alice would not be found to have been the cause of his death.

The *mens rea* of murder is malice aforethought, but it is not clear on the information given exactly what her state of mind was at the time. You would need to look at the line of authorities on the issue of intention and in particular **R v Woollin**. The issue of intoxication will be relevant here, which is discussed at p. 255.

(b) This question required a detailed discussion of both the partial defences of provocation and diminished responsibility. The defences of insanity and self-defence could not be considered on these facts because these are complete defences which would have given rise to an acquittal rather than a conviction for manslaughter. Looking first at provocation, you would need to give a systematic and detailed analysis of the law in this area. Particular consideration would need to be given to the issue of which characteristics of Alice could be taken into account for the objective test. Note that in **R v Morhall** (1995) the House of Lords stated that while being an addict (here to alcohol) could be taken into account, the fact of actually being intoxicated could not. On looking at the law on diminished responsibility the case of **Tandy** was particularly relevant.

(c) The offence of unlawful act manslaughter requires an act, and therefore, while the question asks you to discuss this offence, you must conclude that Alice could not be liable under this heading. The most relevant offence to the facts was gross negligence manslaughter and the leading case of **Adomako** had to be discussed along with later Court of Appeal cases, such as **R v Singh** and **R v Khan and Khan**, that have interpreted and applied this judgment. Ultimately, it would be for the jury to decide whether it felt that Alice's conduct constituted gross negligence. If a court found that she had not been the cause of death for the purposes of murder, then this finding would also prevent her being liable for gross negligence manslaughter.

(d) This question falls outside the scope of this book, but the relevant information can be found in the authors' book *English Legal System*.

(e) Criticisms of the law on murder can be found at p. 51, constructive manslaughter at p. 80 and gross negligence manslaughter at p. 87. In relation to the defences, you will find criticism of the law on provocation at p. 66 on diminished responsibility at p. 70 and on intoxication at p. 261. Make sure you follow the instructions of the examiner to discuss either the offences *or* the defences.

6 Non-fatal offences against the person

The previous chapters have studied offences against the person which result in death. This chapter considers, in order of seriousness, the remaining important offences against the person, where no death is caused.

▶ Assault

The Criminal Justice Act 1988, s. 39 provides that assault is a summary offence with a maximum sentence on conviction of six months' imprisonment or a fine. The Act does not provide a definition of the offence; the relevant rules are found in common law.

Actus reus

This consists of any act which makes the victim fear that unlawful force is about to be used against them. No force need actually be applied; creating the fear of it is sufficient, so assault can be committed by raising a fist at the victim, or pointing a gun. Nor does it matter that it may have been impossible for the defendant actually to inflict any force, for example if the gun was unloaded, so long as the victim is unaware of the impossibility of the threat being carried out.

Words alone can constitute an assault

Until the Court of Appeal decision in **R** *v* **Constanza** (1997) there was some uncertainty as to whether words alone could amount to an assault. **R** *v* **Constanza**, a case involving stalking, confirmed that they could. The House of Lords took this approach on **R** *v* **Ireland and Burstow** (1997) so that silent phone calls could amount to an assault. The offence would, for example, be committed if a man shouted to a stranger 'I'm going to kill you' – there is no need for an accompanying act, such as raising a fist, or pointing a gun. The old case of **Meade and Belt** (1823) which had suggested the contrary must now be viewed as bad law. Some people had gathered around another's house singing menacing songs with violent language and the judge had said 'no words or singing are equivalent to an assault'.

Words can also prevent a potential assault occurring – so, if a person shakes a fist at someone, but at the same time states that they will not harm that person, there will be no liability for this offence. This was the situation in **Tuberville** *v* **Savage** (1669). The defendant, annoyed by the comments someone had made to him, put his hand on his sword, which by itself could have been enough to constitute an assault, but also said, 'If it were not assize time I would not take such language', meaning that since judges were hearing criminal cases in the town at the time, he had no intention of using violence. His statement was held to negative the threat implied by putting his hand to his sword.

Fearing the immediate infliction of force

It has traditionally been said that the victim must fear the immediate infliction of force: fear that force might be applied at some time in the future would not be sufficient. The courts had often given a fairly generous interpretation of the concept of immediacy in this context. In **Smith** *v* **Chief Superintendent, Woking Police Station** (1983), the victim was at home in her ground-floor bedsit dressed only in her nightdress. She was terrified when she suddenly saw the defendant standing in her garden, staring at her through the window. He was found liable for assault, on the grounds that the victim feared the immediate infliction of force, even though she was safely locked inside. The Court of Appeal said:

> It was clearly a situation where the basis of the fear which was instilled in her was that she did not know what the defendant was going to do next, but that, whatever he might be going to do next, and sufficiently immediately for the purposes of the offence, was something of a violent nature. In effect, as it seems to me, it was wholly open to the justices to infer that her state of mind was not only that of terror, which they did find, but terror of some immediate violence.

However, the requirement that the victim must fear the immediate infliction of force was undermined by the Court of Appeal in **R** *v* **Ireland** (1996). The defendant had made a large number of unwanted telephone calls to three different women, remaining silent when they answered the phone. All three victims suffered significant psychological symptoms such as palpitations, cold sweats, anxiety, inability to sleep, dizziness and stress as a result of the repeated calls. He was convicted under s. 47 of the Offences Against the Person Act 1861. This offence is discussed below but what is important here is that for Ireland to have been liable there must have been an assault. Ireland appealed against his conviction on the basis that there was no assault since the requirement of immediacy had not been satisfied. His appeal was dismissed by the Court of Appeal. The court stated that the requirement of immediacy was in fact satisfied as, by using the telephone, the appellant had put himself in immediate contact with the victims, and when the victims lifted the telephone they were placed in immediate fear and suffered psychological damage. It was not necessary for there to be physical proximity between the defendant and the victim. A further appeal was taken to the House of Lords in 1997 and, while the initial conviction was upheld, the House of Lords refused to enter into a discussion of the requirement for immediacy. They said that this was not necessary on the facts of the case as the appellant had pleaded guilty and that, in any case, the existence of immediacy would depend upon the circumstances in each case. It is not sufficient that the victim is immediately put in fear, the fear must be of immediate violence.

In **R** *v* **Constanza** (1997), another stalking case where the victim had been stalked over a prolonged period of time, the Court of Appeal stated that in order to incur liability for assault, it is enough for the prosecution to prove a fear of violence at some time not excluding the immediate future. If the Court of Appeal in **Constanza** is followed, then there would be no need to fear the immediate infliction of force in the sense of a battery; the offence would include fearing some other type of injury, notably psychological damage. The concept of immediacy would also be considerably weakened.

Causation

Note that, as for all these offences against the person, the issue of causation may be relevant if there is any question that the defendant was not the cause of the relevant result – in the case of assault, if the victim was put in fear of immediate and unlawful force, but the defendant did not cause that fear. In such cases the discussion at p. 41 may be relevant.

Mens rea

The *mens rea* of assault is either intention or **Cunningham** recklessness. The defendant must have either intended to cause the victim to fear the infliction of immediate and unlawful force, or must have seen the risk that such fear would be created.

For all the non-fatal offences against the person discussed in this chapter where recklessness is relevant, it is **Cunningham** recklessness that is applied. This was confirmed in the case of **Savage and Parmenter** discussed below. As for the word 'intention' all the case law on oblique intention discussed in the context of murder is potentially relevant here.

▶ Battery

By s. 39 of the Criminal Justice Act 1988, battery is a summary offence punishable with up to six months' imprisonment or a fine, but as with assault, it is left to the common law to define the offence.

Actus reus

The *actus reus* of battery consists of the application of unlawful force on another. Any unlawful physical contact can amount to a battery; there is no need to prove harm or pain, and a mere touch can be sufficient. Often the force will be directly applied by one person to another, for example if one person slaps another across the face, but the force can also be applied indirectly. This was the case in **Fagan** *v* **Metropolitan Police Commissioner** (discussed at p. 9), where the force was applied by running over the police officer's foot in the car.

The force does not have to be applied to the victim's body; touching his or her clothes may be enough, even if the victim feels nothing at all as a result. In **Thomas** (1985), it was stated, *obiter*, that touching the bottom of a woman's skirt was equivalent to touching the woman herself.

Mens rea

Again either intention or recklessness is sufficient, but here it is intention or recklessness as to the application of unlawful force.

▶ Offences Against the Person Act 1861, s. 47

According to s. 47:

> Whosoever shall be convicted upon an indictment of any assault occasioning actual bodily harm shall be liable . . . [to imprisonment for five years].

Section 47 of the Offences Against the Person Act 1861 provides that it is an offence to commit 'any assault occasioning actual bodily harm'. This offence is commonly known as ABH. The crime is triable either way and if found guilty the defendant is liable to a maximum sentence of five years.

Actus reus

Despite the fact that the Act uses the term 'assault' for this offence, s. 47 has been interpreted as being committed with either assault or battery. The first requirement is, therefore, to prove the *actus reus* of assault or battery, as defined above. In addition, the prosecution must show that the assault or battery caused ABH. Both **Ireland** and **Constanza**, discussed in the context of assault, were concerned with this offence as the issue of assault arose in the context of the *actus reus* of a s. 47 crime.

Actual bodily harm has been given a wide interpretation. In **Miller** (1954), the court stated: 'Actual bodily harm includes hurt or injury calculated to interfere with health or comfort.' Thus ABH can occur simply where discomfort to the person is caused. However, this was qualified slightly in **R** *v* **Chan-Fook** (1994), where Hobhouse LJ said in the Court of Appeal: 'The word "actual" indicates that the injury (although there is no need for it to be permanent) should not be so trivial as to be wholly insignificant.'

In **Miller**, it was also accepted that ABH included not just physical harm, but also psychological injury, such as shock. In later cases, the courts have made it clear that psychological injury will only count as ABH if it is a clinically recognizable condition. The defendant, in **R** *v* **Chan-Fook**, aggressively questioned a man he suspected of stealing his fiancée's jewellery. He then dragged him upstairs and locked him in a room. The victim, frightened of what the defendant would do on his return, tried to escape through the window, but injured himself when he fell to the ground. Charged with an offence under s. 47, the defendant denied striking the victim. The trial judge said, for liability to be incurred, it was sufficient if the victim suffered a hysterical or nervous condition at the time and the defendant was convicted at first instance. His appeal was allowed and Hobhouse LJ said: 'The phrase "actual bodily harm" is capable of including psychiatric injury. But it does not include mere emotions such as fear or distress or panic, nor does it include, as such, states of mind that are not themselves evidence of some identifiable clinical condition.'

The offence of causing actual bodily harm has been applied in the context of stalking, but where the stalking consists of a course of conduct over a period of time it can be difficult to identify the actual assault that caused the actual bodily harm. In **R** *v* **Cox (Paul)** (1998) the Court of Appeal did not consider this problem insurmountable. The defendant's relationship with his girlfriend had ended. He started to make repeated telephone calls, some of which were silent, he prowled outside her flat, put through her letter-box a torn piece of a brochure showing details of a holiday she had booked, and, shortly before she was due to depart, he telephoned her to say that she was going to her death and he could smell burning. The complainant began to suffer from severe headaches and stress. The appellant was convicted of assault occasioning actual bodily harm and his conviction was upheld by the Court of Appeal even though it was difficult to identify an act that constituted the assault.

Mens rea

The *mens rea* of assault occasioning ABH is the same as for assault or battery. No additional *mens rea* is required in relation to the actual bodily

harm, as the case of **R** *v* **Roberts** (1978) shows. Late at night, the defendant gave a lift in his car to a girl. During the journey he made unwanted
sexual advances, touching the girl's clothes. Frightened that he was going
to rape her, she jumped out of the moving car, injuring herself. It was
held that the defendant had committed the *actus reus* of a s. 47 offence by
touching the girl's clothes – sufficient for the *actus reus* of battery – and this
act had caused her to suffer actual bodily harm. The defendant argued that
he lacked the *mens rea* of the offence, because he had neither intended to
cause her actual bodily harm, nor seen any risk of her suffering actual
bodily harm as a result of his advances. This argument was rejected: the
court held that the *mens rea* for battery was sufficient in itself, and there
was no need for any extra *mens rea* regarding the actual bodily harm.

The point was confirmed in **Savage and Parmenter** (1991). The defendant went into a local pub, where she spotted her husband's new girlfriend
having a drink with some friends. She went up to the table where the
group was sitting, intending to throw a pint of beer over the woman. On
reaching the table, she said 'Nice to meet you darling' and threw the
beer but, as she did so, she accidentally let go of the glass, which broke
and cut the woman's wrist. The defendant argued that she lacked sufficient *mens rea* to be liable for a s. 47 offence, because her intention had
only been to throw the beer, and she had not seen the risk that the glass
might injure the girlfriend. This was rejected because she intended to
apply unlawful force (the *mens rea* of battery) and there was no need to
prove that she intended or was reckless as to causing actual bodily harm.
The conflicting case of **Spratt** (1991) was overruled on this point.

▶ Offences Against the Person Act 1861, s. 20

This section states:

> Whosoever shall unlawfully and maliciously wound or inflict any
> grievous bodily harm upon any other person either with or without
> any weapon or instrument shall be guilty of an offence triable either
> way, and being convicted thereof shall be liable to imprisonment for
> five years.

Actus reus

The prosecution has to prove that the defendant either inflicted grievous
bodily harm or wounded the victim.

Inflicting grievous bodily harm
In **DPP** *v* **Smith** (1961) the House of Lords emphasized that grievous bodily
harm (GBH) is a phrase that should be given its ordinary and natural
meaning, which was simply 'really serious harm'. This was confirmed in

Saunders (1985) where the Court of Appeal said that there was no real difference between the terms 'serious' and 'really serious'. The point was again made in **R** *v* **Brown and Stratton** (1998) where the Court of Appeal stated that trial judges should not attempt to give a definition of the concept to the jury. The victim was a transsexual who had undergone 'gender reassignment' treatment, and changed her name to Julie Ann. Stratton was the victim's son and he had felt humiliated when his father had come to the supermarket where he worked, dressed as a woman. With his cousin Stratton had gone round to Julie Ann's flat and attacked her with fists and part of a chair, resulting in a broken nose, three missing teeth, bruising, a laceration over one eye and concussion. These injuries were found by the Court of Appeal to amount to grievous bodily harm and the defendants were liable under s. 20. **R** *v* **Ireland and Burstow** (1997) recognizes that a really serious psychiatric injury can amount to grievous bodily harm.

The difference between actual bodily harm under s. 47 and grievous bodily harm in this section is one of degree – grievous bodily harm is clearly the more serious injury.

The meaning of the word 'inflict' in this section has caused considerable difficulty. For many years it was held that 'inflict' implied the commission of an actual assault. Thus, in **Clarence** (1888), the Queen's Bench Division decided that a husband could not be said to have inflicted GBH on his wife by knowingly exposing her to the risk of contracting gonorrhoea through intercourse; the wife had not feared the infliction of lawful force at the time of the sexual intercourse. In **Wilson** (1984) the House of Lords stated that an assault is not necessary, the word 'inflict' simply required 'force being violently applied to the body of the victim, so that he suffers grievous bodily harm'. Thus it was thought that under s. 20 grievous bodily harm had to be caused by the direct application of force. This meant, for example, that it would cover hitting, kicking or stabbing a victim, but not digging a hole for them to fall into. In practice, the courts often gave a wide interpretation as to when force was direct. In **R** *v* **Martin** (1881), while a play was being performed at a theatre, the defendant placed an iron bar across the exit, turned off the staircase lights and shouted 'Fire! Fire!' The audience panicked and, in the rush to escape, people were seriously injured. The defendant was found liable under s. 20, even though strictly speaking it is difficult to view the application of force as truly direct on these facts.

A similarly wide interpretation was given in **Halliday** (1889). In that case, the defendant's behaviour frightened his wife so much that she jumped out of their bedroom window to get away from him. The injuries that she suffered as a result of the fall were found to have been directly applied, so that he could be liable under s. 20.

However, following the decisions in **R** *v* **Ireland and Burstow** (1997), the word inflict no longer implies the direct application of force. Burstow had become obsessed with a female acquaintance. He started to stalk her, following her, damaging her car and breaking into her house. He was convicted for this conduct but after his release from prison he continued to stalk her, following her and subjecting her to further harassment, including silent telephone calls, sending hate mail, stealing clothes from her washing line and scattering condoms over her garden. His behaviour caused his victim to suffer severe depression, insomnia and panic attacks. For this subsequent behaviour he was charged with inflicting grievous bodily harm under s. 20 of the Offences Against the Person Act 1861. The trial court convicted, stating that there was no reason for 'inflict' to be given a restrictive meaning. On appeal against his conviction the appellant argued that the requirements of the term 'inflict' had not been satisfied. The appeal was dismissed by both the Court of Appeal and the House of Lords. The House stated that s. 20 could be committed where no physical force had been applied (directly or indirectly) on the body of the victim.

Wounding

Wounding requires a breaking of the skin, so there will normally be bleeding, though a graze will be sufficient. In **C (a minor)** *v* **Eisenhower** (1984), the defendant fired an air pistol, hitting the victim in the eye with a pellet. This ruptured a blood vessel in the eye, causing internal bleeding, but the injury was not sufficient to constitute a wounding, as the skin had not been broken. This may seem odd given that for this serious offence the *actus reus* can be satisfied simply by pricking somebody's thumb with a pin.

Mens rea

The *mens rea* for this offence is defined by the word 'maliciously'. In **Cunningham** it was stated that for the purpose of the 1861 Act maliciously meant 'intentionally or recklessly' and 'reckless' is used in the **Cunningham** sense.

The case of **Mowatt** (1967) established that there is no need to intend or be reckless as to causing GBH or wounding. The defendant need only intend or be reckless that his or her acts could have caused some physical harm. As Lord Diplock said: 'It is quite unnecessary that the accused should have foreseen that his unlawful act might cause physical harm of the gravity described in the section, i.e. a wound or serious physical injury. It is enough that he should have foreseen that some physical harm to some person, albeit of a minor character, might result.'

In **R** *v* **Grimshaw** (1984), the defendant was in a pub when she heard someone insult her boyfriend. She pushed the glass he was holding into his face. She was found guilty of an offence under s. 20: she had inflicted grievous bodily harm and she had the *mens rea* because she had at least foreseen that he would suffer some harm.

▶ Offences Against the Person Act 1861, s. 18

Section 18 provides:

> Whosoever shall unlawfully and maliciously by any means whatsoever wound or cause any grievous bodily harm to any person, with intent to do some grievous bodily harm to any person, or with intent to resist or prevent the lawful apprehension or detainer of any person, shall be guilty of an offence triable only on indictment, and being convicted thereof shall be liable to imprisonment for life.

This is similar to the offence of s. 20, and, like that offence, requires proof of either grievous bodily harm or wounding. The crucial difference is in the *mens rea*: while recklessness can be sufficient for s. 20, intention is always required for s. 18. It is for this reason that s. 18 is punishable with a life sentence, while the maximum sentence for s. 20 is only five years – a person acting with intent is considered to have greater moral fault than a person merely acting recklessly.

Actus reus

Wounding and grievous bodily harm are given the same interpretation as for s. 20. In **R** *v* **Ireland and Burstow** Lord Steyn said that the word 'cause' in s. 18 and 'inflict' in s. 20 were not synonymous, but it is difficult to see how they differ in practice. Both refer to the need for causation.

Mens rea

As noted above, the prosecution must prove intention. The intent must be either to cause grievous bodily harm (by contrast with s. 20, where an intention to cause some harm is sufficient), or to avoid arrest.

In addition, the section states that the defendant must have acted 'maliciously'. This bears the same meaning as discussed for s. 20, so if the prosecution have already proved that the defendant intended to cause grievous bodily harm, 'maliciously' imposes no further requirement: a defendant who intends to cause grievous bodily harm obviously intends to cause some harm. If the prosecution have proved the other form of intent, the intent to avoid arrest, then the requirement that the defendant acts maliciously does impose a further requirement: an intent to avoid arrest does not necessarily imply intention, or recklessness, as to whether you cause some harm. Therefore, where the prosecution prove intent to avoid arrest, they must also show that the defendant intended to cause some harm, or was reckless as to whether harm was caused.

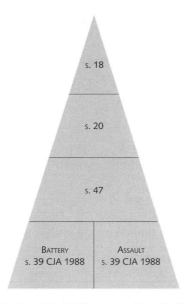

Fig. 3. Non-Fatal Offences Against the Person

▶ Problems with offences against the person

Domestic violence

As these offences show, in theory the criminal law protects those subjected to unlawful violence. In practice, there is a substantial group of such victims for whom there is little protection: women battered by their partners. The extent of this problem can be seen in the results of a survey carried out by Mooney for the Zero Tolerance campaign against domestic violence. Of those men surveyed, only one in three said they would never use violence against their partners, while two in three said they could envisage situations where they would. One in five men said they would react violently 'every time' to situations such as nagging, or housework not being done well enough. Of the women questioned, almost 25 per cent said they had been raped by their partner, 10 per cent had suffered an attempted strangulation, and 7 per cent broken bones. It is perhaps not surprising then to note that 44 per cent of female murder victims are killed by their husband or lover. The proportion of men killed by their partners is 10 per cent.

While the law itself does not distinguish between these victims and the person who gets attacked in the streets by a stranger – the offences above can be committed in just the same way in either situation, providing all the requirements of *mens rea* and *actus reus* are satisfied – in practice the victims of domestic assaults rarely receive the law's protection. The first reason for this is simply that very few domestic assaults – research suggests around 2 per cent – are reported to the police. If they are not reported, obviously they cannot be prosecuted, and the violent partner escapes punishment.

Research among battered wives suggests a variety of reasons for this under-reporting. The women are embarrassed by what the violence says about their relationship, and often blame themselves – a feeling frequently supported by the violent partner's claims that he has been provoked into violence by the woman's behaviour. In the early stages, the woman may make excuses for the man's behaviour, and tell herself that it will not happen again; by the time the violence has been repeated over a long period, she may feel powerless and unable to escape or take any steps towards reporting the offence. American research has suggested that this situation can lead to a recognized psychological state, often called battered woman syndrome, in which the victim loses the ability to see beyond the situation or any means of changing it.

Equally important is the fact that victims may fear that reporting the offence will simply lead to further beatings, given that even if charges are brought, the partner will usually be granted bail, and is highly likely to arrive home and attack her again in revenge for her making the complaint.

These problems are intensified by the traditional police approach to domestic violence, which is to avoid involvement, leaving the partners to sort things out themselves. This is prompted partly by the emphasis on the privacy of the home and the family which has been a traditional part of British culture – 'an Englishman's home is his castle' – and partly by concerns that the intervention of the legal system might lead to increased marriage breakdown. The assumption was that a couple might divorce if a prosecution were brought, but left alone, they would patch up their differences. In addition, the police claimed that, where prosecutions were brought, by the time the case came to court wives and girlfriends were refusing to give evidence, leading to cases collapsing.

In recent years some changes have been made in an attempt to address these problems. A spouse can now be compelled to give evidence against their partner in court proceedings, following the passing of s. 80 of the Police and Criminal Evidence Act 1984, and orders can be made prohibiting violence against a partner and even ousting the violent person from the home, though the effect of such an order in practice may be minimal where the violent partner is really determined to get at the victim.

In 1990, the Home Office published guidelines to encourage the police to take domestic violence seriously. These stress the importance of keeping careful records of incidents of domestic violence and registers of people at risk – similar to those kept for children at risk. They also encourage prosecution rather than attempts at reconciliation in appropriate cases.

The degree to which these measures have helped is unclear. Metropolitan Police figures showed that domestic violence had increased by

66 per cent in 1990–91; this could mean that there was more domestic violence, but it could equally suggest that the degree of violence was much the same as before, but more of it was being reported to the police. What does seem clear is that law and legal procedure alone cannot deal with this problem; a cultural change is required that would make domestic violence as unacceptable as any other kind of violent behaviour.

Definitions of the offences

Criticism is also often made of the way the offences themselves are defined. There is still no clear statutory definition of assault and battery, while the definitions of the more serious offences are contained in an Act passed back in 1861, with much of the vocabulary antiquated and even misleading, such as 'assault' in s. 47 and 'maliciously' in s. 18.

The requirement that the threat must be of immediate force in order to fall within an assault means that there is a gap in the law. Currently, if a person shouts that he or she is going to kill you, that may be an assault; but if the threat is to kill you tomorrow, it is not. The Law Commission has produced a draft Criminal Law Bill in the belief that prompt reform of this area is necessary, and creates an offence that would cover this example.

Seriousness of the offences

The hierarchy of the offences in terms of seriousness can also be criticized. First, while assault and battery can only be punished with a maximum of six months' imprisonment, and s. 47 can be punished by five years, the only real difference between them is that ABH is caused – yet ABH can mean as little as causing discomfort to the person. Secondly, the s. 20 offence is defined a much more serious offence than s. 47, and yet they share the same maximum sentence of five years.

A third problem is that the only significant difference between s. 20 and s. 18 is arguably a slightly more serious *mens rea*, and yet the maximum sentence leaps from five years to life. This can perhaps be justified by the fact that a defendant who intends to cause GBH within s. 18 has the *mens rea* of murder, and it is merely chance which dictates whether the victim survives, leading to a charge under s. 18, or dies, leading to a charge of murder and a mandatory life sentence if convicted.

▶ Reform

In 1980 the Criminal Law Revision Committee recommended that this area of the law should be reformed. Its proposals were incorporated into the draft code of the criminal law prepared by the Law Commission. The Law Commission again considered the matter at the beginning of the

1990s, producing a report and draft Criminal Law Bill on the issue in 1993. In February 1998, the Home Office produced a Consultation Document in furtherance of its commitment to modernize and improve the law. This presents a draft Offences Against the Person Bill modelled largely, but not entirely, on the Law Commission's 1993 Draft Criminal Law Bill. There now looks like a real possibility that legislation may follow. The draft Bill updates the language used for these offences by talking about serious injury rather than grievous bodily harm, and avoiding the words 'maliciously' and 'wounding' altogether. Under the draft Bill s. 18 is replaced by 'intentionally causing serious injury', with a maximum sentence of life (clause 1); s. 20 by 'recklessly causing serious injury', with a maximum sentence of seven years (cl. 2); and s. 47 by 'intentionally or recklessly causing injury' with a maximum sentence of five years (cl. 3). Thus the offence replacing s. 47 would remove the requirement of an 'assault', which would be tidier and avoid the problem of finding an assault where there is a course of conduct (see **R** *v* **Cox (Paul)** on p. 106). The draft Bill still proceeds to use the term 'assault' for conduct which would better be described as two separate offences of assault and battery (cl. 4).

Statutory definitions are given for the mental elements of the offences which would continue to give recklessness a subjective meaning. Difficulties could arise as the statutory definitions differ from the common law definitions and if, for example, a jury was also faced with an accusation of murder, they would have to understand and apply two different tests for intention. The most serious offence in clause 1 could be committed by an omission but not the lesser offences. Injury is defined (cl. 15) to include physical and mental injury, but 'anything caused by disease' is not an injury of either kind, except for the purpose of clause 1. So it would be an offence under clause 1 to intentionally infect another with AIDS but no offence to recklessly do so under clause 2. In support of this solution the Home Office points to the undesirability of discriminating against those who are HIV positive and the danger of discouraging people from coming forward for tests and treatment. But such conduct could fall within clause 2 which is the offence of administering a dangerous substance.

▶ Stalking

The problems of stalking have attracted considerable media attention. 'Stalking', like 'shoplifting' and 'football hooliganism' is not a technical legal concept but one used in everyday language. It describes a campaign of harassment, usually with sexual undertones. Such conduct raises two important questions which have concerned Western legal systems in the late twentieth century: what are the boundaries of acceptable sexual behaviour and how far should psychiatric damage be recognized by the law? So any legal developments in this area are very sensitive.

In response to public concern the Protection from Harassment Act 1997 was passed. As well as enacting certain civil wrongs, it creates several new criminal offences. Section 1 prohibits a person from pursuing a course of conduct which they know or ought to know amounts to harassment of another. This is punishable by a maximum of six months' imprisonment. Section 4 contains the offence of aggravated harassment where, in addition, the defendant knows or ought to know that they placed the victim in fear of violence on at least two occasions. This is punishable with up to five years' imprisonment.

It is questionable whether this piece of legislation was necessary. The Act follows a pattern witnessed in other areas (for example, joyriding and dangerous dogs) of addressing a narrowly conceived social harm backed by a single issue pressure group campaign, with a widely drawn provision which overlaps with existing offences. The new offences in the 1997 Act are broadly defined and there is a danger that they could impinge upon other activities hitherto regarded as legitimate, such as investigative journalism and door-to-door selling. Cases such as **R v Ireland and Burstow** and **R v Constanza** show that the courts were prepared to adapt existing criminal law offences to include this type of harmful conduct. On the other hand, some people feel that these cases artificially distorted the existing law ignoring accepted authorities and that a fresh legislative approach was required with this specific problem in mind. In practice the value of the 1997 Act may be that it includes a power to make restraining orders forbidding the defendant from pursuing any conduct which amounts to harassment and a power of arrest to enforce these orders.

• •

ANSWERING QUESTIONS

1 J who is 17 and K who is 16 years old decide to plan an initiation ceremony for a new student, L, at their college. They agree to blindfold the newcomer and paint his hands and face red. Unfortunately, L is allergic to a chemical in the paint and, when painted, suffers a severe asthma attack. He becomes very unwell, being unable to breathe properly, and nearly faints. J and K become frightened and run off. After twenty minutes L is found and taken to hospital where he recovers after a few days' rest. Should J and K be charged with any offence? How might the courts deal with them on a finding of guilt? *London*
In many cases where there are two possible defendants their liability will need to be discussed separately, but here the defendants have done exactly the same thing so they can be dealt with together – the only difference is their age but as they are both over 14 this does not affect their criminal liability. Note that you are not being asked what offences they may have committed, but specifically with what they should be charged. This means that there are two separate elements to this part of the question: for what offences they might be liable, and whether they should be charged with those offences.

Looking first at the offences for which they may be liable, it is often easiest when answering problem questions to start with the most serious relevant offence and then work your way down to the least serious. Bear in mind that there is no death, so you are only concerned with non-fatal offences. The most serious possible offence would be s. 18 of the Offences Against the Person Act 1861. There is no wounding, so you will need to establish that there is GBH; whether the injuries are sufficient for this will be a question of fact for the jury to decide, but it seems unlikely. There must also be *mens rea* of intention to cause GBH, which again seems unlikely on the facts.

The next offence down is s. 20 for which GBH would again need to be proved. *Mens rea* would be easier to prove as you only need to show intention or recklessness as to causing some harm, but on these facts it would still be possible to find that J and K did not intend to cause any harm at all and neither did they see the risk (remember the recklessness must be subjective). The most likely offence is s. 47, with its wider *actus reus* and *mens rea*. The defence of consent could be relevant and reference should be made to the case of **Jones** concerning horseplay, discussed at p. 290.

Note that whichever offences J and K are liable for committing, they may also be liable for conspiring to commit these – the requirements for conspiracy are discussed on p. 194.

The question of whether or not they should be charged and the issue of sentencing young offenders fall outside the scope of this book, but are dealt with in the authors' book on the English legal system.

2 **It has been suggested by the Law Commission and others that sections 18, 20 and 47 of the Offences Against the Person Act 1861 should be repealed because they are unjust, ineffective, illogical and severely defective. In addition the offences, as they are defined, are incomprehensible to juries. Explain and comment on these suggestions.** *NEAB*
On the issue of the offences being 'unjust', you could look at the criticism of the sentencing structure. On the offences being 'ineffective', consideration could be given to their failure in the context of domestic violence. As regards the offences being 'illogical', you could discuss the word 'wounding' and the fact that it is part of the *actus reus* of the two most serious offences but merely requires a breaking of the skin; and that prior to **R** v **Ireland and Burstow** the courts gave the *actus reus* of s. 20 a narrower definition than the more serious offence of s. 18. The problem of stalking could be considered on the question of whether the offences are 'severely defective', discussing how far it was really necessary for the Government to create new crimes in the field. To consider how far the offences are 'incomprehensible' to a jury you could look at the archaic legislative language, such as 'maliciously' and 'grievous bodily harm'. Finally, you could summarize the Law Commission and Home Office proposals and consider how far they would remedy some of these problems.

7 Rape

Rape is the most serious of the non-fatal, sexual offences against the person. It carries a maximum sentence of life imprisonment. This area of law was amended by the Criminal Justice and Public Order Act 1994 (CJPOA).

▶ *Actus reus*

The *actus reus* of rape is committed where a man has sexual intercourse with a man or a woman without that person's consent. The Sexual Offences Act 1956, s. 1(1), as amended by the CJPOA, provides: 'It is an offence for a man to rape a woman or another man.'

The defendant

Note that only a man can be a defendant to a charge of rape; in law a woman cannot commit rape. However, a woman may be charged with being an accomplice to rape; for example, Rosemary West, wife of the alleged serial killer Frederick West, was initially charged on two counts with aiding and abetting the rape of a girl. In **DPP** *v* **K and C** (1997) two teenage girls were convicted as accomplices to a rape.

In the past, there was an irrebuttable presumption that boys under 14 could not have sexual intercourse and therefore could not be liable for rape. This rule came to look increasingly absurd, as it was clear that in reality such boys could have sexual intercourse. The rule was therefore abolished by s. 1 of the Sexual Offences Act 1993. Young boys can still seek the protection of the general offence of infancy available for all offences and discussed in Chapter 13.

The victim

Until 1994, the offence of rape could only be committed against a woman. Situations where a man was forced to submit to buggery were sometimes described in the media as male rape, but in legal terms they could only be charged as indecent assault or buggery. This was changed by the CJPOA, so that now both women and men can be victims of rape.

Research by Michael King and Gillian Mezey (1992) looked into the issue of male sexual assault before this change in the law. Sexual offences are generally underreported, which means that not only do we not know the true number which are committed, but also that if the offence is not reported, it cannot be prosecuted, so the offenders go unpunished. King and Mezey discovered that sexual assaults on males were even less likely to be reported than sexual offences generally, for a variety of reasons: victims feared that they would not be believed, or that people would assume they were gay, or they blamed themselves, thinking that as men they should have been able to fight off their attacker. Where the offence involved incest, the victims were often under considerable emotional and physical pressure not to report. Finally, in the past male complainants were not guaranteed anonymity so they feared unwanted publicity. It may be that some of these fears will decrease with time now that male rape has received official recognition and anonymity is guaranteed to both male and female victims.

Campaigners on the issue of rape also hope that the extension of the offence to include men will signal a change in perception about rapes of women. As Susan Brownmiller argued in her book, *Against our Will,* 'Women are trained to be rape victims. To simply hear the word "rape" is to take instruction in the power relationship between males and females . . . Girls get raped. Not boys. Rape is something awful that happens to females, and [the suggestion is] unless we watch our step it might become our destiny.' Once it is accepted that rape is not something that only happens to women, there may be less scope for the mistaken idea, still held by some judges, among others, that it is somehow women's responsibility to prevent it, by staying indoors at night, wearing 'respectable' clothing, and so on.

Sexual intercourse

For the purposes of rape, sexual intercourse was limited until 1994 to penetration of the vagina by the penis. This was amended by the CJPOA and it now includes penetration of the anus by the penis. Section 1(2) of the amended Sexual Offences Act 1956 states: 'A man commits rape if – (a) he has sexual intercourse with a person (whether vaginal or anal) who at the time of the intercourse does not consent to it . . .' This means that the offence of rape overlaps with the offence of buggery.

Section 44 of the 1956 Act also provides that the man need not have ejaculated, the offence is committed simply on penetration: '. . . it shall not be necessary to prove the completion of intercourse by the emission of seed, but the intercourse shall be deemed complete upon proof of penetration only'.

Sexual intercourse is treated as a continuing act, so that there can be liability for what might have appeared to be an omission, under the principle laid down in **Fagan** *v* **Metropolitan Police Commissioner**, discussed at p. 9. Thus in **Kaitamaki** (1984) it was stated by the Privy Council that if a victim consented to penetration, but after penetration they ceased to give their consent (in other words the victim wanted to stop), a man would be committing the *actus reus* of rape if he did not withdraw.

Consent

It is the absence of the victim's consent that transforms sexual intercourse into rape. This requirement can be found in s. 1(2) of the SOA 1956, quoted above. Consent is perhaps one of the most difficult issues in a trial. Now that sophisticated forensic methods of investigation mean that denying sexual intercourse took place is less likely to be an option, consent, along with *mens rea*, naturally becomes the obvious line of defence.

The victim's consent must be real and not a mere submission given under pressure. In **R** *v* **Olugboja** (1981) the defendant threatened to keep a girl in his bungalow overnight. He made no explicit threat of violence and she did not resist sexual intercourse. The court said that on the evidence she had not given a genuine consent, but had merely submitted under pressure of his threat. In practice the line between a mere submission and consent is not an easy one to draw.

In the past it had to be shown that the sexual intercourse had been obtained by force, but this is no longer a requirement: the sole question is whether the victim gave a genuine consent. The point was reiterated in **R** *v* **Larter and Castleton** (1995), in which the defendant had sexual intercourse with a woman while she was asleep. The Court of Appeal upheld his conviction for rape, emphasizing that the key issue was whether or not the victim had consented to sexual intercourse; if not, the fact that no force was used would not prevent the act being rape. Evidence of force will be relevant to the issue of consent, but only as evidence – at least in theory. In practice juries have a tendency not to believe victims where there is no evidence of force having been used. A recent case that took the same approach as **R** *v* **Larter and Castleton** is **R** *v* **Malone** (1998). The victim was a 16-year-old girl and the appellant was a friend who lived near her home. She had gone out with some other friends one evening, but had drunk so much wine that she was unable to walk and her friends took her home by car. One of the friends went round to the appellant's house and asked him to help them carry the girl into her bedroom. While the others were downstairs, the appellant went back upstairs. The victim said she became aware of his presence, that he climbed on top of her and inserted his penis into her vagina, which caused considerable pain and she kicked out against the appellant's chest. The appellant was convicted of rape and appealed on the grounds that the judge had made a mistake on the issue of consent where no force, lies or threats had been used and the complainant had offered no resistance. The appeal was dismissed. The Court of Appeal stated that in order to obtain a conviction there had to be some evidence of lack of consent, but this could simply be the assertion of the complainant that he or she did not consent.

The inclusion of anal intercourse within the *actus reus* of rape raises a question that the legislation appears not to answer: if a woman consents to vaginal intercourse, and the man proceeds to penetrate her anus, could this be rape? We would suggest that it should be; to allow consent to one form of intercourse to imply consent to another would be to deny a woman's autonomy over her own body.

Consent obtained by fraud

What is the position if the victim consents to intercourse, but only because of a lie told to him or her by the defendant? For example, the defendant may untruthfully tell his victim that he is not married, so that she consents to intercourse. There are currently only two situations where a deception by the defendant will negative any consent given by the victim. The first is where the defendant pretends to be either the defendant's husband or boyfriend. Section 1(3) of the 1956 Act states: 'A man also commits rape if he induces a married woman to have sexual intercourse with him by impersonating her husband.' Until 1995, it was unclear whether the same approach should be taken where the accused was impersonating a boyfriend rather than a husband. There were two old cases that were relevant, but they conflicted: **Barrow** (1868) suggested that it should not negative consent, **Dee** (1884) suggested that it should. The issue was resolved in **R** *v* **Elbekkay** (1995) with the approach in **Dee** being preferred. The victim lived with her boyfriend. One evening the couple went out for a drink with a friend, returning home very drunk. Her boyfriend fell asleep in the living room, and the victim went to bed. During the night, the friend climbed into the bed with her. Still half asleep, she assumed that it was her boyfriend. The friend started to have sexual intercourse with her, and it was only after he had penetrated her vagina that she realized that it was not her boyfriend, at which point she pushed him away and stabbed him. The Court of Appeal upheld his conviction for rape, stating that the impersonation of boyfriends and husbands should be treated in the same way. Presumably, now that rape extends to male rape, this should include the impersonation of a homosexual partner.

The second situation where fraud can negative the consent of the victim is where the fraud is as to the very nature of sexual intercourse. Thus in **Flattery** (1877) the defendant told the victim that he was performing a surgical operation, when in fact he was having sexual intercourse with her. Her consent to his act was negatived by this lie and he was convicted of rape. The same point was made in **Williams** (1923). The defendant was a singing teacher, who had a 16-year-old pupil. She consented to sexual intercourse when he said it was a method of improving her breathing; as in **Flattery**, the consent was nullified by the fraud and he was convicted of rape.

A contrasting case is **R *v* Linekar** (1995). A woman working as a prostitute was seeking clients outside a cinema in London. The defendant approached her and they agreed that he would pay her £25 for sexual intercourse. They went to the balcony of some flats nearby and had sexual intercourse, but afterwards the defendant ran away without paying. He was eventually found and charged with rape but at the trial it was stated that, as she consented to the sexual intercourse, there was no rape. Although the defendant had lied that he would pay for sexual intercourse in order to gain her consent, he had not impersonated her husband or boyfriend, nor lied as to the nature and quality of the act; the lie that he did tell was not considered sufficient to negative consent.

Even inducing a woman to believe that she is legally married to the defendant when in fact she is not, will not prevent her ensuing consent to sexual intercourse from being valid – **Papadimitropoulos** (1958).

Consent between spouses

Before the CJPOA, the Sexual Offences Act stated that rape required sexual intercourse to be 'unlawful'. For a long time this was understood to mean intercourse that took place outside marriage, which meant that a husband who had sex with his wife without her consent was not guilty of rape (though he might be liable for some lesser offence, such as indecent assault). This idea dated back to the writings of the seventeenth-century legal expert Hale, who stated that in giving her consent to be married, a woman automatically gave consent to sexual intercourse with her husband for the rest of their marriage, and she could not withdraw this consent.

This approach reflected the historical origins of rape, which concerned a view of women as the property of either their father or, on marriage, their husband. Though now seen as an offence against the person, rape was originally a property offence, the rapist having interfered with the property of another man, and, if the woman became pregnant, with the inheritance of family property. For this reason, it was considered acceptable for a man to force his wife to have sexual intercourse, since she was his property to do with as he liked.

Not surprisingly, as attitudes to women and the marriage relationship changed, the law on rape within marriage was increasingly criticized, but it was not until 1991 that it was finally altered, when in the case of **R *v* R**, the House of Lords accepted that times had moved on and marital rape should be an offence. The defendant subsequently appealed to the European Court of Human Rights on the basis that the decision violated article 7 of the European Convention of Human Rights. This article provides that no one can be held guilty of a criminal offence which was not an offence at the time it was committed. The European Court unanimously held that the Convention had not been violated – **CR** *v* **United Kingdom** (1996). It concluded that it did not breach the ban on the imposition of retrospective criminal liability, recognizing that English courts can develop case law provided that any change was 'reasonably foreseeable'. The CJPOA confirms this development in the law.

Even so, some judges have clearly had problems coming to terms with the change. In one 1992 case, Robin David J said he accepted that rape within marriage was 'technically' rape, but argued that it should be differentiated from rape by a stranger. He claimed that a woman's 'sense of outrage' at being raped by her husband could not compare with that of a woman raped by a stranger. The leading criminal law academic Glanville Williams had long been opposed to extending the offence within marriage, partly on the basis that for such an offence it would be difficult to decide the issue of consent. The Criminal Law Revision Committee in its fifteenth report was also in favour of keeping the marital exemption, on the bizarre grounds that it was unwise for the law to interfere in affairs which otherwise might be quickly resolved, and that 'the children might resent what she had done to their father' – the children presumably having no problems with what their father had done to their mother.

However, this development in the law has generally been approved as a positive step forward, and necessary for the proper protection of women. In fact marital rape may be one of the most common forms of rape – research by Hall (1985) suggested that one in seven married women had been forced into sexual intercourse against their will by their husbands.

▶ Mens rea

Section 1(2)(b) of the Sexual Offences Act 1956 states that the defendant's state of mind must be that 'at the time he knows that the person does not consent to the intercourse or is reckless as to whether that person consents to it'.

The case of **R** *v* **Satnam** (1984) established that recklessness for rape is not **Caldwell** objective recklessness (overruling the case of **Pigg** (1982) on the issue). However, in describing the relevant state of mind, the courts have not used the traditional **Cunningham** vocabulary of seeing that the type of risk that did occur might occur, and going ahead anyway. Instead Lord Hailsham in **DPP** *v* **Morgan** (1976) spoke of an 'intention of having intercourse, willy-nilly, not caring whether the victim consents or not'; and in **Taylor** (1984) the Court of Appeal asked, 'Was D's attitude one of "I could not care less whether she is consenting or not, I am going to have intercourse."?' There have been suggestions that this is perhaps a third type of recklessness, different from both **Caldwell** and **Cunningham** recklessness. However, the better approach is probably that this is simply the **Cunningham** test, phrased in slightly different terms.

Mistakes can negative *mens rea*

In **DPP** *v* **Morgan** (1976), a case which caused considerable controversy when it was decided, it was established that where a defendant believes that the victim is consenting, but is in fact mistaken, he will not have *mens rea*, even if the mistake was not a reasonable one to make.

The facts of the case were that Morgan was a senior member of the air force and had been drinking with three junior members of that service. He invited the men to come back to his house to have sexual intercourse with his wife, telling them that his wife might appear to protest, but that they should ignore her as she did not mean it; this was her way of increasing her sexual pleasure. The three men accepted the invitation, and, on arriving in the house, Morgan woke up his wife, who was asleep in their child's bedroom, and dragged her into another room, where the men forced her to have sexual intercourse with them. She struggled and protested throughout, and afterwards she had to go to hospital.

The three men were charged with rape; unfortunately Morgan himself could not be charged with rape because at the time the marital exception applied, though he was charged with being an accomplice. The three men argued that they lacked *mens rea* because Morgan's comments had led them to believe that his wife was consenting, despite her protests. The House of Lords accepted that, if this had been the case, they would not have been liable; their mistake did not need to be reasonable (which it clearly was not), provided it was genuine. However, the convictions were upheld on the grounds that a properly directed jury would not have accepted that the men honestly believed Mrs Morgan was consenting.

The judgment, which was widely publicized, caused considerable public concern. It seemed to imply that any rapist who could create a convincing story demonstrating that he thought the victim was consenting would be able to escape liability. In the light of this concern, the Government set up an advisory group, known as the Heilbron Committee, to review the law of rape. Despite the public concern, the Committee concluded that the **Morgan** judgment reflected the correct approach. It also suggested that the law would benefit from increased clarity and certainty, which could be achieved by putting some of the common law into parliamentary legislation. The result was the Sexual Offences (Amendment) Act 1976, which, among other things, put the decision in **Morgan** into statutory form. To try to appease public opinion, the Committee recommended the inclusion of a provision which became s. 1(2) of the Act. In fact it adds nothing to the existing law but merely stated what was a matter of common sense. Section 1(2) provides:

> If at a trial for a rape offence the jury has to consider whether a man believed that a woman or man was consenting to sexual intercourse, the presence or absence of reasonable grounds for such a belief is a matter to which the jury is to have regard, in

conjunction with any other relevant matters, in considering whether he so believed.

▶ Rules of evidence and procedure

There are special rules of evidence and procedure for rape trials, which have caused considerable controversy.

The corroboration rule

Until 1994, a mandatory corroboration ruling had to be given at a rape trial. This meant that the judge always had to warn the jury that it was unwise to convict on the woman's evidence alone. That did not mean there could be no conviction without evidence corroborating what the woman said, but clearly juries may place great weight on what the judge has to say, and the warning may well have raised doubts where none would have existed without it. The warning seemed to imply that women were liars by nature, and prone to allege rape where none had occurred.

In 1991 the Law Commission recommended that the corroboration rule should be abolished, as did the Royal Commission on Criminal Justice in 1993. In the light of these recommendations, and widespread criticisms of the warning, ss. 32 and 33 of the Criminal Justice and Public Order Act 1994 abolished the mandatory corroboration rule. However, this does not necessarily solve the problem. Although it is no longer mandatory to give the warning, judges may still give it where they feel it is necessary, and given the pronouncements which some of our judges have made on rape (discussed below), it is questionable whether this discretion is safe in their hands.

The victim's sexual history

Evidence of a woman's past sexual experience is sometimes admissible as evidence in court. Section 2 of the Sexual Offences (Amendment) Act 1976 provides:

> **(1)** If at a trial any person is for the time being charged with a rape offence to which he pleads not guilty, then, except with the leave of the judge, no evidence and no question in cross-examination shall be adduced or asked at the trial, by or on behalf of any defendant at the trial, about any sexual experience of a complainant with a person other than the defendant.
>
> **(2)** The judge shall not give leave in pursuance of the preceding subsection for any evidence or question except on an

application made to him in the absence of the jury by or on behalf of a defendant; and on such an application the judge shall give leave if and only if he is satisfied that it would be unfair to that defendant to refuse to allow the evidence to be adduced or the question to be asked.

As a result, evidence of past sexual experience with the particular defendant is always admissible, and evidence of such experience with someone else will also be admissible if the judge concludes that 'it would be unfair to that defendant to refuse to allow the evidence to be adduced or the question to be asked'.

State powers over sex offenders

The maximum sentence for rape is life imprisonment, but concern has been expressed in the past that the courts were, in practice, giving sentences that were too low and which did not reflect the gravity of the offence committed. To try to deal with this criticism, the Court of Appeal laid down sentence guidelines in the case of **R** *v* **Billam** (1986). The court specified that a conviction for rape should normally justify immediate imprisonment, even for a first offence, and that the normal sentence for an 'average' rape should be five years, but aggravating factors such as a gang-rape could justify a much higher sentence.

Reacting to public concern, recent legislation has increased the powers of the state over sex offenders. Under the Crime (Sentences) Act 1997, anyone convicted of a second serious sexual offence will be given an automatic life sentence.

Section 2 of the Crime and Disorder Act 1998 provides that a chief officer of police may apply to the magistrates' court for a sex offender order. Under this order restrictions can be placed on sex offenders after they have been released from prison in order to protect the public from serious harm. Under sections 58–60 of the 1998 Act, a court can impose extended sentences for a sexual offence. This is allowed where a court proposes to impose a custodial sentence but considers that the ordinary licence arrangements would not be adequate to prevent the commission of further offences or secure their rehabilitation. The sentence will consist of the main sentence and the extension period. During the extension period, the offender is subject to a licence. The extension period will be for the time necessary to prevent reoffending or to secure the offender's rehabilitation up to a maximum of 10 years.

The Sex Offenders Act 1997 requires sex offenders to notify the police of their names and addresses, which will be placed on a Sex Offender's register. Failure to do so is an offence. In certain circumstances, the police, following Home Office guidelines, can warn head teachers, youth workers and local agencies of the arrival of a sex offender in their area.

▶ Criticism and reform

Definition of sexual intercourse

The fact that sexual intercourse, for the purpose of rape, only includes penetration of the vagina or anus by the penis means that many harmful and humiliating acts fall outside the most serious sexual offence. Rapists who force their victims to commit oral sex, or who use objects to penetrate the vagina or anus, are no less blameworthy than those whose conduct does currently fall within the *actus reus* of the offence, yet the gravest offence they can be charged with is indecent assault, carrying a maximum sentence of ten years and less social stigma than rape.

In many other European countries, the offence of rape is defined more broadly. In its 1984 report, the Criminal Law Revision Committee opposed any change, arguing that rape was a specific form of conduct which the public recognizes; to extend it would cause confusion, and might weaken the social stigma attached to the offence. It is difficult to see why this should be the case; the concepts involved are perfectly simple to grasp, and there seems no good reason why the social stigma attached to rape should lessen as a result of a change in definition to include such serious misconduct. The CLRC pointed out that with other forms of penetration, there was no risk of pregnancy. The force of this particular argument is difficult to see: there is no risk of pregnancy where a rapist has vaginal intercourse with a little girl, or a woman who has been through the menopause, but presumably the CLRC would not exclude this from falling within rape.

The issue of consent

Consent is the most problematic area of the law of rape. The Heilbron Committee found that this element of the offence encouraged lawyers to bring up evidence of the victim's sexual history, in an effort to prove that she was likely to have consented to sex. As the feminist writer, Carol Smart, points out in *Feminism and the Power of Law*, the implication is that if a woman has consented to sex with various men in the past, she would probably consent to anyone, including the defendant in the case. An American academic, D. Dripps (1992) has suggested that the emphasis on consent is harmful, because of the way it focuses on the victim's state of mind, rather than on the defendant, making it appear that the victim is on trial. To avoid this problem he suggests serious sexual offences should be defined without reference to consent at all; rape would be abolished, and a new sexual offence created, which would be defined as the defendant knowingly presenting the victim with the choice of sex or violence. A second, lesser offence would then be that of knowingly obtaining sexual intercourse with the victim in disregard of a verbally expressed refusal.

An alternative approach would simply be to change the burden of proof, so that it fell on the defendant to prove that the complainant consented. Temkin (1987), an academic who has written extensively on the issue of rape, has argued that a man should have a legal duty to ask if a woman is consenting, though it is debatable how far this proposal is realistic.

S. Box argues in *Power, Crime and Mystification* (1983), that coercion and not consent should be the central issue – where a man is in a position to impose sanctions for refusal, his ability to coerce should be the key question, not her consent. He points out that the law currently focuses on the man's physical superiority, but ignores his social, economic and organizational superiority.

Conviction rates

Very few rapes lead to convictions, because at every stage of the process between the rape itself and a final conviction, there are serious obstacles. First, like other sexual offences, rape is frequently not reported to the police. Hall's 1985 research found that 17 per cent of women questioned had been raped, and a further 20 per cent had been victims of attempted rape; many of these incidents were never reported to the police. A major reason for this underreporting is fear of the criminal justice process itself which, as we have seen, can make the victim feel as though they are the one on trial. The thought of recounting intimate details in front of a court of strangers, and possibly having their sexual history dragged up by an aggressive defence barrister is a significant barrier to reporting the offence.

Even where rape is reported, there is in fact little chance of the offender being tried. This is not just because some rapists are obviously never caught, but also, according to a 1995 report by the pressure groups Women Against Rape and Legal Action for Women, because the Crown Prosecution Service has shown itself reluctant to prosecute in many cases of rape. They point out that during the early 1980s, about half of all reported rapes were prosecuted; by 1993, this had dropped to less than a fifth. In cases studied in the report, the CPS had refused to prosecute on the grounds that evidence was insufficient, inconclusive or uncorroborated, though the pressure groups claim the evidence was actually stronger than in high-profile cases such as that of Austen Donellan (below). The CPS denied that rape was treated differently from any other offence as regards the decision to prosecute.

Those rapes which do come to court are therefore a tiny minority of those actually committed. You might assume this would make them the strongest cases, yet only 10 per cent of them result in a conviction.

The trial

The ordeal of rape complainants is frequently made worse by their experience of the criminal trial process. In court it can often seem that it is the victim who is on trial, rather than the defendant. There are three main concerns in relation to the conduct of rape trials. Firstly, there are worries about the way in which victims are cross-examined by defence lawyers; secondly, there are problems with the direct questioning of victims by defendants; and thirdly, there is concern that irrelevant evidence of a victim's past sexual experience is admitted into court. We will look at each of these issues in turn.

Looking first at the way victims are cross-examined by defence lawyers, in a study conducted by Victim Support in 1996, complainants described their experiences of cross-examination as 'patronising', 'humiliating', and 'worse than the rape'. A number of women complained that they had been asked intrusive and inappropriate questions about their private lives. The personal lives of complainants are subjected to close scrutiny during cross-examination. Sue Lees carried out a study in 1996 on rape trials based upon the transcripts of 31 trials and 116 questionnaires completed by victims of rape. Seventy-two per cent of respondents complained that they had been asked irrelevant and unfair questions during cross-examination and 83 per cent felt that they were on trial and not the defendant. Lees reports that questioning routinely centred on a complainant's lifestyle and 'in more than half the cases where consent was in issue, questioning included whether the complainant was divorced, was an unmarried mother, had a habit of drinking with strangers or drank to excess'. According to Lees, such questioning was directed simply at discrediting the complainant in the eyes of the jury, rather than at eliciting relevant evidence. She argues that the question should not only be whether such evidence is relevant but whether it is of sufficient probative value to counter the potential dangers flowing from its admission. A number of studies suggest that juries are unduly swayed by character evidence. Research conducted by Kalvin and Zeisel (1996) found that there is a danger that juries may be distracted from the real issues in a case by lengthy investigation of a witness's character during cross-examination.

Louise Ellison (1998) has argued that the focus of debate on rape trials is too narrow. She considers that the bullying and browbeating of rape complainants in court is rooted in the adversarial trial process and therefore an inescapable feature of cross-examination. It may be that the assumption that rape complainants are treated differently from other complainants is mistaken. Paul Rock examined proceedings in Wood Green Crown Court in 1993. He found that other crime victims, and prosecution witnesses in general, often feel humiliated, degraded and frustrated by the process of cross-examination. In one case he observed the complainant in an assault trial was described by defence counsel in his closing speech as 'a spiteful, bitchy woman with a drink problem'. In another trial the complainant was cast as a 'deceitful, conniving, drug pushing, lesbian'.

Research conducted by Brereton in 1997 also challenges the assumption that rape complainants are treated differently during cross-examination. Brereton conducted a comparative study of rape and assault trials based upon the transcripts of 40 rape and 44 assault trials. He found substantial similarities in the cross-examination strategies employed by defence counsel in both types of proceedings. Complainants of assault were just as likely as rape complainants to be subjected to attacks upon their character and credibility and to be questioned about their drinking behaviour and their mental stability. He argues that the tactics employed by counsel during cross-examination were 'tools of the trade' rather than unique to rape trials.

On the second issue, the media has recently drawn the public's attention to the plight of victims who are directly cross-examined by their complainants. In one case the complainant, Julia Mason, was subjected to six days of cross-examination by her attacker, Ralston Edwards. She subsequently waived her right to anonymity in order to call for a change in the law and is taking her case to the European Court of Human Rights. The Court of Appeal has indicated that judges have full power to prevent the unacceptable treatment of a complainant by such means as using screens. In **Brown** (1998) the Lord Chief Justice stated that trial judges should take over the cross-examination of complainants where defendants are engaged in repetitious and irrelevant questioning. It was further stated that the Court of Appeal would be very slow in the absence of clear evidence of injustice, to disturb any resulting conviction on the basis that the defendant had been prevented from putting his case.

In the light of the judges clear failure to use these powers in practice, parliament has intervened with the Youth Justice and Criminal Evidence Act to prevent such occurrences in the future. This part of the Act had not been brought into force at the time of writing, but is likely to come into force in the near future. Section 34 would impose an absolute prohibition on any people charged with a sexual offence from themselves asking any question of a complainant with regard to the offence charged or any other offence. Usually this is not a problem as the vast majority of defendants are legally aided and the cross-examination is carried out by a solicitor or barrister. The problem arises where defendants have chosen to act in person, rather than be represented by a lawyer. Under Section 38 a court-appointed defence representative would conduct the cross-examination in this situation.

The reform could create a risk that juries might wrongly convict because they had not heard the complainant cross-examined, and might infringe article 6 of the European Convention of Human Rights which guarantees the right to a fair trial.

On the third issue concerning the admissibility of past sexual history evidence, at the moment about 75 per cent of women who have been raped leading to court proceedings are questioned about their previous sexual encounters with men other than the defendant. Evidence of a woman's past sexual history is used to give the jury a bad impression of the victim and to make it appear that she is not a credible witness – the insinuation being that a woman who has had an active sex life with men other than a husband is immoral and cannot be trusted generally. In addition, it plays up to the belief that only 'good' women deserve protection from rape.

Back in 1975, the Heilbron Committee concluded that urgent reform was necessary. It proposed that evidence of the woman's past sexual experiences should only be admitted if it concerned previous sexual intercourse with the defendant, or the past sexual experience was 'strikingly similar' to that of the alleged incidence of rape. The phrase 'strikingly similar' was rejected by Parliament as too narrow and s. 2 of the 1976 Act was enacted instead (see p. 124). Unfortunately, this section has been given a very broad interpretation by the Courts. In **Lawrence** (1977) the Crown Court stated that the defence could question the complainant about past sexual relationships with other men if such questions 'might reasonably lead the jury, properly directed in the summing-up, to take a different view of the complainant's evidence from that which they might take if the question or series of questions was or were not allowed'. This seems to miss the point: the fact that juries often do take a different view after such evidence is given is precisely why defence lawyers seek to introduce it, but the question is whether such evidence should be the basis on which the jury changes its view.

The Court of Appeal in **Viola** (1982) proceeded to approve this direction. They stated: 'If the questions are relevant to an issue in the trial in the light of the way the case is being run, for instance relevant to the issue of consent, as opposed to credit, they are likely to be admitted'. A recent case on the point is **R** *v* **Cleland** (1995). A rape complainant stated in trial that she had not had unprotected sexual intercourse with her boyfriend. She made no mention to the police that she had had an abortion prior to the rape. At the trial she said that she had an abortion after the rape and that the pregnancy was attributable to the rape. The defence counsel sought permission from the trial judge to question her about these two abortions and about evidence that she had menstruated after the supposed rape but before the second abortion. This application was rejected and the defendant was convicted. An appeal was allowed and a retrial ordered on the basis that these matters were capable of going to the heart of the defendant's credibility. As there was no other evidence against the defendant apart from the complainant's account of the incident and the defendant argued that the complainant had consented, the defendant's credibility was of fundamental importance.

New legislation, the Youth Justice and Criminal Evidence Act 1999, has been passed to replace s. 2 of the Sexual Offences (Amendment) Act 1976. The relevant provisions, sections 41–3, had not been brought into force at the time of writing, but the Home Secretary is likely to bring them into force in the near future. Under s. 41 no evidence of a complainant's previous sexual history will be admissible on the question of whether a complainant consented to sexual intercourse unless the evidence or questioning relates to a specific incident within 24 hours of the alleged offence or is necessary to rebut prosecution evidence. Thus judges will still have the discretion to allow a victim to be questioned about sex with men other than the accused. The campaign group Women Against Rape (WAR) argues that the admission of such evidence gives juries the wrong message: they are being asked to decide, not whether a woman was raped, but whether she is entitled to the protection of the law. WAR would favour the banning of sexual history evidence completely. The Lord Chief Justice has commented 'the simple truth is that on an issue of whether a complainant consented to sexual relations with the defendant, the fact that the defendant has behaved promiscuously on occasion outside the window of 24 hours before and after the commission of the offence allowed by the Bill may well – I emphasise may well – be relevant. So to recognise is not to open the door to abusive, insulting, irrelevant cross-questioning, which in any event is likely to repel any decent modern jury.' He felt that it would be 'a very melancholy reflection on parliamentary confidence in the judiciary of England and Wales, if they are to be denied a . . . . very limited and carefully defined discretion'.

Sentencing

There have been concerns in the past that judges were too lenient when sentencing rapists. While the efforts of the Court of Appeal have generally led to higher sentences for rape, there are still occasional examples of leniency, which call into question the attitudes of the judges concerned to the offence and its victims. In a 1994 case, a trial judge imposed a three-year supervision order, along with a compensation order for £500, so that the 15-year-old victim 'could have a good holiday to get over it'. The prosecution made an appeal against this sentence under the procedures introduced under s. 36 of the Criminal Justice Act 1988, and the sentence was subsequently increased to two years' detention.

Now that the offence has been extended to include male rape, there is concern that the judges may be inclined to pass heavier sentences where there has been a male victim rather than a female victim. The first conviction for attempted male rape occurred in the case of **Richards** (1995). Richards was sentenced to a term of life imprisonment for the attempted rape of an 18-year-old man and an additional six years' imprisonment for assault occasioning actual bodily harm. The sentence attracted a degree of criticism as it was claimed that the case indicated a willingness on the part of the judiciary to treat male rape more seriously than female rape. However, the academics Philip Rumney and Martin Morgan-Taylor (1998) argue that the sentence was entirely consistent with the sentencing guidelines developed in cases of female rape. In particular, they point out that

Richards had previous convictions for sex offences and suffered from a 'psychopathic personality disorder'. In sentencing, the trial judge stated 'this personality defect is one that makes it probable he will commit similar offences in the future if he is not subject to . . . confinement for an indefinite period'. Under the **Billam** guidelines someone posing such a continuing threat may give rise to the imposition of a life sentence. They conclude that the trial judge adopted an approach to sentencing which gave primacy to the facts of the case rather than the sex of the victim, in accordance with Parliament's intentions.

Alternative offences

In Canada they have abolished the offence of rape altogether, and replaced it with a graded offence of sexual assault. Simple sexual assault carries a maximum sentence of ten years; sexual assault accompanied by bodily harm, the use of weapons or of third parties has a maximum sentence of fourteen years; and finally, aggravated sexual assault with wounding, maiming or endangering life has a maximum sentence of life imprisonment. This reform shifts the emphasis away from the sexual element of the offence, to the aggression which it really represents, and puts the victim under less pressure because there is no need to prove such matters as penetration. The grading of the offence also gives more structure to sentences and one of the results has been that sentences have increased.

The sexual offences are currently under review by the Home Office and proposals for a new framework for these offences are likely to be published at the end of 1999. The Home Office minister, Paul Boateng, has stated that the purpose of the review is to provide coherent and clear sexual offences which protect people, especially children and other vulnerable persons, from abuse; to enable abusers to be appropriately punished; and to be fair and non-discriminatory in terms of the European Convention on Human Rights and the new Human Rights Act 1998.

The Sex Offences (Amendment) Bill, currently being considered by Parliament, seeks to introduce new measures including an offence for certain adults to take advantage of their position of trust by entering into a sexual relationship with a child in their care. This would apply in particular to teachers who enter into sexual relations with one of their pupils.

Changing attitudes

Many of the problems surrounding the law of rape arise from attitudes to women and sex, and misconceptions about the offence itself. It is often viewed as a sexual act, so that people express surprise when, for example, very old ladies are raped. But research suggests that in fact rape has little to do with sexual intercourse as understood in everyday life; it is a crime of violence, with the penis being used as a weapon in the same way as another attacker might use a knife. A 1976 study carried out for the Queen's Bench Foundation found that rapists were not primarily motivated by sexual desire: they wanted to dominate and humiliate their victim. As a result, physical attractiveness played little part in the selection of their victim; physical vulnerability was more important.

Another common myth is that rape is something that happens when a stranger jumps out on a woman walking alone in the dark. While it is certainly true that some rapes do happen in situations like this, they appear to be in the minority. Official figures suggest that two in three rapes are committed against women who know their assailants, but in fact the proportion may be even higher, since rapes by someone the victim knows are least likely to be reported: Hall found that 31 per cent of women raped by strangers reported it to the police, compared with 5 per cent when the woman was raped by someone they knew.

It is when the victim is raped by someone they know that outdated attitudes to women and sex have most influence. In the past, these attitudes were responsible for holding back the law on marital rape; currently, they focus on so-called 'date rape', rapes which occur when the victim has had some social contact with the rapist. This was the situation alleged in the case of the university student, Austen Donellan, who was acquitted, and that of the boxer Mike Tyson, who was convicted.

Research by Warshaw (1984) suggests that the incidence of rape and attempted rape in such situations may be high. She surveyed students at an American campus university. One in twelve undergraduate men admitted they had acted in ways that conformed to the legal definition of rape, while 26 per cent had attempted to force intercourse on a woman to the extent that she cried or fought back. Of women undergraduates who had been raped, 84 per cent of them knew their attacker and 57 per cent happened on dates. The psychological harm caused to a woman raped by an acquaintance can be greater than if they are raped by a stranger. One research study suggests that 'women raped by men they knew attribute more blame for the rape to themselves, see themselves in a less positive light, and tend to have higher levels of psychological stress' than women raped by strangers: Parrot and Bechhofer, *Acquaintance Rape* (1991).

In law, conduct which satisfies the definition of rape falls within the offence, whether the rapist is a perfect stranger, a person the victim has met once, or someone she knows well. But whether or not a jury believes the defendant's conduct to fit within that definition may well depend on their own attitudes to the male–female relationship. For example, it is widely believed that once aroused, a man cannot stop himself going on to have sex, and that therefore a woman who arouses a man has only herself to blame if he insists on having sex. Quite apart from the fact that this theory is biologically untrue, it assumes that a woman's rights over her own body are limited; she can say 'No', but only up to a point. In addition, the cultural stereotypes of aggressive men and docile women contribute to the idea that women say 'No' when they actually mean 'Yes', and that it is somehow a man's role in the game to overcome the woman's resistance.

The extent to which these views may be held by juries can be seen in the results of a Gallup poll taken for the *Daily Telegraph* in 1994. One-third of respondents felt that a woman was partly to blame for her own rape if she dressed provocatively, and almost half if she voluntarily went to the man's home or room, or said 'Yes' and then changed her mind. Forty per cent felt a woman was partly to blame if she was under the influence of drink or drugs. It is hard to imagine the same response if people were asked if those who failed to fit security systems were responsible for their own burglaries, or those who chose to cross the street for the injuries suffered if they were run over.

The media coverage of the Austen Donellan case in 1994 revealed similar attitudes. While the evidence in that case was certainly weak, it was not that which caused the outcry, but the fact that the complainant had got drunk and got into bed with the defendant. The *Daily Mail* described the complainant as 'drunk and sexually shameless', while the *Today* newspaper wrote: 'This sort of drunken shenanigans should not be compared to a young girl walking alone in the dark who is raped by a stranger.' The idea seems to be that only two kinds of women deserve protection from rape: the innocent virgin, or those who know their place, accepting that their sexuality belongs not to them but is held on trust for their husband or future husband.

The sociologist Matza (1964) points out that this background culture allows rapists to use techniques of neutralization – justifying their behaviour with claims that 'she asked for it', 'she enjoyed it', 'women are masochists', 'I have a strong sex drive', 'I was drunk', 'she's a prostitute/ or promiscuous so it did not matter to her'. Unfortunately these ideas are all too often backed up by the comments of judges: examples include 'all she has to do is keep her legs shut, and she will not get it without force'; 'women who say "No" do not always mean "No"'; and, of a hitchhiker, 'she was "guilty of contributory negligence"'.

Given these problems, it is perhaps not surprising that there is a high rate of acquittals for rape by acquaintances: the Channel 4 television programme 'Despatches' studied Old Bailey trials and found that two in three acquaintance rapes ended in acquittal.

Only when attitudes towards women change will there ever be any chance of bringing the majority of rapists to justice. Although, sadly, some of these attitudes are held by women as well as men, involving more women in making, interpreting and enforcing the law would be one way to make progress.

Paedophiles

The release from prison of paedophiles such as Sidney Cooke and his friend Robert Oliver produced serious concern amongst the public in general. There is a public perception of a growing threat of sexual abuse to children in society. A study was carried out by Don Grubin, Professor of Forensic Psychiatry at Newcastle University entitled *Sex Offending Against Children: Understanding the Risk.* It looked at research and criminal statistics in the field, while acknowledging the serious limitations of official statistics, which invariably underestimate both the incidence and the severity of sexual offences. He remarked that 'any attempt to arrive at a realistic estimate of the actual rate of child abuse in England and Wales has to rely on assumptions, guesswork and a bit of putting one's finger in the wind.' The criminal statistics available however, show that during the course of a year there are some 4,000 formal cautions or convictions for sexual offences against children, and that of these about one half are for indecent assault of girls under 16. The figures do not confirm the public perception that this sort of crime is increasing. While he notes that the Home Office estimated that there were over 100,000 individuals with convictions for sexual offences against children in 1993, it also appears that the proportion has been declining over a 40-year period. The total number of known offenders represents a decline of some 30 per cent since 1985.

Sex offenders against children represent an extremely diverse group and no clear picture of the 'child molester' emerges. What is certain, however, is that most of the offences do not involve strangers and that about 80 per cent take place within either the home of the victim or the offender. He notes that some research suggests that abusers have often also been the victims of abuse, but he considers a key factor in triggering deviant behaviour may simply be the amount of violence within the family.

Professor Grubin observes that sex offenders have relatively low reconviction rates and that where there is a reconviction it is usually for a non-sexual offence. A study that looked at offenders 21 years after their original conviction in 1973 found that the threat of reconviction for any indictable offence, such as offences against property was around 50 per cent while only 16 per cent were reconvicted for sexual offences against children.

▶ Sex offenders and politics

Recent legislation suggests that sex offenders, particularly paedophiles, are being used as an emotive and vulnerable target to score political points. The large number of legislative measures that have resulted do not necessarily represent the most effective way for a society to be dealing with sexual deviance. In addition to the legislation discussed at p. 125 the Sexual Offences (Conspiracy and Incitement) Act 1996 has been enacted to deal with the problem of 'sex tourism'. It appear that large numbers of children in relatively poor nations are being exploited by tourists from richer countries.

The 1996 Act was enacted in response to concerns about the activities of those involved in the 'sex tourism' industry, to enable prosecutions to be brought in England. The Act targets the organizers of sex tourism and allows prosecutions where the defendant in England encouraged or agreed to carry out one of a list of sexual offences (including rape) abroad. The Act reflects the process of the internationalization in criminal law and challenges the traditional notions of territory and jurisdiction.

In practice, a policy that helps the countries where the abuse is taking place to address the problem, particularly through encouraging local prosecutions, is likely to be more effective than using British laws and courts. The British police can render assistance to the local police to warn them that known offenders are visiting their countries. The offences created in 1996 are likely to prove too impractical to enforce and will therefore have little impact on such sexual deviance.

The provisions in the Sex Offenders Act 1997 in relation to the registration of sex offenders (see p. 125) are similar to those that have recently been passed in America where they are known as Megan's law. Megan was a seven-year-old girl who was raped and murdered by a convicted paedophile who lived on her street in New Jersey. The aim of such legislation is clearly to protect young people, but one has to wonder why a register is being kept purely of sex offenders and not other offenders. It encourages vigilante activity by local neighbourhoods. Efforts at rehabilitation are undermined by the publication of such information as evidence in America suggests that sex offenders are being driven underground to avoid victimization by their neighbours.

Lord Bingham CJ has commented in **R** *v* **Chief Constable of the North Wales Police ex p. Thorpe** (1998):

> It is not acceptable that those who have undergone the lawful punishment imposed by the courts should be the subject of intimidation and private vengeance, harried from parish to parish like paupers under the old Poor Law. It is not only in their interests but in the interest of society as a whole that they should be enabled, and if need be helped, to live normal, lawful lives. While the risk of repeated offending may in some circumstances justify a very limited amount of official disclosure, a general policy of disclosure can never be justified, and the media should be slow to obstruct the rehabilitation of ex-offenders who have not offended again and who are seriously bent on reform.

Professor Grubin in his study discussed above concluded that there is a risk in concentrating too intensely on the minority of offenders known to the authorities. He felt that to be effective and coherent, a policy to tackle sex offences had to emphasize prevention through education, vetting procedures and the provision of services to encourage potential abusers to seek help.

Sex offenders cause considerable harm to their offenders and need to be rehabilitated. If they are simply used as targets for harsh legislation to gain political votes they will not receive the treatment they need and they will become the victims of unjust discrimination.

• •

ANSWERING QUESTIONS

1 Steven is a homosexual and is obsessed with Paul. He invites him for a drink one evening at a wine bar. After the drink Paul allows Steven to come back to his house for a coffee. By midnight Paul is very tired and asks Steven to leave but he refuses and starts to become very violent. He hits Paul across the face and then forces him to have anal intercourse. Paul screams out with the pain and when a neighbour arrives, having heard the noise, Steven runs off. He later claims to friends that Paul obviously fancied him and that while he was saying 'No' to anal intercourse he obviously meant 'Yes'. Discuss the criminal liability of Steven.

The most serious offence here is rape, as this has a maximum sentence of life imprisonment. When discussing the *actus reus*, you should point out that the definition of the offence has been amended to include male rape and anal intercourse. On the issue of consent, Steven's remarks to his friends suggest that he will claim he believed Paul consented. Although the mistake need not be reasonable, the fact that Paul had asked Steven to leave, Steven had used force and Paul had screamed are likely to be evidence which a jury will use to decide whether his mistake was genuine: the case of **Morgan** is obviously relevant. If rape is committed in a place where the rapist is trespassing, there may be liability for burglary (see p. 153), so you should consider whether Steven is a trespasser here. In addition, by hitting Paul across the face, he may have committed a non-fatal, non-sexual offence, such as that defined in s. 47 of the Offences Against the Person Act 1861. With regard to all these offences, you need to consider the defence of intoxication, as they had been out drinking before the incident occurred.

2 Is the current definition of rape satisfactory?

This is a fairly broad essay question, but so long as you remember to take a strongly critical approach, assessing what the law should be, as well as what it is, you can score high marks here. After briefly outlining the offence of rape, you should point out that this is an area where the law has been reformed recently, explaining the problems which the changes were designed to remedy, and stating to what extent these problems have in fact been solved. Then you can go on to point out the problems that still exist, and possible reforms. You could include some of the material on changing attitudes, pointing out that legal reform alone may not be enough to change the problems with rape. See also question 3 of Chapter 8.

8 Non-fraudulent property offences

So far we have considered offences where the target of the wrongdoing is people; in this chapter we will look at offences concerned with property, such as theft and fraud. Until 1968 this area of the law was governed by the common law, and was extremely complex. The Criminal Law Revision Committee identified this field as one suitable for codification, and an attempt to do this was made in the form of the Theft Act 1968. This Act was described as a mini-code, since it covers only the key property offences; a full code would cover criminal law as a whole.

Despite the fact that the 1968 Act was designed to clarify the law, the courts encountered a series of problems with interpretation and application, so that ten years later part of the Act was repealed and the 1978 Theft Act was passed. In 1996 the House of Lords judgment in **R** v **Preddy** drew attention to further problems with the law, leading to the passing of the Theft (Amendment) Act 1996 which amends the two earlier Theft Acts. The mini-code is now contained in the three Acts.

Property offences can be divided into two types: those involving fraud and those not involving fraud. This chapter deals with non-fraudulent property offences where it is not necessary to prove fraud. If fraud does exist there can still be liability for one of these non-fraudulent offences provided the essential ingredients of these offences are established.

THEFT

Theft is the main non-fraudulent property offence, and is defined in s. 1 of the Theft Act 1968: 'A person is guilty of theft if he dishonestly appropriates property belonging to another with the intention of permanently depriving the other of it . . .'

▶ Actus reus

The *actus reus* of theft has three elements: 'property', 'appropriation', and 'belonging to another'.

'Property'

The meaning of 'property' for the purposes of theft is considered in s. 4: 'Property includes money and all other property, real or personal, including things in action and other intangible property.' Intangible property means property that does not exist in a physical sense, and a 'thing in action' (also called a 'chose in action') is a technical term to describe property that does not physically exist but which gives the owner legal rights that are enforceable by a court action. For example, when a bank account is in credit, the bank owes the customer money and if the bank refuses to pay the customer that money when asked, the customer can sue the bank for the amount in the account. This right is the 'thing in action'. Other examples of things in action are shares in a company and copyright.

The approach to be taken with cheques has caused particular problems. The balance of the account reduced when the cheque can be treated as a thing in action if the cheque was drawn on an account which was in credit or within an agreed overdraft facility (**R** *v* **Kohn** (1979)). If the account was overdrawn beyond any agreed overdraft facility then the account holder has no right to money held by the bank which could be treated as a thing in action. The case of **R** *v* **Duru** (1973) suggested that the piece of paper on which the cheque was written could be treated as the property, but this approach was disapproved of in **R** *v* **Preddy** (1996). Professor J.C. Smith (1997) has argued that cheques should be treated as property on the basis that they are a 'valuable security', rather than focusing on a thing in action or a piece of paper. This approach was followed by the Court of Appeal in **R** *v* **Arnold** (1997).

Information cannot be stolen: in **Oxford** *v* **Moss** (1979) a student who stole an exam paper was not liable for the theft of the information contained in it, though he could have been liable for theft of the piece of paper itself, assuming all other elements of the offence were present. This has implications for business, since it means that trade secrets, such as the recipe for Coca-Cola, cannot be stolen (though there are other legal means of dealing with this problem). This area of the law was reviewed by the Law Commission in its Consultation Paper, *Legislating the Criminal Code: Misuse of Trade Secrets* of 1997. It noted that most trade secrets were actually taken in the briefcases of employees leaving to join a competitor or to set up their own business. In other countries such conduct tends to fall within theft. In England, such behaviour could give rise to civil remedies for breach of confidence, but the Law Commission considered this to be an inadequate deterrence and recommended that a separate offence should be created of 'unauthorised use or disclosure of a secret'.

Section 4(2) of the Act states that property does not normally include land or things forming part of the land, and severed from it, such as harvested crops or picked flowers. These cannot therefore usually be stolen. However, there are some circumstances in which land can be stolen:

(a) when the defendant is in certain positions of trust, and 'appropriates the land or anything forming part of it by dealing with it in breach of the confidence reposed in him or her';
(b) when the defendant is not in possession of the land and appropriates anything forming part of the land by severing it or causing it to be severed, or after it has been severed;
(c) when a defendant in possession of land under a tenancy appropriates the whole or part of any fixture or structure let to be used with the land.

An example of (b) would be knocking down your neighbour's brick wall and carrying away the bricks, or shaking apples off someone's tree and taking them, or even picking up fruit which has fallen to the ground. 'Severing' simply means that the item has been detached from the land. However – to complicate matters further – there is no theft if the thing severed is growing wild and it is not taken for commercial purposes. Section 4(3) provides: 'A person who picks mushrooms growing wild on any land, or who picks flowers, fruit or foliage from a plant growing wild on any land, does not (although not in possession of the land) steal what he picks, unless he does it for reward or for sale or other commercial purpose.' For purposes of this subsection 'mushroom' includes any fungus, and 'plant' includes any shrub or tree.

Part (c) is aimed at people who rent premises; they may be committing theft if they remove something which is considered a fixture or structure, such as a fixed kitchen cupboard, and take it with them when they move.

Subsection 4(4) provides that wild animals cannot be stolen unless they have been tamed:

> Wild creatures, tamed or untamed, shall be regarded as property, but a person cannot steal a wild creature not tamed nor ordinarily kept in captivity, or the carcase of any such creature, unless either it has been reduced into possession by or on behalf of another person and possession of it has not since been lost or abandoned, or another person is in the course of reducing it into possession.

The main implication of this is that poaching does not normally fall within the offence of theft.

The human body will only be treated as property if it has been altered for the purpose of medical or scientific examination and thereby acquired financial value. In **R** *v* **Kelly** (1998) the first defendant was an artist who had been granted access to the Royal College of Surgeons so that he could draw anatomical specimens. Aided by the second defendant, a junior technician at the College, he had removed approximately 35 human body parts from the Royal College of Surgeons. They were convicted of theft and their appeals were dismissed.

'Appropriation'

Section 3(1) defines appropriation: 'Any assumption by a person of the rights of an owner amounts to an appropriation, and this includes, where he has come by the property (innocently or not) without stealing it, any later assumption of a right to it by keeping or dealing with it as owner.'

Thus an 'appropriation' means doing something with the property that the owner has a right to do, but which no one else has the right to do without the owner's permission. This could include selling, keeping, damaging, destroying or extinguishing the property; it is not limited to physically taking the property. In **R** *v* **Morris** (1983) it was stated that assuming any one of the owner's rights is sufficient to amount to appropriation. This case has been overruled on another point of law, but is still good law on this issue.

The second half of s. 3(1) makes it clear that appropriation covers a situation in which someone gains possession of property without stealing it, but later assumes some right of the owner – for example, where a person is lent a book by a friend and then later refuses to return it. In this example the appropriation would occur at the moment of refusal.

Where someone buys something in good faith, but ownership does not pass because unknown to them the goods are stolen, they will not be treated as appropriating the goods. In the words of section 3(2): 'Where property or a right or interest in property is or purports to be transferred for value to a person acting in good faith, no later assumption by him of rights which he believed himself to be acquiring shall, by reason of any defect in the transferor's title, amount to theft of the property.'

A situation which caused some problems for the courts was where a defendant assumed some right of the owner, but with the owner's permission. Was this an appropriation? At first glance, the common sense answer might be 'No'; why should it be illegal to do something to property which the owner allows you to do? The case of **R** *v* **Lawrence** (1971) shows that the question is not as simple as that. The case concerned an Italian student, who spoke little English. On arrival in London, he climbed into a taxi at the airport, showing the driver a piece of paper bearing the address of the family with whom he was going to stay. This was not far from the airport, and the fare should have been about 50p. When they arrived, the student tendered a £1 note, but the taxi-driver said that it was not enough. Being unfamiliar with British currency, the student held out his wallet for the taxi-driver to take the correct fare, upon which the driver helped himself to a further £6. The driver was convicted of theft, and appealed on the basis that he had not appropriated the money because the student had consented to his taking it. This argument was rejected by the House of Lords and his conviction upheld.

However, when the question arose again, in **R** *v* **Morris** (1983), the House of Lords said that there could only be an appropriation where the acts of the defendant were 'unauthorized', in other words where the owner had not consented to the defendant's acts. The situation in that case was that Morris took goods from the shelves of a supermarket, and switched their price labels with those of cheaper products. He then took them to the checkout and was charged the lower price on the new labels, which he paid. Charged with theft, he argued that there had been no appropriation on the basis that he had not assumed all the rights of the owner. As pointed out above, the House of Lords held that it was not actually necessary to assume all the rights of an owner, so long as at least one was assumed, and they agreed that an appropriation had taken place. In pinpointing exactly when that appropriation occurred, they stated that it was not when the goods were removed from the shelves, since shoppers had implied permission to do that. Appropriation required some 'adverse interference' with the owner's rights which could not be satisfied if the owner's consent had been given. This appeared to be a direct conflict with the House of Lords judgment in **Lawrence**.

The problem was eventually resolved by the House of Lords in **R** *v* **Gomez** (1993). The defendant was the assistant manager of a shop, who persuaded the manager to sell goods worth £17,000 to Gomez's accomplice. The goods were paid for with cheques which Gomez and the accomplice knew were worthless. This would have been a fairly straightforward case of obtaining property by deception (an offence discussed in the next chapter), but for some reason Gomez was charged with theft instead. The question of whether appropriation could include an act permitted by the owner arose because the accomplice had the owner's authority to take possession. If **Morris** was followed no appropriation would be treated as having occured, and therefore no liability for theft imposed. The House of Lords decided to opt for the principle established in **Lawrence** instead; **Morris** was thereby overruled on this issue and an appropriation can take place even if the assumption of the owner's rights takes place with the owner's consent.

Because the consent of the owner is irrelevant, a person who simply accepts a gift can be treated as appropriating it. This was the view of the Court of Appeal in **R** *v* **Hinks** (1998). The victim was a 53-year-old man of limited intelligence who had been left money by his father. The defendant had befriended the man and was alleged by the prosecution to have encouraged him to withdraw £60,000 from his building society account and deposit it in her account. The defence argued that this money was either a gift or a loan. The defendant was convicted and the subsequent appeal was rejected. The Court of Appeal stated that a valid gift could be an appropriation, which means that the key issue in such cases will be whether the defendant had the *mens rea* of the offence of theft when accepting the gift.

The opposite view had been taken in **R** *v* **Mazo** (1996) where the Court of Appeal was reluctant to apply **R** *v* **Gomez** where there was no deception. Mazo was working as a maid to Lady S. Over a period of two years Lady S made out a number of cheques in her favour to the value of £37,000. On one occasion, when Lady S's bank had telephoned her to query the payments, she had abruptly reaffirmed her instructions. Mazo was subsequently charged and convicted of theft of the cheques on the basis that she took dishonest advantage of Lady S's mental incapacity. On appeal the conviction was quashed on the ground that there could be no theft if a valid gift had been made. This would no longer seem to represent the law, but the danger of the approach in **R** *v* **Hinks** is that there can be a conflict between the criminal law and the civil law, with a convicted thief in theory being able to bring a civil action to recover the stolen property from the alleged victim. Professor J.C. Smith has also argued that this interpretation of the law does not reflect Parliament's intention when it passed the 1968 Act.

Where the gift is not valid in civil law then there is no problem in finding an appropriation. In **R** *v* **Kendrick and Hopkins** (1996) two defendants ran a residential home for old people. Mrs C was 99 years old, very frail and virtually blind. The defendants were accused of having taken control of her financial affairs with the intention of obtaining her assets worth £127,500 for their own benefit. They were convicted of theft and their appeal was rejected as Mrs C was incapable of making a valid gift to the defendants.

Cheques and bank accounts

In relation to transactions involving cheques and bank accounts, in order to determine whether an appropriation has taken place a distinction has to be drawn between where the defendant directly did something themselves to a cheque or bank account and where they induced another, who is not acting on their behalf, to do this. In the former situation there will be an appropriation by the defendant, in the latter there will not be an appropriation immediately, but will be when the defendant subsequently exercises rights over the property after it has been transferred. An illustration of the former situation is **R** *v* **Kohn** (1979) where a company director was authorized to sign cheques on behalf of the company. In fact he signed some cheques for his own benefit and the signing of the cheques amounted to an appropriation. An illustration of the latter situation is **R** *v* **Preddy** (1996) which concerned three appeals that had been joined together as they raised the same legal issues. The appellants had been involved in mortgage frauds, which means that they had made applications for mortgages giving false information, for example, about their income or the value of the property they were seeking to purchase. The mortgage advances were paid by the lenders to the appellants by cheque, telegraphic transfer and the Clearing House Automated Payment System (CHAPS) – a computerized electronic transfer of funds. The House of Lords held that the defendants were not liable for theft, partly because they had not originally appropriated the money themselves, instead this had been done by the mortgage lenders. We will see that once the money had been paid into their accounts they then appropriated this money when they, for example, withdrew it from the bank, but by this stage they were already the owners of the property so another element of the offence was missing (see p. 148).

'Belonging to another'

The property appropriated must belong to another at the time of the appropriation. Section 5 states: 'Property shall be regarded as belonging to any person having possession or control of it, or having in it any proprietary right or interest . . .' Thus if property is treated as belonging to someone under civil law it will also belong to that person for the purposes of theft.

In fact, the definition goes further than this, and includes mere possession without rights of ownership. So if, for example, someone takes a book you have borrowed from the library, they can be said to have appropriated property belonging to you, even though you do not actually own the book.

This means that owners can in some cases be liable for stealing their own goods. The point is illustrated by the case of **R** *v* **Turner** (1971). Turner had taken his car to a garage to be repaired. When the repairs were done, he saw the car parked outside the garage and drove it away without paying for the work that had been carried out. He was liable for stealing his own car, because the garage had possession of the car at the time he took it, and all the other elements of theft existed. In **R** *v* **Marshall** (1998) the defendants had obtained used tickets for the underground from members of the public and resold them. This activity was causing London Underground to lose revenue. The defendants were convicted of stealing the tickets from London Underground. They appealed on the basis that the tickets no longer belonged to London Underground as they had sold them to members of the public. Their appeals were dismissed as on the reverse of each ticket it was stated that the tickets remained the property of London Underground. Thus the company remained owners of the ticket for the purposes of theft after the sale transaction.

A problematic situation is that where employees take advantage of their position to make an illegitimate profit. In the past, under civil law laid down in **Lister** *v* **Stubbs** (1890), such a profit has been treated as belonging to the employee, which means that the employee could not be liable for theft, because of the absence of property belonging to another.

This was the case in **Powell** *v* **McRae** (1977) where the defendant operated an entrance turnstile at Wembley Stadium. A person arrived who did
not have a ticket and the defendant allowed the person in on payment of
£2. He had no authority from his employer to do this and he pocketed
the money himself. No liability for theft was incurred. However, the civil
law may have changed on this point. In **Attorney-General for Hong Kong**
v **Reid** (1993) the Privy Council suggested that if a person makes an
illegal profit from his or her work that profit belongs to the employer. If
this is followed there could be liability for theft.

Keeping property in one's possession

Subsections (3) and (4) of section 5 deal with the specific problem of
where the owner hands someone else their property for some reason,
and this person proceeds to keep the property where there is a moral
obligation to hand it back. According to s. 5(3), where property is handed
over to another, but that other has a legal obligation to deal with the
property in a particular way, the property is treated as still belonging to
the original owner. The sub-section states: 'Where a person received
property from or on account of another, and is under an obligation to
the other to retain and deal with that property or its proceeds in a particular way, the property or proceeds shall be regarded (as against him) as
belonging to the other.' This covers situations such as a builder asking a
client for money to buy materials; under s. 5(3), the money still belongs
to the client, even though the builder has possession of it, and the builder
is obliged to use it to buy bricks; any other use would be appropriation of
property belonging to another. This is only the case where the money is
clearly handed over for a particular purpose, and would not apply if the
builder requested the £100 as a deposit or part-payment. In such a situation the builder would not be liable for theft even if the building work
was never actually carried out, because by having possession of the money,
he or she would be treated as its owner (on the other hand the builder may
have committed a fraudulent offence, and in any case the client would
have a civil remedy).

The obligation to treat the property in a particular way must be a legal
obligation recognized under civil law. This was the view of the Court of
Appeal in **R** *v* **Breaks and Huggan** (1998). The defendants worked for a
company which placed insurance on behalf of clients with Lloyds of London through Lloyds' brokers. They were charged with theft in relation to
premiums received from clients in respect of business negotiated with a
firm of Lloyds' brokers but to whom no payments were made. The prosecution case was that the premiums received by the company remained
the property of the clients, being destined for the onward transmission to
the brokers, and the company owed an obligation to the clients to use
the payments for that purpose but did not do so, spending them in some
other way. The trial judge had ruled that the purpose of section 5(3) was

to avoid provisions of the civil law and accordingly there was a case to go to the jury. The defendants were convicted and appealed against conviction on the grounds that the judge's ruling was wrong. Their appeal was allowed and the Court of Appeal stated that the civil law determined whether or not a duty to deal with property in a particular way existed. Judges in criminal cases are understandably reluctant to become involved with the civil law; but in cases of this kind they will have to do so.

R *v* **Hall** (1972) is an example of a case that fell outside s. 5(3). A client had paid a travel agent a deposit for a holiday. The money had been paid into the company's general account, but the agent went bust, leaving the client unable to recover the deposit. It was held that the travel agents had not stolen the deposit because, for the purposes of the Theft Act 1968, the money belonged to them, so they could not appropriate it. Section 5(3) did not apply as they had no legal obligation to spend the money in a particular way; it was simply security for them against the client cancelling.

In **Davidge** *v* **Bunnett** (1984), the defendant was one of a group of people sharing a flat. His flatmates gave him money to pay certain household bills, but he spent the money on himself, leaving the bills unpaid. He was held liable for theft; the money was given to him for the specific purpose of paying the bills, and since that meant it still belonged to his flatmates, his alternative use of it amounted to appropriation. This authority was applied by the Court of Appeal in **R** *v* **Wain** (1996). The appellant had raised almost £3,000 for a 'Telethon' organized by Yorkshire Television. He opened a separate bank account under the name 'Scarborough Telethon Appeal' and deposited the money into the account. With the permission of the telethon organizers, he was permitted to transfer the money from this account to his own and then wrote out a cheque to the organizers for the sum due. The cheque was dishonoured and he was convicted of theft. His appeal failed, and the court stated that Wain was under an obligation to retain at least the proceeds of the sums collected, if not the actual notes and coins: he had to keep in existence a fund sufficient to pay the bill. Therefore the sums credited to his own account remained property belonging to another because of s. 5(3).

In **R** *v* **Klineberg and Marsden** (1998) the Court of Appeal stated that s. 5(3) could be used to avoid the problems of **R** *v* **Preddy** in appropriate cases. In **R** *v* **Preddy** s. 5(3) could not apply because the money had been lent for the purposes of a mortgage and it was used in this way. In **R** *v* **Klineberg and Marsden** the money was lent to buy timeshares in apartments in Lanzarote. The money was not used in this way and s. 5(3) could apply. J.C. Smith in his commentary on this case in the *Criminal Law Review* has argued that the reasoning of the Court of Appeal was wrong because s. 5(3) requires that the property has been 'received' and he considers that as there has not been an obtaining for the purposes of s. 15 (discussed in the next chapter) there has not been a receipt. However, with all due respect, his reasoning is flawed – there was an obtaining under s. 15 in **Preddy** but it was simply not of property belonging to another. Thus there is also a receipt, and s. 5(3) deems that the property shall be treated as having belonged to another.

Section 5(4) provides that if a person receives property by mistake and has a legal obligation to give it back, then for the purposes of the 1968 Act, it will be treated as belonging to the original person who handed it over by mistake – so that failure to hand it back will count as appropriation. In **Attorney General's Reference (No. 1 of 1983)** (1984), a police officer received an extra £74 in her wages, due to an accounting error by her employer, and failed to alert anyone or give it back. The Court of Appeal held that this amounted to appropriation.

Passage of ownership

The point at which appropriation occurs is important in situations where ownership will pass to the thief, since if appropriation happens after ownership has passed, the property appropriated does not belong to another. Prior to **Gomez**, this caused frequent problems. In **R** *v* **Dip Kaur** (1981) the defendant was in a shoe shop where some of the shoes were £4.99 and some were £6.99. She noticed that one shoe which should have been priced at £6.99 bore a label saying £4.99. Carefully positioning this shoe on top, she went to the cash desk hoping that the cashier would not notice the incorrect price label. The cashier did not notice and sold the shoes at the lower price. When the mistake was discovered the defendant was charged with theft. Her conviction was quashed on appeal on the basis that by the time the appropriation took place at the cash till, the shoes already belonged to her because the cashier had authority to accept the lower price and did so.

Recent cases avoid this problem by interpreting appropriation as taking place at a very early stage – as soon as any right of an owner has been assumed, even if the owner consented to that assumption. **Dip Kaur** would probably be decided differently now since the decision in **Gomez** established that the shop's consent to the appropriation was irrelevant. In the light of **Gomez** it could be argued that the appropriation took place when the defendant assumed the right of the owner to have possession of the goods by taking them off the shelves, even though this is an action to which the shop had consented. At this earlier time it is clear that the goods still belonged to the shop so today a conviction might be upheld if the same facts of **Dip Kaur** were to appear before a court.

The issue of passage of ownership can still be relevant in relation to goods which lose their own identity when supplied to another – such as food when consumed, or petrol when poured into the tank of a car. Because it is no longer possible to take back the original goods, they are treated in civil law as belonging to the receiver as soon as they lose their identity; while with other types of goods this usually occurs only at the time of payment. Therefore such items can only be stolen before they lose their identity; all the elements of theft must be present at this point. This was the ground for the decision in **R** *v* **McHugh** (1976), which concerned the theft of petrol. By contrast in **Corcoran** *v* **Wheat** (1977) the defendant was not liable for theft when he ate a meal and only afterwards formed the dishonest intent not to pay. During the time when the property belonged to another he lacked the *mens rea* of theft, and when he did have the *mens rea* for theft, he could not commit the *actus reus* because by then the property belonged to him.

Cheques and bank accounts

In **Preddy** the House of Lords took the view that where a transfer takes place from one bank account to another the balance in the first account is a thing in action which belongs to the victim. With the transfer this thing in action ceases to exist and a completely new thing in action is created which has only ever belonged to the defendant. We saw on p. 144 that in relation to transactions involving cheques and bank accounts, where a defendant simply induced another to do something to the cheque or bank account who is not acting on their behalf there will not be an appropriation immediately, but will be when the defendant exercises rights over the property after it has been transferred. In order for there to be a theft the property must belong to another at the time of the appropriation. In this situation, by the time there is an appropriation the only property that has been appropriated belongs to the defendant, so he or she cannot be liable for theft.

▶ Mens rea

The *mens rea* of theft has two elements: intention permanently to deprive, and dishonesty.

Intention permanently to deprive

The defendant must have the intention of permanently depriving the other of the property. The victim need not actually be deprived permanently of the property, so long as the prosecution can prove that the defendant intended permanent deprivation.

Merely borrowing without permission does not amount to theft. For this reason, although cars count as property which can be stolen, there are a number of specific property offences dealing with the taking of cars, because cars are so frequently taken with the intention of driving them for a while and then dumping them, otherwise known as 'joyriding'.

Section 6 contains certain exceptions where a mere borrowing will be sufficient to constitute a theft. The Court of Appeal observed in **R** *v*

Fernandes (1996) that the critical notion in s. 6 is whether a defendant intended 'to treat the thing as his own to dispose of regardless of the other's rights'. Everything else in the section is merely specific illustrations of this point, rather than restrictions on where s. 6 applies. Section 6(1) provides:

> A person appropriating property belonging to another without meaning the other permanently to lose the thing itself is nevertheless to be regarded as having the intention of permanently depriving the other of it if his intention is to treat the thing as his own to dispose of regardless of the other's rights; and a borrowing or lending of it may amount to so treating it if, but only if, the borrowing or lending is for a period and in circumstances making it equivalent to an outright taking or disposal.

This section was applied in **Chan Man-sin *v* Attorney-General for Hong Kong** (1988). The defendant was a company accountant. He drew a forged cheque on the company's account knowing that the company would not be permanently deprived of their money because the bank would have a legal obligation to reimburse them for any money paid out as a result of such a trick. This knowledge, he argued, meant he lacked any intention permanently to deprive the company of its property. The Privy Council held that his situation fell within s. 6(1); he intended to treat the company's property as his own to dispose of regardless of the company's rights.

The specific illustration of where s. 6(1) can arise, that is where a defendant borrows property for a period and in circumstances making it equivalent to an outright taking or disposal, was the focus of **R *v* Lloyd** (1985). The defendant removed films from a cinema for a few hours, made illegal copies of them, and then returned them. He argued that since he intended all along to return the films, he had no intention permanently to deprive; nor had he borrowed the films in circumstances making the borrowing equivalent to an outright taking or disposal. Lord Lane CJ in the Court of Appeal felt that to fall within this part of s. 6(1) there must be an intention 'to return the "thing" in such a changed state that it can truly be said that all its goodness or virtue is gone'. Just what this situation would cover is still unclear: would it, for example, include borrowing someone's season ticket without permission and returning it when it has almost – but not quite – expired?

Section 6(2) states:

> Without prejudice to the generality of subsection (1) above, where a person, having possession or control (lawfully or not) of property belonging to another, parts with the property under a condition as to its return which he may not be able to perform, this (if done for purposes of his own and without the other's authority) amounts to

treating the property as his own to dispose of regardless of the other's rights.

This subsection is most likely to apply where someone has pawned another's property without their permission and is uncertain whether they will be able to satisfy the condition for the property's return.

Conditional intent

A person has conditional intent if he or she intends to do something providing certain conditions are satisfied. In **R** *v* **Easom** (1971), it was held that such an intent was not sufficient for theft; the person will only start to intend permanently to deprive when the condition is satisfied and they go on to carry out their intention. The defendant was in a cinema, where the victim had placed her handbag on the floor. He picked up the bag, intending to steal if there was anything worth taking in it. In fact there were only a few tissues and aspirins inside, so he put the bag back. Unknown to him, the owner of the bag was a policewoman in plain clothes; the bag was attached to her wrist by a piece of thread and she was fully aware of what was happening. The defendant was charged with theft, but his conviction was quashed on the grounds that he had no intention permanently to deprive the victim of any property. This may be considered to be a rather lenient interpretation of the law.

Intention to return similar property

By contrast, the courts have taken a very harsh view of defendants who take property, intending to return similar property in the future: for example, a cashier who takes £5 out of the till, intending to pay it back later. Even if the person actually replaces the money, they can be treated as intending to deprive the shop permanently of the specific banknote that was removed – **R** *v* **Velumyl** (1989). In such cases the defendant may plead that they lack the other element of the *mens rea*: dishonesty.

Dishonesty

The 1968 Act only provides a partial definition of dishonesty, leaving some discretion to the courts. Unusually, the statutory definition, contained in s. 2(1), makes use of examples, stating three situations in which a defendant should not be deemed dishonest:

  (a) if he appropriates property in the belief that he has in law the right to deprive the other of it, on behalf of himself or of a third person; or

  (b) if he appropriates the property in the belief that he would have the other's consent if the other knew of the appropriation and the circumstances of it; or

(c) (except where the property came to him as trustee or personal representative) if he appropriates the property in the belief that the person to whom the property belongs cannot be discovered by taking reasonable steps.

If the facts of a particular case do not fall within any of these examples, the courts have to look to the common law to decide whether the defendant has been dishonest. Following a period of uncertainty, the Court of Appeal laid down a test for dishonesty in **R *v* Ghosh** (1982). Lord Lane said:

> In determining whether the prosecution has proved that the defendant was acting dishonestly, a jury must first of all decide whether according to the ordinary standards of reasonable and honest people what was done was dishonest. If it was not dishonest by those standards, that is the end of the matter and the prosecution fails. If it was dishonest by those standards, then the jury must consider whether the defendant himself must have realized that what he was doing was by those standards dishonest.

Thus, the court should first ask whether the defendant had been dishonest by the ordinary standards of reasonable and honest people. If the answer was 'Yes', the court should then ask whether the defendant realized that he or she had been dishonest by those standards. If the answer to this second question was also 'Yes', there was dishonesty. Where a court feels it necessary to give a **Ghosh** direction, it was stated in **R *v* Hyam** (1997) that it was preferable, though not compulsory, for that court to use Lord Lane's precise words.

▶ **Sentence**

The maximum sentence for theft is seven years' imprisonment.

• • • • • • • • • • •
ROBBERY

This offence is defined by s. 8 of the Theft Act 1968: 'A person is guilty of robbery if he steals, and immediately before or at the time of doing so and in order to do so, he uses force on any person or puts or seeks to put any person in fear of being then and there subjected to force.'

Robbery is most simply described as aggravated theft, as it usually involves theft accompanied by force or a threat of force. This can cover anything from a mugging in the street to a big bank robbery with guns.

▶ Actus reus

The *actus reus* of robbery is the *actus reus* of theft, plus using force against a person or seeking to put him or her in fear of being subjected to force ('the threat of force').

Force is not defined in the Act, so its definition has been left to the common law, which has established a fairly wide interpretation. In **R v Dawson and James** (1978) it was said that it was an ordinary English word and its meaning should be left to a jury. A mere nudge so that someone lost their balance could be sufficient.

The force or threat of force must be used in order to steal, so there is no robbery if the force is only used when trying to escape after the theft, or if the force was accidental. The force or threat of force must also be used immediately before or at the time of the theft. The theft occurs at the time of the appropriation, but again the courts have taken a very flexible approach to this rule. In **R v Hale** (1979) the two defendants broke into a house. While the first defendant went upstairs and stole a jewellery box, the second stayed downstairs and tied up the owner of the house. It was impossible to say whether these activities took place at precisely the same moment or whether the jewellery box was taken after the force was applied. Despite this, the Court of Appeal upheld the convictions on the basis that appropriation was a continuing act, and it was open to the jury to conclude on these facts that it was still continuing at the time the force was applied.

The case of **Hale** was confirmed in **R v Lockley** (1995). The appellant and two others took cans of beer from an off-licence and when the shopkeeper approached they used violence. It was submitted on appeal in the light of **Gomez** that the theft was complete before the force was used and the robbery charge should not have been left to the jury. Their appeal was dismissed because actually **Gomez** was irrelevant to this point and **Hale** was still good law that appropriation was a continuing act.

In the case of a threat, the threat must be of force 'then and there', rather than at some time in the future.

▶ Mens rea

The defendant must have the *mens rea* of theft. This requirement led to surprising results in **R v Robinson** (1977). The defendant threatened his victim with a knife in order to obtain payment of money he was owed. He was convicted of robbery, but the conviction was quashed by the Court of Appeal because the defendant lacked dishonesty according to the Theft Act; he fell within s. 2(1)(a) of the Act because he honestly believed he had a legal right to the money, even though he may have known that his mode of seeking repayment was dishonest.

▶ **Completion of the offence**

The question has arisen as to when the offence of robbery is completed; in other words when a person is liable for the full offence and not just its attempt. It was held in **Corcoran** *v* **Anderton** (1980) that the full offence takes place when the appropriation is complete. In that case, two defendants tried to take a woman's handbag by force. They managed to grab hold of the bag, but then dropped it and ran off. The court held that the appropriation was complete when the defendants got hold of the handbag, and therefore they were liable for robbery and not just attempted robbery, regardless of the fact that they had failed to run off with the bag.

▶ **Sentence**

The maximum sentence for robbery is life imprisonment.

BURGLARY

Burglary is generally thought of as the typical situation of someone breaking into a private home and stealing from it. In law, burglary covers this situation, but it also goes further. Section 9 of the Theft Act 1968 defines the offence:

(1) A person is guilty of burglary if—
(a) he enters any building or part of a building as a trespasser and with intent to commit any such offence as is mentioned in subsection (2) below; or
(b) having entered any building or part of a building as a trespasser he steals or attempts to steal anything in the building or that part of it or inflicts or attempts to inflict on any person therein any grievous bodily harm.
(2) The offences referred to in subsection (1)(a) above are offences of stealing anything in the building or part of a building in question, of inflicting on any person therein any grievous bodily harm or raping any person therein, and of doing unlawful damage to the building or anything therein.

As there is a higher maximum sentence available if the property burgled was a dwelling, s. 9 technically creates four offences:

- s. 9(1)(a) of a dwelling
- s. 9(1)(a) of a non-dwelling
- s. 9(1)(b) of a dwelling
- s. 9(1)(b) of a non-dwelling.

The offences in ss. 9(1)(a) and 9(1)(b) will be considered in turn.

▶ Burglary under s. 9(1)(a)

The s. 9(1)(a) offences are committed by entering any building or part of a building as a trespasser, and with intent to commit theft, grievous bodily harm, rape or criminal damage.

Actus reus

There are three elements: trespass, entry, and a building or part of a building.

Trespass

Trespass is a civil law concept which essentially means being on someone else's property without authority. A person who has authority to be on land is not a trespasser there, but someone who has authority to enter the land for a particular purpose will become a trespasser if they enter it for some other purpose. This was the case in **R v Jones and Smith** (1976). The defendant had left home, but had his father's permission to visit whenever he liked. One night the son came home and stole the television. The Court of Appeal upheld his conviction for burglary because, while he had permission to enter the house, in stealing the television he had gone beyond what he had permission to do, and was therefore a trespasser at the time of the theft.

Entry

In order for there to be a burglary the defendant must enter property. This may seem a straightforward concept, but the question of exactly what entering entails has caused quite a lot of judicial debate. In **R v Collins** (1972) the defendant had been out drinking, and at the end of the evening decided to find a woman with whom he could have sex, without her consent if necessary. Seeing an upstairs light on in a house, he climbed up a ladder and saw a girl asleep naked on her bed. He went back down the ladder and took off all his clothes, except for his socks, then climbed back up the ladder and stood on the windowsill, intending to climb inside. At this point the girl woke up, and mistaking him for her boyfriend, invited him in. She then consented to sexual intercourse and it was only afterwards that she realized her mistake. In order for the defendant to be liable for burglary under s. 9(1)(a), he had to have entered the house as a trespasser with the intention to rape. Once the girl invited him in, he was no longer a trespasser, so he could be liable only if he had entered before that invitation was made. The court stated that for there to be an entry it must be 'substantial' and 'effective'. The appeal was allowed as there had been a misdirection at the trial.

However, two subsequent cases suggest that the entry need be neither substantial nor effective. First in **R v Brown** (1985), a shop window had been broken and the defendant was found standing on the pavement, with the top half of his body inside the shop, rummaging among the goods inside. According to the Court of Appeal in that case the critical question was whether the entry had been 'effective'; they considered the word 'substantial' an unhelpful addition. On the facts, the jury were entitled to conclude that there was an effective entry and the defendant's appeal against conviction was rejected.

Secondly, in **R** *v* **Ryan** (1996) the appellant was found with his head and right arm trapped in a downstairs window in the middle of the night. He was subsequently convicted of burglary. He appealed on the ground that there had not in law been an entry. His appeal was rejected on the basis that his partial entry was sufficient, and that it was irrelevant whether he was capable of stealing anything, which raises doubts as to whether the entry must be 'effective'.

Building or part of a building

The place which the defendant enters as a trespasser must be a building or part of a building. A building is not defined, but s. 9(3) states that it includes inhabited vehicles or vessels (for example, caravans and houseboats).

The term 'part of a building' was considered in **R** *v* **Walkington** (1979). The accused entered a department store during open hours. This was not a trespass, since everyone has implied permission to enter open shops (although if it could be proved that the defendant was entering with the intention to steal, he may have been entering as a trespasser as he would have been exceeding his authority to enter – **Jones and Smith** (1976)). The defendant then went behind a counter – an area where customers did not have permission to go – and took money from a till. The court held that the counter area was part of a building and having entered this area as a trespasser, the defendant was liable for burglary.

Coincidence in time

The defendant must be a trespasser *at the time of entry* into the building or part of the building. In **R** *v* **Laing** (1995) the defendant had been found in the stockroom of a department store after the store had been closed. Initially he was convicted of burglary but on appeal his conviction was quashed because the prosecution had relied on his entry into the shop and had failed to provide evidence that at that time he was a trespasser. There was no doubt he was a trespasser when he was found, but he needed to have been a trespasser when he entered. This problem could have been avoided if the prosecution had relied on his entry into the stockroom as they had relied on the 'entry' into the area behind in the counter in **R** *v* **Walkington**.

Mens rea

There are two elements: intention or recklessness as to the trespass, and intention to commit the ulterior offence.

Intention/recklessness as to the trespass
In civil law there is no need for *mens rea* to be proved in relation to a civil trespass, but in criminal law it is necessary in the context of burglary. The relevant form of *mens rea* is intention or **Cunningham** recklessness. In the case of **Collins** the defendant probably lacked intention or recklessness to trespass if he entered the house after the girl had invited him in.

Intention to commit the ulterior offence
The defendant must intend to commit one of the offences listed in s. 9(2), known as the ulterior offences: theft; inflicting grievous bodily harm; rape; unlawful damage to the building or anything in it. The intention must exist at the time of entry. Provided the defendant enters with the relevant intention, the full offence of burglary is committed at the point of entry; the defendant need not actually proceed to commit the ulterior offence.

Conditional intent It was observed above that conditional intention is probably not enough for theft. However, for burglary, conditional intention can be sufficient; so if, for example, a defendant breaks into a house intending to steal if he or she finds anything worth taking, or to commit grievous bodily harm to a particular person if that person is in the house, then that intention may be sufficient for burglary.

Some confusion over this issue was caused by the case of **R** *v* **Husseyn** (1977). The defendants opened the door of a van in which there was a holdall containing valuable sub-aqua equipment. They were charged with attempted theft of that equipment, and the indictment specified that they had opened the van door with the intention of stealing the equipment. The Court of Appeal allowed their appeal, saying: 'It cannot be said that one who has it in mind to steal only if what he finds is worth stealing has a present intention to steal.' As a result, it was thought for a time that conditional intention was not sufficient for burglary, despite the fact that this would cause serious practical problems for prosecutors, since it is quite common for burglars to intend stealing only if they find something worth the trouble once they have broken in. The issue was reconsidered in **Attorney-General's References (Nos 1 and 2 of 1979)**, and the Court of Appeal made it clear that the remark in **Husseyn** quoted above should be understood as a criticism of the indictment in that case, which had been inaccurate: the defendants could not have opened the van door intending to steal the equipment since they did not know it existed. Had the indictment simply stated that the defendants opened the van door with the intention of stealing the contents of the van, the problem could have been avoided. The outcome is that there can be a conviction where the defendant only has conditional intent, so long as the indictment is appropriately worded.

▶ Burglary under s. 9(1)(b)

The s. 9(1)(b) burglary offences are committed where the defendant enters any building or part of the building as a trespasser, and then steals, attempts to steal, inflicts or attempts to inflict grievous bodily harm.

Actus reus

The prosecution must prove all the elements of the *actus reus* of a s. 9(1)(a) offence, and in addition prove that the *actus reus* of the ulterior offence (in this case stealing, attempting to steal, inflicting or attempting to inflict grievous bodily harm) has been carried out. This offence is committed not at the time of entry but at the time of committing the ulterior offence.

Mens rea

As for the s. 9(1)(a) offence, the prosecution must prove intention or recklessness as to the trespass. In addition, they must prove the *mens rea* of the ulterior offence (in grievous bodily harm this includes recklessness). The defendant need not have the *mens rea* of this ulterior offence at the time of entry, but must have it when the ulterior offence is committed.

▶ Sentence

For both types of burglary, the maximum sentence is fourteen years where the property burgled is a dwelling, and ten years where it is not a dwelling. The Crime (Sentences) Act 1997 provides for the introduction of a minimum sentence of three years for repeat burglars, but this has not yet been brought into force. How effective this reform will be is a matter of debate. Research suggests the level of property crime is more likely to be reduced through methods of prevention and by tackling drug addiction rather than the use of heavier sentences, particularly as Home Office statistics show that only 2 per cent of offences lead to a conviction. For example, in the 1990s security was tightened up for the use of credit cards, with better card design and card distribution. This reduced plastic fraud by almost half from £166 million in 1991 to £97 million in 1996.

• •
AGGRAVATED BURGLARY

Aggravated burglary is defined in the Theft Act 1968 s. 10:

A person is guilty of aggravated burglary if he commits any burglary and at the time has with him any firearm or imitation firearm, any weapon of offence, or any explosive; and for this purpose—
(a) 'firearm' includes an air gun or air pistol, and 'imitation firearm' means anything which has the appearance of being a firearm, whether capable of being discharged or not; and
(b) 'weapon of offence' means any article made or adapted for use for causing injury to or incapacitating a person, or intended by the person having it with him for such use; and
(c) 'explosive' means any article manufactured for the purpose of producing a practical effect by explosion, or intended by the person having it with him for that purpose.

▶ Actus reus

Aggravated burglary essentially involves committing a burglary when equipped with a weapon. The defendant must be in possession of the weapon at the time of the burglary (as was noted above, the moment at which the burglary occurs depends on whether it is a s. 9(1)(a) or a s. 9(1)(b) offence).

So long as the defendant was in possession of the weapon when the offence was committed, it does not matter that they only armed themselves seconds before. This point was made in **R v O'Leary** (1986). The accused entered a house as a trespasser, then took a knife from the kitchen and went upstairs. He proceeded to use the knife to force the victim to hand over some of his property. Liability was incurred for aggravated burglary, because the accused fell within the aggravated form of a s. 9(1)(b) offence, which is committed at the time the ulterior offence is committed, by which point he was equipped with the knife.

▶ Mens rea

The defendant must have the *mens rea* of burglary and also know that he has the weapon. In **R v Russell** (1984), the defendant had known he had a weapon, but by the time of the burglary had forgotten it was there. He was only liable for the burglary and not for aggravated burglary.

There is no need to prove that the defendant had any intention to use the weapon. In **R v Stones** (1989) the defendant was equipped with a kitchen knife at the time of committing the burglary, but argued in his defence that he had no intention to use the knife during the burglary; he said he was carrying it because he feared being attacked by a gang. Nevertheless, he was held liable for the aggravated offence.

▶ Sentence

The maximum sentence for aggravated burglary is life imprisonment.

● ● ● ● ● ● ● ● ● ● ● ● ●
BLACKMAIL

Blackmail is defined in s. 21 of the Theft Act 1968:

> A person is guilty of blackmail if with a view to gain for himself or another or with intent to cause loss to another, he makes any unwarranted demand with menaces, and for this purpose a demand with menaces is unwarranted unless the person making it does so in the belief—
> (a) that he has reasonable grounds for making the demand; and
> (b) that the use of the menaces is a proper means of reinforcing the demand.

▶ *Actus reus*

There must be a demand supported by menaces. In **Harry** (1974), the organizers of a student rag week wrote to shopkeepers requesting donations to charity, and stating that shopkeepers who gave donations would be given immunity from the inconvenience of rag week activities. These activities included throwing flour and water and tickling people with feathers. The court held that while there was a demand, the activities threatened were not sufficiently grave to be classified as menaces.

▶ *Mens rea*

The defendant must intend to make his or her demand with menaces, and s. 34(2) specifies that this demand must be made with a view to making a financial gain or causing a financial loss.

Section 21 contains a statutory defence that a person will not be liable for blackmail if the demand was warranted. A demand will only be warranted if the defendant believes that he or she has reasonable grounds for making the demand *and* that the means used to reinforce the demand are proper. The scope of this defence has been narrowed by the case of **R** *v* **Harvey** (1981). The appellant had paid £20,000 to the victim who promised to supply him with cannabis. In fact the victim had no intention to supply any cannabis, and simply pocketed the money. When the appellant realized this, he threatened to kill, maim and rape unless he was repaid. The appellant claimed that his demand for repayment was warranted, but the court held that the means used to make the demand were clearly not proper, since it could not be proper to threaten to do something that was known to be unlawful or morally wrong.

▶ Sentence

The maximum sentence for blackmail is fourteen years' imprisonment.

HANDLING

The definition of handling can be found in s. 22 of the Theft Act 1968:

> A person handles stolen goods if (otherwise than in the course
> of the stealing) knowing or believing them to be stolen goods he
> dishonestly receives the goods, or dishonestly undertakes or assists
> in their retention, removal, disposal or realization by or for the
> benefit of another person, or if he arranges to do so.

The most obvious type of handling is where someone receives stolen goods, but the offence actually covers a much wider range of activities. While there is only one offence of handling, there are 18 different potential ways that it can be committed, and in practice almost anything a person does with stolen goods may be classified as a handling, provided it takes place after the original theft ('otherwise than in the course of stealing'). Thieves can be liable for handling the goods they have stolen, provided that they are dealing with those goods in a totally separate incident from the original theft (for example selling them on to someone else).

▶ *Actus reus*

The *actus reus* may be committed in any of the following ways: (a) receiving stolen goods; (b) arranging to receive them; (c) undertaking the keeping, removing, disposing of or realizing of stolen goods by or for the benefit of another person, or helping with any of those things; (d) arranging to do any of the things in (c).

Stolen goods are very broadly defined in s. 24 of the Act. They include goods obtained not just by theft but also by blackmail or under the fraud offence defined in s. 15 of the Theft Act 1968 (discussed in the next chapter).

In **R** *v* **Kanwar** (1982) a wife was held liable for handling because she lied to the police in order to protect her husband who had brought stolen goods into the house. She was held to be assisting in the retention of those goods.

▶ Mens rea

The handler must know or believe the goods to be stolen and have behaved dishonestly. The concept of 'dishonestly' for these purposes has the common law meaning laid down in **Ghosh** and s. 2(1) of the Theft Act 1968 does not apply.

▶ Sentence

The maximum sentence for this offence is fourteen years' imprisonment.

TAKING WITHOUT CONSENT

Section 12 of the Theft Act 1968 is the most appropriate offence for joyriders. Such offenders are not normally liable for theft of the car as they have no intention to permanently deprive. Section 12(1) states:

> . . . a person shall be guilty of an offence if, without having the consent of the owner or other lawful authority, he takes any conveyance for his own or another's use or knowing that any conveyance has been taken without such authority, drives it or allows himself to be carried in or on it.

Any passengers as well as the driver can be liable for this offence. The vehicle must have been taken, simply using it, for example, to sleep does not suffice. The vehicle must move, but it need not be driven. Thus in **Bow** (1977) there was a 'taking' when the defendant had released the handbrake of the car and coasted some 200 yards down a hill. But in **Stokes** (1982) the defendant had not 'used' the car when for a joke he pushed a car round a corner in order to create the impression that it had been stolen.

In relation to the *mens rea* of the offence there is no requirement to prove dishonesty, nor an intention to permanently deprive. Section 12A of the 1968 Act contains an aggravated form of this offence which arises when a person commits the s. 12 offence in various aggravating circumstances such as driving dangerously, injuring someone or damaging property, including the vehicle. In **Marsh** (1997) the accused had taken a car and was driving it when a woman stepped out in front of the car and was knocked down. The accused was guilty of the aggravated offence despite not being at fault for the accident.

RETAINING A WRONGFUL CREDIT

The Theft (Amendment) Act 1996 inserts a new offence of retaining a wrongful credit under s. 24A of the Theft Act 1968. This offence occurs when a person's bank account is wrongfully credited, and knowing or believing this to be the case they dishonestly fail to take reasonable steps to secure that the credit is cancelled. A credit is 'wrongful' if it derives from any of the following offences: theft, blackmail, stolen goods, or an offence under s. 15A (discussed in the next chapter). This offence is very similar to the offence of handling and was introduced to criminalize people who benefited from the proceeds of a s. 15A crime.

CRIMINAL DAMAGE

The offence of criminal damage is contained in the Criminal Damage Act 1971. The basic offence of criminal damage is contained in s. 1(1) of that Act: 'A person who without lawful excuse destroys or damages any property belonging to another intending to destroy or damage any such property or being reckless as to whether any such property would be destroyed or damaged shall be guilty of an offence.'

▶ Actus reus

This consists of destroying or damaging property that belongs to another. The definition of property is different from that of theft, in that it includes land, but does not include intangible property – so you can cause criminal damage to a field but not to a company share. The question of whether the property belonged to another is essentially the same as for the law of theft.

The damage caused must not be purely nominal. In **A (a juvenile)** *v* **R** (1978), the defendant spat on a policeman's raincoat. The spit was easy to remove from the coat by wiping it with a damp cloth and so the damage was considered insufficient to amount to criminal damage. Similarly, in **Morphitis** *v* **Salmon** (1990), a scratch on a scaffolding bar was held not to be criminal damage because it did not affect the value or usefulness of the scaffolding. By contrast, in **Hardman** *v* **Chief Constable of Avon and Somerset Constabulary** (1986) the defendant had drawn a large painting with water soluble paints. If it had been left in place, rain would eventually have washed it away, but the local authority incurred expense by washing it off. Due to this expenditure, the painting was held to constitute criminal damage. In **Lloyd** *v* **DPP** (1991) the defendant's car had been clamped for illegal parking and in trying to remove it he damaged the clamp, which amounted to criminal damage.

▶ **Mens rea**

Section 1(1) of the 1968 Act, quoted above, requires that the defendant must have either intended or been reckless as to the criminal damage. **Caldwell** recklessness applies in this context, since that case was itself concerned with an offence contained in the Criminal Damage Act 1971. **Chief Constable of Avon and Somerset Constabulary** *v* **Shimmen** (1986), discussed at p. 17, is an example of recklessness being found for this offence.

▶ **Defence**

Section 1(1) provides that the defendant is only liable if the damage was done 'without lawful excuse'. A defendant will have a lawful excuse if they can prove some general defence (such as self-defence) or if their conduct falls within one of the categories of behaviour listed in s. 5(2) of the Act, which states that a person has a lawful excuse:

> (a) if at the time of the act or acts alleged to constitute the offence he believed that the person or persons whom he believed to be entitled to consent to the destruction of or damage to the property in question had so consented, or would have consented to it if he or they had known of the destruction or damage and its circumstances; or
> (b) if he destroyed or damaged . . . the property in question . . . in order to protect property belonging to himself or another . . . and at the time of the act or acts alleged to constitute the offence he believed—
> (i) that the property, right or interest was in immediate need of protection; and
> (ii) that the means of protection adopted or proposed to be adopted were or would be reasonable having regard to all the circumstances.

Section 5(3) states that, for the purposes of this statutory defence, it is immaterial whether the relevant belief is justified or not, so long as it is honestly held.

While (a) is a purely subjective test, the courts have introduced in **Hill and Hall** (1989) an objective element to (b), despite the subjective wording of that subsection. The appellants had been involved in the longstanding demonstrations against the presence of American weapons in the UK, best known by the activities of the Greenham Common women. They were convicted of an offence under the Criminal Damage Act because they had equipped themselves to cut the perimeter fence of the military base, so that they could stage a demonstration on the site. In their defence it had been submitted that they had a lawful excuse within the meaning of s. 5(2)(b), as they had acted in order to protect the property of those living nearby, which would be destroyed in the event of the kind of attack which they felt the presence of the weapons rendered highly likely. By encouraging the authorities to remove the military equipment such a threat would be removed. This argument was rejected both by the trial court and the Court of Appeal. The Court of Appeal said that in determining whether the defence was made out, two questions had to be asked: first, whether the defendants did think they were protecting property; and secondly, whether as a matter of law they were protecting homes in the vicinity. The court concluded that the answer to the second question was 'No', because the threat of harm to the property concerned was too remote. This result has been criticized by some as distorting the clear wording of the Act for political ends.

▶ Criminal damage endangering life

Section 1(2) of the Criminal Damage Act 1971 defines an aggravated offence of criminal damage, which contains all the elements of ordinary criminal damage, with an additional requirement that the defendant intended or was reckless as to the endangering of life. This offence has a maximum sentence of life imprisonment.

There is no need to prove that life was in fact endangered, so long as it is proved that the defendant intended such danger, or was reckless as to whether it occurred. There must be a connection between the destruction of or damage to property and the intention or recklessness to destroy life. This link was not proved in **R** *v* **Steer** (1987). The defendant fired a gun at someone, intending to hurt them, but missed. The bullet ricocheted off the window, damaging it. He was held not liable under s. 1(2); the shooting had both endangered life and caused criminal damage, but the danger to life was not caused by the criminal damage.

▶ Arson

Arson is another form of aggravated criminal damage, committed where all the elements of s. 1(1) of the 1971 Act are proved but in addition the destruction or damage was caused by fire. Again the maximum sentence is life imprisonment as fire is seen to be an unusually dangerous weapon, given its tendency to get out of control very quickly. Both **Caldwell** and **Elliott**, discussed at pp. 14 and 16, were concerned with this offence.

In **Hunt** (1977) the defendant was charged with arson and he argued that he fell within the statutory defence of having a lawful excuse. He was a deputy warden in an old people's home, and had been concerned about the fire risks posed by the building. Unable to persuade the fire officer to improve the conditions, he decided to set fire to the property to show the authorities what the risks were, in the hope of prompting them to take action. He was held to fall outside the defence under s. 5 as he was not acting to protect property.

• •

ANSWERING QUESTIONS

As a general comment make sure you do not make the mistake of talking about offences under, for example, s. 2 or s. 6 of the Theft Act 1968. These sections are not offences in their own right, they are merely elements that may need to be proved for the offence of theft.

1 **What offences, if any, have been committed as a result of the following occurrences in the Heaton department store?**
(a) D, who works in the electrical department, borrows an electric drill, without telling his supervisor, for the weekend. When he returns the drill its motor has burnt out. *(10 marks)*
(b) E, a cleaner of low intelligence, finds a diamond ring in the ladies' cloakroom. She keeps the ring. When this is discovered she says she did not realize it would be possible to find the owner. *(10 marks)*
(c) F, the flower department manager, picks daffodils growing wild in nearby woods. He sells them in the store and keeps the proceeds. *(10 marks)*
(d) G, a customer in the self-service food department, takes a number of items from a shelf and places them into the wire basket provided by the store. G then takes a tin of salmon from the shelf and places it into his coat pocket. G is detained by a store detective before he leaves the food department. G admits it was his intention to take the salmon and the other items in the basket from the store without payment. *(20 marks) Oxford*
Part (a): the most relevant offence here is theft. While all the elements of this offence would need to be mentioned – the dishonest appropriation of property belonging to another with the intention of permanently depriving – the issues of intention and dishonesty would need particular consideration on these facts. Section 6 should be looked at closely. You could also discuss liability for criminal damage.

No other property offences would appear to have been committed. There is no fraud offence because nobody has been deceived; D simply fails to tell his supervisor anything about borrowing the drill. Nor are there any of the aggravating factors to bring the incident within burglary (no trespass) or robbery (no force or threat of force).

Part (b): this is also concerned with theft. Given the cleaner's low intelligence, and her belief that the owner could not be found, dishonesty is a key issue here, and in particular its definition in s. 2(1)(c). Note that it is the defendant's actual belief that is important for s. 2(1)(c): it is a subjective and not an objective criterion.

Part (c): the first question is whether there has been a theft of the daffodils, and the crucial issue is whether the daffodils constitute property, as defined by s. 4(3). Because they were picked for commercial purposes they are treated as property. F may also be liable for theft of the illegal profit, if **Attorney-General for Hong Kong** v **Reid** is preferred over **Lister** v **Stubbs**. The fact that customers consented to handing over the money will not prevent there being an appropriation: **Gomez**.

F might also be liable for obtaining property by deception (discussed in the next chapter), the deception being the implied representation that he had authority to sell the daffodils. A crucial question will be whether the obtaining was by the deception (**Laverty**) as it may be that the customers did not care whether he had authority or not; all they may have been interested in was the quality of the flowers.

Part (d): here we are again concerned with theft. Your answer will be clearer if you deal with the items in the basket and the tin of salmon separately. The critical issue in both cases will be whether G's conduct is sufficient to constitute an appropriation. In the light of **Gomez**, both acts are likely to suffice, because G only needs to have assumed a right of an owner, and here he has done that by taking possession. The old idea that theft could only be committed if the person had left the store or gone past the point of payment is no longer true. Before **Gomez**, only the salmon would have been appropriated because putting the other items in the basket was authorized conduct – **R** v **Morris**. As a result of **Gomez**, it no longer matters that the owner had impliedly consented to these actions.

2 Bill and Tim go to their local hypermarket. On an earlier visit, the hypermarket manager told Tim he was not to return again as he suspected him of being connected with a spate of thefts which his store had recently suffered. As they are about to enter the hypermarket, Bill and Tim agree that they will unplug all the freezers in the store, thus spoiling the frozen foods which they contain. They each enter the store, Bill heading for the freezers in the meat department and Tim heading for the freezers in the dairy produce department. Bill unplugs several freezers and spoils £1,000 worth of meat. On his way out, he enters a room marked 'Staff only' and takes £25 from an unattended handbag. As he is leaving the room, a store detective challenges him, whereupon Bill strikes him on the nose and makes good his escape. As Tim is about to unplug a freezer full of cheeses, he is challenged by Mary, a shop assistant. Knowing that Mary is having a secret affair with the manager, Tim threatens to reveal this fact to Mary's husband if she stops him. He then unplugs the freezer, spoiling its contents, Mary being too frightened to intervene.

Consider the criminal liability of
(a) Bill (25 marks) **and**
(b) Tim (25 marks)
ignoring any possible offences of conspiracy and secondary participation.
Oxford

The key offences here are criminal damage and burglary, along with the blackmail of Mary and a non-fatal offence against the storekeeper. Take them one at a time, working through the ingredients for liability in the order you find them in this chapter. Notice that you are not required to discuss conspiracy or secondary participation – this means you will get no marks for comments on these points, so do not waste your time, even if you are dying to show off your knowledge in the field!

In discussing burglary it is important to discuss s. 9(1)(a) and s. 9(1)(b) burglary, both are relevant on these facts. You should also consider whether the defendants are trespassers and both **Collins** and **Jones and Smith** can be analysed on this point.

3 **Peter went back to the house he had shared with his former girlfriend, Rachel, as he believed that some of his tapes were still in the house. Unknown to Peter, Rachel had changed the locks so he could not gain access with his key. Peter therefore broke a window and gained access to the house.**

Whilst looking for the tapes, he came across Rachel who was in a drugged stupor. He then had sexual intercourse with Rachel 'for old time's sake', as sexual activity whilst she was drugged had been quite usual and accepted by Rachel whilst they were living together. He then left the house taking with him Rachel's photograph album.

Analyse the offences that Peter might be charged with. *NEAB*

There are a range of offences that Peter appears to have committed on these facts both against the person and against property. Taking the problem question chronologically, the first offence that he commits is criminal damage when he breaks the window, though you could discuss the statutory defence in s. 5. He does not seem to be liable at the time of entering the property for a s. 9(1)(a) burglary because he appears to lack the *mens rea*. There is then an issue as to whether he has committed rape when he has sexual intercourse with Rachel. She is unlikely to be considered to have consented in the light of **R** *v* **Larter and Castleton**. As regards *mens rea* he was probably at least reckless as to whether or not she was consenting though if the jury were satisfied that in the light of her past behaviour he had made a genuine mistake he would avoid liability – **DPP** *v* **Morgan**. Depending on his *mens rea* he could incur liability for burglary under s. 9(1)(b) with the ulterior offence being that of stealing. He could also be found liable for theft in its own right provided the jury found his conduct to be dishonest.

9 Fraudulent property offences

These offences concern situations where the defendant obtains something, usually property, by lying – described in the legislation as deception or fraud.

OBTAINING PROPERTY BY DECEPTION

This is the main fraudulent property offence. It is defined in s. 15 of the 1968 Act: 'A person who by any deception dishonestly obtains property belonging to another with the intention of permanently depriving the other of it, shall on conviction on indictment be liable to imprisonment for a term not exceeding ten years.'

Most of the elements of this offence have already been discussed when we looked at theft, and there is a clear overlap between these two offences.

▶ *Actus reus*

There are four elements: obtaining, property, belonging to another, and deception.

Obtaining

Section 15(2) provides: 'For the purposes of this section a person is to be treated as obtaining property if he obtains ownership, possession or control of it, and "obtain" includes obtaining for another or enabling another to obtain or retain.'

This concept of 'obtaining' serves a similar function to the idea of 'appropriation' in the law of theft. In the past, the main distinction between the two was that appropriation could not take place if the owner of the property consented, whereas obtaining could (in many fraud cases there will be consent, because the deception will be used to get the victim's consent). The decision in **Gomez** has abolished this distinction, and there

168

is now very little difference between the concepts of obtaining and appropriation. As a result, there is also less difference between a s. 15 offence and a theft, apart from the element of deception in the definition of the former. In practice where there is a s. 15 offence there will usually also be liability for a theft, though the reverse is not true because, of course, theft can be committed without deception.

Property

The definition of property for theft given in s. 4(1) of the 1968 Act also applies to this offence, though in this context property can include land, wild animals and plants.

Belonging to another

The definition here is also the same as for theft, and contained in s. 5(1) of the 1968 Act. The House of Lords has drawn attention to the fact that this requirement is not always satisfied where a 'thing in action' is transferred from the victim to the defendant. It handed down an extremely important judgment in **R** v **Preddy** (1996) which concerned three appeals that had been joined together as they raised the same legal issues. The appellants had been involved in mortgage frauds, which means that they had made applications for mortgages giving false information, for example, about their income or the value of the property they were seeking to purchase. The mortgage advances were paid by the lenders to the appellants by cheque, telegraphic transfer and the Clearing House Automated Payment System (CHAPS) – a computerized electronic transfer of funds. The House of Lords allowed their appeals. Lord Goff concluded that the debiting of a bank account and the corresponding crediting of another's bank account did not amount to an obtaining of property belonging to another. This was because the initial bank balance in the lender's account was a thing in action. This initial thing in action did not simply pass to the borrower. Instead, it was extinguished and a completely new thing in action was created that belonged to the borrower. The new property that the appellants had obtained was not the property that had belonged to the victim and therefore no property that had belonged to another had been obtained for the purposes of s. 15. This was true for all three modes of payment. The old case of **R** v **Danger** (1857) on this point was followed and that of **R** v **Duru** (1973) was overruled.

The Court of Appeal subsequently applied this approach to the law in **R** v **Graham** (1997). In that case the court commented that where the reasoning in **Preddy** was fatal to a conviction of obtaining property by deception, it was likely to be fatal on a conviction of theft as well. However, if one looks at the facts of **Preddy** there may well have been a theft committed in that very case: while s. 15 requires an obtaining, theft merely requires an appropriation, and appropriation is so broadly defined that it could include the extinguishing of property as to extinguish property is a right of the owner. The victim might also be treated in law as having an interest in the new 'thing in action'. This would be imposed by equity and is known as a constructive trust: **Westdeutsche Landesbank** *v* **Islington BC** (1996). Section 3(1) could then apply so that any later assumption of a right to the property by the defendant would amount to an appropriation for the purposes of theft and this would belong to the defendant because of the constructive trust (s. 5).

By deception

The property belonging to another must have been obtained by deception. Section 15(4) states: 'For the purposes of this section "deception" means any deception (whether deliberate or reckless) by words or conduct as to fact or as to law, including a deception as to the present intentions of the person using the deception or any other person.' The fact that the deception must be 'deliberate or reckless' relates to an issue of *mens rea* and will be discussed later.

Deception essentially means a lie, though this need not be in words; behaviour can also be deceptive. For example, if someone wearing a police uniform tells you to do something, they are, by implication, suggesting they are a police officer entitled to give you that order. If this is not true, the behaviour is a deception. The point is illustrated by the case of **R** *v* **Laverty** (1970). The defendant changed the number plates on a car and then sold it. It was held that there was an implied representation that the car was the original car to which those numbers had been assigned.

The issue of implied representations has been particularly important in relation to the use of cheques, cheque cards and credit cards. When you go into a shop and buy something, you do not usually say 'This is my credit card', or anything else about your entitlement to use the method of payment you present to the cashier; you simply hand over your card or write your cheque. If the card turns out to be stolen, or for some other reason you are not entitled to use it, you cannot be said to have '*told*' a lie, since you have said nothing; but can your behaviour be interpreted as a deception? The courts have decided that in such cases, the act of using one of these methods of payment can be said to imply two statements: that the person paying has an account with the relevant bank/credit card company; and that they are authorized to use the chequebook and/or card. If either of these representations is untrue, then there is a deception.

This interpretation of the law was first given in **Metropolitan Police Commissioner** *v* **Charles** (1977). Mr Charles's account was overdrawn, and he was told by his bank manager not to cash more than one cheque a day, and for no more than £30. That night Charles used his cheque card to back 25 cheques for £30 each at a casino. He was charged with the offence of obtaining a pecuniary advantage by deception under s. 16 of the 1968 Act (discussed below), which has the same definition of deception as the s. 15 offence. The House of Lords held that by using his chequebook and card, he was implying that he had an account with the bank, and was authorized to use the chequebook and card. As the second of these representations was false, because he did not have authority to cash so many cheques, his conviction was upheld.

In **R** *v* **Lambie** (1981), the House of Lords concluded that the same rules applied to the use of credit cards. Ms Lambie had a Barclaycard, and was authorized to use it up to a specified credit limit. Knowing she had already exceeded that limit, she used the card to buy more goods. She was charged with a deception offence (the particular offence has since been repealed but the case is still relevant on the issue of deception). The House of Lords considered that by using the card, she had made the two implied representations specified in **Charles**, and the second one was untrue because she did not have authority to use the card while she was over her credit limit; therefore she had committed a deception.

The prosecution must not only prove that there was a deception, but that property was obtained as a result of that deception. In **R** *v* **Laverty** (above), the conviction was quashed on the basis that while there had been a deception there was no evidence that the number plates had influenced the victim in buying the car, and therefore the defendant had not obtained the money for the car as a result of the deception. The defendant in **DPP** *v* **Ray** (1974) went to a restaurant initially intending to pay for the meal. Having finished his food he then dishonestly decided to leave without paying. He waited until the waiter had left the dining room and then ran off. The House of Lords ruled that the waiter was induced to leave the room by the defendant's implied representation that he was an honest customer intending to pay his bill.

Property cannot be obtained by deception if the deception occurs after the obtaining. In **R** *v* **Collis-Smith** (1971) petrol was put into the defendant's car. He then falsely stated that he was using the car for business purposes and that his firm would pay on account. He was originally convicted of obtaining the petrol by deception under s. 15, but on appeal his conviction was quashed. The petrol had already been obtained before he said his company would pay and therefore the obtaining was not brought about by the deception. A case with almost identical facts, **R** *v* **Coady**, arose in 1996 and the Court of Appeal reached the same conclusion that the defendant was not liable under s. 15 as there was no evidence of an obtaining prior to the deception.

In **R** *v* **Rozeik** (1996) the Court of Appeal considered how far a company could be deceived for the purposes of s. 15 if one of its employees was not so deceived. The appellant had been convicted of obtaining cheques by deception from finance companies. The deception involved in the provision of false information about equipment acquired by him under hire purchase agreements. The branch managers of the finance companies may have been aware of the falsity of the information when they signed some of the cheques to the defendant. On appeal the appellant argued that the finance companies were not deceived if these employees had not been deceived. The appeal was allowed. The Court of Appeal stated that a company was fixed with the knowledge acquired by one of its employees only if the employee had its authority to act in relation to the particular transaction in question. On the facts of this case the employees with such authority were those who signed the cheques, not simply those who typed them out or delivered them. It did not matter how many other employees were deceived. On the other hand, if an employee was a party to the fraud they could not be acting with the company's authority, so their knowledge would not prevent the company from being deceived. On the facts the company had not been deceived as the branch managers had authority to carry out the transaction, knew of the deception and (surprisingly) it had not been shown that they were a party to the fraud.

▶ Mens rea

There are three elements: deliberate or reckless deception, dishonesty, and intention permanently to deprive.

Deliberate or reckless deception

It was thought that **Cunningham** recklessness was applied here, with the prosecution having to prove the defendant was aware they might be lying. Following **R** *v* **Goldman** (1997) **Caldwell** recklessness may be applied.

Dishonesty

The definition of dishonesty is found in the common law test laid down in **Ghosh**. The provisions of s. 2(1) on dishonesty in theft do not apply here.

Intention permanently to deprive

The provisions of s. 6 apply, with all references to 'appropriating' being substituted with the phrase 'obtaining by deception'.

OBTAINING A MONEY TRANSFER BY DECEPTION

This offence was created by the Theft (Amendment) Act 1996 following concerns raised by the House of Lords judgment of **R** *v* **Preddy** and implementing proposals made by the Law Commission in its report *Offences of Dishonesty: Money Transfers* (1996).

Following **R** *v* **Preddy** there can be no offence under s. 15 where money is transferred from one account to another. Section 1 of the 1996 Act inserts section 15A into the 1968 Act so that this situation can fall within the new offence of obtaining a money transfer by deception. The offence applies to payments made by cheques and electronic transfer, by deception. It is immaterial whether any of the accounts are overdrawn before or after the money transfer is effected.

OBTAINING A PECUNIARY ADVANTAGE BY DECEPTION

This offence is contained in s. 16 of the 1978 Act: 'A person who by any deception dishonestly obtains for himself or another any pecuniary advantage shall on conviction on indictment be liable to imprisonment for a term not exceeding five years.'

The offence is similar to s. 15, obtaining property by deception, except that a pecuniary advantage must have been obtained rather than property.

▶ *Actus reus*

There are three elements: obtaining, a pecuniary advantage, and deception. Obtaining and deception have the same meaning as when they are used in the s. 15 offence. The only new element is the concept of a pecuniary advantage, which is narrowly defined in s. 16(2)(b) and (c):

(2) the cases in which a pecuniary advantage within the meaning of this section is to be regarded as obtained for a person are cases where—
(b) [the defendant] is allowed to borrow by way of overdraft, or to take out any policy of insurance or annuity contract, or obtains an improvement of the terms on which he is allowed to do so; or
(c) he is given the opportunity to earn remuneration or greater remuneration in an office or employment, or to win money by betting.

The 1968 Act originally contained a subsection 16(2)(a), but this proved too complex and was repealed and replaced by provisions in the 1978 Act, to be discussed later.

Provided that the above criteria are met, the defendant need not actually gain any financial advantage from the deception. So if, for example, someone used a deception to gain the opportunity to win money by betting, but in fact does not win on the bet, the offence may still have been committed – **DPP** *v* **Turner** (1974).

The different transactions covered by the offence (overdrafts, insurance policies, annuity contracts, an opportunity to earn remuneration or to win money by betting) have little in common with each other; they are collected together under one offence mainly for reasons of convenience, and because they are all areas which have caused problems in imposing liability in the past. **Metropolitan Police Commissioner** *v* **Charles** is an example of s. 16(2)(b), as Charles was charged and convicted for obtaining the pecuniary advantage of an overdraft by deception.

▶ Mens rea

There are two elements: deliberate or reckless deception and dishonesty. Both are defined as for the s. 15 offence. In **R** *v* **Clarke** (1996) the defendant was a private investigator who falsely told a group of potential clients that he was a former fraud squad officer and a court bailiff. In the light of these false representations he was employed to trace funds which the group had lost through a fraud. The judge indicated that he intended to direct the jury that the defendant would be guilty of the s. 16 offence if he made the representations, they were false, and they were the reason why he was employed by the clients: he would thereby have obtained a pecuniary advantage, namely the opportunity to earn remuneration for employment through deception. In the light of this indication the defendant changed his plea to guilty. He then appealed arguing that the issue of dishonesty had effectively been withdrawn from the jury. A person is not automatically dishonest because they lied. The jury should have been directed that in deciding whether he was dishonest, they must consider the defendant's submission that he believed he was able to do the work, intended to do so, and went ahead and did it.

There is no need to prove an intention permanently to deprive for this offence.

▶ Sentence

The maximum sentence is five years' imprisonment.

•
OBTAINING SERVICES BY DECEPTION

This is the first of the fraud offences contained in the Theft Act 1978, and is defined in s. 1 of that Act: 'A person who by any deception dishonestly obtains services from another shall be guilty of an offence.'

It is very similar to the s. 15 offence, except that services are obtained rather than property. An example of the type of situation at which it is aimed would be where someone takes their car to a garage to be repaired, stating (untruthfully) that their company will be paying the bill.

▶ Actus reus

There are three elements: obtaining, a service and deception. Obtaining and deception have the same meaning as for the s. 15 offence, and the only new element is the concept of a service. This is defined very broadly by s. 1(2) of the 1978 Act: 'It is an obtaining of services where the other is induced to confer a benefit by doing some act, or causing or permitting some act to be done, on the understanding that the benefit has been or will be paid for.'

The definition is therefore wider than the everyday meaning of services, and there is often an overlap between this offence and other offences such as s. 15. The Court of Appeal in **R** *v* **Shortland** (1995) emphasized the need for evidence that there is an understanding that the service has been or will be paid for: the obtaining of a free service is not sufficient. Shortland had opened two bank accounts using false names. No evidence had been provided at the trial of an understanding as to payment so the appeal was allowed, for this could not just be assumed as the trial judge had suggested.

It was held in **R** *v* **Halai** (1983) that a mortgage advance could not be described as a service. This judgment was heavily criticized. For example, the Lord Chief Justice stated in **R** *v* **Graham** (1997) that the decision in **Halai** 'has lain like a sunken wreck impeding navigation but difficult, laborious and expensive to remove'. **R** *v* **Halai** was subsequently overruled by the Court of Appeal in **R** *v* **Cooke** (1997). Cooke had been convicted of obtaining property by deception contrary to s. 15 arising from a series of fraudulent mortgage applications. On appeal the Crown conceded that these convictions could no longer stand in the light of **R** *v* **Preddy**. Instead they submitted that the convictions should be substituted with alternative offences, including s. 1 of the Theft Act 1978. The Court accepted this submission and ruled that **R** *v* **Halai** should no longer be followed. The wording of s. 1(2) of the Theft Act was apt to cover inducement of a financial institution to advance money since it was expected that payment would be made in the form of interest charges, an arrangement fee or both.

The Theft (Amendment) Act 1996 has now added a new subsection (3) to section 1 of the 1978 Act. This makes it clear that services for the purpose of s. 1 include loans where there is an understanding that the loan will be or has been paid for, whether by way of interest or otherwise. There is therefore no longer any doubt that **R** *v* **Halai** is bad law.

▶ Mens rea

The two elements of *mens rea*, deliberate or reckless deception and dishonesty, are both defined as for the s. 15 offence. Like the s. 16 offence, there is no need to prove an intention permanently to deprive.

▶ Sentence

The maximum sentence is five years' imprisonment.

• •

EVASION OF LIABILITY BY DECEPTION

This description applies to three offences defined in s. 2 of the Theft Act 1978, all of which are concerned with dishonest debtors. The subject was previously covered by s. 16(2)(a) (mentioned above), which was repealed and replaced by this section as the previous law had got into a very confused and unsatisfactory state. Section 2 has proved problematic in its turn, and the continuing difficulties call into question whether this is an area that the criminal law should cover at all, given that there are civil remedies available in this context.

▶ Remission

The first offence, defined in s. 2(1)(a), states that a person commits an offence if he or she 'dishonestly secures the remission of the whole or part of any existing liability to make payment whether his own liability or another's'. It concerns the situation where a victim knows that they are owed something but, as a result of deception by the defendant, agrees to let the defendant off repayment. For example, a person who owes a friend £100 might lie about losing his or her job to avoid paying the money back.

Actus reus

There are three elements: a debt, remission of the debt, and deception. The debt must be a legally enforceable one. Use of a stolen credit card has been held to be securing remission of a debt. In **Jackson** (1983), the defendant paid for petrol with a stolen credit card, which meant that the garage would then look to the credit card company for payment, rather than to Jackson. Deception has the same meaning as for s. 15.

Mens rea

The two elements, deliberate or reckless deception and dishonesty, have the same meaning as in s. 15.

▶ Wait for or forgo

The second offence, s. 2(1)(b), applies when the defendant uses deception to make someone 'wait for or forgo payment' of a debt.

Actus reus

There are three elements: a debt, inducing another to wait for or forgo payment, and deception. Deception has the same meaning as for the s. 15 offence.

There has been a certain amount of debate as to the difference between a 'remission' and a 'forgoing'. It seems that, whereas for a remission, the victim knows of the debt and consciously agrees to let the defendant off payment, when forgoing, the creditor does not know they are owed anything, or does not agree to let the defendant off the debt. For example, in **R** *v* **Holt** (1981) the defendant dined in a restaurant, and when asked to pay, said he had already paid another waiter. The restaurant was thereby induced to forgo payment of the debt owed for the meal because they did not know that it was still owing.

Writing a dud cheque counts as making someone wait for payment due to s. 2(3) of the 1978 Act.

Mens rea

The three elements, deliberate or reckless deception, dishonesty and intention permanently to deprive are defined as for the s. 15 offence.

▶ Exemption or abatement of liability

The third offence, s. 2(1)(c), covers situations where a defendant avoids payment of an existing or future debt ('exemption') or gets the amount of the debt reduced ('abatement'). Unlike the two previous offences, in this case the debt need not have actually been in existence at the time of the offence. An example might be where a person lies about his or her income in order to make themselves liable for a lower rate of income tax.

Actus reus

There are three elements: an existing or future debt, an exemption or abatement of liability and deception. Section 15(4) provides the definition of deception.

Mens rea

The two elements, deliberate or reckless deception and dishonesty, have the same meaning that they have in s. 15.

▶ Sentence

All three offences have a maximum sentence of five years.

• •

MAKING OFF WITHOUT PAYMENT

This crime is defined in s. 3(1) of the Theft Act 1978: 'Subject to subsection (3) below, a person who, knowing that payment on the spot for any goods supplied or service done is required or expected from him, dishonestly makes off without having paid as required or expected and with intent to avoid payment of the amount due shall be guilty of an offence.'

An obvious example of this offence occurs where a defendant sits down to a restaurant meal and then leaves without paying the bill, but it could also cover, among other things, putting petrol in a car and then driving off without paying, or even having a haircut and refusing to pay afterwards. It is a useful offence for prosecutors because there is no need to prove deception nor that property belonged to another at the time that it was obtained.

▶ *Actus reus*

There are three elements: goods supplied or service done, making off from the spot, and failure to pay as required or expected.

Goods supplied or service done

The Act does not define either of these, and they are therefore to be given their ordinary, everyday meaning, influenced by similar concepts elsewhere in the Theft Acts.

Makes off from the spot

R *v* **Brooks and Brooks** (1983) observes that 'to make off' simply means 'to depart'; there is no need for the person to have run away. Where exactly 'the spot' is will depend on the particular facts of the case. In **R** *v* **McDavitt** (1981), where the defendant left a restaurant without paying, 'the spot' was regarded as being the restaurant itself, so the defendant was only liable for an attempt to make off without payment, because he was stopped as he reached the door. On the other hand, in **Brooks and Brooks**, 'the spot' was treated as being the 'spot where payment is required', which would normally be the cash register. It is not clear which authority will be preferred in the future.

Fails to pay on the spot as required or expected

The offence can only take place if the defendant makes off at or after the point where payment is required or expected. In **Troughton** *v* **The Metropolitan Police** (1987), the defendant was drunk. He got into a taxi and asked the driver to take him home, which he said was somewhere in Highbury. When the taxi reached Highbury, the defendant failed to give more precise directions so the driver drove to the police station. The man then tried to leave and he was charged with making off without payment. His conviction was quashed by the Court of Appeal on the basis that as the driver had not completed his part of the contract by taking the man home, payment was not yet required at the point when the defendant tried to make off.

▶ *Mens rea*

There are three elements: knowing that payment on the spot was required or expected, dishonesty and intention permanently to avoid payment.

Knowledge that payment on the spot is required or expected

There must be some obvious indication that payment on the spot is required or expected – either a specific statement, or a well-known practice, such as the tradition of paying for taxi rides, haircuts and restaurant meals once those services are finished. In **Troughton** *v* **The Metropolitan Police** it could also have been argued that the defendant did not know that payment on the spot was required, since this would usually only be the case when the destination was reached.

Intention to avoid payment permanently

Section 3 does not state that there must be an intention to avoid payment permanently, but this requirement was implied by the House of Lords in **R** *v* **Allen** (1985). In that case the appellant left a hotel without paying his bill. He argued that he was prevented from paying by temporary financial difficulties, and intended to pay as soon as he received the proceeds from a certain business venture. The trial judge said that this argument was in law irrelevant, but the House of Lords accepted that it was relevant, because the prosecution had to prove an intention to avoid payment permanently. The issue should therefore have been left to the jury and the conviction was quashed.

Dishonesty

This is defined by the common law test laid down in **Ghosh**.

▶ **Sentence**

Being regarded as a relatively minor offence, it carries a maximum sentence of only two years.

▶ **Problems with the Theft Acts**

As was observed at the start of Chapter 8, the 1968 Theft Act was created because the previous law on the property offences was complex and confused. It had developed in a piecemeal way, and in many cases the law was stretched to fit behaviour which the courts perceived as dishonest, leading to a mass of fine distinctions and overlapping offences. The 1968 Act was designed to be a completely new start, bringing together all the relevant law in a clear, accessible mini-code.

Unfortunately, this ambitious aim was not fulfilled. One area of the Act, s. 16, which covered certain deception offences, was so obscure and difficult to use that just four years after the Act was passed, the Criminal Law Revision Committee (CLRC) was asked to look at amending it. There were also clear gaps in the coverage of the Act. The 1978 legislation was passed to remedy both problems, repealing the troublesome part of s. 16, and creating the new deception offences of obtaining services by deception, evasion of liability by deception, and making off without payment.

More recently problems with the legislation have been highlighted by the House of Lords judgment in **R** *v* **Preddy** (1996). While some of the difficulties arising from this case have been dealt with by the Theft (Amendment) Act 1996, some problems still remain and the Theft Acts still fall short of the high hopes that were held for them. There are now twice the number of fraud offences and the area of law still raises major problems of interpretation and application. Professor J.C. Smith, an expert on the law of theft who attended CLRC meetings during its work on the proposed 1968 Act, has commented that the difficulties have been partly due to poor prosecuting decisions, and, in particular, to charging defendants with theft when it was clear that a s. 15 offence would have been more appropriate. Compounding the problem is the reluctance of the courts in such cases to acquit a person who has acted dishonestly, even though the facts do not quite fit the legal pigeonhole that would establish liability. One result of this has been the problems with 'appropriation', where the courts have tended to adopt whatever interpretation would lead to the conviction of the dishonest defendant, even though that might lead to difficult precedents. An example of this tendency is the issue of appropriation where the owner has consented to the conduct of the accused, as seen in **Lawrence**, **Morris** and **Gomez**. In all three cases, a deception offence would have been a more appropriate charge, and the decision to charge theft instead left the courts with the unpalatable choice of acquitting defendants who were clearly guilty of dishonest behaviour, or stretching the concept of appropriation to fit the facts, and creating problematic precedents in the process.

In interpreting the Acts, the courts have tried to give words their ordinary everyday meaning, in order to steer clear of unnecessary technicality. This is not a problem in itself – in fact it seems sensible – but it has led in practice to a tendency to leave the interpretation of terms used in the Acts to juries, which can lead to a lack of consistency. It is hard to ensure that like cases are treated alike when juries are given such a large degree of discretion.

Professor Smith also points out a difficulty which perhaps no Theft Act, however carefully drawn, could eliminate. This is the fact that legislation delimiting the property offences is necessarily concerned with the civil law of property; you cannot define stealing unless you can define what is or is not yours to take. The civil law in the field is complicated – not because it is badly drawn, but because the issues themselves are complex. It is this difficulty which is partly responsible for some of the problems with appropriation, the difficulties highlighted in **Preddy** and the intricacies found in s. 2 of the 1978 Act (evasion of liability by deception). The latter offences also raise the question of whether, given the mass of civil law in the area of debt, it is actually necessary for the criminal law to intervene.

The implications of these problems extend further than just the Theft Acts. For some time, there has been an intention to codify the whole of the criminal law, though little progress has been made. Given the difficulties which remained after the limited codification of the Theft Acts, it might be concluded that the criminal law may simply be unsuitable for such a process.

▶ Reform

In 1999 the Law Commission published a consultation paper making proposals to simplify and clarify the law in relation to fraud and in particular credit card fraud. It considers that the current law is difficult to prosecute in practice. But it has provisionally rejected a single offence of 'dishonesty' partly because it is uncertain whether this would be too loosely drafted to satisfy the European Convention on Human Rights. It has also rejected the idea of a general deception offence. It makes several proposals, including that there should be an offence of depriving someone of property, irrespective of whether anyone else obtains it. In an effort to bring the law up to date with technological changes and the development of the Internet, reforms are suggested to make sure that liability for obtaining a service by deception can be imposed where a machine is deceived. Finally, it proposes that the requirement of a 'representation' being made before finding a deception offence proved should also be scrapped.

▶ White-collar crime

Fraud offences have given rise to some controversy because of the different response to the problem of fraud compared with non-fraudulent property offences. Some have argued that fraud is a 'white-collar crime', that it tends to be carried out by middle or upper class professionals and is therefore dealt with more leniently than other property offences, despite the huge sums that are often involved. The Fraud Advisory Panel, set up by the private sector to assist the government in dealing with fraud, has observed that fraud often takes place within commercial businesses and these companies tend to prefer not to report this conduct to the police. The reasons for this are varied. The company may simply be embarrassed and prefer to deal with the issue behind the scenes. It may fear damaging the company's reputation and a resulting loss of clients and profit. It may not have a clear idea as to what constitutes criminal fraud. The management may feel there is no benefit for the company of reporting the fraud as the amount of employee time and effort required to establish that a crime has been committed would be disproportionate to the perceived benefits. Or the senior management might themselves have been involved in the fraud and it may not have been detected.

Because much of this fraud is unreported it is difficult to assess the extent of the problem in the UK. Police and private sector estimates vary from £400m to £5bn a year. The Association of British Insurers puts the total at nearer £16bn. As the Fraud Advisory Panel notes: 'It is difficult to know what level of resources to devote to fighting the problem of fraud, without some sense of the scale and nature of the problem.' As much of the offending activity does not come to the attention of the police the deterrent effect of any existing legislation, or proposed changes, may be lost or at least not well targeted.

•
ANSWERING QUESTIONS

Property offences are popular subjects for problem questions and, when answering these, you should note that a lot of these offences now overlap. That means it is not sufficient to pull out the most obvious offence that has been committed; you need to discuss the whole range of possible offences, while allocating more time to the ones that fit the facts most closely. In particular, if you believe that an offence has been committed under s. 15 of the Theft Act 1968, in the light of **Gomez** it is also likely that theft has been committed. Bear in mind that wherever, on the facts, there has been some kind of deception or lie you will usually need to consider s. 15 and some of the fraud offences contained in the 1978 Act.

1 T orders a taxi to take him to the railway station. What offences, if any, does T commit in the following separate situations:
(a) T resolves not to pay before ordering the taxi. The journey is completed and T does not pay *(10 marks)*;
(b) T falsely tells the driver during the journey that he is unemployed and homeless. The driver feels sorry for him and does not require payment *(15 marks)*;
(c) at the end of the journey T threatens to assault the driver and takes £50 from the driver's wallet *(10 marks)*;
(d) at the end of the journey T discovers he has left his money at home. Too embarrassed to explain, he runs away from the taxi intending to trace and pay the driver later *(15 marks)*. Oxford

Part (a): the main offence here is obtaining services by deception under s. 1 of the 1978 Act. Making off without payment under s. 3 of the 1978 Act could be discussed more briefly. Theft and s. 15 are only relevant if you can pinpoint some property that has been appropriated/obtained; the only such property here would be the petrol the taxi-driver uses, and given the existence of a deception, the Crown Prosecution Service are unlikely to pursue this approach. Section 16 is not relevant because of the narrow definition of a 'pecuniary advantage'.

Part (b): the most relevant offence is s. 2(1)(a), as the driver knew that a debt was owing but agreed because of the deception to let T off. Section 1 of the 1978 Act was relevant in relation to the driving (services) after the false hard-luck story had been told. Again making off without payment may be possible though this will depend on whether the courts are prepared to include within this offence people who depart by making a fraudulent representation.

Part (c): the main offence to consider is robbery because of the threat of force. You could also discuss assault and theft.

Part (d): the most appropriate offence on these facts is making off without payment. On the issue of T's intention to pay later, the case of **Allen** is particularly important.

2 Charles steals a video recorder and puts it in his garage. Three days later he offers to sell it to Bernard, who owns a shop selling used electrical equipment. Bernard bought a video recorder from Charles two weeks ago, and thinks it is possible that this second one might have been stolen, especially since Charles does not have the remote-control unit belonging to the recorder. However, it is a high-specification machine, and Bernard knows that he can make a good profit on it if he gives Charles £75. Bernard asks no further questions, and buys it for £75. Bernard, who is disabled, asks Charles to place it in a prominent position in the shop window. Charles does so.

Five days later John, from whom the video had been stolen, notices the machine in Bernard's shop. He examines it closely and is almost certain that it is his video because of a small but distinctive blemish on the casing. John's insurance company has already agreed to settle his claim for the theft for a sum which will allow John to buy the latest, improved model. He decides that he will not raise the matter with Bernard. Later that day a police officer telephones John to tell him that they still have no news about his stolen property, and asks whether John has any further information about the theft. As John does not wish the arrangement with the insurance company to be jeopardized he does not tell the policeman that he believes he has seen the video recorder in Bernard's shop. Two days later John receives a cheque from his insurance company for the agreed sum of £550.

Consider the criminal liability, if any, of Charles (for any offence other than theft), Bernard and John. Include in your answer your assessment of how appropriate the law is in these factual circumstances. *NEAB*

Normally for a problem question your main goal is to apply the law correctly. However, you are specifically asked to assess how appropriate the law is in this situation as well as applying the law. You could do this at the same time as applying the law or you could deal with this as a second part to your answer.

You should consider the possible liability of each defendant in turn. Looking first at Bernard, you could consider his liability for handling. The issue of *mens rea* will be particularly important. The offence is committed when the defendant handles goods 'knowing or believing them to be stolen goods'. Wilful blindness can be sufficient, that is to say where the defendant has every opportunity to know something but chooses not to.

As regards Charles, when he sells the video recorder to Bernard and places it in the window he might fall within handling. You would need to discuss in particular the fact that the handling must be 'otherwise than in the course of stealing'.

In looking at handling and how appropriate the law is you could consider whether it is defined too broadly. We have seen that there are currently eighteen different ways that it can be carried out. It includes 'assisting' – which would describe Charles's conduct when he placed the video recorder in the window – but this would be an offence anyway under the principles of secondary participation (discussed in Chapter 11).

In relation to the insurance money, you need to consider the implications of the case of **Preddy** for liability under s. 15 of the 1968 Act. The deception could be John's failure to tell the police that he has seen the video. You could also consider the issue of obtaining services by deception as the insurance company will have to do acts on the understanding that they will be paid for as a result of the deception.

The concept of services is particularly open to criticism because of its very broad definition so that it includes situations that would not be viewed in everyday language as a 'service'. You could criticize the complexity of the deception law in general and the confusion that has arisen with some of the case law, leading to the Theft (Amendment) Act 1996.

3 **Explain, illustrate and comment on what is meant by appropriation in the law of theft.** *NEAB*

You could start this essay by pointing out that appropriation is an essential element of the *actus reus* of theft, and give a brief definition of what is meant by it. Point out that the most obvious type of appropriation is simply taking something away, but that appropriation is wider than this. This is the 'explain' part of the question.

Then you need to 'illustrate' what is meant by appropriation. Give some examples from case law, such as label switching.

In order to 'comment' on the law in this field you could then go on to discuss some of the refinements that have been made to the definition, including the fact that it need not be an assumption of all rights of the owner – one will suffice (**Morris**); and the issue of consent (**Lawrence**, **Morris** and **Gomez**). Since **Gomez** has made such an important change to the law, you might spend some time considering its effect.

4 **O found a ring in the street one day when he was walking to work. He decided to keep it and had just picked it up and was about to put it in his pocket when R ran past and snatched it from him. O was so angry about this that he went up to the next person he saw, who happened to be S, and shouted very loudly in her ear, causing her to jump backwards, trip and twist her ankle. This left her with a painful bruise. He then went to a coffee bar where he ordered a cup of coffee and a piece of cake. After he had been served, he realized that he had not brought any money out with him. When he had finished the coffee and cake, he ordered more coffee and told the cashier that he was just going to buy a newspaper from the shop next door and would return immediately. As soon as he was outside, he walked away rapidly. Having borrowed some money from a colleague at lunch time, he went to a bar and drank four pints of beer in fifteen minutes. When he left the bar, he took a briefcase which looked very much like his own, forgetting that his own was at work, and kissed a customer who violently objected but whom he was convinced was an old friend.**

Are O and R guilty of any offences? Would O be able successfully to plead any defences? *London*

We will consider the liability of O first of all and then the liability of R. The first issue is whether O could be liable for theft of the ring. When he picked up the ring this could amount to an appropriation regardless of the fact that he had not put it in his pocket: he had taken possession of the ring – even though only momentarily – which is an assumption of the right of an owner. A critical issue will be whether O had the *mens rea* of theft. Section 2(1)(c) of the Theft Act 1968 is particularly relevant here as it states that a person is not dishonest

'. . . if he appropriates the property in the belief that the person to whom the property belongs cannot be discovered by taking reasonable steps'. The nature of the ring, where and when it was found and how long it might have been there will all be relevant in examining this issue. We are told that he had decided to keep it. If he thought the ring had been abandoned by its original owner then he would have no intention of permanently depriving this owner; if he just thinks it has been lost by its owner then he does have an intention to deprive permanently.

When O shouts very loudly in S's ear this could probably be an assault. We saw at p. 102 that it looks increasingly likely that an assault can be committed by words alone, though it would need to be shown that S feared immediate personal injury and that O intended her to do so, or was reckless as to her doing so. On hearing O's shout, S jumped backwards, tripped and twisted her ankle. If there has been an assault, O could be liable for an offence under s. 47 OAPA as his assault caused the actual bodily harm. The case of **R v Roberts** could be considered on this issue.

When O went to a coffee bar and ordered a cake and coffee no property offence was committed initially because he had behaved honestly, believing that he had the money to pay and intending to pay. When he subsequently ate the cake and coffee, while it could be said that he had the *mens rea* of the offence, he probably lacked the *actus reus* as the food and drink probably already belonged to him. When he ordered more coffee and left without paying he could be liable for the offences of making off without payment, obtaining property by deception and obtaining services by deception. The conduct also amounted to an evasion of liability by deception under s. 2(1)(b) of the Theft Act 1978 as his deception induced the cashier to delay payment. The deception was either the lie that he was just popping out to buy a paper, or alternatively the false representation that he was going to pay for the second coffee.

In relation to the briefcase the relevant offence is theft. He would argue that he was not dishonest as he believed the briefcase to be his own and that he had no intention to permanently deprive anyone. If he made these mistakes because of his intoxication then you need to look at this defence which is considered at p. 255. The kiss was potentially a battery and again the defence of intoxication would need to be considered.

As regards R's liability, he could be liable for theft as the ring will be treated as belonging to O who had possession for the purposes of this offence.

10 Inchoate offences

The inchoate offences – attempt, conspiracy and incitement – are concerned with the preparatory stages of other criminal offences. A person may be convicted of an inchoate offence even if the main offence was never actually committed: in some circumstances he or she may be guilty of an inchoate offence even if it would for some reason have been impossible to commit the complete offence. Where a person is convicted of an inchoate offence and the full offence has actually been committed, they may also be liable as a principal or a secondary party to the full crime.

One of the reasons for the existence of inchoate offences is that without them the police would often have to choose between preventing an offence being committed, and prosecuting the offender – it would be ridiculous, for example, if they knew a bank robbery was being planned, and had to stand by and wait until it was finished before the robbers could be punished for any offence. In addition, the person would have had the *mens rea* for the commission of the offence, and it may often merely be bad luck that he or she did not complete the crime – for example, if a planned bank robbery did not take place because the robbers' car broke down on the way to it.

All the inchoate offences are offences in their own right, but they can only be charged in connection with another offence (which from now on we shall call the main offence), so a person would be charged with incitement to rob, or attempted murder, or conspiracy to blackmail, but not with 'attempt', 'conspiracy' or 'incitement' alone.

ATTEMPT

The criminal law does not punish people just for intending to commit a crime, but it recognizes that conduct aimed at committing an offence may be just as blameworthy if it fails to achieve its purpose as if it had been successful – the person who tries to kill someone but for some reason fails is as morally guilty as someone who succeeds in killing, and possibly just as dangerous.

The difficulty for the law on attempts is to determine where to draw the line – how far does someone have to go towards committing an offence before his or her acts become criminal? Over the years the common law proposed various tests to answer this question, but all have been problematic. Consequently, much of the common law was replaced by the Criminal Attempts Act 1981, which laid down statutory rules instead.

▶ *Actus reus*

Section 1(1) of the Criminal Attempts Act 1981 provides that: 'If with intent to commit an offence to which this section applies, a person does an act which is more than merely preparatory to the commission of the offence, he is guilty of attempting to commit the offence.'

The question of whether an act is 'more than merely preparatory' is a matter of fact and, in a trial on indictment, will be for the jury to decide. The judge must consider whether there is enough evidence to leave this question to the jury, but s. 4(3) of the Act states that, the judge having concluded that there is, the issue should be left completely to the jury.

What the jury have to ask themselves is whether the accused was simply preparing to commit the offence or whether the accused had done something that was more than merely preparatory to the commission of the offence. Clearly, there will be many cases where it is difficult to prove that the accused has crossed this line. In **Campbell** (1991) the accused was arrested by police within a yard of the door of a post office, carrying a threatening note and a fake gun. He admitted that he had originally planned to rob the post office, but said he had changed his mind and was going back to his motorbike when he was arrested. His conviction for attempted robbery was quashed because, rather surprisingly, it was held that there was no evidence on which a jury could safely find that his acts were more than merely preparatory to committing the offence.

Similarly, in **Gullefer** (1987), the accused had backed a greyhound and, once the race was started, it became clear that the dog would probably lose. The accused thought that by disrupting the race, so that it would be declared null and void, he would get his stake money back, so he ran on to the track. The Court of Appeal held that there was no evidence that this act was more than merely preparatory, as the accused had clearly not started on 'the crime proper' – the offence consisted not of stopping the race, but of using that disruption to get his money back, and he had not yet started to get that money back.

Attempting the impossible

Before the Criminal Attempts Act 1981, impossibility was a defence to a charge of attempts – **Haughton** *v* **Smith** (1975) – which effectively meant that if an accused reached into someone's bag, intending to steal a purse, but found no purse in there, they were not guilty of attempted theft.

Many commentators found this ridiculous, and now s. 1(2) of the Act states: 'A person may be guilty of attempting to commit an offence to which this section applies even though the facts are such that the commission of the offence is impossible.'

Though generally viewed as more sensible than the position prior to the Act, this concept has caused some problems for the courts. In **Anderton v Ryan** (1985), the defendant bought what she thought was a stolen video recorder, and then went and confessed as much to the police. She was charged with, among other things, attempted handling of stolen goods, but when the evidence was examined, there was no proof that the video recorder had in fact been stolen. The Divisional Court held that the Act indicated that although the facts meant it was impossible for the full offence to have been committed, this was not a defence to the charge of attempted handling. The House of Lords reversed the decision, which they considered absurd, and the conviction was quashed, thus rendering impossibility a defence despite the apparently clear wording of the Act.

However, their Lordships swiftly (by legal standards) overruled their own decision. In **Shivpuri** (1987), the accused was arrested by customs officers and confessed that there was heroin in his luggage. After forensic analysis, it transpired that in fact the substance was only harmless ground vegetable leaves, but Shivpuri was nevertheless convicted of attempting to be knowingly concerned in dealing with a controlled drug. The House of Lords held that on an accurate construction of s. 1(1) of the Criminal Attempts Act 1981 **Shivpuri** was guilty. Lord Bridge, who had also been a judge in **Anderton v Ryan**, admitted that he had got the law wrong in that case. He said that if the accused intended to commit the offence he was charged with attempting, and had done an act that was more than merely preparatory to committing the intended offence, he was guilty of attempt, even if the offence would be factually or legally impossible for any reason. It was stated that **Anderton v Ryan** had been wrongly decided.

As a result of **Shivpuri** a criminal attempt would be committed if Ann put her hand into a pocket intending to steal whatever was in there, but found it empty; or when Ben stabbed Chris intending to kill him not knowing that he had already died of a heart attack.

The only case in which impossibility can now be a defence is where the accused attempts to commit what they think is an offence, but which actually is not against the law. In **Taaffe** (1984), the accused imported foreign currency into the UK, believing it to be a crime. In fact it is not against the law, so although Taaffe was in his own mind attempting to commit an offence, he could not be liable.

▶ Mens rea

The Criminal Attempts Act 1981 specifies that intention is required to commit this offence. Case law has made it clear that an accused can only be liable for an attempt if they act with the intention of committing the complete offence – recklessness as to the consequences of the act is not enough. This means that, even if the offence attempted can be committed recklessly, there will be no liability for attempt unless intent is established – for example, for most non-fatal offences against the person, reckless-ness is sufficient *mens rea*, but it is not enough for a charge of attempting to commit any of them.

In attempted murder, the only intention that suffices for liability is an intent to kill; despite the fact that intention to cause grievous bodily harm is a sufficient *mens rea* for the full offence of murder, for an attempt you must intend to commit the complete offence, and the complete offence of murder requires the killing of a human being. In **Whybrow** (1951), the accused was convicted of the attempted murder of his wife. He had wired up a soap dish to the mains electricity supply, with the result that she received an electric shock while in the bath. Whybrow claimed that in fact that wiring arrangement had been designed to pro-vide an earth for a wireless set he kept in his bedroom, so any electric shock received by his wife had been purely accidental. The Court of Appeal reaffirmed that to be liable for attempted murder, the accused must have intended to kill. On the facts the conviction was upheld, as the jury had clearly not believed his explanation.

Where the definition of the main offence includes circumstances, and recklessness as to these circumstances is sufficient for that aspect of the *mens rea*, then it will also be sufficient for an attempt to commit that offence (though intention will still be required for the rest of the *mens rea*). For example, liability for the main offence of rape is imposed if a man intends to have sexual intercourse with a man or a woman knowing that they are not consenting, or being reckless as to whether or not they are consent-ing. With attempted rape the absence of the victim's consent is viewed as a circumstance of the offence; so long as the accused intends to have unlawful intercourse, it will suffice that he is reckless as to the fact that the victim may not be consenting – he does not have to know for certain that there is no consent. Thus in **Khan and others** (1990), a 16-year-old girl left a disco with five youths, going with them in a car to a house, where they were joined by other youths. Three of them had sexual intercourse with the girl without her consent, and four others, the appellants, tried to do so but failed. The four were convicted of attempted rape, and appealed, contending that the judge had misdirected the jury by telling them that a man who intended to have sexual intercourse with a woman (the result of the crime) and did not know she was not consenting, but was reckless about whether she was or not, and nevertheless attempted to have inter-course with her, was guilty of attempted rape. The Court of Appeal held that this direction was correct, and the convictions were upheld.

The point was confirmed in the case of **Attorney-General's Reference (No. 3 of 1992)**. The defendant had been charged with attempting to commit aggravated arson. This offence essentially consists of intentionally or recklessly causing damage to property by fire with the intention of endangering life or being reckless as to whether life was endangered. The Court of Appeal stated that to attempt this offence the defendant must have intended the criminal damage by fire, but endangering life was merely a circumstance of this crime and so recklessness as to that issue was sufficient. A problem with this concept is that it is difficult to predict what elements of an offence will be treated as a mere circumstance, and in fact s. 1(1) of the 1981 Act makes no reference to recklessness, referring only to an 'intent to commit an offence'. The *actus reus* of an inchoate offence will be limited as the main offence was never carried out, so *mens rea* is fundamental to the imposition of criminal liability. It is therefore questionable whether the *mens rea* requirement should have been lowered in this way.

Conditional intention

The concept of conditional intention has caused the courts problems in the past. Conditional intention arises where a person intends to do something if a certain condition is satisfied, for example, they intend to steal a wristwatch from a woman if it is a genuine Rolex. The question is, will this intent be sufficient to be the *mens rea* of an attempt? Doubt was raised by the case of **R v Husseyn** (1977). The defendants had seen a parked van and decided to break into it, intending to steal if there was anything worth stealing inside. In fact the van contained a bag full of sub-aqua equipment, which the defendants did not steal. At their trial the indictment said that they had attempted to steal the sub-aqua equipment. On appeal Lord Scarman said in the Court of Appeal that 'it cannot be said that one who has it in mind to steal only if what he finds is worth stealing has a present intention to steal'; their conditional intention was found to have been inadequate to impose liability.

This case caused considerable concern, because it seemed to leave a significant gap in the law. However, in **Attorney-General's References (Nos 1 and 2 of 1979)** it was said that the judgment in **Husseyn** could be explained by the fact that the indictment had specified that the attempted theft was theft of the sub-aqua equipment. If it had simply said, for example, that they intended to steal anything of value in the van then they could have been convicted. In conclusion, conditional intention is sufficient to impose liability for an attempt provided the indictment is carefully worded.

▶ Offences which may not be attempted

There are some offences for which liability for attempts cannot be imposed. The Criminal Attempts Act covers all indictable offences, and either way offences when they are tried on indictment, but for summary offences, there is no liability for attempts unless Parliament creates a specific statutory provision stating that there should be – for the offence of drink-driving for example, the Road Traffic Act 1988 provides that it is an offence to 'drive or attempt to drive' after drinking more than the prescribed limit.

There is no liability for attempting to be a secondary party to a crime – so there is no offence of attempting to aid, abet, counsel or procure the commission of an offence. Nor is it an offence to attempt to conspire, though it is possible to attempt to incite (one exception to this rule is aiding and abetting suicide, as charged in **Reed** (1982) – below – as this is a full offence in its own right rather than an inchoate offence, and therefore can be attempted).

Some offences cannot be attempted because of their *mens rea*. The most obvious example is manslaughter. An attempt requires intention to commit the full offence; if the accused has the intention to kill, the attempted offence would be attempted murder, and not attempted manslaughter.

Section 1(1) of the Criminal Attempts Act 1981 describes an attempt with the words 'does an act'. It is thought to be impossible to attempt any crime where the *actus reus* is an omission – it is difficult to imagine how you can attempt not to report an accident for example. Nor is it possible to attempt an offence where the *actus reus* is a state of affairs – you cannot, for example, attempt to be found in possession of a controlled drug.

It is possible for an act done in another country to amount to an attempt to commit a crime in England. In **DPP** *v* **Stonehouse** (1978) the accused went to Miami, and there falsely staged his own death, so that his wife in England (who knew nothing of the plan) could claim on his life insurance policies. He was convicted of attempting to enable his wife to obtain property by deception.

▶ Sentence

Under s. 4(1) of the 1981 Act the maximum sentence that can be imposed for an attempt is usually the same as that for the main offence.

▶ Criticism and reform

The narrow interpretation of the *actus reus*

The limited approach taken to the meaning of 'more than merely preparatory' has unfortunate implications for efforts at crime prevention and protecting the public. The police can still lawfully arrest anyone behaving as the defendant did in **Campbell**, for example, on the basis that they have reasonable grounds for believing that he or she is about to commit an arrestable offence, but it appears that in order to secure a conviction for attempt in such circumstances, they would have to hold back until that person has actually entered the post office and approached the counter before arresting him or her. Clearly this may mean putting post office and other staff, the general public and police officers, at unnecessary risk.

The dangers of this approach are highlighted in **R** *v* **Geddes** (1996). The accused had entered some school premises including the boys' toilets. On being discovered he ran away discarding a rucksack which was found to contain rope, masking tape and a large kitchen knife. He was charged with attempted false imprisonment and the trial judge ruled that there was a case fit for the jury's consideration. The accused was convicted but his appeal was allowed. While there was no doubt about the appellant's intention, there was no evidence of the *actus reus* of the offence. The evidence showed that he had made preparation, got himself ready and put himself in a position to commit the offence of false imprisonment, but he had not made contact with any pupil. He had not moved from the role of preparation and planning into the area of execution or implementation.

The decision in *Shivpuri*

This case has been criticized on the grounds that it allows the law to punish people merely on account of their intentions. However, it should be remembered that to incur liability, the accused must have done something which is more than merely preparatory to committing the offence, and may in fact have tried very hard to commit an offence, failing to do so only through carelessness, chance or the intervention of the police. In such cases incurring no liability would simply give potential offenders the opportunity to try harder next time.

Sentencing

Some have argued that the maximum sentence for an attempt is too harsh. In certain US states, for example, the maximum that can be imposed is usually only half that for the main offence. Arguments in favour of the English position include the fact that the defendant had the *mens rea* for the complete offence, and may be equally dangerous. The academic Becker (1974) argues that whether an offence is actually committed or merely attempted, the same type of harm can be caused: disruption to social stability. On the other hand another academic James Brady (1980) has suggested that the harm is not the same and so they do not justify the same sentence. In practice the judge still has a discretion and most of the time judges choose to impose a lower sentence if the offence was not completed.

Attempts at omission

The draft Criminal Code proposes that it should be possible to attempt offences where the *actus reus* is an omission.

A defence of withdrawal

In the USA, a defence of withdrawal is widely accepted. This allows a defendant to avoid liability if he or she voluntarily chooses not to go on and carry out the offence. At the moment in England this defence is available to accomplices, but not to those charged with attempts. This means that, once a person has done something that is more than merely preparatory to the commission of the offence, they might just as well carry on and finish the job, since stopping at that point will not necessarily reduce their liability.

The Law Commission is opposed to the idea of a defence of withdrawal, arguing that this issue can be left to mitigation in sentencing.

. . . .
CONSPIRACY

Conspiracy covers agreements between two or more people, usually to commit a crime. Until 1977, conspiracy was a purely common law crime, but there were difficulties with the definition of the offence. One of the problems was that its definition was extremely broad and included situations where two or more people had simply agreed to commit a tort. Thus, in **Kamara** *v* **DPP** (1974), where the defendants had reached an accord to commit the tort of trespass to land together, they were liable for the criminal offence of conspiracy. This was felt to be extremely harsh and consequently the 1977 Criminal Law Act abolished most of the common law offences of conspiracy, and created a new statutory offence of conspiring, which is limited to an agreement between two or more people to commit a crime.

But Parliament was not prepared to abolish the whole of the common law of conspiracy because it was concerned that this might leave a gap in the law, where people had not agreed to commit a crime but their agreement was of a type that still required criminal liability to be imposed. Therefore they chose specifically to preserve two small areas of the old common law of conspiracy. The result is that there are now two categories of conspiracy: statutory conspiracy and common law conspiracy.

With one exception, statutory and common law conspiracy are mutually exclusive, and statutory conspiracy takes priority; if the act the conspirators agree to do is an offence, the charge will necessarily be statutory conspiracy. The exception is conspiracy to defraud.

▶ **Statutory conspiracy**

Statutory conspiracy is an agreement by two or more people to do something that will amount to a crime.

Actus reus

The Criminal Law Act 1977 s. 1(1) provides:

> Subject to the following provisions of this Part of this Act, if a person agrees with any other person or persons that a course of conduct shall be pursued which, if the agreement is carried out in accordance with their intentions, either:
> (a) will necessarily amount to or involve the commission of any offence or offences by one or more of the parties to the agreement, or
> (b) would do so but for the existence of facts which render the commission of the offence or any of the offences impossible, he is guilty of conspiracy to commit the offence or offences in question.

There must be an agreement that the planned actions will be committed by one or more parties to that agreement; so long as this is the case, the conspirators will be liable even if they never act upon their plan. It can be argued that there should be liability only when the agreement is carried out, as is largely the case in US law, because there is no real threat to society until the conspirators start acting on the agreement. In practice, though, it will be rare for conspirators who have not taken any action to be convicted, simply because it would be difficult to prove the agreement existed.

The fact that a conspirator has second thoughts and withdraws does not provide a defence. If the main offence is carried out, the defendants will not usually be charged with conspiracy as well, unless the additional charge is felt necessary to show the seriousness of what they have done.

Who can conspire?
Section 2 of the 1977 Act provides:

> (1) A person shall not by virtue of section 1 above be guilty of conspiracy to commit any offence if he is an intended victim of that offence.
> (2) A person shall not by virtue of section 1 above be guilty of conspiracy to commit any offence or offences if the only other person or persons with whom he agrees are (both initially and at all times during the currency of the agreement) persons of any one or more of the following descriptions, this is to say:

(a) his spouse;
(b) a person under the age of criminal responsibility; and
(c) an intended victim of that offence or of each of those offences.

Spouses cannot therefore be liable for conspiring with each other, though they may both be liable for a conspiracy involving one or more people besides the two of them. Nor is there a conspiracy where two people agree to commit a crime for which one has a defence; there must be more than one person who has no defence.

Where an offence is designed to protect certain groups of people, such as minors or the mentally ill, members of those groups cannot be convicted of conspiring to commit those offences against themselves – so a girl under sixteen cannot be liable for conspiring with her boyfriend to have under-age sex, even though she planned it with him, and he was guilty of the main offence.

Conspiracy to do the impossible

Section 1(1)(b) of the 1977 Criminal Law Act (quoted above) makes it clear that the fact that the crime agreed on turns out to be impossible to commit does not prevent a conviction for conspiracy.

Mens rea

The parties must intend that the agreement will be carried out and the crime committed by one or more of the conspirators. In **Edwards** (1991), the accused had agreed to supply amphetamine but appeared to have intended to supply a different drug, ephedrine, which was not a controlled drug. According to the Court of Appeal, the judge had rightly directed the jury that they could only convict of conspiracy to supply amphetamine if it was proved he had agreed to supply amphetamine and he intended to supply that drug – merely agreeing with no intention of actually supplying the controlled substance was not enough. His conviction was upheld.

The issue was somewhat confused by the House of Lords judgment in **Anderson** (1985) which seemed to suggest that defendants must personally intend to play some part in carrying out the agreement, but that also they did not need to intend that the crime would actually be committed. The accused had been in prison with Andaloussi, a man who was awaiting trial for serious drug offences. Anderson, who was expecting to be released on bail quite quickly, agreed to take part in a plan to free Andaloussi. His part in the scheme was to supply diamond wire, to be used to cut through bars in the prison, for which he was given a down payment of £2,000, to be followed by another £10,000 on delivery of the wire. Anderson gave evidence that he had never believed that the escape plan would actually work, and that after supplying the wire he had intended simply to take the money and leave the country for Spain, playing no further part in helping Andaloussi to escape. Nevertheless, his conviction was upheld on appeal. Lord Bridge said:

> The appellant, in agreeing that a course of conduct be pursued that would, if successful, necessarily involve the offence of effecting Andaloussi's escape from lawful custody, clearly intended, by providing diamond wire to be smuggled into the prison, to play a part in the agreed course of conduct in furtherance of that criminal objective. Neither the fact that he intended to play no further part in attempting to effect the escape, nor that he believed the escape to be impossible, would, if the jury had supposed they might be true, have afforded him any defence.

While this approach gave a satisfactory outcome in the particular case, it could cause difficulties in some situations. Conspiracy charges are extremely useful with regard to organized crime. For example, in a mafia-style organization, there is often a 'Mr Big', who may initiate the whole criminal enterprise, but never actually become involved in committing the criminal acts himself – he will pay others to smuggle drugs, or kill his enemies rather than risk doing it himself. The approach in **Edwards** would ensure that such a person could still be liable for conspiracy as he had been party to the agreement, and intended it to be carried out and the crime committed, but under the apparent *ratio* of **Anderson** he would avoid liability because he would intend to play no part himself. However, in **R** *v* **Siracusa** (1990) the court said that **Anderson**, despite its fairly clear dicta, did not mean that the defendant had to intend to play any part in the carrying out of the agreement; and in **Yip Chiu-Cheung** *v* **R** (1994) the Privy Council assumed that the defendant only needed to intend that the crime be committed by someone. On the whole it makes most sense to view **Anderson** as an aberration, and regard the *mens rea* of statutory conspiracy as that laid down in **Edwards**.

We saw that in relation to attempts, recklessness as regards the circumstances of the main offence is sometimes sufficient. This is not the case with conspiracy. Section 1(2) of the Criminal Law Act 1977 states:

> Where liability for an offence may be incurred without knowledge on the part of the person committing it of any particular fact or circumstance necessary for the commission of the offence, a person shall not be guilty of conspiracy to commit that offence . . . unless he and at least one other party to the agreement intend or know that fact or circumstance shall or will exist at the time when the conduct constituting the offence is to take place.

It can be seen from this section that only intention or knowledge concerning all the circumstances of the *actus reus* will be satisfactory for a charge of conspiracy. This is the case even if the agreement involves committing a crime for which recklessness is sufficient *mens rea*. For example, in relation to the offence of rape, recklessness as to whether the woman was consenting to sexual intercourse is sufficient *mens rea*, but to be liable for a conspiracy to rape, the accused must have known that the woman was not consenting. Even where an offence imposes strict liability, intention or knowledge will be required for conspiracy to commit that offence.

Both parties to a conspiracy (or if there are more than two, at least two of them) must have *mens rea* – so if A and B agree to take C's car, but B believes that A has C's permission to do so, there is no liability for conspiracy for stealing the car. Interestingly, in **Yip Chiu-Cheung** *v* **R**, the conspiracy concerned the importation of controlled drugs, and the co-conspirator was an undercover drug enforcement officer, participating in the offence in order to detect and report the crime. The operation never progressed further than a conspiracy because on the morning that the officer was supposed to undertake the actual smuggling, he overslept and missed the plane. Despite the fact that he was an honest police officer doing his job, he was treated as having the *mens rea* of the offence, on the grounds that his motive was irrelevant, which meant that the co-conspirator could be liable. Theoretically, the law enforcement officer could have been prosecuted and convicted as well, but his protection would be that the prosecution authorities would exercise their discretion and not proceed in such situations.

Where a conspiracy involves more than two people, it is not necessary for everyone to know what all the others are doing, but each defendant will only be liable for conspiracy to commit those crimes which he or she knows about – so if A, B and C conspire to steal from D, but A and B also agree to kill D, C is liable for conspiracy to steal but not for conspiracy to murder.

Conditional intention

In some cases two or more people may agree to do something that would amount to a crime, but decide that they will only carry out the plan on condition that certain circumstances exist – this is the idea of conditional intention already discussed in the context of the property offences. In **Reed** (1982), the defendants had agreed that one of them would visit individuals who they knew were thinking about committing suicide and, after assessing the circumstances in each case, would either try to persuade them out of it, or actively help them to kill themselves. It was held that they were guilty of conspiring to aid and abet suicide.

In explaining the decision, the court drew a distinction between situations where the intention to commit the offence if necessary is only incidental to the plan, and where it could be said to be the whole object of the exercise. They gave the example of a pair of motorists who agree to drive from London to Edinburgh within a specified time. This journey can only be achieved without speeding if the traffic is exceptionally light, and the two have therefore agreed that if the traffic conditions are not sufficiently favourable, they will drive above the speed limit, committing an offence. Their main purpose, the court said, would not be to break the speed limit, but to get to Edinburgh. By contrast, for the defendants in **Reed**, aiding and abetting suicide, where they thought the circumstances warranted it, could be said to be their main purpose, and so conditional intent would suffice for conspiracy.

Acquittal of the alleged conspirators

Section 5(8) of the Criminal Law Act provides that a person can be convicted of conspiracy even if his or her alleged co-conspirators have been acquitted, unless such a conviction is inconsistent with the fact that the others have been acquitted. This protects against guilty conspirators going free because another party has been acquitted due to evidential problems or procedural irregularities at trial.

Conspiracy and secondary parties

At the moment, the law is unclear about whether you can conspire to aid, abet, counsel or procure. The issue arose in **Hollinshead** (1985), but the House of Lords held that the facts of that case did not make it necessary to decide the issue there and then, and left it to be decided in some future case.

Sentencing

The sentence for a statutory conspiracy may not exceed the maximum penalty for the crime that the conspirators agreed to commit.

▶ Common law conspiracy

Actus reus

The main principles discussed in relation to the *actus reus* of statutory conspiracy also apply here. The only difference is that instead of agreeing to commit a crime, the defendants agree to do one of the two things laid down in s. 5 of the Criminal Law Act 1977. This provides:

> (1) Subject to the following provisions of this section, the offence of conspiracy at common law is hereby abolished.
> (2) Subsection (1) above shall not affect the offence of conspiracy at common law so far as relates to conspiracy to defraud.
> (3) Subsection (1) above shall not affect the offence of conspiracy at common law if and in so far as it may be committed by entering into an agreement to engage in conduct which:

(a) tends to corrupt public morals or outrages public decency; but
(b) would not amount to or involve the commission of an offence if
carried out by a single person otherwise than in pursuance of an
agreement.

Thus s. 5 makes two exceptions to the abolition of common law conspiracies. We will look at each of these in turn.

Conspiracy to defraud

This is a property offence, mainly used to deal with the situation where a
person dishonestly obtains someone else's property, but his or her behaviour is not covered by the Theft Acts. It therefore helps the courts to keep
pace with ever-increasing methods of fraud, which may develop too quickly
to fall within the existing legislation. For example, conspiracy to defraud
was the charge used against the Maxwell brothers, inheritors of their
father's publishing empire, with regard to their transactions concerning
the Maxwell pension funds. It is a popular charge with the Serious Fraud
Office because it avoids some of the complexities of the Theft Acts.

Conspiracy to defraud need not necessarily involve deceiving anyone.
In **Scott** *v* **Metropolitan Police Commissioner** (1974), the defendants
copied films, without securing the consent of the copyright owners. They
planned to make money by charging others to watch them, and therefore
clearly intended to cheat the copyright owners out of funds that should
rightfully have been paid to them. They could not be charged under the
Theft Acts, because they had stolen nothing, nor had there been any deception. Because they had only conspired to commit a civil wrong and not a
criminal offence, they could not be liable for statutory conspiracy either.
However, the House of Lords held that an agreement by two or more
people to deprive another dishonestly of something to which that person
would normally be entitled could constitute the common law offence of
conspiracy to defraud.

In **Adams** *v* **R** (1995) the Privy Council said that the offence could only
be committed where the victim had some right or interest capable of being
prejudiced. The case involved a complicated fraud on a large company.
As the company had a legal right to recover secret profits made by its
directors they had a sufficient interest for these purposes.

When the 1977 Act was first passed, defendants could not be charged
with the common law offence of conspiracy to defraud if they could be
charged with statutory conspiracy. So, for example, a couple of defendants
who conspired to do something which would amount to burglary would
have had to be charged with the statutory offence of conspiracy to burgle
under s. 1 of the 1977 Act, rather than the common law offence of conspiracy to defraud. This caused problems in practice, because defendants
were being acquitted on the technical basis that they should have been
charged with statutory conspiracy rather than common law conspiracy to

defraud. So, in 1987, the law was changed. Statutory conspiracy and conspiracy to defraud are no longer mutually exclusive; a conspiracy to commit an offence such as theft may be covered by either offence, and the prosecution may choose which to charge.

Conspiracy to corrupt public morals or outrage public decency

The Act provides that there is still a common law offence of conspiracy to do an act which is likely to corrupt public morals or outrage public decency, where that act would not in itself be a criminal offence. For some time after the legislation was passed, it was not clear whether these activities were offences in their own right or whether criminal liability could only be imposed if there was a conspiracy to do them. Recent cases make it clear that outraging public decency is an offence in itself, and a conviction for this was upheld by the House of Lords in **R** *v* **Gibson** (1990), where the defendant exhibited earrings made from freeze-dried human foetuses of three or four months' gestation.

As a result of **Gibson**, outraging public decency is itself an offence, which means that in the light of the terms of s. 5(3)(b) above this should be charged as a statutory conspiracy and not a common law conspiracy. This appears to mean that only conspiracy to corrupt public morals is left as a common law offence. This approach is supported by the Court of Appeal in **R** *v* **Walker** (1995) where no objection was raised to the conviction of an individual defendant for outraging public decency on his own, though the appeal was allowed on a different ground.

The kind of behaviour required for liability for these two conspiracies has rarely been defined. As regards conspiracy to outrage public decency, in the case of **R** *v* **Walker** the defendant was accused of having committed the offence of outraging public decency in his own home. The complainant was a ten-year-old girl. The Court of Appeal allowed his appeal on the basis that this offence must be carried out in a place of public resort and that two or more persons must have been able to see the incident.

In **Shaw** *v* **Director of Public Prosecutions** (1962), the publication of a directory listing the names, addresses and photographs of prostitutes, with details of any unusual sexual practices they were willing to pursue, was held to be conduct liable to corrupt public morals, and in **Knuller** (1973) the same view was taken of an agreement to publish advertisements designed to secure sexual partners for homosexual men.

In **Knuller**, Lord Simon suggested that conduct tending to corrupt public morals had to be more than just behaviour which might 'lead morally astray'; it should be conduct which a jury 'might find to be destructive of the very fabric of society'. He also defined conduct likely to outrage public decency, stating that it would have to 'go beyond offending the susceptibilities of, or even shocking, reasonable people', and that in deciding what kind of conduct fitted the definition, juries should remember that they lived in a society which aimed to tolerate minorities.

Impossibility

Section 1(1)(b) of the 1977 Act does not apply to common law conspiracies, so this issue is still governed by case law. It is therefore likely, in the light of the cases on impossibility and incitement discussed below, that impossibility can still be a defence.

Mens rea

The *mens rea* for statutory and common law conspiracy is the same, except that conspiracy to defraud requires an extra element of *mens rea*: dishonesty (**Scott**, above). Dishonesty for the purposes of the Theft Acts was defined in **Ghosh** (1982) and it has been held that the same test should be applied in cases of conspiracy to defraud. Defendants are therefore dishonest if their conduct would be considered dishonest by ordinary decent people, and the defendants realize that it would be so regarded.

Sentence

Conspiracy to defraud has a maximum sentence of ten years. There is no set maximum for the other form of common law conspiracy; it is left to the discretion of the judge.

▶ Criticism and reform

Evidential rules

Special evidential rules can be used in conspiracy charges, which allow evidence against one party to be put forward against the others – this would not be permitted if they were charged for separate offences. These rules mean that a conspiracy charge can be brought where there is not enough evidence to charge one or more of the parties individually with the main offence, and while this may be a useful way of ensuring that guilty conspirators do not go free due to evidential problems, it is open to abuse by the prosecution.

Conspiracies not put into action

It is questionable whether there is a need for the crime of conspiracy to cover cases where the conspirators take no action to put their agreement into practice, since this appears to pose no threat to anyone. On the other hand, one of the principal reasons for the offence is the state's fear of criminals getting together as they are seen as a greater threat to society when they co-ordinate their activities.

Conspiracy and attempts

In many cases, a conspiracy will be committed prior to an attempt: it is the agreement that precedes the conduct. As a result it can be argued that if the law of attempts is broadly defined there is no need for the offence of conspiracy. On the other hand, this would leave a gap as regards 'Mr Big' who does not himself become involved in the criminal activity. In addition, where there is some degree of organized crime, the actual offences may be quite minor – shoplifting by gangs, for example – but the profit to be made by the person running the operation can be enormous. The charge of conspiracy enables the judge to see the whole picture and appreciate the seriousness of their conduct.

One benefit of the conspiracy charge is that an agreement is more concrete than such concepts as 'more than merely preparatory'.

Outraging public decency and corrupting public morals

The desirability of maintaining the offences of conspiracy to corrupt public morals or outrage public decency is debatable. Both are potentially extremely wide and the Law Commission favours their abolition.

Conspiracy to defraud

Conspiracy to defraud is very broadly defined, and while this is clearly useful for the prosecution, it may cause injustice to the defendant. However, the Law Commission has concluded that the offence bridges important gaps and should be retained.

Sentencing

The wide sentencing discretion has been criticized particularly in the context of the common law conspiracies.

The draft Criminal Code

The draft Criminal Code largely restates the current law on conspiracy, except that there is no specific exemption for agreements made between spouses; and a party would not be acquitted of conspiracy purely on the grounds that the only other party to the agreement has a defence to the crime they conspired to commit.

INCITEMENT

Incitement means encouraging others to do something which would amount to a crime. For example, if Ann instructs Ben, a contract killer, to murder someone, Ann will immediately be liable for incitement to murder, even if the killing is never carried out. Incitement is not defined in any statute but remains a common law offence.

▶ Actus reus

There must be real encouragement of another to commit a crime – more than just a suggestion. This may be by means of advice, persuasion, threats or pressure, communicated in writing, speech, or through signs.

The defendant need not be inciting any particular person; the incitement may be addressed to a group, or to people in general. In **R *v* Most** (1881), it was held that an article in a revolutionary newspaper encouraging revolutionaries all over the world to assassinate their heads of state, could be an incitement to murder.

Nor does incitement have to be explicit – an implied encouragement to commit an offence may be enough. In **Invicta Plastics Ltd *v* Clare** (1976), the defendants manufactured a device called a Radatec which could detect wireless transmissions, including those used by the police radar traps designed to catch speeding motorists. They advertised the product in a motoring magazine, the advertisement showing a road with a speed limit sign, seen through a car windscreen. The court held that this was an implied incitement to use the device without a licence, constituting an offence under the Wireless Telegraphy Act (1949). The fact that the company's advertisement did point out that to do so would be an offence did not prevent liability being incurred.

The act incited must be one which would be a crime if it was committed by the specific person incited. In **Whitehouse** (1977) a father tried to persuade his daughter to have sexual intercourse with him, though in the event no sex took place. The father could not be prosecuted for inciting the girl to commit incest, since she would not have been committing a crime if she had done so (though he would have been).

The rule in **Tyrell** (1894) (see p. 226) that where an offence is created in order to protect a certain group of people (such as minors), members of that group cannot be guilty of abetting that offence against themselves, applies in the same way to incitement: a girl under 16 who incited a man to have sexual intercourse with her would not be liable for inciting the full offence, although the man would be liable for the full offence if he committed it.

Inciting the impossible

In **McDonough** (1962), it appeared that a person could be liable for inciting an offence even though it would not have been possible to go on and commit the actual full offence. McDonough had been convicted of inciting another to handle stolen lamb carcasses. He had believed that the meat in question was in cold store, but in fact it did not even exist (and therefore could not have been either stolen or handled). The Court of Appeal upheld his conviction.

By contrast, in **R v Fitzmaurice** (1983) the Court of Appeal held that a person would not be liable for inciting offences that were impossible to commit, but that if the incitement was in general terms, the fact that the precise plan visualized by the inciter was impossible would not necessarily mean that the offence itself was impossible. Fitzmaurice's father had asked him to recruit people to commit a robbery near a bank in Bow, on a woman whom he said would be carrying a lot of money. Fitzmaurice found one person, who recruited two others, and then put all three in touch with his father. Unknown to Fitzmaurice, his father had no intention of bringing about the crime he had described, and in fact planned to claim reward money by reporting his son's activities to the police.

Fitzmaurice was convicted of incitement to rob, and the Court of Appeal upheld his conviction, because the incitement was in general terms and the offence of robbery was not impossible to carry out – even if the men could not rob the particular woman whom Fitzmaurice's father had appeared to have in mind, they could still have robbed someone else coming out of the bank.

The court reconciled this principle with **McDonough** on the (rather dubious) basis that the offence in that case was not impossible to commit since the meat might have existed at some point in the future.

▶ Mens rea

The *mens rea* required for incitement is intention that the end result of the crime should occur, and knowledge of, or wilful blindness to, the circumstances which make the act incited illegal. In other words the inciter must intend that the crime will be committed, without needing to know that it is a crime – ignorance of the law is never a defence.

Where the full offence is actually committed, the inciter can only be liable if the person incited actually had the required *mens rea* for the full offence. If Abdul incites Bob to commit a crime, knowing that Bob does not have *mens rea*, Abdul is not liable for incitement, but is in fact the principal offender, and is using Bob as an innocent agent (see p. 211). In **Curr** (1968), the accused was charged with inciting women to commit offences covered by the Family Allowances Act 1945. He had provided loans, taking family allowance books as security, and persuaded women to cash the books for him. He was acquitted of incitement because the prosecution could not prove that the women had the knowledge that was the necessary *mens rea* of the statutory offence. If Curr had been charged as a principal he might have been liable, since he had *mens rea* and therefore the women could have been treated as innocent agents.

Where the full offence is not committed, it is not entirely clear whether the court must conclude that the person incited would have had the *mens rea* if the offence had gone ahead, though this does appear to be a logical extension of **Curr**.

▶ Criticism

Evidential problems

This crime can be committed merely by speaking, giving rise to obvious dangers that evidence can be fabricated by the police.

Impossibility and incitement

Under the Criminal Attempts Act 1981, the fact that committing the main offence may be impossible is no defence to either statutory conspiracy or attempt, yet according to **Fitzmaurice**, it is still possible for impossibility to be a defence to incitement if the incitement is in specific rather than general terms. The Law Commission report that led to the passing of the 1981 Act clearly intended that impossibility should not be a defence to any inchoate offence; but it was not thought necessary to include a provision on incitement and impossibility in the Act, since it appeared that **McDonough** already prevented impossibility from being a defence to incitement. There appears to be no logical reason for maintaining the current distinction.

Sentencing

Where an accused is convicted of incitement after being tried on indictment, the court can impose a sentence of imprisonment which is greater than the maximum penalty for the crime incited – so, for example, a person convicted of incitement to batter could theoretically be given a sentence of anything up to life imprisonment, while the person who actually committed the battery could be punished with up to six months' imprisonment only. In the past there was a similar provision in the law on conspiracy, but this was reformed. The reasoning behind maintaining it for incitement is said to be that in some cases the inciter may be more at fault, and more of a risk to society, than the person incited – as for example where the ringleaders of a gang encourage members to commit crimes, without necessarily taking part themselves.

Mens rea of the person incited

The draft Criminal Code takes the approach that in cases like **Curr**, it should be irrelevant whether or not the person incited had *mens rea;* the issue should be whether the inciter believed that he or she did.

The offence may be unnecessary

It can be argued that a specific offence of incitement is not necessary, given that, if the person incited agrees to commit the crime, there will be a conspiracy, and it is only when there is such an agreement that any real threat to society arises. Where the person incited does not agree, this could be treated as an attempted conspiracy, though at the moment this offence is abolished by s. 1(4) of the Criminal Attempts Act 1981. Thus if incitement is abolished there need not be any gap in the law, merely a simplification.

• •

ANSWERING QUESTIONS

1 **'The criminal law does not punish people for their guilty thoughts alone but only for overt conduct accompanied by those guilty thoughts.' Assess the validity of this statement with reference to the offence of attempt.** *Oxford*
Again, this should not be used as an opportunity to write all you know about attempts – or anything else for that matter! As always, there is no right or wrong answer, but one approach might be to divide the essay into the following three parts. First, consider whether the law of attempt requires 'overt conduct'. This will be a matter of looking at the 'more than merely preparatory' test. Secondly, discuss the fact that you do need guilty thoughts by looking at the *mens rea* of the offence. Finally, consider whether the current law gets the right balance, pointing for example to the fact that you can be liable for attempting the impossible, and looking at some of the relevant criticisms of the law. Errors to avoid are writing purely about the issue of impossibility when the question was intended to be much broader than this; and discussing incitement and conspiracy when the question was limited to attempts.

2 **Should there be criminal offences of incitement and conspiracy?**
To keep your essay clear, it would be wise to divide it into two halves, considering first incitement and then conspiracy – make it clear in your introduction that this is what you will be doing. To tackle this question, you need a clear statement of the current law, and some critical material.

When explaining what the law is, link your points to the question, pointing out the public policy reason why these are types of conduct which the state currently feels should be penalized with criminal liability. You can also show how the boundaries of the offences have changed, for example the abolition of most of common law conspiracy and the extension of conspiracy to include conspiracy to do the impossible. Some time could be spent considering the particular uses of conspiracy to defraud and the uncertain role of the other head of common law conspiracy. The criticism and reform sections for both these topics will be of particular use in answering this question.

Inchoate offences can also arise as part of a problem question – obviously they cannot form problem questions on their own, because by their nature they must be linked with another complete offence. Part of the skill in answering problem questions which give rise to such issues is simply recognizing that this set of facts gives rise to the issue, and if you spend some time looking at past papers, you should soon begin to pick up the key situations which suggest that the examiners want you to consider inchoate offences. For example, where you are told that a person tries to commit an offence but fails, you will usually be required, among other things, to consider that person's liability for an attempt. On the other hand, if the problem question only mentions the activities of one individual then it is unlikely to raise issues of incitement or conspiracy. For example: 'David walked into a bank with a gun and asked the cashier to hand over the money in the till. She refused to do so and set off the emergency alarm. He panicked, shot her dead and ran off.' Among other offences, David can be liable for attempted robbery, as what he did would amount to something more than merely preparatory to the commission of the complete offence of robbery and he intended to steal by seeking to put someone in fear that force would be used.

Similarly, if you spot someone encouraging or asking someone else to commit an offence, you should consider incitement. If in the above example, David had gone to rob the bank after being asked to by someone else, or if David himself had tried to persuade a friend to join him in committing the robbery, incitement should be discussed. If more than one person is involved in an offence, you should also be aware of the possibility of conspiracy.

3 Paul was released from prison yesterday, having completed a 15-year sentence for an armed bank robbery involving £100,000 in bank notes. Five years ago Richard was in the same prison as Paul and, in the course of their friendship, discovered that Paul had given the money to a trusted friend for safe-keeping in a foreign bank account in the friend's name which had been opened for this purpose. However, Richard did not know the authorization code which was to be used to allow Paul or his nominee to collect the money on Paul's release from prison. Paul was pleased to see Richard when he visited Paul's house last night, and he invited Richard in. When Paul left the room to get some more drinks Richard started to hunt through Paul's cupboards and drawers to try to find some reference to the authorization code. Eventually he found a document, memorized the code, and replaced the document. Paul came back into the room and saw Richard closing a drawer. He asked Richard what he was doing; Richard became alarmed and hit Paul very hard, causing him to fall and lose consciousness when he hit his head on the edge of the table. Richard left the house and the following afternoon sent an instruction, including the authorization code, to the foreign bank to transfer the money to his own UK bank account. The foreign bank informed Richard's bank that the account had been closed two hours earlier when all the money had been transferred to Paul's UK account. Consider the criminal liability, if any, of Paul and Richard. *NEAB*

We will consider Richard's liability first, and take each incident in turn. As regards the code, the question will be whether by memorizing it he has committed theft. The answer in the light of **Oxford v Moss** is 'No', as you cannot steal information.

When he hits Paul you will need to look at his liability for a non-fatal offence. In relation to s. 18, it will be a question for the jury whether they consider Paul's injury was sufficient to constitute grievous bodily harm. Alternatively, it is not clear whether he was cut by the hit or the table to constitute a wounding. If the *actus reus* is found to exist for a s. 18 offence, it is still not clear whether Richard had sufficient *mens rea*: it is uncertain whether Richard intended to cause Paul grievous bodily harm when he hit him hard, we are simply told that he was alarmed. It might be argued that he was intending to avoid lawful apprehension (the alternative head of *mens rea*) but it is unlikely that he thought Paul would want to involve the legal authorities in this incident given the criminal circumstances that Paul himself was in.

Moving on to s. 20, OAPA 1861, in the light of **Burstow** the *actus reus* is the same as for s. 18 and would not need to be repeated in detail. The *mens rea* is intention or subjective recklessness as to the causing of some harm. From the facts we are given it is not clear whether Richard satisfies either of these criteria.

If he falls within neither s. 18 nor s. 20 he is highly likely to be found liable for a s. 47 offence.

As regards his contacting the bank to obtain the funds, he was unsuccessful and therefore we are looking at an attempt. You would need to consider what offence he was attempting. You could look at theft, obtaining property by deception, obtaining services by deception and handling. On the issue of attempt you would need to consider whether what he had done 'was more than merely preparatory' in the light of, for example, **R v Gullefer**. There would seem to be no problem with him having *mens rea*.

The offence to consider in relation to Paul's conduct of transferring the funds to his UK account is handling.

4 H was 25 and his brother, I, was 19. H had five previous convictions for offences ranging from minor assault to theft and burglary, for the last of which he had been sentenced to six months imprisonment. I had two cautions for minor offences but no previous convictions. They agreed that they would go to a supermarket on the edge of town and get as much food as they could without paying for it. They had to walk and had only just got inside the store when they were told that the shop was closing and they had a very short time to buy what they wanted. Because they were closely observed by security guards and staff trying to close the store, they were unable to take anything and went away empty-handed. H suggested to I that, instead of walking back, they should take a car from the store's car park. When I seemed uncertain about doing so, H threatened to beat him up if he did not help. I was too frightened to resist and they looked around for a car. Eventually they saw J,

an old woman, getting into her car. H told her that if she did not get out and give him her keys he would smash the car up. They then drove off and later dumped the car on some waste ground.

What offences have H and I committed and how should they be dealt with by the court? *London*

The second part of this question ('how should they be dealt with by the court') is concerned with sentencing and the relevant area of law is considered in Chapter 10 of the authors' book *English Legal System*. We will only consider here the first part of the question.

There was first of all a conspiracy to commit theft and burglary. The conduct in the supermarket may have amounted to an attempted theft, provided a court finds that they have done acts that were more than merely preparatory to the commission of the offence. Note that unlike the defendant in **Campbell**, H and I had entered the shop where they intended to carry out the offence. In addition they have committed a burglary under s. 9(1)(a) as they entered the shop as trespassers (**R v Jones and Smith** at p. 154) with intent to steal. If they are guilty of attempted theft then they will also be guilty under s. 9(1)(b).

In relation to J's car, H and I committed the offence of taking without consent (p. 161). H also assaulted J when he threatened to smash the car up because he was probably reckless at causing her to fear personal injury, though he merely threatened to damage property. When H demanded the keys backing his demand with threats this would fall into blackmail. There is unlikely to be a theft of the car since they appear to have lacked the intention to permanently deprive as they dump the car on some waste ground. There might however be a technical theft of the petrol.

H's threat to beat up I would amount to an assault. I may be able to plead the defence of duress which is discussed at p. 270, though the issue of self-induced duress would need to be examined closely.

11
Accomplices

The person who actually commits the *actus reus* of an offence may not be the only one who is liable for it. If other people play a part in the crime, they too may incur liability as secondary parties – so, for example, a woman who hires a contract killer to murder her husband cannot escape liability merely because she did not physically take part in the killing.

THE PRINCIPAL OFFENDER

The principal is the main perpetrator of the offence, and usually the person who commits the *actus reus*. Where more than one person is directly responsible for the *actus reus*, there may be more than one principal, they are known as joint principals. The test of whether someone is a joint principal or a secondary party is whether they contribute to the *actus reus* by their own independent act, rather than simply playing a supporting role.

▶ Innocent agents

In some circumstances the principal may not directly carry out the *actus reus*, but instead use what is called an innocent agent. There are two situations in which the person committing the *actus reus* may be considered an innocent agent.

Where someone lacks the *mens rea* for the offence

If, for example, Ann wants to kill Ben, Ann might give Chris a poisonous drug, telling Chris it is an asprin and asking Chris to give it to Ben. If Chris does so, Chris will be committing the *actus reus*, but as an innocent agent – because Chris, with no idea that the drug is poison, has no *mens rea*. He therefore incurs no criminal liability. Ann is the principal offender since she brought about the innocent agent's act. Similarly, a terrorist who sends a letter bomb which kills the recipient will be the principal, and the postman who unknowingly delivers the parcel is merely an innocent agent.

211

Where someone has a defence

If Ann persuades Ben to shoot and kill Chris, by convincing Ben that the target is a bear rather than a human being, Ben is an innocent agent and can rely on the defence of mistake; Ann will be the principal offender. The same applies if the principal uses someone below the age of criminal responsibility to bring about the *actus reus*.

Offences to which the concept of an innocent agent cannot apply

It has been suggested that there are some crimes which, by their nature, need to be carried out personally and to which the idea of an innocent agent cannot apply. This is because, for that offence, it would be wrong in logic to describe a person who did not carry out the *actus reus* of the offence as the principal offender. Murder is not such a crime so in the poisoning example above, there is no problem in saying that Ann killed Ben, even though Ann did not actually give Ben the poison. On the other hand, if we take bigamy, for which the *actus reus* is marrying while still married to someone else, it would seem inappropriate to rely on the doctrine of an innocent agent. If Mary persuades Peter to marry Kate, when Mary knows such a marriage would be bigamous because Peter's wife is alive though Peter does not know that, Peter cannot be liable as a principal offender because he lacks the *mens rea* of the offence. It has been argued by academics that Peter should not be treated as an innocent agent nor Mary as the principal, because it is not possible to say that Mary had married Kate while she was married to someone else. She may, however, still be a secondary party.

This problem was ignored in the case of **R *v* Cogan and Leak** (1976). The case concerned the offence of rape which, like bigamy, one would have expected to be an offence that had to be committed in person. Leak made his wife have sexual intercourse with Cogan. Mrs Leak did not consent to this, but Cogan thought she did. Cogan's mistake meant he lacked the *mens rea* of rape, so he was not liable for the offence. But he was treated as an innocent agent and Leak was liable as the principal offender in the rape of his wife. The case has been heavily criticized but the philosophy behind the case is supported by the decision in **DPP *v* K and C** (1996) which is discussed below.

• • • • • • • • • • • • • • • • • • • •
SECONDARY PARTIES

This chapter is primarily concerned with looking at the liability of secondary parties – often described as accomplices or accessories. The key provision for indictable offences is s. 8 of the Accessories and Abettors

Act 1861. This states: 'Whosoever shall aid, abet, counsel or procure the commission of any indictable offence, whether the same be an offence at common law or by virtue of any Act passed or to be passed, shall be liable to be tried, indicted and punished as a principal offender.' Section 44 of the Magistrates' Courts Act 1980 lays down a similar provision with respect to summary offences. As the provisions are so similar, we will concentrate on the 1861 Act.

A secondary party is essentially a person who helps or encourages the principal offender before the offence is committed, or at the time when it is committed. Help or encouragement given after the principal has committed the offence – to enable the principal to escape or to sell stolen goods, for example – does not amount to secondary participation, though it might amount to some other offence.

Under s. 8 such a person can generally incur the same liability as the principal offender, for the section states that he 'shall be tried, indicted and punished as a principal offender'. The extent of each party's involvement in a crime will usually be taken into account for sentencing purposes (except where the penalty is fixed, as in murder), but, technically, helping or encouraging someone else to commit a crime can attract the same punishment as actually committing the crime.

The implications of this principle can be seen in the controversial case of **R** *v* **Craig and Bentley** (1952), the story of which was made into the film *Let Him Have It*. Bentley was caught and arrested after the pair were chased across rooftops by police. Craig had a gun, and Bentley is alleged to have said to Craig, 'Let him have it.' Craig then shot and killed a policeman. Craig was charged with murdering a police officer (at that time a hanging offence) and Bentley was charged as his accomplice. In court Bentley argued that when he shouted 'Let him have it', he was telling Craig to hand over his gun, rather than, as the prosecution claimed, encouraging him to shoot the police officer. Nevertheless, both were convicted. Craig was under the minimum age for the death sentence, and was given life imprisonment. Bentley, who was older, was hanged. The conviction was subsequently overturned by the Court of Appeal in July 1998, following a long campaign by his family. But the error by the trial judge had simply been that his summing up was too harsh to the defendant and the legal principle in relation to equal liability for secondary parties as for the principal still stands.

Because the secondary party 'shall be tried, indicted and punished as a principal offender' the prosecution do not have to establish whether the accused was the principal offender or a secondary party, provided it is proven that he was definitely one or the other. In **R** *v* **Galliano** (1996) the accused was charged with the murder of his wife. There was evidence that either he carried out the killing himself or a killer carried it out on his behalf. The accused's appeal against his conviction was dismissed.

▶ *Actus reus*

A principal offence

Unlike a person who incurs liability for an inchoate offence, a secondary party cannot (with one exception) be liable if the principal offence is not committed. So if Ranjit encourages Jill to kill Lisa, Ranjit will be immediately liable for inciting murder but will only be liable as a secondary party to the murder if Jill goes ahead and kills Lisa.

In **Thornton** *v* **Mitchell** (1940) a bus driver was charged with careless driving after an accident. The conductor of the bus had been giving directions to help the driver reverse when the accident occurred, and was charged as a secondary party. The driver was acquitted on the basis that he had not been careless; this meant that the *actus reus* of the offence had not been committed, and so the conductor could not be liable either.

Provided that the prosecution prove that the offence was carried out by someone, a secondary party may be convicted even if the principal is unknown, or has not been caught. Secondary parties can also be convicted where the principal is acquitted. This is because an acquittal does not necessarily mean that the principal has not committed the offence; they may be acquitted because there is a lack of evidence against them, or some procedural defect occurred in the trial (assuming the parties are not tried together), or because they have a defence which accepts the offence was committed but excuses the conduct in the circumstances. In **R** *v* **Bourne** (1952), the accused forced his wife to commit buggery with a dog. Because the wife had acted under duress (see p. 270), she was not liable as a principal offender, but as an *actus reus* had been committed Bourne was liable as a secondary party.

The exception to the rule that the secondary party can only be liable if the principal offence is committed applies to the particular type of secondary party conduct known as 'procuring' which is discussed in more detail in the next section. Where the secondary party procured the principal offence, only the *actus reus* and not the *mens rea* of the principal offender need be proved. In **R** *v* **Millward** (1994) the appellant instructed an employee to drive a vehicle on a public road. The appellant knew that the vehicle was in a dangerous condition but the employee did not. Driving the vehicle caused a collision which resulted in a death. The employee was acquitted of causing death by reckless driving (an offence that has since been repealed) since he lacked the *mens rea* of the offence; the appellant was convicted as a secondary party as it was sufficient that he had procured the *actus reus* of the principal offence.

This approach was approved in **DPP** *v* **K and C** (1996). Two girls aged 14 and 11 were charged with procuring the offence of rape of a young girl by an unidentified boy. The two girls had imprisoned and robbed the victim when they were joined by the boy. They ordered the victim to remove her clothes and have sexual intercourse with the boy who partially penetrated her. The magistrates found that the boy could have been under 14 and might have lacked the *mens rea* of the principal offence so the girls were acquitted. On appeal by way of case stated, it was held that it did not matter if the principal lacked *mens rea*, the girls could still be liable for procuring the principal offence.

Aid, abet, counsel or procure

Section 8 of the Aiders and Abettors Act 1861 provides that liability as a secondary party lies on 'Whosoever shall aid, abet, counsel or procure'. Thus there are four types of secondary liability: aiding, abetting, counselling, and procuring.

Up until 1975, it was generally assumed that these particular words had no specific meaning and were interchangeable. This interpretation had to be reconsidered following the case of **Attorney-General's Reference (No. 1 of 1975)**. This stated that these four words describe four different types of behaviour, though their meanings may overlap, and each word should be given its ordinary and natural meaning. In summary, aiding means helping at the time of the principal offence; abetting means encouraging at the time; counselling means encouraging prior to the commission of the principal offence and procuring means helping prior to its commission.

In practice, the courts often fail to draw this distinction. For example in **Gillick** *v* **West Norfolk and Wisbech Area Health Authority** (1984) the House of Lords considered the issue of doctors providing contraceptives to girls under the age of 16. It is an offence for a man to have sexual intercourse with a girl under that age, and the judges considered whether in giving contraceptives to girls under 16, doctors were aiding and abetting this offence. It has since been pointed out that in the light of **Attorney-General's Reference (No. 1 of 1975)**, aiding or abetting means providing help or encouragement at the time the offence is committed, and it is highly unlikely that doctors would be present when sexual intercourse actually took place. It would have been more appropriate to talk about counselling or procuring, which take place prior to the commission of the offence.

An accused may often have committed more than one of these offences, and can be charged with more than one in the same proceedings, the most obvious example being aiding and abetting. We will now look in detail at the meanings of the different words, whether the accomplice must have caused the commission of the main offence, and whether the principal offender needs to have been aware of the accomplice's conduct.

Aiding

Aiding signifies helping the principal at the time when the offence is committed. Providing that some help is given, the prosecution do not have to prove that the help caused the principal to commit the offence, nor that the principal even knew about it.

Abetting

Abetting comprises encouragement to commit the crime, which is given at the time that the crime is committed. The principal probably needs to be aware of this encouragement though the encouragement need not have caused the principal to go ahead and commit the principal offence.

Simply being present at the scene of a crime and failing to stop it or report it to the police is not usually sufficient to constitute aiding the principal, but can it constitute encouragement at the time of the offence and thus abetting? The conclusion from the authorities seems to be that mere presence is not enough, the prosecution must prove something more in order for a court to conclude that this conduct amounted to encouragement. In **R** *v* **Clarkson** (1971), the defendants were soldiers who stood and watched a girl being raped by another soldier in their barracks. It was held that this did not amount to abetting the rapist; in order for it to do so the soldiers must have intended that their presence should encourage the rapist to continue, and it must have in fact encouraged him.

In **Allan** (1963), the accused was present when some of his friends got into a fight. He stayed at the scene and decided that he would help his friends if it became necessary, but in the event his assistance was not needed. The court held that presence at the scene combined with a secret intention to participate was not abetting, provided nothing was done to show that intention.

The defendant in **Coney** (1882) attended an illegal prize fight (a fight that is not carried out in accordance with the Queensberry Rules) and the court said that while without the spectators there would be no fight, there was insufficient evidence to constitute an abetting.

By contrast, in **Wilcox** *v* **Jeffrey** (1951), a well-known saxophone player came into the UK from America on a tourist visa. This visa prohibited him from working in England, but he breached its terms by taking part in a musical performance. The defendant not only attended the performance, but also met the saxophonist at the airport, and wrote a favourable review of the performance afterwards. It was held that these things together were sufficient to make him liable for abetting the commission of the offence.

Where an accused has a right to control someone else's actions and deliberately fails to do so, that failure may be a positive encouragement to the other to commit an illegal act, and therefore amount to an abetting. In **Tuck** *v* **Robson** (1970), the defendant was the licensee of a public house who let his customers commit the offence of drinking after hours. Because he was in a position of authority and control, the fact that he did not prevent his clientele from consuming drinks after hours was held to have abetted the offence.

Counselling

This encompasses encouraging the principal to commit the crime. Since encouraging someone at the scene of the crime is abetting, counselling covers giving such encouragement before the crime takes place. The principal must at least be aware that they have the encouragement or approval of the secondary party to commit the offence, and there must be some causal link between the encouragement and the commission of the offence. On the other hand, it is not necessary to prove that without the counselling, the offence would not have been committed.

In **R** *v* **Calhaem** (1985) the defendant was charged with murder. She had been infatuated with her solicitor and hired another person, Zajac, to kill the solicitor's girlfriend. At her trial, she was alleged to have counselled Zajac to commit murder. In his evidence, Zajac said that, although Ms Calhaem had indeed told him to carry out the killing, he had never had any intention of doing so – he was simply intending to go to her home and pretend that he meant to kill her, so that Ms Calhaem would think he had tried to carry out the plan and pay him his money. However, the victim had screamed a great deal, and he had gone 'berserk' and killed her. On appeal, the court held that it was not necessary to prove that the counselling caused the offence; a less direct causal link would suffice, and here that was satisfied by the fact that Zajac would never have gone to the girlfriend's flat if Ms Calhaem had not asked him to do so. Ms Calhaem's conviction was upheld.

Procuring

In **Attorney-General's Reference (No. 1 of 1975)** the Court of Appeal specified that to procure means 'to produce by endeavour'. This suggests that procuring an offence means causing it, or bringing it about, and this does not necessarily require the agreement or knowledge of the principal. In the case, the principal offender was caught driving with a blood-alcohol level over the prescribed limit. The secondary party had 'spiked' the principal's drink with alcohol, knowing that the principal would be driving, and was held to be guilty as a secondary party, even though the principal was not aware of what the secondary party had done.

	Encourage	Help
Before	Counsel	Procure
At the time	Abet	Aid

Fig. 4. Liability of Secondary Parties

▶ *Mens rea*

Once the prosecution have established that the secondary party did an act or acts which could help or encourage the principal to commit the crime, they must prove that the accomplice had the *mens rea* to be liable as a secondary party. It has to be shown that the defendant knew that acts and circumstances constituting a crime would exist (they do not need to know that these acts or circumstances would be a crime, because ignorance of the law is no defence). For example, a woman who tells a man to have sexual intercourse with another woman, knowing that he may have sexual intercourse with that woman, and aware of the circumstance that that woman might not be consenting at the time, could be liable for counselling the offence of rape.

The level of *mens rea* required is very low, because there is no need to prove that the defendant intended to help or encourage the principal. While the courts sometimes talk of 'intending' the help or encouragement, all this appears to mean in this context is that the person acted voluntarily – that they intended to do what they did, rather than that they intended its effect on the principal. Thus, for example, if Peter sells Beatrice a gun, knowing that she intends to kill Jane but not wanting her to do so, and Beatrice proceeds to kill Jane, then Beatrice will be liable for murder and Peter will be liable as a secondary party. The prosecution do not need to prove that Peter intended to help Beatrice, simply that he intended to sell the gun.

If a person acts in complete ignorance of a principal offender's plan to commit a crime they will not be liable as accomplices. For example, if Bill tells Mohammed that he has locked himself out of his house, and Mohammed helps Bill break into the house, Mohammed will not be liable as a secondary party to the burglary if it later transpires that Bill was breaking into his neighbour's house.

This approach was laid down in the leading case of **National Coal Board** *v* **Gamble** (1959). An employee of NCB operated a weighbridge at a colliery. His job included checking the loaded weights of lorries leaving the colliery, since it was an offence to take on to the road a lorry which was overloaded. On seeing that one lorry was over the weight limit, he informed the driver, but the driver replied that he was prepared to take the risk. The weighbridge operator proceeded to give him the ticket with which he was able to leave the colliery. Under the principle of corporate liability and, more specifically, vicarious responsibility (discussed in Chapter 12), the Board were liable for their employees' acts, and were thus secondary parties to the offence committed by the lorry driver. The employee may not have intended to help the driver commit the offence but this did not need to be proved. He had committed the *actus reus* of the crime and all that had to be proved in addition was his awareness of the risk that the acts and circumstances constituting the offence existed.

An example of a secondary party lacking *mens rea* because he was unaware of the circumstances that constituted the offence occurred in **Ferguson** *v* **Weaving** (1951). The defendant was the licensee of a pub, and had been charged with aiding and abetting customers to commit the offence of consuming intoxicating liquor on licensed premises outside permitted hours. As he did not know that the customers were drinking after closing time he was not liable.

While defendants need not intend the help or encouragement, they must know that their acts were capable of assisting or encouraging. This point was confirmed in **R** *v* **J.F. Alford Transport Ltd** (1997). A company, its managing director and its transport manager were charged with aiding and abetting lorry drivers employed by them in the making of false entries on tachograph record sheets. The prosecution claimed that the defendants, as managers of the company, must have known and accepted, if not actively encouraged, what the drivers did. They were convicted and appealed arguing that the trial judge's summing-up suggested to the jury that passive acquiescence would suffice for the purpose of secondary party liability. The Court of Appeal held that to impose liability on a secondary party, it had to be proved that the particular defendant intended to do the acts which he knew to be capable of assisting or encouraging the commission of the principal offence. He did not need to intend that the crime be committed. A defence that the management turned a blind eye in order to keep the drivers happy rather than to encourage them to produce false tachograph records would therefore fail. Where the defendant knew of the offence the prosecution had to show in addition that the defendant had made a deliberate decision not to prevent its commission. On the facts there was insufficient evidence of knowledge so the appeal was allowed.

The secondary party does not have to want the crime to be committed, and may in fact be very much against it, and yet still be liable. In **Director of Public Prosecutions for Northern Ireland** *v* **Lynch** (1975), Lynch was ordered by a man called Meehan, to drive him and some others to a place where they planned to kill a policeman. Meehan was known to be ruthless and extremely violent, and apparently made it clear to Lynch that it would be extremely dangerous for him to disobey – in fact Lynch testified that he believed he would himself have been shot if he refused to drive. Lynch did as he was told, staying in the car during the shooting, and driving the killers away afterwards. The court held that although he might not have condoned the plan, and may even have been horrified by it, the fact that he drove the principal to the appointed place, knowing of the relevant circumstances that constituted the offence, meant he could be liable for aiding and abetting (the appeal against his conviction as a secondary party to murder was, however, allowed on a different point).

Merely knowing that some kind of illegal activity is being planned is not sufficient to impose liability as a secondary party. In **Bainbridge**

(1960), the accused purchased some cutting equipment for a man called Shakeshaft which was later used in a bank robbery. Bainbridge admitted that he suspected Shakeshaft wanted the equipment for some illegal act, but said he thought it would be breaking up stolen goods rather than a bank robbery. It was held that, for the defendant to be liable as a secondary party to the robbery, he would at least have to know that the equipment was for some form of robbery, though he need not know which bank was going to be robbed and when. In fact, Bainbridge's story was not believed and his conviction was upheld.

In a situation like the one presented in **Bainbridge**, a secondary party will not escape liability by practising 'wilful blindness' – if someone sells a sawn-off shotgun to a person he knows to be a bank robber, and the gun is used in such a robbery, he or she will not escape liability as a secondary party to the crime on the grounds that the buyer did not actually say that the gun was to be used in a bank robbery, and the seller did not ask.

The Court of Appeal in **Bainbridge** talked about the defendant needing to foresee the risk that that 'type' of offence would be committed. But, there are difficulties in trying to divide offences into types. Is burglary the same type of offence as robbery? Is grievous bodily harm the same type of offence as murder? While not overruling this dictum, in **DPP for Northern Ireland** *v* **Maxwell** (1978) the court talked about the offence committed having to fall within the range of offences contemplated by the defendant. The accused was a member of a terrorist organization which ordered him to drive some men to a public house. He realized that he was being asked to take the men there for some illegal and probably violent purpose, but did not know the specific details of what they planned to do. The men in fact planted a bomb, and Maxwell was convicted of abetting an act done with intent to cause an unlawful explosion. The House of Lords held that Maxwell's knowledge that the men were terrorists and would intend to endanger life or property, was sufficient for liability as a secondary party; he did not need to know precisely what kinds of weapons or methods the terrorists planned to use. The offence committed was within the range of offences that he must have contemplated the men were likely to commit.

▶ Joint enterprise

The courts have shown themselves more willing to impose criminal liability on secondary parties where they feel that the defendants were involved in a joint enterprise, sometimes described as a joint plan. So what is a joint enterprise? In **Petters and Parfitt** (1995) the Court of Appeal said that for a joint enterprise to exist, the defendants must have a common purpose or intention. It is not sufficient that they both separately intend the same thing; they must have made it clear to each other, by their actions or words, that they have this common intention, though this might not be communicated until just before or at the point of committing the offence. The two defendants in the case had arrived separately at a car park, where they proceeded to attack the victim. The victim died as a result of a kick in the head, but it was not clear which one of the defendants had given the fatal kick, since they both admitted punching the victim, but denied kicking him at all. An appeal against their convictions was allowed on the grounds that it had not been made clear to the jury that, in order for there to be a joint enterprise, the two defendants had to have communicated their common intention to each other.

The significance of the existence of a joint enterprise for liability has caused some debate. **R** *v* **Stewart and Schofield** (1995) concerned a robbery that went badly wrong. Stewart had suggested to Schofield and a third man that they should rob a shop. Stewart went armed with a knife and the third man with a scaffolding pole, while Schofield played the role of lookout. During the robbery, the owner of the shop was killed by a blow from the scaffolding pole. The third man was found liable for murder, and the other two were convicted for manslaughter. On appeal, while rejecting their applications, Hobhouse LJ suggested that the law on joint enterprise was separate to the law on secondary participation:

> The allegation that a defendant took part in the execution of a
> crime as a joint enterprise is not the same as an allegation that
> he aided, abetted, counselled or procured the commission of
> that crime. A person who is a mere aider or abettor etc, is truly a
> secondary party to the commission of whatever crime it is that the
> principal has committed although he may be charged as a principal.
> If the principal has committed the crime of murder, the liability of
> the secondary party can only be a liability for aiding and abetting
> murder. In contrast, where the allegation is joint enterprise, the
> allegation is that one defendant participated in the criminal act
> of another.

The Court of Appeal also appeared to support this distinction in **R** *v* **O'Brien** (1995), which concerned a secondary party to the attempted murder of a policeman. The Law Commission took a similar approach, suggesting that the law of secondary parties could be abolished while retaining the law on joint enterprises. However, leading criminal law academics have severely criticized this analysis, arguing that joint enterprise is clearly part of the law on secondary participation, the only distinction being that where a joint enterprise exists, it will usually be easier to find the elements of helping or encouraging and the relevant *mens rea*. The leading authority on joint enterprises is now **R** *v* **Powell and English** (1997) which gave no support to the suggestion that liability for participation in a joint enterprise was separate to liability as a secondary party.

Thus the preferred approach is that the law on joint enterprises is part of the law on secondary party liability, and **Stewart and Schofield** should now be seen as bad law on this point. The main significance of the presence of a joint enterprise is simply to lower the threshold of *mens rea* required by a secondary party.

We have seen that under the principle laid down in **National Coal Board** *v* **Gamble** (1959) you normally need to prove knowledge to impose liability on a secondary party. The existence of a joint enterprise means that liability can be imposed where there is mere foresight rather than knowledge. Where there is a joint enterprise and someone commits an offence that goes beyond the scope of the joint enterprise, the others will be liable as secondary parties to that offence if they foresaw it might be committed. If Pat and Jill have agreed to rob a bank and in the process Pat goes outside their plan and kills a member of the public, Jill will be liable not only for the robbery but also as a secondary party to the murder if she foresaw the risk that Pat might commit murder.

In **R** *v* **Powell and English** two separate appeals were heard together before the House of Lords. On the issue of the *mens rea* required to be liable as part of a joint enterprise, Lord Hutton stated: 'It is sufficient to found a conviction for murder for a secondary party to have realised that in the course of the joint enterprise the primary party might kill with intent to do so or with intent to cause grievous bodily harm.'

In the first appeal, three men visited a drug dealer and the dealer was shot. The prosecution was unable to prove which of the three shot the victim, but agreed that all three participants were guilty because the two who did not fire the gun nevertheless knew that the third man had a gun and realized he might use it to kill or cause serious injury. Their appeal against conviction was rejected.

In the second case, English was involved in a joint enterprise to attack a police officer with wooden posts. The principal offender went beyond the joint enterprise by stabbing the officer to death with a knife. English's appeal was allowed as the House of Lords stated that where the lethal act by the primary party was fundamentally different from the acts foreseen by the secondary party, the latter would only be liable for a homicide if the weapon used was as dangerous as the one contemplated. **Powell and English** has been followed closely by the Court of Appeal in **R** *v* **Greatrex** (1998) and **R** *v* **Uddin** (1998).

Saunders and Archer (1573) is a very old case in this field. Saunders wanted to kill his wife, and Archer supplied him with poison for this purpose. Saunders, who was presumably an avid reader of fairy tales, put the poison into an apple and gave the apple to his wife. She took a bite from it, but then passed it to their daughter, who finished off the apple and died as a result. Saunders was found liable for the murder of the daughter, but Archer was acquitted as a secondary party, because he could not have foreseen that Saunders would fail to intervene. If the same facts were to occur today, the doctrine of transferred malice would probably mean that Archer would be liable.

In **Davies** *v* **DPP** (1954) two gangs of boys were involved in a brawl on Clapham Common. One of them, E, had a knife, and ended up stabbing and killing someone. Davies was charged as a secondary party to the murder but it was held that as there was no evidence that he knew E had a knife, he could not have contemplated the risk that E might use it. Therefore he was not a party to the murder, though he was guilty of common assault. A similar conclusion was reached, on different facts, in **Mahmood** (1994). The defendant was 'joyriding' with a friend, who was driving the car. The police spotted the car and pursued it, and the friend drove recklessly in order to get away. Finally the two boys jumped out of the car, leaving it in gear. The car mounted the pavement, killing a baby in its pram. The defendant was charged as a secondary party to manslaughter. On appeal, the Court of Appeal concluded that he would have been liable if death had occurred while the car was being driven recklessly, but there was no evidence that he had foreseen that the friend might abandon the car while it was still in gear.

While a defendant can be liable on the basis of foresight that someone else would behave in a certain way, it needs to be decided what degree of foresight is required. Sir Robin Cooke commented in **Chan Wing-Siu** (1985): 'Various formulae have been suggested – including a substantial risk, a real risk, a risk that something might well happen. No one formula is exclusively preferable.' However, he said, risks that the defendant had merely considered 'fleetingly or even causing him some deliberation' were not sufficient. The three defendants in the case were charged with murder. They had gone to the victim's flat in order to enforce payment of a debt, and the victim had been stabbed during the ensuing fight. One of the three said he had not realized the other two had knives. The Privy Council held that, where the principal was convicted of murder, secondary parties could be liable for the same offence, if they foresaw that it was more probable than not that the principal might kill or cause grievous bodily harm. Therefore, all the parties in the case were liable if they foresaw a substantial risk that one of their accomplices might have a knife and use it with the intention of inflicting serious injury, even though they did not intend or want this to happen.

The Court of Appeal upheld the conviction of the defendant in **R** *v* **O'Brien** (1995) as a secondary party for the attempted murder of a policeman. He had been the driver in the car when the policeman had been shot by his co-defendant. As regards his *mens rea* it only had to be proved he knew that in the course of committing the agreed crime the principal offender *might* act with an intent to kill. It was not necessary for him to know that the principal offender *would* act with such an intent.

▶ Strict liability offences

In strict liability crimes the secondary party must have *mens rea*, even though the principal can be convicted without it. In **Callow** *v* **Tillstone** (1900) a butcher was liable as a principal offender for exposing unfit meat for sale, which is a strict liability offence. The defendant was a vet who had examined the carcasses at the butcher's request and certified that the meat was sound. He was convicted of aiding and abetting the offence, but this verdict was quashed on appeal, because he had not known the meat was unfit.

▶ Liability of a secondary party for a different offence

Until 1986 the courts took the approach that a secondary party could not be convicted of a more serious offence than the principal. In **R** *v* **Richards** (1974) the defendant hired two men to attack her husband, telling them to 'put him in hospital for a month'. She was convicted as a secondary party to wounding with intent under s. 18 of the Offences Against the Person Act 1861, but the two men were acquitted of that offence, and instead convicted of unlawful wounding, a lesser offence. The Court of Appeal quashed Mrs Richards's original conviction and substituted a conviction for unlawful wounding, holding that as a secondary party, she should not be liable for a more serious offence than the two principals.

However, Lord Mackay pointed out in **R** *v* **Howe** (1986) that sometimes this would cause the law to be unduly lenient on a secondary party. As an example of this, consider a situation in which Ann hands Ben a gun, telling him that it is loaded only with blank cartridges, and asking him to fire it at Clare, just to scare her. Ann actually knows that the gun is loaded with live ammunition, and wants Ben to kill Clare. When Ben fires the gun at Clare she dies instantly. Ben, as the principal offender, can only be liable for manslaughter, because he did not intend to kill nor to cause grievous bodily harm to Clare. If the *ratio* of **Richards** were applied, Ann would also only be liable for manslaughter, even though she did intend to kill Clare. Because of this anomaly, the case of **Richards** was overruled by **R** *v* **Howe**.

▶ Withdrawal

An alleged secondary party who withdraws from a joint enterprise before the offence is committed and decides not to take part (or take any further part) may escape liability. Where the criminal conduct is spontaneous they can withdraw, and thereby avoid liability, without communicating it to the principal offender, for example, by simply walking away. In **R** *v* **Mitchell** (1999) there had been some trouble inside an Indian restaurant. A fight ensued between staff and three customers outside the restaurant. One member of staff was killed and all three customers, including Mitchell were charged with his murder. There was some evidence that after the deceased had been repeatedly kicked and hit, the three accused had walked away from the deceased leaving him on the ground. Mitchell had then turned back, picked up a stick and hit the victim several more times. It was possible that these constituted the fatal blows. In their defence the other two defendants argued that they had withdrawn from the joint enterprise by the time the fatal blows were struck. The trial judge directed the jury that someone participating in a joint enterprise could only withdraw by communicating his withdrawal to the principal offender. They were convicted and appealed. The Court of Appeal held that for an effective withdrawal from the criminal conduct communication was not required where the criminal enterprise was spontaneous rather than pre-planned. The appeals were allowed and a retrial ordered as it was possible that the death had resulted from the injuries incurred before Mitchell returned with the stick.

Where the criminal conduct is planned, a person can only withdraw from the plan and avoid criminal liability if their withdrawal happens at a sufficiently early stage and the secondary party communicates their withdrawal to the principal offender and does everything they reasonably can to prevent the crime from going ahead. What constitutes sufficient withdrawal depends on the facts of each case and is for the jury to decide. In **R** *v* **Becerra** (1975), the accused took part in a burglary, armed with a knife. He and his accomplice had agreed that if they were caught in the act, Becerra should use the knife, but when they saw someone approach, Becerra changed his mind, said 'Let's go' and ran away. The other burglar used the knife, killing the victim. The court held that Becerra's words were not enough in themselves to constitute a withdrawal from the crime. At such a late stage only more definite action, such as attempting to take away the knife, could have amounted to repentance.

The defendant in **Rook** (1993) was involved in a plan to murder. He later changed his mind and decided not to take part; so on the day that the murder was to take place he made sure that he was not at home when the other parties to the plan came round to collect him. This conduct was held to be insufficient to constitute an unequivocal communication of his withdrawal, and so he was still liable as a secondary party to the murder.

Defendants who change their minds and do not take part in a planned crime may still be liable for incitement or conspiracy as already discussed in Chapter 10.

Who did it?

Sometimes the prosecution can establish that a victim died as a result of a wound, and that a group of people were involved in the attack but it cannot be established which person caused the fatal blow. In this situation they can be convicted of murder if the prosecution can show that they foresaw that the fatal blow would be carried out by one of them. It does not matter that the prosecution cannot identify precisely who administered the fatal blow as under s. 8 of the Accessories and Abettors Act 1861 they are all treated as if they are the principal offender.

▶ Victims as secondary participants

Some statutes are passed specifically to protect a particular group of people, such as minors. People who fall within such groups cannot be held liable as participants in the criminal offence created by the statute. In **Tyrell** (1894), the defendant was a girl under 16 years old. It was stated that she could not be held guilty of aiding or abetting a male to commit the offence of having unlawful sexual intercourse with her, or of inciting him to commit that offence, however willing she might have been for the offence to be committed.

▶ Criticism

Joint enterprises

The simple requirement of foresight where there is a joint enterprise seems hard to reconcile with **Moloney**, which stressed that liability for murder requires an intent to kill or cause grievous bodily harm and that foresight was only evidence of intention. Since secondary parties may be punished as if they were a principal, it seems unjust that they should be convicted without the same *mens rea* as that required for the principal. Despite this, the approach was approved in **R** *v* **Powell, R** *v* **English** due to the need to protect the public from criminals operating in gangs.

Deviations from the plan

The distinction highlighted in **R** *v* **Bamborough** (1996) between those who foresaw the harm but contemplated it would be committed in a different way and would be secondary parties; and those who avoid liability because the principal offender went beyond the agreement is a very fine distinction which will be difficult to apply in practice.

Sentencing

The current law treats the secondary party as if he committed the actual crime. This is very harsh and can be seen as lowering the threshold of criminal liability. Under German law the accessory has a lower maximum sentence than the principal.

▶ Reform

Terminology

The draft Criminal Code uses the terms 'procures, assists or encourages'. These are clearly more in tune with everyday language than 'aids, abets, counsels or procures', and each clearly has a distinct meaning. The new terms would all be inchoate offences, so that the final offence need never be committed, and liability would arise as soon as the procuring, assisting or encouraging took place. This would avoid problems of deciding what the relationship should be between the accomplice's conduct and the final offence.

• •

ANSWERING QUESTIONS

1 **Using cases to illustrate your answer, critically consider whether the words 'aid, abet, counsel and procure' each have a separate meaning.** *Oxford*
An answer to this question might start by pointing out that these words come from s. 8 of the Accessories and Abettors Act 1861 and point to the leading case of **Attorney-General's Reference (No. 1 of 1975)**. Most of the material discussed under the subheading 'Aid, abet, counsel or procure' is of relevance to this essay, including the fact that the *mens rea* in relation to those words is much the same, apart from perhaps for procuring. You are asked to consider the law 'critically', so you need to draw out some of the confusion that still exists, illustrated by the case of **Gillick** and the problems with joint enterprises. You should also discuss the reform proposals in the draft Criminal Code.

2 **'... if four words are employed here, "aid", "abet", "counsel" or "procure", the probability is that there is a difference between each of those four words ...'** (Lord Widgery CJ, in Attorney-General's Reference (No. 1 of 1975))
Do you agree that each of the four words should have a separate meaning? *(10 marks)*
Do the four words together satisfactorily summarize the law relating to secondary participation? *(15 marks) Oxford*
This is a situation where it would have been tempting to talk generally on the subject without really answering the question.

In fact this question can be answered quite precisely, if you plan your answer carefully. For the first part, you can say what the law is on the meaning of the four words, but you must also say whether you think there should be a separate meaning. You are free to answer in favour or against, but you should point to confusion from the cases, intricate distinctions which merely complicate the law without adding much of substance, problems for the jury and so forth. Again, the draft Criminal Code will be relevant.

For the second part (which you should spend slightly longer on as it is worth more marks), you are free to take any approach you want, but one line of argument would be that the words are misleading, old-fashioned and give little clue as to the intricate distinctions that are drawn between them. For example, there seems no linguistic reason why aiding should not require any causal connection while abetting does.

3 **David and Shirley are members of the Animals Have Rights organization. In order to draw attention to their demands they decide to blow up a farm house. They persuade Niel, a former member of the organization who had not participated in its affairs for a year, to supply bomb-making equipment, by threatening to kill his girlfriend and son if he refused. They persuaded Ian, a timorous taxi-driver, to take them to the farm. David and Shirley planted the explosive device with a three-minute time fuse and shouted a warning that the occupants had three minutes to get out. The bomb exploded prematurely, killing Liz and seriously injuring Tony.**
Consider the criminal liability of David, Shirley, Niel and Ian.
In this question David and Shirley do exactly the same things, so they can be dealt with together. As they are principal offenders, it is probably best to deal with them first, and to start with their liability for complete offences before looking at their liability for inchoate offences.

The most serious complete offence they could be liable for is the murder of Liz. They have committed the *actus reus* of murder (causation is not an issue on these facts as there is no intervening event) so the only debate will be whether they had the *mens rea* of murder. As they shout a warning and the bomb goes off prematurely, the key question will be whether they foresaw that death or personal injury were virtually certain to result from their conduct (though remember to point out that the *mens rea* required is intention, and foresight will only be evidence of this intention). The key cases of **Moloney** and **Nedrick** will need to be discussed. Remember that in discussing *mens rea*, motive (such as helping animals) is irrelevant.

If David and Shirley are found to have the *mens rea* of murder, there is nothing to suggest that they would fall within the defences of provocation or diminished responsibility (or any other defence), so voluntary manslaughter is not an issue. Although murder is the likely offence, it would also be worth considering involuntary manslaughter as a fall-back position in case a jury found that they did not have the *mens rea* of murder.

Next, you should consider the non-fatal injury to Tony. We are told that he is seriously injured, but it is not clear whether this would be sufficiently serious to fall within s. 18 of the Offences Against the Person Act 1861. If it does, David and Shirley can only be liable for this if they were also liable for murder, since if they lacked the *mens rea* for murder, they would also lack the *mens rea* for s. 18 of the Offences Against the Person Act 1861. They might have the *mens rea* of a s. 20 offence, if they foresaw the risk of causing some physical harm to a person. If Tony's injuries are not sufficient to constitute GBH then David and Shirley are likely to be liable under s. 47.

David and Shirley will also be liable for criminal damage and aggravated criminal damage, as they were reckless as to the endangering of life. Note that the relevant form of recklessness is **Caldwell**, which should be easy to prove on these facts.

As for inchoate offences discussed in Chapter 10, David and Shirley will be liable for conspiring to commit at least criminal damage. They will also incur liability for inciting the commission of criminal damage in relation to their behaviour towards Niel and Ian.

Moving on to Niel, he is obviously not the principal offender, as he does not personally carry out the *actus reus* of the principal offences, so his potential liability is that of a secondary party. He provides assistance prior to the time of the commission of the offence so his role would be that of a procurer. Procurers are thought to require knowledge of the acts and circumstances of the crime. He would probably have the *mens rea* as a secondary party to the criminal damage, but would he have the *mens rea* of a secondary party to murder? The fact that he provided a three-minute time fuse may be relevant here. Niel is also likely to argue that he acted under duress (see p. 246), but note that this defence is not available to secondary parties to murder (**Howe**) so it would only be possible in relation to the lesser offences. You need to consider the fact that he did originally join the organization.

Ian is potentially liable as a secondary party. His role was to provide help at the time of the *actus reus* so he might be labelled an abettor. On the issue of *mens rea*, foresight of the acts and circumstances of the offence would be sufficient. The case of **Lynch** makes it clear that the fact that Ian does not want the bombing to happen may not help him. Like Niel, he will also seek to rely on the defence of duress, and in this case it is not self-induced. Note that in applying the second limb of the **Graham** test of duress, the court could not take into account that Ian was timorous because the reasonable person must be treated as someone of reasonable firmness.

4 E was queuing to get into a club with his friend, F, when G tried to push past him and then called him a big-nosed brainless idiot when E would not let him through. E turned away to avoid further trouble but F became angry and kicked G in the groin. G took a bottle of beer from his pocket, smashed it against a wall and thrust it at F's face. E managed to pull G off balance and, as he fell, F kicked him three or four times. E and F then ran off, leaving G apparently unconscious. An ambulance was summoned, but by the time that it arrived, G had revived and refused to go to hospital. However, he was still feeling unwell the next day and he went to the hospital's casualty department. There, no X-rays were taken and he was sent home with painkillers. In fact, he had suffered a broken skull and he suddenly collapsed and died later that day.

Discuss what offences E and F may have committed, and whether any defences may be available. *London*

As E and F's conduct has been quite different you need to discuss their liability separately. It would be wise to start with F first of all as his conduct has been the most serious, and you will be looking at whether E is a secondary party to offences committed by F, so it would help to have decided first what offences F has committed. We will consider F's conduct in chronological order. First of all F kicked G in the groin. This could be a non-fatal offence of either battery or s. 47 of the Offences Against the Person Act 1861, depending on the gravity of the harm caused. When G fell, F kicked him three or four times leaving G unconscious and with a broken skull. F could be liable for a s. 18 OAPA if he intended to cause G grievous bodily harm.

G later dies. The most serious offence that F could then be liable for is murder. This would depend on whether he is found to have been the cause of the death or whether the intervening conduct, of G initially refusing to go to hospital or the apparently negligent medical treatment, would have broken the chain of causation. You would need to look in detail at the case law in this field and in particular the case of **Cheshire**. A court is likely to find that the injuries inflicted by F were still operative at the time of G's death and that F was therefore a cause of his death. There would also be a debate as to whether F had the *mens rea* of murder. If F satisfied the elements of murder then he would want to argue the partial defence of provocation because of G's initial conduct in the queue. As the court might find that he lacked the *mens rea* for murder you would also need to consider his liability for involuntary manslaughter and on these facts unlawful act manslaughter would be particularly relevant.

As regards E's liability, when he pulled G off balance he may have committed a battery. A major issue would be whether E could be liable as a secondary party to the murder or manslaughter of G by F. You would need to look at **Peters and Parfait** and consider whether there was a joint enterprise on these facts and whether he had foreseen that death or grievous bodily harm might be committed by F. As G had just thrust a bottle at F he would probably succeed with a public or private defence discussed at p. 263.

12 Corporate liability

Criminal offences may not only be committed by individual people, but also by companies. This raises obvious problems regarding the existence of *mens rea* – how do you define the state of mind of a company? Consequently the law has developed two devices by which criminal liability can be imposed on a corporation: vicarious liability and the doctrine of identification.

▶ Vicarious liability

In practice this type of liability tends to be applied where the law is faced with a regulatory offence. Vicarious liability means the liability of one legal person for the acts of another (a 'legal person' may be a company or a group, as well as an individual human being). The law rarely imposes liability on one person for acts done by someone else, but there are three types of situation where vicarious criminal liability can arise.

* In strict liability offences, where the statutory description of the *actus reus* can be interpreted in such a way as to cover someone other than the actual perpetrator. An example might be where the offence involves 'selling' goods – when shop assistants 'sell' food, it can reasonably be said that at the same time their employer is also selling it, even if the owner of the shop is not present. By contrast, if a lorry driver was charged with an offence using the word 'driving' – driving a lorry with worn tyres perhaps, or driving over the speed limit – liability could not be shifted to the driver's employer, because the term used is not capable of this extended meaning; in normal language we would not say the employer 'drove' the lorry.
* Where the possibility of vicarious liability is expressed or implied in a statute. An example of vicarious liability being expressly allowed for in a statute is the Licensing Act 1964 which states that 'A person shall not, in pursuance of a sale by him of intoxicating liquor, deliver that liquor, either himself or by his servant or agent.'

- In cases of delegated management. If an employer is under a statutory duty, and delegates that duty to one of his or her employees, the employer will be vicariously liable for any criminal offence which the employee commits while carrying out the delegated duty, even one which requires *mens rea*. In **Allen** *v* **Whitehead** (1929), the owner of a café was charged with knowingly permitting prostitutes to meet together and remain in a place where refreshments were sold. The café was run by a manager who knew about the prostitutes; the accused had no knowledge of them. The court held that the café owner had delegated his statutory duty, and was therefore vicariously liable, so that his manager's *actus reus* and *mens rea* could be assigned to him.

▶ The doctrine of identification

This doctine applies to all offences to which vicarious liability does not attach. Identification allows certain senior people within a company to be recognized for legal purposes as being the company, so that any criminal liability they incur while going about the company's business can be assigned to the company.

The House of Lords in **Tesco Supermarkets** *v* **Nattrass** (1972) adopted a rather narrow attitude towards the kind of employee who could be identified with the company. It stated that only individuals who had some power of control within the organization, including some discretion over the activity with which the offence is concerned, would fall within this doctrine. This would only include 'the board of directors, the managing director and perhaps the superior officers of a company carrying out the functions of management and speaking and acting as the company'. It would not normally cover a sales assistant. As a result, the larger a company, the more difficult it would be to convict it of an offence, unless the offence was one where vicarious liability applied.

In the case, Tesco were charged with an offence under the Trade Descriptions Act 1968. The company had advertised that they were selling a particular soap powder at a specified (reduced) price. An old age pensioner had tried to buy a packet at the advertised price, but in his local branch the packets were all marked at the full price. The shop refused to sell him the soap powder at less than the full cost. It appeared that the failure to display the goods at the reduced-price was the fault of the branch manager, so the issue in the case was whether he could be considered to be representing the company by his acts – if he was not, Tesco were not liable. The House of Lords found that Tesco exercised strict controls over its branch managers, allowing them no power of control over pricing policy, and therefore the branch manager could not be identified as the company, and Tesco were not liable.

This restrictive approach to identification liability has been challenged by the Privy Council in **Meridian Global Funds Management Asia Ltd** *v* **Securities Commission** (1995). Two men were employed in New Zealand by Meridian as investment managers. Under New Zealand legislation any person becoming a substantial security holder in a public company had to give notice of the fact. The employees used Meridian's funds to acquire such an interest and failed to give the relevant notice. The Court of Appeal in New Zealand ruled that the knowledge of the employees could be attributed to Meridian, and so Meridian were liable for breaching the legislation. An appeal to the Privy Council was rejected. Lord Hoffmann suggested that in attributing knowledge, a court should not take too literal an approach to the concept of a 'directing mind'. It was relevant to examine the language of the particular statute, its content and underlying policy to decide how it was meant to apply to a company. Since, in this case, the policy was to compel disclosure of a substantial security holder, the knowledge should be that of the person who acquired the relevant interest, in other words the person who was actually in charge of the matter. This would include people who fell outside the nerve centre of command who could be taken into account under **Tesco** *v* **Nattrass**. Privy Council judgments are not binding on the domestic courts but are only persuasive, and it is therefore not certain whether this approach will be followed in the future.

▶ Offences for which corporations are never liable

A corporation can only be held liable for an offence which may be punished by a fine – so, for example, a corporation cannot be liable for murder, since the mandatory sentence is life imprisonment. In **R** *v* **Coroner for East Kent, ex parte Spooner** (1987), an application for judicial review arising from a coroner's inquest into the deaths caused by *The Herald of Free Enterprise* ferry disaster, it was accepted that a corporation could be convicted of manslaughter, though the consequent prosecution was dropped due to lack of evidence.

It is unlikely that corporate liability would ever be imposed for more personal crimes, such as rape or bigamy.

▶ Why is corporate liability needed?

There are several reasons for the imposition of corporate liability.

* Without it, companies might escape regulation by the criminal law, and individuals could be prosecuted for offences which were really the fault of company practices.

- In some cases it is more convenient for procedural purposes to prosecute a company than its employee(s).
- Where an offence is serious, a company may be more likely to be able to pay the required level of fine than an individual employee would be.
- The threat of criminal prosecution may encourage shareholders to exercise control over the activities of companies in which they invest.
- If a company has made a profit through an illegal practice, it should be the one to pay the price, not an employee.
- Corporate liability can discourage companies from putting pressure on employees, directly or indirectly, to raise profits by acting illegally – for example, if a haulage firm sets its drivers targets for delivery times that those drivers could not meet without speeding, imposing corporate or vicarious liability would be a way of ensuring that the company does not get off scot-free if the driver is charged with speeding.
- Adverse publicity and fines may act as a deterrent against acting illegally – this might not be the case if an individual was prosecuted.

▶ Criticisms of corporate liability

Corporate manslaughter

The failings of the law of corporate liability have been highlighted in the context of corporate manslaughter. While over the last 40 years 22,000 people have been killed at work or through business related disasters, there has only ever been two successful prosecutions for corporate manslaughter, noteably following the Lyme Bay canoeing disaster, **R** *v* **Kite and OLL Ltd** (1994). P & O were indicted for manslaughter following the drowning of 188 people in 1987 when their ferry *The Herald of Free Enterprise* capsized. This tragedy occurred because the bow doors were left open when leaving Zeebrugge harbour. The employee responsible for shutting the doors had fallen asleep. An inquiry set up following the disaster (the Sheen inquiry) found that the company's own regulations made no reference to the closing of the doors and this was not the first occasion on which the company's ships had gone to sea with their doors open. The inquiry concluded that the company's management shared responsibility for the failure in their safety system, but the criminal case against the company collapsed. The prosecution had been unable to satisfy the doctrine of identification.

Another high profile case in which the prosecution collapsed was that against Great Western Trains Company (GWT). On 19 September 1997 a high-speed train travelling from Swansea to London was racing at 125 mph about 10 minutes from Paddington when it passed a red light.

Soon afterwards it collided with a freight train. Seven people were killed and 151 injured. The train was being operated with its automatic warning system switched off because it did not work, and the automatic train protective system was also inoperative. Furthermore there was no second driver in the cab. The subsequent train accident in 1999 at Ladbroke Grove, and the public anger against Railtrack, highlights the need for the criminal law to provide effective deterrence, so that companies are not tempted to make savings through safety cuts.

Punishment

The courts do not usually set fines in proportion to the profit a company may have made as a result of their illegal practice – ignoring health and safety regulations, or anti-pollution laws can save companies a great deal of money. Fines themselves may only deter companies from offending if they are higher than the profits to be made from illegal activity – so if, for example, it is cheaper for a company to pay fines for polluting the environment than to improve their waste-disposal processes, the fines may be regarded as no more than a business expense.

The fact that corporate liability can only be punished by fines can mean that the guilty company simply shifts the financial burden on to the consumer. By charging higher prices, the company can make up the cost of the fine, so that the only penalty it really suffers is bad publicity and a slight dent in its competitiveness – though even this is ineffective where the company has a monopoly on the supply of particular goods or services.

Lack of deterrence

In large companies shareholders are very rarely able to exercise control over firms with regard to the kinds of issues likely to come before the courts, so corporate liability may have little effect in promoting better control.

As with strict liability, the success of corporate liability in encouraging companies to ensure that their employees maintain high standards depends largely on the possibility of being caught; unless there is a good chance of illegal activity being discovered and prosecuted, the fact that corporate liability will be imposed if it is, may carry little weight.

Individual responsibility

Where serious offences such as manslaughter are concerned, bringing a prosecution against a company may allow the individuals responsible to go free. For example, the owner of a company who deliberately neglects safety precautions in order to maximize profits is just as morally guilty for the resulting death of an employee as the careless driver who kills a pedestrian, yet the second is likely to end up in prison, while the first may only suffer the prosecution of their company and the consequent fine, rather than being prosecuted personally and possibly imprisoned.

▶ Reform

Management failure

An alternative model of corporate liability would look at corporate systems, practices and policies rather than focus on the wrongdoing of a particular employee. The Law Commission has recommended the creation of an offence of corporate killing which would be based on 'management failure'. Under the draft Bill prepared by the Law Commission a company would be guilty of a corporate killing if:

(a) management failure by the corporation is the cause or one of the causes of a person's death; and

(b) that failure constitutes conduct falling far below what can reasonably be expected of the corporation in the circumstances.

There is a management failure by the company 'if the way in which its activities are managed or organized fails to ensure the health and safety of persons employed in or affected by those activities'. The penalty for this offence would be a fine together with the possibility of making a remedial order. The Government has announced that they intend to introduce this reform.

Statutory vicarious liability

The draft Criminal Code retains the principle of vicarious liability but would apply it only where specifically written into a statute. It abolishes the principle of delegated authority, and provides that a company would not be liable where the controlling officer was acting against the interests of the company.

Gross negligence manslaughter

In the Great Western Trains case, the leading barrister, Mr Richard Lissack QC, put forward a novel argument to the court. He argued that there had been a change in the law on corporate manslaughter following the House of Lords judgment in **R** *v* **Adomako** on gross negligence manslaughter. His case was that today the test for guilt for involuntary manslaughter (excluding constructive manslaughter) was purely objective – was the defendant grossly negligent, that is, criminally careless judged by ordinary reasonable standards? Accordingly, it was no longer necessary to look for any directing mind of the company because a defendant's mind is not in question. All that needs to be focused upon is the company's conduct, and the question whether, measured against reasonable conduct, the company's behaviour was so bad as to warrant the label 'criminal'. This argument was rejected by the trial judge and the Crown Prosecution has announced that it will appeal his ruling through an Attorney-General's reference. While it is unlikely that **Adomako** did make this change, such a reform could be made by Parliament. The advantage of this approach is it focuses on the company as a whole, rather than on the *mens rea* of an individual employee. As Mr Lissack observed:

> If a company is large, with responsibility for safety assumed by no one and avoided by everyone, it may conduct its undertaking as negligently as it wishes, knowing that, unless the prosecution can prove beyond doubt that a directing mind of the company personally authorised, procured or directed the specific wrong, that neither that individual nor the company could ever be convicted of manslaughter, with all that a conviction for that offence conveys.

Civil liability

It has been suggested that some of the offences for which companies are likely to incur responsibility should be taken out of the criminal system, with companies being sued through the civil courts for damages, rather than being fined under the criminal law. Civil awards of damages could be made to reflect the harm caused more easily than fines, which often have a statutory maximum.

Alternative punishments

Where a fine does not reflect the harm done, nor appear to offer a sufficiently strong deterrent, companies could be punished with sanctions other than fines. Steven Box, in his book *Crime, Mystification and Punishment*, suggests the following:

- Requiring companies to advertise the details of their convictions, at their own expense. This has been tried in the USA, but large corporations got round the punishments by advertising only in publications which were unlikely to be read by their target consumers; consequently strict supervision would be needed.
- Nationalizing the company for a specific period, so that all its profits during that time would go to the state, or forcing it to sell a proportion of its products at cost price (meaning without making a profit) to underprivileged sections of the community.
- Putting companies 'on probation' by appointing teams of accountants, lawyers, managers and technical staff (depending on the nature of the company) who would monitor any of the company's working practices which might be relevant to the offence committed, and then make recommendations for improvement. If these recommendations were not followed, the company would be

returned to court for resentencing. The 'probation officers' would be paid for (but not chosen) by the offending company.

- Imposing a community service order. Just as individual offenders can be ordered to take part in work for the community, companies could be required to undertake projects of social importance, such as building a new hospital, or paying for a new school or library, at their own expense.
- Preventing corporate crime, by means of training in health and safety for example, may be more useful than criminal charges in relevant cases.
- Increasing a company's chances of being caught acting illegally, for example by increasing the number of Health and Safety Inspectors, and requiring offences resulting in death or serious injury to be investigated by the police, would strengthen the deterrent effect.

ANSWERING QUESTIONS

Is the current law on corporate liability for criminal offences inadequate?
This is a straightforward question which you could answer in much the same order as this chapter. A logical approach would be to say first what the law is, then look at some of the criticisms of this to decide whether or not the law is 'inadequate'. Then if you had time you could look quickly at possible reforms that might make the law more satisfactory.

13 General defences

There are several ways in which accused persons may try to prevent themselves from being found guilty of a crime, reduce their liability for the alleged offence, or lower their sentence if convicted. When pleading not guilty, they may challenge the evidence on matters of fact – by arguing that they have an alibi for the time of the offence, or that witnesses who have identified them are mistaken. Alternatively, defendants may admit the offence, but argue that there is some reason why they should be leniently sentenced – this is an argument that there are mitigating circumstances. Finally, they may raise a substantive defence, such as self-defence, duress or necessity. The effect of a substantive defence is usually to assert that although the accused may have committed the *actus reus* with *mens rea*, there is a legal reason why he or she should not be liable.

Complete and partial defences

Some defences, such as self-defence, may result in an acquittal; they are described as complete defences. Others result in conviction for a lesser offence – for example, successfully pleading diminished responsibility or provocation on a charge of murder leads to a conviction of manslaughter. These are sometimes known as partial defences.

General and specific defences

Substantive defences may be either general or specific. Specific defences are linked to particular crimes, and cannot be applied to other offences – for example, provocation is a defence only to murder. General defences can be used for a range of different crimes.

The burden of proof

In a criminal case, the burden of proof always lies with the prosecution: they must prove beyond all reasonable doubt that the defendant committed the offence, rather than defendants having to prove themselves innocent. On the other hand, defendants who claim they have a substantive defence will be required to provide some proof of it – they cannot simply claim to have acted in self-defence, or under duress, and expect the court to leave it at that.

The precise nature of the burden of proof depends on the defence which is put forward. Where it is self-defence, provocation, duress, necessity, automatism or intoxication, defendants bear an evidential burden, which means that they must produce some evidence to support the claim. Once this evidence is produced, the burden of proof passes back to the prosecution, who have to disprove the defence in order to prove their case. Where the defence put forward is either insanity or diminished responsibility, defendants bear not only an evidential but also a legal burden: as well as producing evidence of this defence, they also have to prove to the jury that it was more likely than not that factors amounting to such a defence existed (this is called proving on a balance of probabilities, a standard of proof usually associated with civil actions).

INFANCY

Children under 10 cannot be criminally liable. When they appear to have committed an offence, the social services can be informed but they cannot be prosecuted.

If the young person is aged 10 or over, but under 14, there used to be a presumption that they could not form *mens rea* (known in Latin as *doli incapax*). This presumption could be rebutted if the prosecution proved that the young person knew that what they had done was seriously wrong – a young person with this knowledge was described as having mischievous discretion. The Divisional Court had suggested, in **C (a minor) v DPP** (1995), that the presumption against criminal liability for the under-14s no longer existed, on the grounds that with compulsory education young people matured much more quickly than in the past. On appeal the House of Lords rejected this approach, stating that there was a line of cases dating back many years making it clear that the presumption did exist; if such an important and drastic change in the law were to be made it should come from Parliament, not the courts. The House observed that, while the Law Commission had proposed abolishing the presumption in 1985, the Government chose not to adopt this proposal in its 1990 review of the law. The defendant's appeal was allowed because, on the facts, the prosecution had failed to provide clear and positive evidence that the child in the case knew what he was doing was wrong.

However, in 1998 Parliament enacted s. 34 of the Crime and Disorder Act which abolished the presumption of *doli incapax,* as part of the Government's fight against youth crime. Section 34 states:

The rebuttable presumption of criminal law that a child aged 10 or over is incapable of committing an offence is hereby abolished.

This would appear to be short and simple but in fact there seems to be some confusion as to whether the abolition of the presumption implies with it the abolition of the defence, or whether the defence was separate from the presumption and survives after its abolition. Nigel Walker (1999) has argued that all that was abolished was the common law presumption, and that the defence remains. Thus it would still be open to the defence to prove that a child lacked mischievous discretion. If this approach was accepted then the only change made by the legislation would be a change in the burden of proof, from the prosecution to the defence. The Solicitor-General appeared to take this view during the Second Reading of the Bill before the House of Lords, when he said:

> The possibility is not ruled out, where there is a child who has genuine learning difficulties and who is genuinely at sea on the question of right and wrong, of seeking to run this as a specific defence. All that the provision does is remove the presumption . . . (*Hansard*, 1997 December 16, column 596).

There is therefore an element of doubt in this field, and we will have to wait for a case to reach the courts on this issue before the matter can be clarified.

▶ Criticism

In favour of the abolition of the presumption of *doli incapax* is the fact that the children who avoided criminal liability under the test – those who did not know right from wrong – might be those who were most in need of control. Glanville Williams had argued that the test was also out of line with current sentencing practice. In the past, when conviction was likely to lead to severe punishments, it was right to save children who, through no fault of their own, did not know right from wrong; but these days, such a test only kept them from probation officers or foster parents who might be able to help them. On the other hand, there is evidence that juvenile offenders diverted from the criminal justice system at an early stage are less likely to reoffend. Also, when a child of 10 commits a criminal offence this might be more a reflection of the failings of their parents than any fault of their own.

INSANITY

The defence of insanity, also known as insane automatism, actually has little to do with madness, or with any medical definition of insanity; the concept is given a purely legal definition. As a result, it has been held to include conditions such as sleep-walking and epilepsy, despite the fact that doctors would never label such conditions as forms of insanity. Where the defence of insanity is successful a special verdict will be given of 'not guilty by reason of insanity'. In order for this verdict to be given the prosecution must have proved the *actus reus* of the offence but not the existence of the *mens rea*. The defendant's state of mind will only be relevant to the issue of insanity – **Attorney General's Reference No. 3 of 1998** (1999).

As well as being put forward by the accused, a defence of insanity may be raised by the prosecution, if the defendant makes their mental state an issue in the case, for example by raising a defence of automatism or diminished responsibility. In such situations the prosecution can then try to prove that the defendant was insane when the offence was committed, rather than suffering from diminished responsibility or automatism. A judge may raise the issue of insanity in very exceptional circumstances. In **Dickie** (1984), the accused was charged with arson and introduced evidence of extreme hyperactivity. The judge decided that this evidence required a direction to the jury on insanity. The Court of Appeal allowed an appeal against the verdict, saying that the judge should only interfere if all the medical evidence suggested insanity and the defence were deliberately evading the issue.

The case of **R v Horseferry Road Magistrates' Court ex p. K** (1996) made it clear that the defence is available to summary as well as indictable offences. The defence of insanity is not available for strict liability offences. Thus, in **DPP v H** (1997) the defendant was charged with drink driving. He suffered from manic depressive psychosis, but he had no defence of insanity as drink driving is a strict liability offence.

In the past, successfully pleading insanity meant only one possible result: a hospital order under which the accused could be detained for an indefinite period of time. Consequently, once the death penalty was abolished, most defendants preferred to plead guilty to an offence rather than raise the defence of insanity, on the grounds that the punishment was unlikely to be worse than being locked away in a mental hospital with no fixed date for their release. When the defence of diminished responsibility was introduced for murder in 1957, this defence could be raised instead of pleading insanity, and insanity is now successfully put forward in only two or three cases a year.

The Criminal Procedure (Insanity and Unfitness to Plead) Act 1991 has altered the situation by introducing various sentencing options. Where the offence is murder, the court *must* still make a hospital order, under which the accused can be detained for an indefinite period. For any other crime, the court *may* make:

- a hospital order and an order restricting discharge either for a specified time or for an indefinite period;

- a guardianship order under the Mental Health Act 1983;
- a supervision and treatment order under Schedule 2 of the 1991 Act;
- an order for absolute discharge.

These changes are likely to encourage defendants to put forward the defence of insanity in the future.

▶ The M'Naghten rules

The rules on the defence of insanity were laid down in the **M'Naghten** case back in 1843. Daniel M'Naghten was obsessed with the then Prime Minister, Sir Robert Peel, and tried to kill him. He actually killed Peel's secretary instead, and was charged with the secretary's murder. He was found not guilty by reason of insanity, and this verdict produced enormous public disapproval. One result of the outcry was that the judges outlined their reasoning on insanity as a defence, producing what became known as the M'Naghten rules.

The starting point of the rules is that everyone is presumed sane. In order to rebut this presumption the accused must prove, on a balance of probabilities, that, when the offence was committed, they were suffering from a defect of reason, caused by a disease of the mind, so that either: (a) they did not know the nature and quality of their act; or (b) they did not know that what they were doing was wrong in law. In essence, this is saying that the defendant did not know what they were doing.

Defect of reason

A defect of reason means being deprived of the power to reason, rather than just failing to use it. In **Clarke** (1972), Mrs Clarke was accused of shoplifting, and argued that she had been acting absentmindedly because she was suffering from depression. The court ruled that this evidence meant she was denying *mens rea*, rather than raising the defence of insanity.

It does not matter whether the defect of reason was temporary or permanent. Thus, in **R v Sullivan** (1984), the defendant was treated as suffering from a defect of reason when he suffered from an epileptic fit which is inevitably a temporary state.

Disease of the mind

This is a legal definition, not a medical one, and covers states of mind which doctors would be highly unlikely to characterize as diseases of the mind. In legal terms it means a malfunctioning of the mind, and this has been held to include a hardening of the arteries, which is called arteriosclerosis – **R** *v* **Kemp** (1957); epilepsy – **R** *v* **Sullivan** (1984); diabetes – **R** *v* **Hennessy** (1989); and sleep-walking – **R** *v* **Burgess** (1991).

In **Kemp**, the defendant hit his wife with a hammer, causing her grievous bodily harm. He was suffering from arteriosclerosis, which caused temporary blackouts. Evidence showed he was devoted to his wife, and could not remember picking up the hammer or attacking her. In medical terms, arteriosclerosis is not considered to be a disease that affects the brain, but the court held that for the defence of insanity, the 'mind' meant 'the ordinary mental faculties of reason, memory and understanding', rather than the brain in the physical sense.

The courts are now drawing a distinction between a disease of the mind caused by an internal factor and one caused by an external factor. In the former the relevant defence is insane automatism; in the latter it is automatism. An example of a situation in which a disease of the mind is caused by some external factor is where someone is knocked on the head or undergoes hypnotism. This distinction was drawn in **Sullivan**. The appellant kicked and injured a friend during an epileptic fit, and was charged with inflicting grievous bodily harm. Medical evidence suggested that he would not have been aware, during the fit, that he was kicking anyone. The House of Lords held that epilepsy was a disease of the mind, because during a fit mental faculties could be impaired to the extent of causing a defect of reason. The internal/external divide was applied strictly in **R** *v* **Burgess** (1991). Burgess and a friend, Miss Curtis, had spent the evening watching videos at her flat. She fell asleep and while sleeping Burgess hit her over the head with a bottle and the video recorder and then grasped her throat. She cried out and he seemed to come to his senses, showing considerable distress at what he had done. Having been charged with wounding with intent under s. 18 of the Offences Against the Person Act 1861, he argued that he fell within the defence of automatism. The judge said the appropriate defence on the facts was insanity. Burgess was found not guilty by reason of insanity and ordered to be detained in a secure hospital. His appeal was dismissed on the grounds that as his sleep-walking was caused by an internal factor, the judge had given the correct direction.

Even diabetes, a disease which is in no medical sense a disease of the brain, has been treated as legal insanity. Diabetes is a disease which affects the body's ability to use sugar. It is usually controlled by injections of insulin, the substance which the body uses to break down sugar. Problems can arise where diabetics either fail to take their insulin, causing high blood sugar and what is known as a hyperglycaemic episode, or take the insulin and then drink alcohol, or fail to eat when they should; this causes low blood sugar and is known as a hypoglycaemic episode. Either situation may lead the diabetic to behave aggressively, which is why the problem has been brought to the attention of the courts. The result has been a rather odd approach, in which hyperglycaemic episodes are regarded as insanity, because they are caused by an internal factor – the action of the diabetes when insulin is not taken – while hypoglycaemic episodes are regarded as non-insane automatism, because they are caused by an external factor, the insulin.

In **R** *v* **Hennessy** (1989), the accused was a diabetic, charged with taking a vehicle and driving while disqualified. He gave evidence that at the time of the offence, he had failed to take his usual dose of insulin due to stress and depression, and as a result was suffering from hyper-glycaemia, which it was argued put him in a state of automatism. The trial judge ruled that since this state had been caused by diabetes, a disease, the proper defence was one of insanity under the M'Naghten rules. Hennessy then pleaded guilty (since successfully pleading insanity would have led to committal to a mental institution), and then appealed against his conviction. His appeal was dismissed.

By contrast in **Quick** (1973), the diabetic defendant was a nurse at a psychiatric hospital, who attacked a patient. He claimed that due to hypoglycaemia, brought on by not eating after taking insulin, he had acted without knowing what he was doing. The judge directed that this was a plea of insanity, upon which Quick changed his plea to guilty. On appeal, it was held that the alleged mental condition was not caused by diabetes, but by the insulin used to treat it, and his appeal was allowed.

The disease of the mind may need to manifest itself in violence. In **Bratty** *v* **Attorney-General for Northern Ireland** (1963) Lord Denning said, 'Any mental disorder which has manifested itself in violence and is prone to recur is a disease of the mind.' Thus some mental disorders which do not manifest themselves in violence, such as kleptomania (a compulsion to steal) are not diseases of the mind for the purposes of the defence of insanity. On the other hand, Lord Denning's statement that the mental disorder must be 'prone to recur' was not followed by Lord Lane in **Burgess**. The expert evidence in that case was that there was no reported incident of a sleep-walker being repeatedly violent. As Lord Lane concluded that the mental disorder need not be 'prone to recur' the defendant still fell within the defence of insanity.

Once a suitable disease of the mind has been proved, the defence must also prove that the disease of the mind meant that the defendant lacked knowledge as to the nature and quality of the act, or that the act was wrong.

The nature and quality of the act

In **Codere** (1916) this was held to mean the physical, rather than the moral nature of the act. A classic example of not knowing the nature and quality of an act is where the defendant cuts the victim's throat under the delusion of slicing a loaf of bread – it is not that they do not realize cutting someone's throat is wrong, but that they do not know they are cutting someone's throat.

Knowledge that the act was wrong

This has been held to mean legally rather than morally wrong. In **Windle** (1952) the accused killed his wife with an overdose of aspirin. When giving himself up to the police, he said, 'I suppose they will hang me for this.' There was medical evidence that although he was suffering from a mental illness, he knew that poisoning his wife was legally wrong. The Court of Appeal upheld his conviction and he was hanged.

▶ Criticism

Medical irrelevance

The legal definition of insanity stems from an 1843 case, and has not developed to take account of medical and legal progress since then. As long ago as 1953, medical evidence given to the Royal Commission on Capital Punishment showed that even then the rules were considered by doctors to be based on 'an entirely obsolete and misleading conception of the nature of insanity'. In the Victorian period when the test was developed, insanity was associated with a failure of the power to reason. But doctors now recognize that insanity does not just affect the power to reason and understand, but the whole personality, including the will and the emotions. A medically insane person may well know the nature and quality of his or her act, and know that it is wrong, but commit the offence all the same because of the mental illness.

Though the courts maintain that the legal definition of insanity can reasonably remain separate from medical definitions, it is difficult to uphold this distinction without absurdity. The most striking anomaly is that the courts claim a purely legal definition suffices, yet still impose mandatory committal to a mental institution in cases of murder; if a defendant is not medically insane, or even mentally ill, there is little point in imposing medical treatment. The current law may well be in breach of the European Convention on Human Rights. Article 5 of the Convention, which protects the right to liberty, states that a person of unsound mind can only be detained where proper account of objective medical expertise has been taken. This is likely to come to the attention of the British courts when the Human Rights Act 1998 comes into force.

The fact that diabetes has been held to give rise to a defence of insanity when it causes hyperglycaemia, but not when it causes hypoglycaemia, shows how absurd the application of the defence can be. The charitable organization MIND has criticized the link being drawn between epilepsy and insanity, saying that it encourages a dangerous and outdated approach to epileptics, who form 0.5 per cent of the population and, for the most part, lead lives which bear no relation to the cases in which epilepsy has featured.

Burden of proof

The fact that the defence must prove insanity, even though only on a balance of probabilities, conflicts with the principle that the burden of proof should always be on the prosecution, and the accused be innocent until proven guilty. It could be argued that the question of whether the accused knew what they were doing, and knew that it was wrong, is part of *mens rea* and should therefore be for the prosecution to prove. The Criminal Law Revision Committee and the Committee on Mentally Abnormal Offenders of 1975 (the Butler Committee) have recommended that the burden of proof should be on the prosecution.

Ineffectiveness

The purpose of the test for insanity is to distinguish between the accused who is a danger to society and to themself, and one who is not, but the rules appear not to be an effective way of doing this. They are so narrow that they rule out those whose mental illness makes them behave in ways that they know are wrong, yet wide enough to include people such as diabetics and epileptics, who are rarely likely to be a recurring danger to others. The divisions made by the rules seem to bear little relation to the purpose of the test: why should a diabetic with high blood sugar be more dangerous than one with low blood sugar, when the results are medically similar? Why should a 'defect of reason' be more dangerous when caused by a disease than when caused by a blow to the head? Diseases such as diabetes and most forms of epilepsy can be controlled by modern drugs. If the reason for the rules is to catch those defendants whose illnesses mean that unlawful behaviour is likely to recur, then as far as diabetes and other controllable diseases are concerned, the relevant issue is whether the accused has failed to take medication through some isolated lapse (in which case it is clearly less likely to recur), or through unwillingness or inability to accept the need for medication, in which case some help may be needed. The M'Naghten rules take no account of this kind of issue.

Sentencing for murder

The standard penalty for a successful plea of insanity where the charge is murder greatly limits use of the defence. Even though the sentence for murder is life imprisonment, most defendants would prefer this to an unlimited time in a mental institution (especially as in practice they will usually only serve around 12 years in prison), and so may plead guilty to an offence which they have not committed rather than raise the plea. This has two undesirable results: defendants who are neither morally liable for their actions nor medically insane are forced to plead guilty rather than be found legally insane; and defendants who know what they are doing and know that it is wrong, but cannot stop themselves, might really need the help that could be given by a mental institution, yet fall outside the legal definition of insanity (though they may come into the definition of diminished responsibility if the charge is murder).

▶ Proposals for reform

Abolition of the rules

The British Medical Association recommended to the Royal Commission on Capital Punishment 1953 that the M'Naghten rules ought to be abolished or, at least, amended so that they were more in line with current medical knowledge. This was not done, though the creation of the defence of diminished responsibility for murder has gone some way towards meeting their criticisms.

Despite this evidence the Royal Commission concluded that the issue of whether a person was suffering from a disease of the mind should be determined neither by medicine nor the law, but was a moral question to be decided by the jury. Alternatively, they proposed an extension of the definition of insanity to include where the defendant 'was incapable of preventing [themself] from committing it'.

A new defence of mental disorder

The Butler Committee recommended a new defence, leading to a verdict of 'not guilty on evidence of mental disorder'. This terminology would avoid the stigma of being labelled insane. The new defence would apply where:

- evidence of mental disorder was put forward, and the jury find that the accused has committed the *actus reus* but without *mens rea*; and
- at the time of the act the accused was suffering from one of a range of severe mental illnesses or abnormalities, which are defined in line with medical knowledge.

No causal link would have to be proved between the mental illness and the act, as the illnesses covered by the defence would be sufficiently serious to make it reasonable to presume such a link. The draft Criminal Code substantially adopted the Butler Committee's proposals though it does require a causal connection to be proved.

Extending automatism

In cases of diseases which can be controlled by drugs, and/or by following certain rules about eating and drinking, attacks brought on by those diseases could all be treated under the defence of automatism, with liability imposed in cases where the attack has been brought on by the defendant's own carelessness, but not where it has happened through no fault of their own. This may seem rather harsh on those who suffer from such diseases, but is actually no different from the fact that the law expects people who know they become violent when drunk to prevent themselves from getting drunk, rather than making allowances for them when they do.

Abolish the defence

In the USA, there have been claims that defences referring to insanity should be abolished completely. The issue hit the headlines after the attempted assassination of the then President, Ronald Reagan, by John Hinckley. At his trial, Hinckley claimed that he was obsessed by the actress Jodie Foster, and in carrying out the killing he had been under the delusion of acting out a movie script. He was found not guilty by reason of insanity, and critics argued that this was simply because he was able to pay for a very good psychiatrist. They have also pointed out that insanity defences cause procedural problems, with expert evidence often conflicting, making the trials very lengthy, and that the criminal justice system is not the ideal place to determine mental health. Perhaps not surprisingly, President Reagan himself gave his support to restrictions being placed on the defence.

One suggestion is that a mental disorder should be purely relevant to the issue of *mens rea*, and could be taken into account as mitigation in sentencing. However, the proposal ignores the fact that where defendants have mental problems, there may be little to gain by punishing them.

• • • • • • • • • • • • • • •
AUTOMATISM

Often known as non-insane automatism, this defence seeks to prove that the crime was committed by an involuntary act caused by an external factor.

▶ Involuntary act

As was noted in Chapter 1, a basic requirement for criminal liability is that the *actus reus* of an offence must have been committed voluntarily (p. 8). Therefore defendants will have a complete defence if they can show that at the time of the alleged offence, they were not in control of their bodily movements, rendering their conduct involuntary.

The defence was discussed by the Court of Appeal in **Bratty *v* Attorney-General for Northern Ireland** (1963):

> No act is punishable if it is done involuntarily and an involuntary act in this context – some people nowadays prefer to speak of it as 'automatism' – means an act which is done by the muscles without any control by the mind such as a spasm, a reflex action or a convulsion; or an act done by a person who is not conscious of what he is doing . . . [However] to prevent confusion it is to be observed that in the criminal law an act is not to be regarded as an involuntary act simply because the actor does not remember it . . . Nor is an act to be regarded as an involuntary act simply because the doer could not control his impulse to do it.

The law gives the defence a very narrow interpretation, emphasizing that there must be a total loss of voluntary control. The case of **Broome *v* Perkins** (1987) shows the limited scope of the defence. The accused got into a hypoglycaemic state and, during this period, drove home very erratically from work, hitting another car at one point. Afterwards he could remember nothing about the journey, but seeing the damage to his car, reported himself to the police. Medical evidence suggested that it was possible for someone in his state to complete a familiar journey without being conscious of doing so, and that although his awareness of what was going on around him would be imperfect, he would be able to react sufficiently to steer and operate the car, even though not very well. The court held that since the accused was able to exercise some voluntary control over his movements, he had not been acting in an entirely involuntary manner, and therefore the defence of automatism was not available.

This decision was heavily criticized as being too harsh, but it was nevertheless followed in **Attorney-General's Reference (No. 2 of 1992)**. When driving a lorry down a motorway, the accused crashed into a car parked on the hard shoulder, killing two people. Expert evidence showed that while he had not fallen asleep at the wheel, he had been put into a trance-like state by the repetitive vision of the long flat road which reduced, but did not eliminate, awareness of what he was doing. On acquittal the prosecution raised the case as an issue of law in the Court of Appeal. That court concluded that his state did not amount to automatism, again implying that reduced awareness cannot amount to the defence. Thus, the trial court got the law wrong and the defendant should probably not have been acquitted.

▶ External cause

The inability to control one's acts must be caused by an external factor, such as being banged on the head with a hammer. If it is due to an internal factor, the defence of automatism is not available, but if that internal factor is a disease of the mind it has been seen that there may be a defence of insanity.

It was on this basis that the courts distinguished between **Quick** and **Hennessy** (see above), stating that Hennessy's hyperglycaemia was triggered by an internal factor (his diabetes) and was therefore within the legal definition of insanity, but the causes of Quick's hypoglycaemia were the insulin he had taken and the fact that he had drunk alcohol and not eaten, all external factors, and so he could successfully raise the defence of automatism.

Hennessy's counsel had argued that the hyperglycaemia was caused by the defendant's failure to take insulin, which in turn was caused by stress and depression, which, it was suggested, were external factors. But in the Court of Appeal Lord Lane stated: 'In our judgment, stress, anxiety and depression can no doubt be the result of the operation of external factors, but they are not, it seems to us, in themselves separately or together external factors of the kind capable in law of causing or contributing to a state of automatism.' The Court of Appeal pointed out that they were prone to recur and lacked the feature of novelty or accident. The kind of external factors the law required would be something like a blow to the head, or an anaesthetic.

If a jury rejects evidence of insanity, they may still consider automatism. Since the Criminal Procedure (Insanity and Unfitness to Plead) Act 1991, the difference between the two verdicts has lost some of its importance.

▶ Self-induced automatism

The defence of automatism may not be available if the automatism was caused by the accused's own fault. Where someone loses control of their actions through drinking too much, or taking illegal drugs, the defence is unavailable, for obvious reasons of policy. Where the accused brings about the automatism in some other way, the availability of the defence will depend on whether they knew there was a risk of getting into such a state.

In **Bailey** (1983) the defendant was a diabetic, who attacked and injured his ex-girlfriend's new boyfriend during a bout of hypoglycaemia. Feeling unwell beforehand, he had eaten some sugar but no other food. The Court of Appeal held that self-induced automatism (other than that caused by drink or drugs) can provide a defence if the accused's conduct does not amount to recklessness, taking into account his knowledge of the likely results of anything he has done or failed to do. In Bailey's case this meant that he would have a defence if he did not realize that failing to eat would put him into a state in which he might attack someone without realizing it. If he was aware of this, and still failed to eat, he was reckless and the defence ought not to be available.

Should a defendant take drugs which normally have a soporific or sedative effect, and then commit a crime involuntarily, the defence of automatism may be available, if their reaction to the drug was unexpected. In **Hardie** (1984), a person whose condition of automatism was due to taking Valium (a tranquillizer) could rely on the defence, even though the drug had not been prescribed by a doctor.

▶ **Criticism**

Irrational distinctions

Distinguishing between internal and external causes has been criticized as leading to absurd and irrational distinctions – such as that drawn between **Hennessy** and **Quick** above. The main reason given for the difference in treatment is that automatism caused by an internal factor, namely a disease, is more likely to recur than such a state caused by an external factor. This may be true of a comparison between an automatic state caused by a long-term mental illness, and one caused by a blow to the head, but as the cases on diabetes show, the distinction can be tenuous, to say the least.

Possibility of wilful action

Criminal law writers, Clarkson and Keating, have drawn attention to the fact that some psychiatrists believe that, even when unconscious, people can act voluntarily. For example, Robert White recorded an incident during the Second World War, in which a soldier set off to take a message to a place where there was a lot of fighting and enormous danger. Some hours later, he found himself pushing his motorcycle through a coastal town nearly a hundred miles away, but had no idea how he had got there. Thoroughly confused, he gave himself up to the military police, who used hypnotism to try to discover what had happened. Under hypnosis, the soldier recalled that he had been knocked over by an explosion, got back on his bike and headed straight for the coastal town, asking directions and studying road signs in order to get there. Despite his genuine amnesia, he had acted rationally throughout; the amnesia had simply enabled him to do what he wanted to do, which was to escape without having to face up mentally to the consequences of being a deserter.

The implication of this argument is that perhaps automatism should not give rise to a complete acquittal. Automatism rests on the idea that the person acts without thought, but if it is the case that many everyday actions are carried out automatically without there being any distinctive thinking process involved, this situation is not as exceptional as the defence suggests.

Reform

The draft Criminal Code

The draft Criminal Code proposes maintaining the law on automatism as it stands, on the grounds that the public interest is best served by the complete acquittal of anyone who acts while in a condition of non-insane automatism. While this may be reasonable for the one-off offender, it offers no public protection against someone who is prone to recurring states of automatism through some external factor – though in this case the accused's own awareness of the dangers might lead to liability being imposed, on the grounds that he or she has behaved recklessly.

Abolition of the external/internal distinction

The distinction between internal and external causes could be abolished. Reform of the insanity defence to bring it in line with medical thinking would go some way towards this; behaviour which was allegedly automatic but clearly did not fall within medical definitions of insanity could then be considered solely in the light of the danger of recurrence, and the element of recklessness in the accused's behaviour.

MISTAKE

The issue of mistake is relevant in two contexts: it may mean that the accused could not have had *mens rea*, or it may be relevant in deciding whether a person has another defence such as self-defence.

Mistake and *mens rea*

In some cases, a defendant's mistake may mean that they lack the *mens rea* of the offence. For example, the *mens rea* of murder requires that the defendant intends to kill or cause grievous bodily harm to a person. If the defendant makes a mistake and thinks that the victim is already dead before they bury their body, then they would not have the *mens rea*, because when they buried what they thought was a dead person they could not have intended to kill or cause grievous bodily harm to that person.

The mistake must be one of fact, not of law, and a mistaken belief that your conduct is not illegal will not suffice as a defence. In **R** *v* **Reid**

(1973) a motorist had been asked to take a breathalyser test. Mistakenly believing that the police officer had no legal right to ask him to take such a test in the particular circumstances, he refused to provide a specimen. The courts held that his mistake as to the law was no defence against a charge of refusing to provide the specimen.

The *mens rea* must be negatived by the mistake; a mistake which simply alters the circumstances of the offence is not enough. If a defendant thinks that they are stealing a silver bangle, but in fact it is made from platinum, for example, they still have the *mens rea* of theft and so the mistake is irrelevant. If, however, they mistakenly thought that the bangle was their own, or that the owner had given permission to take it, the required *mens rea* is not present, and the mistake will provide a complete defence.

For offences of strict liability, there is no *mens rea* to negative, so mistake will be irrelevant in this context and not serve as a defence. Thus, if it is a strict liability offence to sell bad meat, and a butcher sells infected meat under the mistaken impression that it is perfectly all right, that mistake will be no defence because no *mens rea* is needed.

Some offences provide that liability will be incurred where there was either intention or recklessness, and in these cases, an accused will be able to rely on mistake as a defence only if it meant that they had neither type of *mens rea* – so if a mistake meant that there was no intention, but the accused could still be considered reckless, mistake will not be a defence.

▶ Reasonableness of the mistake

For many years it was considered that a mistake could only be relied on as a defence if it was a reasonable mistake to make. Thus, in **Tolson** (1889) a woman who reasonably believed that her first husband was dead, remarried, only to discover later that the first husband was in fact alive. She was accused of bigamy, but acquitted because her mistake had been both honest and reasonable.

However, this requirement of reasonableness was ruled out in **Morgan** (1972). Morgan had been drinking with some colleagues and during the evening he invited them to have sexual intercourse with his wife, saying that if she resisted or screamed, they should ignore this as it was only her way of adding to her sexual pleasure. The men duly ignored the woman's protests and had sexual intercourse with her. They were charged with rape and pleaded not guilty, on the grounds that they had believed she was consenting, but were convicted and appealed.

The House of Lords stated that if the accused honestly believed their victim was consenting, they did not have the *mens rea* for rape, even though they were mistaken in that belief and their mistake could not even be said to be a reasonable one. On the facts of the case their Lordships found that the jury would have convicted the defendants if they had been correctly directed, so the convictions were allowed to stand. The decision in **Morgan** with regard to mistake and rape was confirmed in the Sexual Offences (Amendment) Act 1976.

It was established in **Kimber** (1983) that the rule in **Morgan** concerning unreasonable mistakes applied not just to rape, but to all offences requiring a subjective *mens rea*. Thus, where an offence requires intention or **Cunningham** recklessness, an honest mistake, however unreasonable, will be a defence. Where the standard is the objective test of negligence the situation is different. Making an unreasonable mistake is clearly negligent, so only a reasonable mistake will be a defence to crimes of negligence. In the light of **Reid** the same also seems to be true of **Caldwell** recklessness; if a person thinks about whether there is a risk and due to a grossly unreasonable mistake decides there is none, they fall outside the lacuna and are **Caldwell** reckless, the mistake providing no defence.

In reality, of course, juries are unlikely to acquit on the basis of a mistake which to them seems unreasonable, since its unreasonableness is likely to be taken as evidence that the accused did not actually believe it – as the House of Lords realized in **Morgan**.

Since proving *mens rea* is the responsibility of the prosecution, the defendant does not legally have to introduce evidence to support a claim of mistake which negatives *mens rea*, though in practice it is obviously sensible to do so, since without such evidence the jury are more likely to believe the prosecution.

▶ Mistake and other defences

The issue of mistake can also arise in the context of other defences, and these situations are considered in the discussion of the relevant defences.

INTOXICATION

Intoxication can be caused by alcohol or drugs or a combination of the two; the same legal principles apply whichever the cause. The defence of intoxication poses something of a problem for the law. On the one hand, it can be argued that when intoxicated, people are not in full control of themselves, and do not think rationally, so they should not be held as liable for their actions as when they know exactly what they are doing. On the other hand, there are obvious policy reasons for not allowing people to use intoxication to excuse their criminal behaviour, not least the sheer numbers of crimes, particularly crimes of violence against the person, which occur as a result of intoxication. For this reason, the defence of intoxication is only allowed in a limited number of circumstances, and only where it means that the defendant lacked the *mens rea* of the offence.

▶ Absence of *mens rea*

The starting point is that if the defendant did actually have the *mens rea* of the crime, then intoxication cannot be a defence. This was made very clear by the House of Lords in **R v Kingston** (1994), overturning an unexpected decision in the case by the Court of Appeal. The defendant was attracted to young boys, but he normally managed to control these tendencies and prevent himself from acting on them. Unfortunately, his business associates decided to set him up so that he could be photographed in a compromising situation with a young boy, which could then be used to blackmail him. The defendant was invited with a 15-year-old boy to a flat, where their drinks were laced with drugs; when they were both intoxicated, the defendant indecently assaulted the child. Kingston admitted that, at the time of committing the assault, he intended it, but argued he would not have committed the offence if he had been sober. The House of Lords held that an intoxicated intent was still an intent, and the fact that the intoxication was not voluntary made no difference to that. He had the *mens rea*, and so the intoxication was no defence and he was liable.

▶ Specific and basic intent crimes

Even where intoxication means that the accused lacks the *mens rea* of a crime, in some circumstances they can still be found liable, forming an exception to the rule that both *mens rea* and *actus reus* are required. In this respect, the courts distinguish between crimes of basic intent and crimes of specific intent; intoxication will usually be a defence to crimes of specific intent where the defendant lacked *mens rea*, but not usually to crimes of basic intent.

The leading case in this area is **DPP v Majewski** (1977). The accused had spent 24 hours getting drunk and taking drugs, and then smashed windows and attacked a police officer. Majewski argued that he had been so intoxicated that he could not remember the incidents at all, and therefore could not have formed the necessary *mens rea*. The trial judge ruled that intoxication was only a defence to crimes of specific intent, and that, since the accused was charged with offences of basic intent, his intoxication gave him no defence.

In deciding whether the defence of intoxication is available we, therefore, need to know which crimes are classified by the courts as ones of basic intent and which of specific intent. This sounds straightforward, but unfortunately the courts have been far from clear about which crimes fall into which category, and why.

In **Majewski** the House of Lords attempted to explain the concepts but there now seem to be two possible approaches. The first is that if the offence can only be committed intentionally, it is a crime of specific intent, but if it can be committed with some other form of *mens rea* such as recklessness, it will be a crime of basic intent.

The second possible approach is slightly more complex. On this analysis specific intent offences are those where the required *mens rea* goes beyond the *actus reus*. A simple example of the distinction can be made by contrasting assault and assault with intent to resist arrest. The *actus reus* of assault is the doing of an act which causes another to apprehend immediate and unlawful violence, and the *mens rea* is intention to cause another to apprehend immediate and unlawful violence, or recklessness as to whether the other would be caused to apprehend immediate and unlawful violence. Clearly the two correspond exactly and on this analysis would be treated as crimes of basic intent. In assault with intent to resist arrest, however, the *actus reus* remains the same, but the *mens rea* has the additional element of intention to resist arrest. This is therefore an offence of specific intent.

Obviously these two tests are quite different, and will not always produce the same result, so that certain crimes may be offences of basic intent under one test, and specific intent under the other. Where there is such a conflict, it is not clear which test should be applied. For example, take the offence of criminal damage with intent to endanger life. The *mens rea* is intention or recklessness, so under the first test this should be an offence of basic intent. Yet the *mens rea* – intention or recklessness as to the damaging or destroying of property and as to endangering life – extends beyond the *actus reus*, damaging or destroying property, making this an offence of specific intent under the second test.

In fact the courts do not appear to apply either of the two rules very strictly, making it extremely difficult to predict whether a crime will be treated as one of basic or specific intent. The only reliable method of classifying an offence seems to be to see how offences have been defined when cases have come before the courts. The following list details some of the more important offences, and the case (or one of several cases) in which the distinction was made.

Offences of basic intent include:

- Involuntary manslaughter – **Lipman** (1970);
- Rape, Sexual Offences Act 1956, s. 1 (**Majewski**);
- Maliciously wounding or inflicting grievous bodily harm, Offences Against the Person Act 1861, s. 20 (**Majewski**);
- Criminal damage, Criminal Damage Act 1971, s. 1(1) (**Caldwell**);
- Assault occasioning actual bodily harm, Offences Against the Person Act 1861, s. 47 (**Majewski**);
- Common assault, Criminal Justice Act 1988, s. 39 (**Majewski**).

Offences of specific intent include:

- Murder – **DPP** *v* **Beard** (1920);
- Wounding or causing grievous bodily harm with intent, Offences Against the Person Act 1861, s. 18 – **Bratty** (1963);
- Theft, Theft Act 1968, s. 1 (**Majewski**);
- Burglary with intent to steal, Theft Act 1968, s. 9 – **Durante** (1972).

An example of the application of the rules on intoxication is **Lipman** (1970). The accused and his girlfriend had taken LSD at his flat. The effects of this drug include hallucinations and, while under its influence, the accused attacked the girl under the illusion that he was descending to the core of the earth and being attacked by snakes. He stuffed a sheet into her throat, with the result that she suffocated. At his trial for murder, the accused said that he had no intention of harming his victim, for he had not known what he was doing while under the influence of LSD. It was accepted that this gave him a defence against murder, since this was a crime of specific intent and he clearly had not formed the intention to kill or to cause GBH, but his intoxication was not allowed as a defence against manslaughter, which was a crime of basic intent. The Court of Appeal said that if a person deliberately takes alcohol or drugs in order to escape from reality – to 'go on a trip' – they cannot plead that self-induced disability as a defence to a criminal offence of basic intent.

Liability for lesser offences

For most offences of specific intent there is a similar crime for which basic intent suffices, providing a fall-back position – so that if, for example, intoxication means that an accused cannot be convicted of the specific intent crime of murder, they can be charged with the basic intent offence of manslaughter (as in **Lipman**). However, where there is no appropriate basic intent offence, intoxication can become a complete defence. This approach was confirmed in **Majewski**.

▶ Involuntary intoxication

If the defendant is treated as being involuntarily intoxicated then intoxication may be a defence to any crime, whether one of basic or specific intent, provided the defendant lacks *mens rea*. There are three situations where a person will be treated as involuntarily intoxicated.

Prescribed drugs

Taking drugs on prescription from a doctor is not regarded by the courts as reckless, so intoxication as a result of taking them will be a defence.

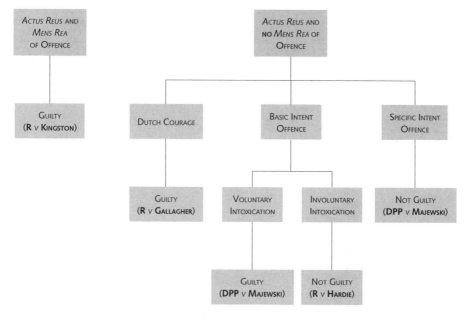

Fig. 5. The Defence of Intoxication

Soporific drugs

Where the accused has taken drugs that normally have a soporific effect, making the user relaxed or sleepy, they will be treated as involuntarily intoxicated. In **Hardie** (1985), the accused had been living with a woman at her flat, but the relationship broke down and she wanted him to leave. Very upset, the accused tried to calm his nerves by taking Valium, a tranquillizer which had been prescribed for the woman. He then started a fire in a bedroom, while the woman and her daughter were in the living room. He was prosecuted for damaging property with intent to endanger the life of another or being reckless whether another life would be endangered, contrary to s. 1(2) of the Criminal Damage Act 1971. On appeal, the Court of Appeal confirmed that, as a general rule, self-induced intoxication from alcohol or a dangerous drug could not be a defence to ordinary crimes involving recklessness, since the taking of the alcohol or drug was itself reckless behaviour. However, the court stated that where the normal effect of a drug was merely sedative, different rules applied. The issue, according to the court, was whether the taking of Valium had itself been reckless, taking into account the fact that the drug was not unlawful in prescribed quantities; that the accused did not know the drug was likely to make him behave as he did; that he had been told it would do him no harm; and that the normal effect of the drug was soporific or sedative. In this case Hardie was held to have a defence.

Laced drinks

Involuntary intoxication also arises where the defendant was unaware that they were consuming the intoxicant, for example, because drinks were laced (in **Kingston**, above, the defendant's drinks were laced, but he could still not rely on the defence because he had the *mens rea* of the offence). The provision is quite tightly interpreted; in **Allen** (1988), the defendant voluntarily drank wine, but was unaware that the wine he was drinking had a high alcohol content. It was held that simply not knowing the precise strength of the alcohol did not make his intoxication involuntary.

▶ 'Dutch courage'

There is one circumstance where intoxication will not even be a defence to an offence of specific intent. This is where a person gets intoxicated in order to summon up the courage to commit a crime – often called getting 'Dutch courage'. In **Attorney-General for Northern Ireland** *v* **Gallagher** (1963), Gallagher wanted to kill his wife. He bought a knife and a bottle of whisky, which it seems he drank to give himself Dutch courage. He got so drunk that he would have been incapable of forming the *mens rea* for murder (possibly because the drink also brought on a mental condition from which he already suffered). In this state he killed his wife with the knife. The House of Lords held that drunkenness is no defence for a sane and sober person who, being capable of forming an intention to kill, and knowing it would be legally wrong to do so, forms the intention to kill and then gets so drunk that when he does carry out the attack he is incapable of forming that intention.

▶ Intoxication and automatism

An accused who appears to have acted involuntarily, and was intoxicated at the time, is in legal terms considered to be acting voluntarily (assuming that the intoxication was voluntary), and the defence of automatism will not be available. Such a person may, however, have the defence of intoxication.

▶ Mistake and intoxication

Mistake will not be a defence if it was made as a result of intoxication. In **O'Grady** (1987), the accused had drunk a considerable amount of cider. In his drunken state, he killed his friend, believing (apparently mistakenly) that the friend was trying to kill him. If he had been sober, this mistake could have allowed him a defence, but because he had voluntarily got drunk, the courts held that he should be found liable.

▶ Criticism

The basic/specific intent distinction

As we have seen, the distinction between basic and specific intent appears neither logical nor consistently applied. It can be said that drunkenness should either be relevant or irrelevant, but not arbitrarily relevant for some aspects of some crimes.

In theory, the issue in all crimes is, did the accused have the required mental state to constitute the *mens rea* of the offence? One approach would be to acquit all defendants who were unable to form the *mens rea* because they were so intoxicated. However, from the point of view of policy, this approach has obvious drawbacks. Would we really want a rapist to be acquitted if he deliberately got himself so drunk that he could not know that his victim was not consenting? Or if a drunken brawl results in someone's death, would we want to allow the participants to go free because they were too drunk to realize that they might kill someone?

Most people would agree that this would not be a desirable state of affairs. But the problem is not solved by pretending that logical distinctions can be drawn on the basis of types of *mens rea*; by trying to avoid openly discussing policy considerations, the courts have created a series of anomalies (just one example is that intoxication can be a defence to attempted rape, but not to rape itself), and made the law on this important issue uncertain. One suggested solution is to recognize that policy issues are involved, and leave the question of when intoxication should be a defence to the facts of each case and the common sense of juries.

Accused's attitude to intoxication

No distinction is drawn between the person who intends to lose all self-control, and one who intends no more than social drinking but in the event ends up very drunk. On the normal principles of criminal liability, the first would seem more blameworthy than the second.

Difficulties for juries

The state of the law at the moment can require juries to enter the world of fantasy and guess what might have happened if the person had not been intoxicated. Where an accused is charged with a crime of basic intent, a jury may have to disregard their intoxication when deciding whether they committed the offence. In **Lipman**, for example, the jury were asked to decide whether the accused would have realized that what he was doing was dangerous if he had not been under the influence of LSD; yet if the accused had not been so heavily drugged, it seems highly unlikely that he would have tried to stuff a bedsheet down his girlfriend's throat anyway.

Inconsistency

The fall-back position which allows an intoxicated offender to be convicted of a similar, lesser offence can act as a reasonable compromise, but for some specific intent offences there is no corresponding crime of basic intent – for example, theft. This leads to a situation in which intoxication is a complete defence to some crimes but not to others, apparently with no logical reason for the distinction.

▶ Reform

A full defence of intoxication

In Australia intoxication is a full defence on the basis that the accused lacks the necessary *mens rea*; there are obvious policy objections to this approach.

An intoxication offence

The Butler Committee suggested the creation of a new offence of dangerous intoxication. This would come into effect where an accused was, due to their intoxication, acquitted of a sexual assault, an offence against the person, or criminal damage endangering life. Where the jury found that the accused had committed the *actus reus* of the offence charged, but was so intoxicated as to be unable to form *mens rea*, they could find the accused guilty of dangerous intoxication. Whatever the offence originally charged, the maximum sentence for dangerous intoxication would be one year for a first offence, and three for subsequent convictions.

A special verdict

In the Criminal Law Revision Committee's Fourteenth Report, a minority of its members recommended the introduction of a special verdict that the offence was committed while the defendant was intoxicated. The defendant would then be liable to the same potential penalty as if they had been convicted in the normal way (except where the charge was murder, where the penalty would be that for manslaughter). Sentencing could then both reflect the harm done, and take the intoxication into account where appropriate.

Miscellaneous proposals

Other proposals have included the introduction of a crime of negligently causing injury; retaining the current law on specific and basic intent but creating some new offences to ensure every specific intent offence has a corresponding 'fall-back' offence of basic intent; and treating persistent drunken offenders outside the criminal law system, on the basis that treating their drinking problems would be more helpful in preventing crime than repeatedly punishing them.

PUBLIC AND PRIVATE DEFENCE

These defences, which include the well-known defence of self-defence, can apply where a person does something which would normally be a crime, but their reason for doing it is to prevent crime in one of several specified ways, or to protect themself, someone else, or property.

▶ Public defence

This is a statutory defence contained in s. 3 of the Criminal Law Act 1967. This section allows a defence to any person who uses such force as is reasonable in the circumstances to prevent crime, or lawfully to arrest or assist the lawful arrest of offenders, suspected offenders or persons unlawfully at large (such as escaped prisoners). For example, if you saw someone snatch a bag, chased that person and then caught them with a rugby tackle, your action would normally be an assault, but because you were attempting to make a lawful arrest, the public defence would probably allow you to avoid liability.

▶ Private defence

This term covers the common law defences of self-defence, defence of another or defence of property, again using such force as is reasonable in the circumstances. Situations where this defence might be appropriate include hitting someone who seems about to attack you or someone else.

These two defences sometimes overlap and the same basic principles, discussed below, apply to both.

▶ Necessity for action

Defendants can only rely on these defences if their action was necessary because of a threat of unjustified harm to themselves, to someone else or to property, or because of a need to prevent crime in one of the ways listed above. In deciding whether or not the behaviour was necessary, the courts will take into account three key issues: whether the person could have retreated from the situation; whether the threat was imminent; and whether the defendant made some mistake which caused them to think the action was justified.

Possibility of retreat

At one time it was believed that in order for these defences to apply, the accused must have retreated as far as possible from the situation before using force – so that a person who had a chance to run away from an attacker but instead chose to fight back might not be covered by the defence. But in **McInnes** (1971), it was stated that failure to make use of a chance to retreat is simply evidence which the jury can use to decide whether it was necessary to use force, and whether the force used was reasonable. The Court of Appeal said that the jury should have been directed that, in order for force to be considered reasonable in the circum- stances, the defendant's behaviour should certainly have demonstrated that he did not want to fight, but simply failing to take an opportunity to run away did not in itself make the defence unavailable.

The law recognizes that in the kind of situations where the defence is used, there is rarely much time to consider what should be done. As Lord Morris put it in **Palmer** (1971), 'a person defending himself cannot weigh to a nicety the exact measure of his necessary defensive action'.

Imminent threat

A defendant will only be justified in reacting to a threat which is immin- ent. This does not mean that the defendant has to wait until they are hit, for example, before hitting back, but it does mean there must be some immediacy about the threat. The balance which the courts have sought to establish in this area can be seen from the following two cases.

In **Attorney-General's Reference No. 2 of 1983**, the defendant owned a shop in an area where there had been extensive rioting. He made up some petrol bombs, and kept them ready to defend his property if required. The court found that a defence was available to him as the threat was sufficiently imminent. By contrast, in **Malnik** *v* **DPP** (1989) the defend- ant went to visit a man who was believed to have stolen some valuable cars belonging to an acquaintance of the defendant. The suspected thief was known to be violent, so the defendant took with him a rice flail – a martial arts weapon consisting of two pieces of wood joined together by a chain. He was arrested while approaching the man's house, and the court rejected the argument that carrying the weapon was justified because he was in imminent danger of attack, pointing out that he had himself created the dangerous situation by choosing to go to the man's house.

Mistake

If a defendant makes a mistake which leads them to believe there are circumstances which make defensive action necessary, the courts will assess the necessity of the defence on the basis of the facts as the defendant believed them to be, even if the mistake is not a reasonable one to make. In **R** *v* **Williams (Gladstone)** (1987) a man saw a youth rob a woman in the street. He grabbed the youth and a struggle ensued, at which point the defendant arrived on the scene, and, not having seen the robbery, attempted to help the youth. The first man claimed to be a police officer, and told the defendant that he was arresting the youth for a mugging; in fact he was not a policeman so, when the defendant asked to see some police identification, he was unable to produce it. As a result, the defendant concluded that the man was simply attacking the youth without justification, and in an attempt to defend the youth, he punched the man in the face. He was charged with occasioning actual bodily harm under s. 47 of the Offences Against the Person Act 1861. The court held that, in deciding whether or not he had a defence, the facts should be treated as he honestly thought them to be; if the man had been attacking the youth, the defendant would have had a defence, so he was not liable.

If a mistake is induced by intoxication then the mistake has to be ignored in relation to the defence. In **O'Connor** (1991) the defendant got drunk in a pub, and started arguing with the victim. Mistakenly believing that he was about to be attacked, he head-butted the victim about three times. The victim died from his injuries and the defendant was convicted of murder, but appealed. The Appeal Court stated that because his mistake was produced by intoxication, it could not be taken into account when considering self-defence, though it was relevant to the defence of intoxication and the issue of whether he had *mens rea* (discussed above). In fact the appeal was allowed because the trial judge had made a mistake.

▶ Reasonable force

What constitutes reasonable force is a matter for the jury to decide, balancing the amount of force used against the harm the accused sought to prevent – so that, for example, force considered reasonable for protecting a person might be considered excessive if used to protect property.

Strictly speaking, the defence is all or nothing: if the accused used reasonable force, they are not guilty; if the force was unreasonable, often described as excessive, the defence is unavailable. However, in considering this issue, the courts place great emphasis on the fact that defendants are not expected to perform precise calculations in the heat of the moment. In **Attorney-General for Northern Ireland's Reference** (1977) a soldier in Northern Ireland stopped a man, who started to run away. Mistakenly thinking that the man was a member of the IRA, the soldier shot and killed him. He was charged with murder and argued that he had both the public and private defences. The House of Lords said it was a question for the jury whether the force used by the soldier was reasonable or excessive, and in deciding this they had to take into account the limited time for reflection in these types of circumstances. In this case, they would have to balance the high risk of death or serious injury to the man running away, against the harm which could be avoided by preventing the man's escape if he were a terrorist:

> it would not be unreasonable to assess the level of harm to be averted by preventing the accused's escape as even graver – the killing or wounding of members of the patrol by terrorists in ambush and the effect of this success by members of the Provisional IRA in encouraging the continuance of the armed insurrection and all the misery and destruction of life and property that terrorist activity in Northern Ireland has entailed.

Mistake as to the degree of force

This issue has been subject to much recent confusion. The original position – laid down in **Williams** (1987) – was that the matter had to be decided objectively and the mistake of the defendant could not be taken into account in deciding whether reasonable force had been used. A dramatic change appeared to have been brought about by the case of **Scarlett** (1993). Scarlett was the licensee of a pub. The victim came into the bar extremely drunk, and Scarlett asked him to leave. He refused to go, and a struggle ensued. In such a situation licensees are legally entitled to use reasonable force to eject the person. Scarlett pushed the man out through a swing door, into a lobby which gave on to some stairs; the victim fell down the stairs and died. Scarlett was convicted of constructive manslaughter, but his appeal was allowed on the basis that he could rely on the private defence. At the trial he had given evidence that he thought he was behaving reasonably, and he had not believed there was any risk of the victim falling down the stairs. Beldam LJ stated that the jury should be told to acquit 'unless they were satisfied that the degree of force used was plainly more than was called for by the circumstances as [the defendant] believed them to be – and, provided he believed the circumstances called for the degree of force used, he is not to be convicted even if his belief was unreasonable'. This was thought to impose a subjective test: if the defendant used excessive force but, owing to a mistake, honestly believed it to be reasonable force, the defence would still be available, and the reasonableness of the force would be judged on the facts as the defendant believed them to be.

However, in 1995 the issue arose again before the court in **R** *v* **Owino**. The appellant had been convicted of assaulting his wife, occasioning her actual bodily harm under s. 47 of the Offences Against the Person Act 1861. She had suffered injuries to her head and thumb but he claimed, in his defence, that any injuries he caused her were the result of reasonable force used to restrain her and to stop her assaulting him. He appealed against his conviction on the basis that the judge had misdirected the jury in failing to point out that the test of whether reasonable force was used was subjective. The appeal was rejected and it was stated that **Scarlett** did not in fact impose a subjective test, it merely stated the old law as laid down in **Williams**.

▶ **Criticism**

The 'all or nothing' approach

The 'all or nothing' approach to the defence can work harshly in murder cases. For other offences, if the accused cannot be acquitted because they have used excessive force, but it is obvious that some force was justified, this can be taken into account as a mitigating factor in sentencing. The mandatory sentence for murder means that there can be no such mitigation. It has been suggested that more flexibility in sentencing could be gained by allowing juries to convict of manslaughter rather than murder in such circumstances (as is done, for example, when an accused successfully raises the defence of provocation). This was the law in Australia for a time, but was later rejected as being too difficult for juries to understand.

The case of the soldier, Sargeant Lee Clegg, has highlighted such concerns over the current law of self-defence. In **R** *v* **Clegg** (1995), Clegg was on duty at a Northern Ireland checkpoint, when a car containing joyriders failed to stop. Although Clegg admitted he did not think the car contained terrorists, he shot at the car four times, killing one of the passengers. He was convicted of murder. At his trial he said he had shot at the car, three times from the front and once from the side, because it was driving towards a soldier and he thought that the soldier's life needed protecting. The soldier in question was found to have an injured foot after the incident, and the suggestion was that the car had driven over it. In fact, the soldier's injury was later discovered to have been caused by someone stamping on his foot, in an attempt to fabricate evidence to support Clegg's defence. Forensic examination of the bullet holes in the car showed that the fourth shot had not been fired from the side, but from behind, after the car had passed and when there could have been no danger to the other soldier. Clegg admitted in court that he did not believe there was any justification for shooting at the car from behind. In the light of this evidence, the logical conclusion of the House of Lords was that Clegg had used excessive force in shooting from behind, and because he realized this, he could not rely on **Scarlett** as it was then understood. His conviction for murder was upheld with its mandatory life sentence, but after a campaign by tabloid newspapers in England, he was released after serving only four years' imprisonment. The case has caused enormous political controversy, to which Clegg's release has added. Sympathizers with Clegg argued that British soldiers should not be locked up for 'doing their duty' when IRA terrorists were causing much more harm, while those who opposed Clegg's release state that the family of the girl who died have been denied justice.

In the light of the controversy the case aroused, the Home Secretary announced the Home Office would carry out a review of the law of public and private defence. This review has been criticized by the academic Andrew Ashworth in an editorial comment to the 1995 *Criminal Law Review*. His criticism is that the review has been confined to cases where police officers or members of the armed forces use excessive force in situations where some force would be allowed. He points out that the law should be neutral as to the status of the individual, and that there are grave dangers in having one law for private individuals and another for representatives of the state. Certainly the Lee Clegg campaign itself reflected the attitude which lies behind the problem Ashworth highlights. It was noticeable that the same British newspapers which campaigned for the release of Clegg, who had definitely killed somebody whatever one thinks of the circumstances, took little interest in campaigns for the release of the Guildford Four, the Birmingham Six and other Irish victims of miscarriages of justice. These people were guilty of nothing at all – in fact when they were released, several papers asked where was the justice for the bomb victims, as though releasing those who had nothing to do with the bombings in some way increased the injustice for the victims. It is hard not to conclude that the complaints about the law arising from **Clegg** have less to do with problems in the law than they do with political interests in Northern Ireland.

Mistake and intoxication

The case of **O'Grady** creates an exception to the rule in **Williams** that a person has the defence of self-defence if they are acting under a mistake of fact. This creates an anomaly in that, on the one hand, an accused who is so drunk that they cannot form *mens rea* will be acquitted of murder, since it is an offence of specific intent; on the other hand, if the accused was drunk and this caused them to believe they were being attacked by the victim, they cannot rely on self-defence. **O'Grady** is thus out of line with cases which allow a defence of intoxication to offences of specific intent.

Sexual discrimination

It is arguable that the public and private defences are more likely to succeed for male as opposed to female defendants. The defences are usually raised in the context of offences against the person, and most reported violent crime is between young males, typically when they are out drinking in the evening. While there is probably just as much violence against women – if not more – most of it takes place in the domestic setting, and often goes unreported. Because of this, the cases which have developed the rules for these defences have been concerned primarily with male defendants, which means that, as with the defence of provocation, there is a danger that they have been shaped with male responses to danger in mind, when female responses may be quite different. In particular, the lesser strength of a woman may mean she has to use a weapon to defend herself even if her attacker is unarmed, whereas a man can usually fight fists with fists, so making his response proportionate to the attack.

As with provocation, this type of difference has caused problems with the use of the defences by battered women. Ewing studied 100 cases of battered women who killed their partners, and found a number of common features: they had been the victims of violence for many years; had received insufficient help from the community and the police; felt unable to leave the situation though they had often made unsuccessful attempts to do so, and the killing was committed in anticipation of further violence in the future. In the past, the mere fact that they did not leave the situation could make the defence unavailable. **McInnes** should change this, but there are still problems: if a woman acts in anticipation of further violence, it may be held that the threat cannot be described as 'imminent'; and if she uses a weapon when her partner is unarmed, the force may be considered excessive.

▶ Reform

Abolish the rule in O'Grady

For the reasons stated above, the Law Commission has recommended that the **O'Grady** principle should be abolished.

The draft Criminal Code

The draft Criminal Code, in line with the approach recommended by the Law Commission and the Criminal Law Revision Committee, provides that where excessive force is used in self-defence, this should reduce murder to manslaughter, a proposal also put forward by the House of Lords Select Committee on Murder and Life Imprisonment in 1989.

Remove the requirement of an imminent threat

The Law Commission in its draft Bill would abandon the requirement that there must be an imminent threat. This might go some way towards meeting the problems of the defence for battered women.

• • • • • • • • • •
DURESS

Duress is the defence that applies where a person commits a crime because they were acting under a threat of death or serious personal injury to themself or another. By allowing the defence the criminal law is recognizing that the defendant had been faced with a terrible dilemma. In **R** *v* **Symonds** (1998) it was observed that the same facts could fall within both the defence of duress and self-defence. It felt that self-defence should be preferred for offences against the person and duress for other offences (such as dangerous driving). At one time the defence of duress only covered acts done as a result of an express threat to the effect of 'do this or else', but modern cases have introduced the concept of duress of circumstances, which arises from the situation that the person was in at the time. There are thus now two forms of this defence: duress by threats and duress of circumstances.

▶ Duress by threats

This traditional defence of duress covers situations where the defendant is being forced by someone else to break the law under a direct threat of death or serious personal injury to themself or someone else.

▶ Two-part test

In order to try to find the balance between the seriousness of the harm threatened to the accused and the seriousness of the consequent illegal behaviour, a two-part test was laid down in **Graham** (1982). The test is similar to that used in the defence of provocation as it involves both a subjective and an objective criterion:

1 Was the defendant forced to act as they did because they feared that otherwise death or serious personal injury would result?

2 Would a sober person of reasonable firmness, sharing the accused's characteristics, have reacted to that situation by behaving as the accused did?

Graham was a homosexual who lived with his wife and his lover, King. In the past King had behaved violently, for example tipping Graham and his wife off the settee when he found them cuddling. Threatened by King, Graham took part in the strangling of his wife with an electric flex. On the facts the Court of Appeal did not consider duress existed, as the threats were not sufficiently grave.

The subjective part of the test

Seriousness of the threats

Whether the threats will constitute a valid defence depends on the balance between the seriousness of the harm threatened to the accused, and the seriousness of the offence they commit as a result. Modern authorities suggest that where the offence committed is a serious one, the defence will only be allowed if the harm threatened was of death or serious personal violence. In **R** *v* **Valderrama-Vega** (1985), the accused was charged with taking part in the illegal importation of cocaine from Colombia. He argued that he was acting under duress, in that a mafia-type organization in Colombia had threatened to kill or injure him or his family, and to expose his homosexuality; he was also under great pressure financially, facing ruin if he did not take part in the smuggling. The courts held that only the threats of death or personal injury could constitute duress, although it was not necessary that those threats should be the only reason for the accused's behaviour. The threat need not actually be serious as long as the defendant perceived it to be. Thus a mistaken belief of the defendant that there is a serious threat will be taken into account. **R** *v* **Cairns** (1999) was a case on duress of circumstances but it is equally relevant here. The victim had been drinking excessively with friends when he climbed on to the bonnet of the defendant's car with his friends following alongside. He fell off when the defendant braked at a speed hump and landed in front of the car. The appellant drove over him, causing a fracture of his spine and then continued home. At the defendant's trial the victim's friends said they had been running alongside the car to stop the foolish behaviour of the victim, though their conduct may have appeared hostile to the defendant. In leaving the issue of duress to the jury the trial judge said the jury had to consider whether what the defendant did was 'actually necessary' to avoid the evil in question? He was convicted of inflicting grievous bodily harm and dangerous driving and appealed on the grounds that the judge was wrong to require that the defendant's conduct have been 'actually necessary'. The Court of Appeal stated that the defendant only needed to show that he acted as he did because he reasonably perceived a threat of death or serious physical injury. This he had established. He did not have to prove that there was, in fact, a real threat. Accordingly, the appeal was allowed.

Threats to property will not usually be sufficient for duress to be treated as a defence to a serious crime; it may still be possible to argue that an extremely serious threat to property might excuse a very minor crime, but there is no authority on the point.

An imminent threat

There must be an imminent threat of harm. In **Gill** (1963) the defendant was told to steal his employer's lorry, and threatened with violence if he failed to do so. At his trial for theft, the court stated, *obiter*, that he probably would not have been able to rely on the defence of duress: between the time of the threat and his carrying out the crime he had the opportunity to inform the police of the threat, so the threat was not sufficiently immediate to justify his conduct.

Later cases have taken a more lenient approach, stating that a threat will be counted as imminent if, at the time of the crime, it was operating on the accused's mind, even though it could not have been carried out there and then. In **Hudson and Taylor** (1971), the defendants were two teenage girls who had been the main witnesses for the prosecution at the trial of a man charged with wounding. In court, neither identified the accused as the attacker, and both falsely testified that they did not recognize him. On being charged with perjury, they explained that before the trial they had been threatened with serious injury if they told the truth, and during the trial they had noticed in the public gallery a member of the gang who had made those threats. The threat to injure was held to have been immediate, even though it obviously could not have been carried out there and then in the courtroom. It was pointed out that the defence of duress would be unavailable where the accused could have taken reasonable steps to prevent the threatened harm, for instance by going to the police. Whether or not it was reasonable to expect the accused to take such steps would depend on the facts, taking into account the age and circumstances of the accused, and any risks to themselves in taking such action.

In **R** *v* **Abdul-Hussain** (1999) the defendants were Shia Muslims from Southern Iraq who were fugitives from the Iraqi régime. For a while they lived in Sudan but they feared that they and their families would be deported to Iraq where they would almost certainly have been executed. In desperation, using fake weapons made of plastic, they hijacked a plane that was going to Jordan, which after negotiations landed in Stansted airport. After 8 hours the hostages were released and the defendants gave themselves up. At their trial, the judge ruled that the defence of duress (duress of circumstances on these facts) should not be left to the jury because the threat was insufficiently close and immediate to give rise to a virtually spontaneous reaction to the physical risk arising. They were all convicted of the statutory offence of hijacking. The defendants appealed against their convictions on the ground that the judge had made a mistake in withdrawing the defence of duress from the jury's consideration. Their appeal was allowed. The Court of Appeal stated that the imminent threat of death or serious injury to the defendants or their families had to operate on the mind of the defendants at the time they committed the act so as to overbear their will, but the execution of the threat need not be immediately in prospect. The period of time which elapsed between the inception of the threat and the defendant's act was a relevant but not determinative factor. The appellants were in no immediate danger of death or serious bodily harm, but the threat was hanging over them, it was 'imminent'. The trial judge had interpreted the law too strictly in seeking a virtually spontaneous reaction. In summary, the threat must be imminent but it need not be immediate. The court gave a vivid and persuasive example to support its decision based around Anne Frank, the Jewish girl whose diaries have been published describing her life hiding from the Nazis during the Second World War:

> If Anne Frank had stolen a car to escape from Amsterdam and been
> charged with theft, the tenets of English law would not, in our
> judgement, have denied her a defence of duress of circumstances,
> on the ground that she should have waited for the Gestapo's knock
> on the door.

Self-induced duress

The defence will not be available if the defendant has voluntarily joined the criminal association which makes the threats, such as a terrorist organization or the Mafia. In **R v Sharp** (1987), Sharp had joined a gang and became a party to a conspiracy with them to commit a robbery. He gave evidence that, as soon as he realized the others were armed with guns, he had tried to withdraw from the plan, but one of the gang, E, threatened to blow off his head if he pulled out. Sharp therefore took part in the robbery and, during it, a member of the public was killed by E. Sharp's conviction for manslaughter was upheld after a jury rejected his defence of duress. The Court of Appeal pointed out that the defence might still be available to an accused who had been forced to join an organization, or who joined one without knowing that there was a risk of being coerced into criminal activity.

In **R v Ali** (1995), Ali had become a heroin addict during a visit to Pakistan. Back in England, a man, X, supplied him with heroin. Their arrangement was that Ali could use some of the heroin himself, in return for selling the rest and giving the proceeds back to X. Naturally the amount of heroin Ali needed began to increase, and one day he used all the heroin himself, which left him in debt to X. He moved house to try to avoid X, but X caught up with him, gave him a gun and told him to go and rob a bank or building society or else he would be killed. The Court of Appeal found that at his trial for armed robbery he could not rely on the defence of duress, as he had voluntarily become involved in a criminal enterprise with a man he knew was of a violent disposition. He did not need to know that he would be forced to commit an armed robbery, only that he would be involved in some criminal activity.

The objective part of the test

In applying the second, objective, limb of the **Graham** test, the reasonable person can be given some of the characteristics of the defendant but not all. In **R** *v* **Bowen** (1996) the defendant was accused of obtaining services by deception, having dishonestly obtained electrical goods on credit. In his defence he argued that throughout he had been acting under duress, as two men had threatened to attack him and his family with petrol bombs if he did not obtain the goods for them. The trial judge directed the jury that, in applying the objective limb of the **Graham** test, they could take into account the age and sex of the defendant. On appeal it was argued that the jury should also have been directed to take into account his very low IQ. The appeal was rejected. The Court of Appeal stated that the mere fact that an accused is pliable, vulnerable, timid or susceptible to threats are not characteristics which can be invested in the reasonable person. On the other hand, if a defendant is within a category of persons who the jury might think less able to resist pressure than people not within that category – such as being of a certain age or sex or suffering from a serious physical disability, recognized mental illness or psychiatric condition (including a post traumatic stress disorder) – then this could be treated as a characteristic of the reasonable person. A low IQ, short of mental impairment or mental defectiveness, cannot be treated as such a characteristic. In **R** *v* **Hurst** (1995) expert evidence was inadmissible on the issue that the defendant had suffered sexual abuse as a child, resulting in lack of firmness in their personality, though not amounting to a psychiatric disorder. The court said:

> . . . we find it hard to see how the person of reasonable firmness can be invested with the characteristics of a personality which lacks reasonable firmness.

The Court of Appeal stated in **R** *v* **Flatt** (1996) that a self-induced characteristic of the defendant would not be given to the reasonable person. Flatt was charged with possession of a prohibited drug with intent to supply. He argued in his defence that he was acting under duress. As an addict to crack cocaine, he owed his supplier £1,500. Seventeen hours before the police searched his flat, his drug dealer ordered him to look after the drugs subsequently found in his possession, saying that if Flatt refused, he would shoot Flatt's mother, grandmother and girlfriend.

On appeal it was argued that the judge had misdirected the jury. In assessing the response of the hypothetical reasonable person to the threats, the judge had not told the jury to consider how the reasonable drug addict would have responded to the threats. His appeal was dismissed as drug addiction was a self-induced condition and not a characteristic. Also there was no reason to think that a drug addict would show less fortitude than any other member of the public when faced with such threats. This would appear to conflict with the approach the House of Lords took in **Morhall** (see p. 63) to drug addiction for the purpose of provocation.

A complication in **Graham** (above) was that the accused had been drinking alcohol and taking Valium before the killing took place; the court held that the fact that a defendant's will to resist threats had been reduced by the voluntary consumption of drink or drugs or both could not be taken into account when assessing whether he had behaved as a reasonable person would have done. In other words, he had to be assessed on the basis of how a reasonable person who was sober would have behaved.

To which crimes does duress allow a defence?

Duress applies to most crimes, but not to murder (**Abbott** (1977)) – including involvement in a murder as a secondary party – nor to attempted murder. The principle that duress should never be a defence to murder was laid down as far back as the sixteenth century, with the legal writer Blackstone stating that a person under duress should die themself rather than escape by means of murdering an innocent person.

It was thought at one time that duress might be available as a defence where the accused was only an accomplice to the murder, and in 1975, the House of Lords confirmed this in **R *v* Lynch**. This led to some illogical distinctions, given that the principal in a murder may not always be the most morally culpable of the parties. Therefore, in **Howe** (1986), the House of Lords overruled **Lynch** (1975) and stated that duress was not available as a defence to any of the parties to an offence of murder. Howe had fallen under the evil influence of a man called Murray and, as a result, had assaulted one person who had been killed by another, and then actually killed a man on Murray's orders. It was held that the defence of duress was available to neither the murder that he had carried out as principal, nor the murder where he was merely a secondary participant.

In **Gotts** (1992) the House of Lords specified that duress was also unavailable as a defence to attempted murder. In that case the accused, aged 16, seriously injured his mother with a knife. He argued that he was acting under duress because his father had threatened to shoot him unless he killed his mother, but his defence was rejected.

▶ Duress of circumstances

The basic rules for this defence are the same as for duress by threats, except that it applies where there is no express threat of 'do this or else' but the circumstances threatened death or serious personal injury unless the crime were committed.

The defence is relatively new, originating in **R v Willer** (1986). Willer was charged with reckless driving, and pleaded that he had to drive in such a way in order to escape from a gang of youths who appeared to be about to attack him. Driving up a narrow road, he had been confronted by the gang, which was 20 to 30 strong, and heard shouts of 'I'll kill you Willer', and threats to kill his passenger. With the gang surrounding the car, the only means of escape was to drive along the pavement and into the front of a shopping precinct. After the trial judge ruled that the defence of necessity was not available, Willer changed his plea to guilty and appealed. On appeal it was held that the issue of duress should have been left to the jury, and Willer's conviction was quashed. The Court of Appeal did not use the term 'duress of circumstances', but clearly the case was different from the 'do this or else' scenario previously associated with the defence: Willer was threatened, but he was not told that the threats would be carried out unless he drove on the pavement.

This extension of the defence was subsequently considered in **R v Conway** (1989) where the label 'duress of circumstances' was introduced. After being followed in his car by an unmarked vehicle, Conway had driven off in a reckless manner when two men, who were police officers in plain clothes, got out of the car and started to approach him. Conway's passenger, Tonna, had earlier been in a car in which someone had been shot, and when he saw the two men running towards the car (not knowing that they were policemen), believed that he was about to be attacked. Consequently he yelled 'Drive off' and Conway, also failing to realize the men were police officers, responded accordingly, believing that Tonna was indeed about to be attacked. Conway's conviction for reckless driving was quashed on appeal because the defence of duress of circumstances should have been put to the jury. It was said that this defence was available only if, from an objective viewpoint, the defendant could be said to be acting in order to avoid a threat of death or serious injury to himself or someone else.

The defence was discussed in **R v Martin** (1989) where Martin had been disqualified from driving. One morning, while the driving ban was still in force, his stepson was late for work and Martin's wife, who had been suicidal in the past, started to bang her head against a wall and threatened to kill herself unless he drove the boy to work. Martin was charged with driving while disqualified, and argued that he had reasonably believed that his wife might carry out her threat. The trial judge refused to allow the defence of duress, but the Court of Appeal held that the defence of duress of circumstances should have been put before the jury, who should have been asked two questions. First, was the accused, or may he have been, compelled to act as he did because what he reasonably believed to be the situation gave him good reason to fear that otherwise death or serious physical injury would result? Secondly, if so, would a sober person of reasonable firmness, sharing the characteristics of the accused, have responded to that situation by behaving as the accused did? If the answer to both of these questions was 'Yes', the defence was proved and the jury should acquit.

All the cases discussed so far have been concerned with road traffic offences. But in **R** *v* **Pommell** (1995) the Court of Appeal explicitly stated that the defence did not just apply to road traffic cases, but applied throughout the criminal law. The police obtained a search warrant and burst into the defendant's London flat at eight o'clock in the morning. They found him in bed holding a loaded gun and he was charged and convicted of possessing a prohibited weapon without a licence. Defence counsel argued that the night before someone had visited Pommell with the gun, intending to go and shoot some people who had killed a friend. Pommell had persuaded the man to leave the weapon with him to avoid further bloodshed. This happened at one o'clock in the morning, so he had decided not to take the gun straight to the police, but to sleep and take it in the morning. The police had arrived before he was able to do so. His conviction was set aside on appeal as the defence of duress of circumstances would technically be available in these circumstances. In the case of **R** *v* **Abdul-Hussain** (1999) the Court of Appeal found that the defence could be available for the offence of hijacking.

As with duress by threats, duress of circumstances only usually applies where death or serious bodily harm is feared. In **R** *v* **Baker** (1997) the Court of Appeal stated that the defence of duress of circumstances could not be extended to cover situations where serious psychological injury was feared. The father of a child had refused to return the girl at the end of a contact visit. Her mother along with her husband had gone round to the father's house and, hearing a child crying, they feared for the girl's psychological health and proceeded to pound on the front door. The mother and her husband were convicted of criminal damage and their appeals were rejected, as the defence of duress of circumstances only applied where there was a fear of an imminent death or serious physical injury.

▶ Criticism

Arguments against duress

A case can be made for abolishing the defence altogether. In their 1978 report, the Law Commission recognized the following arguments against duress as a broad general defence:

- doing wrong can never be justified;
- it should not be up to individuals to weigh up the harm caused by their wrongful conduct against the harm avoided to themselves or others;
- duress could be classified as merely the motive for committing a crime, and the criminal law does not take motive into consideration for the purposes of conviction;
- the criminal law is itself a system of threats (if you commit a crime you will be punished), and that structure would be weakened if some other system of threats was permitted to play a part;
- allowing the defence helps such criminals as terrorists and kidnappers.

Despite recognizing these points, the Law Commission did not recommend that the defence should be abolished (see below).

Duress and murder

The refusal to allow duress as a defence to murder can apply harshly in some cases, notably those where terrorist organizations have coerced individuals into committing crimes for them by threatening to harm their families. The policy argument for such severity is that, without it, the terrorists' job would be made easier, but in practice this seems unlikely; where a person's family is seriously threatened, the possibility of prosecution is unlikely to be an issue in that person's decision whether or not to help those making the threats.

In **Howe** the House of Lords put forward four grounds for its decision that duress should not be a defence for secondary parties to murder.

1 An ordinary person of reasonable fortitude was expected to lay down their own life rather than take that of someone else.
2 In choosing to kill an innocent person rather than die themselves, defendants could not be said to be choosing the lesser of two evils.
3 Parliament had not chosen to make duress a defence to murder when recommendations had been made that this should be done.
4 Difficult cases could be dealt with by applying a discretion not to prosecute.

Smith and Hogan refute all four points.

1 The criminal law should not expect heroism, and in any case the defence is only available on the basis of what the reasonable person would do.
2 There are circumstances in which murder could be seen as the lesser of two evils. One example might be committing an act (such as planting a bomb) which causes death rather than having your family killed, where there is a chance that your act may not cause

death, and little or no chance that your family will be spared if you fail to do it.
3 We should not assume lack of action by Parliament to represent its intention that the law should not be changed – it might, for example, be that reform was put off because of pressures on parliamentary time.
4 Leaving the issue to administrative discretion is not a satisfactory substitute for clear and just legal provisions.

Psychiatric illness

We saw at p. 274 that in applying the objective test the courts will only take into account 'recognized' psychiatric illnesses. This is a move that has also been seen in the case of **R** *v* **Chan-Fook** (1994) in the context of non-fatal offences against the person. An interesting discussion on this matter has been provided by Alec Buchanan and Graham Virgo in an article published in the Criminal Law Review in 1999 entitled *Duress and Mental Abnormality*. They observed that the requirement for the psychiatric illness to be a 'recognized' illness demonstrates a wariness on the part of the courts – no one talks about recognized heart attacks or recognized broken legs. This wariness may reflect the widespread perception that psychiatric illnesses are less 'real' than other illnesses, and that their victims are better able to help themselves. The judges may also have been concerned that psychiatric symptoms are less amenable to verification: a heart attack can be diagnosed by blood tests and a broken bone by an X-ray, but the diagnosis of a psychiatric condition depends partly on observation but largely on listening to what the patient says. The danger is that people could avail themselves of the defence of duress simply by describing symptoms that did not exist. Buchanan and Virgo state that developments in psychiatry mean that the diagnosis of a psychiatric illness by a psychiatrist is often primarily based on the description of symptoms by the patient, thus increasing this danger. They also point out that the labelling of a psychiatric illness by a medical professional is aimed at treatment and not at the needs of the criminal law, here the identification of characteristics which affect a defendant's ability to withstand a threat.

▶ Reform

The Law Commission

The Law Commission (1978) recommended that duress should be a general defence, and applicable to all crimes including murder. A threat of harm to the accused or another should be sufficient to constitute duress, but a threat to property should not be. Under the draft Criminal Code, defendants would not have the defence if they brought the circumstances of duress on themselves.

Duress and murder

In relation to murder, an obvious compromise would be for duress to operate in the same way as provocation, providing a limited defence to murder resulting in a conviction for manslaughter.

Abolish the defence

Remarks made *obiter* in **Howe** and **Gotts** suggest that the defence of duress should be abolished, and the circumstances of the offence taken into account as mitigation when sentencing. But this would take an important issue away from juries and the standard of proof beyond reasonable doubt.

NECESSITY

This defence essentially applies to situations in which defendants are faced with the choice of committing a crime, or allowing themselves or someone else to suffer or be deprived in some way. Public and private defence and duress can be seen as specific forms of the necessity defence. As far as a general defence of necessity is concerned, the courts have been very careful to impose tight restrictions on its scope. The judiciary have frequently expressed their concern that a wider, generally available defence of necessity might be seen as going too far towards providing excuses for law-breaking.

A leading case laying down restrictions on the application of necessity as a defence is **R** *v* **Dudley and Stephens** (1884). Three sailors and a cabin boy were shipwrecked and cast adrift in an open boat, a thousand miles from land, with only a small amount of food. After twenty days, the last eight with no food, two of the sailors killed the cabin boy, the smallest and weakest among them, and the three ate him. After four more days, they were rescued by a passing ship. Once the story was revealed, they were tried for murder, but the jury refused to convict, returning instead a statement of the facts which they found had been proved: there was little chance that the four could survive for much longer without killing and eating one of them; the cabin boy was the weakest, and least likely to survive; he was killed and eaten by the defendants; without eating him they would probably not have survived. The Divisional Court found that, on these facts, the accused were guilty of murder. The judges acknowledged the defendants had been in a truly desperate situation, but stated that even these circumstances could not afford them a defence. Although the court felt that the defence of necessity could not be allowed, it did alter the usually mandatory death sentence to six months' imprisonment.

A more modern case in which the courts discussed the restrictions on necessity is **Southwark London Borough Council *v* Williams** (1971). This concerned a homeless family who had squatted in an empty council flat. Mr and Mrs Williams and their children had been forced to leave the boarding house in Kent where they lived when the landlady died. Unable to find local accommodation they could afford, they had gone to London, where they thought accommodation might be easier to find. After a couple of nights spent with friends, and one with a kind stranger, they found themselves on the streets, the local council having been unable to help. Scared that their homelessness would mean their children being taken from them by social services, they approached a squatters' association, which helped them make an orderly entry into a council house that neighbours said had been empty for years. The court heard that hundreds of other council homes in the borough were also standing empty, awaiting repairs, yet the council had a waiting list of around 9,000 people.

The council applied for an order for immediate possession, which would allow them to eject the squatters. Mr Williams gave evidence that he did not want to squat, but saw no other way to find a home for his family. The Williams family contended that the council was in breach of its statutory duty to provide accommodation for people in emergency situations. While expressing sympathy, the court granted the council the order it required. Lord Denning explained that, while a defence of necessity had always been available 'in case of imminent danger in order to preserve life', such a defence had to be carefully circumscribed. Otherwise, he said, 'Necessity would open a door which no man could shut . . . If hunger were once allowed to be an excuse for stealing it would open a way through which all kinds of disorder and lawlessness would pass. If homelessness were admitted as a defence to trespass, no man's house would be safe . . . The plea would be an excuse for all sorts of wrongdoing. So the courts must, for the sake of law and order, take a firm stand. They must refuse to admit the plea of necessity to the hungry and the homeless and trust that their distress will be relieved by the charitable and the good.'

The precise extent of the defence of necessity is not clear, and in fact some legal academics have asserted that English law does not recognize a defence of necessity at all, largely on the grounds that if it was not allowed as a defence to a crime in the desperate circumstances of **Dudley and Stephens**, the courts would be unlikely to allow it in any other circumstances. However, in **Richards** (1986), Lord Goff commented that there was no doubt that a defence of necessity existed, even though its scope was not well established.

The defence of necessity has been recognized in three types of cases.

- The criminal act is done in the public interest. A traditional example would be the fact that, during the Great Fire of London, people were allowed to pull down buildings without securing the owners' permission, in order to stop the fire spreading. More recently, the courts held in **Johnson** *v* **Phillips** (1975) that a police constable could direct motorists to disobey traffic regulations if it was necessary to do so in order to protect life or property.
- A person commits a criminal act in order to protect themselves or their property. An example might be a prisoner escaping from prison because it is burning down – this actually happened in an old American case, and the judge ruled that the prisoner should not be hanged because he would not stay to be burnt – **US** *v* **Kirby** (1869).
- The criminal conduct involves assisting someone without their consent. This application of the defence of necessity has been used in some very controversial cases. In **F** *v* **West Berkshire Health Authority** (1989), F was a 36-year-old patient in a mental hospital who suffered from a very severe mental disability. She had formed a sexual relationship with a male patient. There was medical evidence that pregnancy would be disastrous for her mental condition, but there were serious obstacles to her using any ordinary type of contraception. She was incapable of giving consent to a sterilization operation, so her mother sought a declaration that the absence of her consent would not make sterilization an unlawful act. It was confirmed by the House of Lords that the operation was lawful because it was in the best interests of the patient. Lord Brandon said: 'In my opinion the principle is that, when persons lack the capacity, for whatever reason, to take decisions about the performance of operations on them, or the giving of other medical treatment to them, it is necessary that some other person or persons, with the appropriate qualifications, should take such decisions for them.'

Another dramatic illustration is the case of **Mrs S** (1992). Mrs S was a pregnant woman, whose doctors had advised that a Caesarean section was necessary to save the life of her unborn child. Mrs S, who was mentally competent to give consent, refused to allow the operation because it was against her religious beliefs. Her husband supported the decision. After hearing medical evidence that both mother and child could die without the operation, and that if their lives were to be saved it would have to be carried out very quickly, the High Court granted a declaration that it was lawful for surgeons to carry out the surgery without the woman's consent. They did so, and Mrs S survived but the child died.

▶ Should there be a general defence of necessity?

There are arguments both for and against a general defence of necessity.

Arguments against

An excuse for wrongdoing
The argument most often offered against a defence of necessity is that it would simply be an excuse for crime, and that there would be no end to its use; see, for example, **Southwark London Borough Council *v* Williams** (above).

The reasoning in *Dudley and Stephens*
In **Dudley and Stephens**, the judges gave the following reasons why necessity should not afford a defence in the case which involved the offence of murder:

- There was no authority for allowing necessity as a defence to killing an innocent person.
- To allow the defence to such a serious crime would be straying too far from morality.
- The defence was a dangerous one due to the difficulty of measuring one life against another. By what measure is the comparative value of lives to be measured? Is it to be strength, or intellect, or what?
- On the facts of the case, there was no moral reason why it should have been the cabin boy who died. Some commentators have suggested that the defence might have been available if the choice of victim was made in a fair way, by drawing lots for example, but in fact the court specifically stated its disapproval of an American case where this had happened.

Discretion over prosecution
In **Buckoke *v* GLC** (1971), Lord Denning said, *obiter*, that if the driver of a fire engine, who could see a person in a burning building 200 yards down the road, was faced with a red traffic light between them and the building, it would be an offence not to stop at the light, even though not stopping would clearly be the right thing to do. Lord Denning's solution to the problem was that the driver should simply not be prosecuted for the offence, and in fact it appears that this is one way in which the harshness of the law is evaded. Thus, during the inquest following the Zeebrugge ferry disaster, one witness gave evidence that he and numerous other passengers had been trapped in the sinking ferry, and their only means of escape was a rope ladder. The way up the ladder was blocked by a man who, paralysed by fear, could move neither up nor down. After attempting,

in vain, to persuade him to move, the witness, an army corporal, had
ordered those nearest the man to push him off the ladder; he fell into
the water and apparently drowned. The rest of the passengers were then
able to climb the ladder to safety. No criminal charges have ever been
instituted against either the corporal or the passengers who pushed the
man off the ladder. In other cases, the circumstances in which an offence
was committed can be taken into account when considering what sentence would be appropriate.

Duress of circumstances
In recent years the courts have developed a defence of duress of circumstances, which bears a strong similarity to the traditional idea of necessity.
In some cases this has met the need for a general defence of necessity,
but it is limited to situations in which there has been a threat to life, or
one of personal injury.

Arguments for

Relevance of motive
The law accepts that people should only incur criminal liability for those
acts which they do of their own free will, but critical legal theorists argue
that by ignoring the motive behind the act, the law's view of free will is
too narrow. Alan Norrie, writing in *The Critical Lawyer's Handbook*, points
out that the defence of necessity tends to be raised in cases where the
accused's motive for acting as they did is the result of social or natural
circumstances beyond their control (such as the homelessness suffered
by the Williams family), and therefore it is difficult to argue that they
acted of their own free will.

Inconsistency
Duress is allowed as a defence to most crimes and it seems contradictory
for the law to allow some kinds of coercion to excuse wrongdoing, but
not others, when both kinds may equally mean that the accused has not
acted freely. Even the doctrine of duress of circumstances only seems to
allow a defence where the duress is applied by other people, not by natural
or social circumstances. Yet, if the result of duress is that the accused is
not acting of their own free will, why should it matter whether the duress
was caused by a person or not?

The issue of duress of circumstances first arose in **Willer** (1986) (see
above), where it was accepted that the defence could justify the accused
in driving on the pavement to escape a gang of youths who were about
to attack him and his passengers. Previously, duress was only available
as a defence in situations where the accused had been threatened to the
effect that they should commit a particular offence 'or else'. Since this

was not precisely the case in **Willer** it can be argued that it should not matter whether the accused drove on the pavement to escape human attackers, or to avoid a rampaging herd of cows, so long as their conduct aimed to escape death or serious injury. Yet, technically, the law distinguishes between these two circumstances, allowing a defence in one and not the other.

Similarly, the argument that a defence of necessity would become an excuse for all kinds of lawless behaviour (as put forward by Lord Denning in **Williams**) seems difficult to justify given the existence of public and private defences (it is interesting to note that in the eyes of the law, physically injuring someone who might damage your property is apparently more excusable than stealing food because your child has nothing to eat). Public and private defences could equally be seen as potential excuses for crime, but are in practice limited by the courts to those situations in which it might be said that the accused had no alternative. Necessity could be limited in a similar way.

Impossible standards

The lack of a defence of necessity in a case as desperate as **Dudley and Stephens** suggests that the law requires people to behave heroically – in that case the court appears to have felt that all four people should simply have allowed themselves to die. This seems a strangely high standard to set in a legal system that on the other hand recognizes no general duty of care, and would not, for example, impose liability on a healthy adult who fails to help a child drowning in shallow water (see p. 9).

Discretion on prosecution insufficient

It is argued above that the possibility of not prosecuting those who have acted from necessity, or of allowing their circumstances to act as mitigating factors in sentencing, means there is no need for a defence of necessity. There are, however, several arguments against this view.

First, it is against the interests of justice to convict people of a criminal offence, no matter how lightly they are eventually sentenced, when by normal standards they have done nothing wrong, and may even have acted in the interests of others, or of the general public. Where the offence is murder the sentence is mandatory, so the circumstances in which the accused acted cannot be used to lessen the sentence anyway.

Secondly, it is absurd to make rules (or not to allow exceptions to rules) which discourage people in difficult situations from taking actions which are in the public interest – such as Lord Denning's hypothetical firefighter ignoring the red light in order to save people from a burning house.

Finally, leaving the issue to the discretion of prosecuting authorities seems an undesirably vague and subjective way of dealing with the matter – while deciding not to prosecute in such cases may be the best outcome for all concerned, there is no way of ensuring that such decisions are made in every appropriate case, and so the need for a defence may remain.

Other jurisdictions

A general defence of necessity is recognized in many other parts of the world, apparently without the results envisaged by Lord Denning in **Williams**. For example, many American states have adopted the American Model Penal Code, which provides that conduct which the defendants believe to be necessary to prevent harm to themselves or another is justified, providing that the harm they are aiming to prevent is greater than that which the law seeks to prevent by prohibiting the act committed (though it has to be said that even this is not entirely satisfactory – how would it apply, for example, where defendants have been told to kill someone else, or be killed themselves?).

▶ Reform

A limited defence

A limited general defence of necessity could be created, which would apply only where an offence was committed in order to avoid death or serious personal injury to oneself or another, regardless of whether the harm anticipated would be caused by a human being or not. This would make the law on necessity more consistent with that on self-defence and duress, and, if the issue were left to juries to decide, could build a sense of mercy into the law, without leading to the mass criminality envisaged by Lord Denning in **Williams**.

No necessity defence

In 1977 the Law Commission stated its opposition to a defence of necessity, and proposed that any common law defence of this kind should be abolished. This proposal was subsequently severely criticized, and the draft Criminal Law Bill 1993, drawn up by the Law Commission, explicitly retains any defence of necessity that currently exists at common law.

Cannabis for medicinal purposes

There has been some debate as to whether it should be legal to use cannabis for medicinal purposes, for example to soothe the pain of arthritis sufferers. Judges could do this through accepting a defence of necessity in these circumstances, but they have been reluctant to do so. But there is growing evidence that juries are now prepared to accept this defence. Alan Blythe supplied cannabis to his suicidal wife to reduce the pain and discomfort she experienced as a result of multiple sclerosis. He was prosecuted in April 1998 for several drug offences. At his trial expert evidence was given that cannabis can relieve the symptoms of this disease and a jury acquitted. Another man was acquitted by a jury in Manchester who admitted cultivating cannabis to relieve his back pain.

A working party on the therapeutic uses of cannabis has been established by the Royal Pharmaceutical Society of Great Britain and the Home Office has granted limited permission for experiments involving cannabis and related substances. It may be that in the future cannabis will be made available to patients on prescriptions as was the case until 1971.

CONSENT

A victim's consent to the defendant's behaviour can exempt the defendant from liability. The issue normally arises in relation to non-fatal offences against the person, and has already been touched upon in the context of rape where, instead of being viewed as a defence, it is treated as part of the definition of the offence.

By recognizing a defence of consent, the courts are acknowledging that individuals should be independent and free to control their own lives, but there are limitations to this principle, which seem to depend on the nature and degree of harm to which the victim has consented.

▶ Genuine consent

For the defence to be allowed the consent must be genuine. In **R v Richardson** (1999) the defendant was a registered dental practitioner who was suspended from practice by the General Dental Council. Whilst still suspended she carried out dentistry on a number of patients, one of whom complained to the police. A prosecution was brought for assault occasioning actual bodily harm. She was convicted and on appeal she argued that she had the defence of consent as the complainants had consented to their treatment. The appeal was allowed. It was accepted that consent had the same meaning as a defence as it did in the context of the rape offence. For rape we saw at p. 120 that a consent is not treated as a genuine consent if it has been obtained by the defendant lying about their identity – pretending to be the victim's husband or their boyfriend. The prosecution argued that the concept of the identity of the defendant should be extended to cover their qualifications. The Court rejected that contention. In **R v Olugboja** (discussed in relation to rape) it was pointed out that a mere submission is not a consent.

Sometimes parents or the court can give consent on behalf of a child or an incompetent adult, particularly in relation to surgery which is needed in an emergency. In **Gillick** *v* **West Norfolk AHA** (1986) the House of Lords said that a parent continues to be able to give consent on behalf of their child until 'the child achieves a sufficient understanding and intelligence to enable them to understand fully what is proposed', a situation now known as being 'Gillick competent'. The case concerned the question of whether doctors could give girls under sixteen contraceptives if the girls consented, without having also to seek their parents' consent. The answer was that doctors could if the girl was 'Gillick competent'.

The scope of the Gillick competence test has since been restricted to situations where the child gives a positive consent; if a Gillick competent child refuses treatment then a parent's consent can override that refusal. In **Re W** (1993) a 16-year-old girl was suffering from anorexia nervosa, and refused medical treatment which would have saved her life. The court was prepared to override her refusal even though she was regarded as being Gillick competent.

▶ The nature and degree of harm

In deciding whether to allow the defence the courts will look at the nature and degree of harm consented to by the defendant. This is primarily a question of public policy, and the courts seek to strike a balance between the seriousness of the harm consented to, and the social usefulness, if any, of the conduct.

The courts are never prepared to allow a victim's consent to their own death to provide a defence for the person who brings about that death. This would be euthanasia, and as a matter of public policy the victim's consent does not provide a defence in Britain, though it does in some other countries. Deliberate euthanasia (also described as mercy killing) would normally leave the perpetrator liable to murder, though sometimes liability can be reduced to manslaughter on the basis of diminished responsibility.

In the light of **Airedale National Health Service Trust** *v* **Bland** (1993) (discussed on p. 10) a distinction has to be drawn between active euthanasia and passive euthanasia. In that case it was held that hospital authorities could legally terminate the treatment which was keeping Tony Bland alive. The courts did not acknowledge that the Trust had the defence of consent, but justified their conclusion on the basis that it was in the best interests of the patient and that switching off the life support machine only constituted an omission to act. In similar situations in the USA, courts admit that they are substituting their judgement for that of the patient, and therefore consenting on behalf of that person.

A victim cannot consent to injury (other than assault and battery) unless the activity causing that injury falls into certain exceptions which are considered to have some social usefulness, in which case the defendant can consent to conduct which might otherwise constitute a serious offence. In **Leach** (1969) the victim had arranged to be crucified on Hampstead Heath. The defendants, at his request, nailed him to a wooden cross, piercing his hands with six-inch nails. They were found liable under s. 18 of the Offences Against the Person Act 1861 and were not allowed to rely on the victim's consent as a defence. This was because he had suffered serious injury and there was no social benefit from the activity.

Considerable controversy has been caused by the case of **Brown** (1993) which is now the leading House of Lords judgment on the law of consent. The case arose when police officers by chance came across a private party in the home of one of the defendants. The guests were homosexuals who enjoyed sado-masochistic experiences, and the party had involved activities such as whipping, caning, branding, applying stinging nettles to the genital area, and inserting sharp objects into the penis. The whole event took place in private, with the consent of everyone there; none of the men had suffered permanent injury or infection as a result of these practices, nor sought any medical treatment, and no complaint had been made to the police. Despite this, the men were charged with offences under s. 47 and s. 20 of the Offences Against the Person Act 1861. They were convicted, the defence of consent being rejected. Lord Templeman said:

> In principle there is a difference between violence which is
> incidental and violence which is inflicted for the indulgence of
> cruelty. The violence of sado-masochistic encounters involves the
> indulgence of cruelty by sadists and the degradation of victims.
> Such violence is injurious to the participants and unpredictably
> dangerous. I am not prepared to invent a defence of consent for
> sado-masochistic encounters which breed and glorify cruelty and
> result in offences under sections 47 and 20 of the Act of 1861 . . .

The House of Lords concluded that defendants can only rely on a victim's consent to serious injury if the activity falls within certain recognized exceptions, but the exact *ratio* of the judgment is unclear. The academic J.C. Smith has argued that the *ratio* could be limited to where the harm is intentionally imposed, so that situations where the *mens rea* was recklessness would not be excluded from the defence. Alternatively, it might be further limited to its facts, and so only affect sado-masochistic encounters, though this seems unlikely.

An appeal against the House of Lords judgment was taken to the European Court of Human Rights in **Laskey** *v* **United Kingdom; Jaggard** *v* **United Kingdom; Brown** *v* **United Kingdom** (1997). The European Court of Human Rights concluded that the law as laid down in the House of Lords judgment did not breach the European Convention on Human Rights. Article 8 of the Convention provides for the right to respect of a person's private life, though this right can be restricted where it is 'necessary in a democratic society'. The court found that Article 8 had not been breached as interference by a public authority in the consensual activities of a sado-masochistic group was necessary in a democratic society for the protection of health. The state authorities were entitled to rely on the criminal law in regulating the infliction of physical harm; the authorities could consider the potential for serious harm that might result from the extreme activities of the men. Such conduct could not be viewed as purely a matter of their own private morality. The level of the sentences given and the degree of organization involved in the group meant that the interference in the men's private lives could not be viewed as disproportionate.

The extent of the exceptions where the defence of consent will be allowed for serious harms mentioned by the House of Lords in **R v Brown** is not clear, despite the fact that the House described them as 'recognized' exceptions. Serious injuries sustained during a fight are known to fall outside these exceptions. In **Attorney-General's Reference (No. 6 of 1980)** two men had got into an argument and had proceeded to have a fist fight; it was held that although they both fought voluntarily, they could not rely on the defence of consent. On the other hand, fights that take place within the Queensberry Rules do fall within a recognized exception, as do tattooing, surgery, ear-piercing, and ritual circumcision. Sports activities are viewed as having social usefulness, and so defendants are treated as having consented to even serious injuries provided they occurred when the players were acting within the rules of the game, as in **Billinghurst** (1978) where the defence was allowed in the notoriously violent game of rugby.

The defence has also been allowed where serious injuries occur following what the courts described as 'rough horseplay' though others might call it bullying. In **Jones** (1986) a gang of schoolboys threw their victims up to ten feet into the air, with the result that one victim suffered a ruptured spleen and broke his arm. The defence was allowed on the basis that there was no intention to cause injury, and on appeal convictions for grievous bodily harm were quashed.

R v Wilson (1996) is the first major case of the Court of Appeal to interpret the implications of **R v Brown** on the law of consent. Wilson had, at his wife's request, used a hot knife to brand his initials onto her buttocks. The scars were found during a medical examination and he was subsequently charged with the offence of assault occasioning actual bodily harm contrary to s. 47 of the Offences Against the Person Act 1861. At the trial it was argued in his defence that his wife had consented to his conduct. The judge felt bound by **R v Brown** to rule that the defence of consent was not available on the facts. Wilson was convicted but his appeal was allowed by the Court of Appeal which stated that this conduct fell within the recognized exception identified by **R v Brown** of tattooing. In addition, the court observed that it was not in the public interest to impose a criminal sanction on such consensual activity between husband and wife carried out in the privacy of their matrimonial home and without any aggressive intent.

There is no need to rely on the defence of consent where the defendant lacked the *mens rea* for an offence anyway. This point was made in a first instance decision of **R *v* Simon Slingsby** (1995). The defendant met a woman in a night club. They later had vaginal and anal intercourse to which she consented. She also consented to him penetrating her vagina and anus with his hand. Neither of them thought about the fact that he was wearing a signet ring but the ring caused her internal cuts. She did not realize the seriousness of her injuries, which went septic and caused her death. Slingsby was charged with unlawful and dangerous act manslaughter. The trial judge ruled that **Brown** could be distinguished, as in the case before him the defendant lacked the *mens rea* for any offence, thus there was no need to consider the defence of consent.

▶ Criticism

Inconsistency

The academic David Feldman (1993) has highlighted the inconsistency of allowing the defence for the bullying behaviour in **Jones**, to which it is hard to see any real consent, and not for the fully consensual behaviour in **Brown**. He points out that while bullying is reckless behaviour with substantial risks being foolishly taken, sado-masochistic activity is very ritualistic and disciplined, so that risks are carefully calculated and minimized. In addition, free expression of sexuality is considered desirable in a free society, whereas bullying is merely an expression of aggression.

Under proposals by the Law Commission the defence would not be available for horseplay and it would continue to be unavailable for sado-masochistic activity.

Serious injury and consent

It has been questioned how a person can have a defence of consent to assault and battery but no defence to s. 47 of the Offences Against the Person Act 1861, when an essential element of the latter offence is proof of either of the former.

Informed consent

The defence could be improved by adding a requirement that the consent is an informed consent, which would cover cases such as **Clarence** (1888), where a husband had sexual intercourse with his wife when she did not know he had a sexually transmitted disease. As the law stands, provided her injury was not too serious, he would not be liable for a crime against the person because she had consented to the sexual intercourse. If there was a requirement that her consent had to be informed, meaning that her consent would only be valid if she knew of the relevant circumstances, then the defence would not be available. This issue is of particular importance in the context of AIDS. If informed consent was required the outcome would have been different in the case of **R** *v* **Richardson** (1998) which is the case that concerned the dentist discussed at p. 287. As the law currently stands if the defendant had had no qualifications and had masqueraded as a qualified dentist she would still have been acquitted.

Individual autonomy

Peter Tatchell, a spokesperson for the gay rights group *Outrage*, has commented, following the House of Lords judgment in **R** *v* **Brown**: 'The state has no legitimate business invading the bedrooms of consenting adults and dictating how they should have sex.'

Consent and euthanasia

There is an ongoing debate as to whether euthanasia should be legalized. Those in favour of euthanasia have argued it offers a person the opportunity to select the time and manner of their dying in order to secure a peaceful end to their life, unencumbered by intrusive medical technology. The practice of providing patients with potentially lethal drugs is becoming increasingly common. A recent survey of three hundred doctors carried out for the *Sunday Times* (*Doctor will you help me die? Sunday Times*, 15 November 1998) suggests that 15 per cent of Britain's 36,000 GPs have assisted patients to die. Technically in England the act of euthanasia can give rise to liability for murder, though in the case of **Tony Bland** (see p. 10) the courts accepted that liability could be avoided if there was merely an omission. This can place doctors in a delicate position when treating terminally ill patients. The law in this field is based on the concept of 'double effect'. This doctrine attempts to distinguish between the primary and secondary consequences of an action or course of treatment. It was first formulated by Devlin J in 1957 in the case of Dr John Adams. This doctor had been tried for the murder of an 84-year-old woman who he had injected with a fatal dose of narcotics when she was terminally ill. In his summing up, Devlin J stated:

> If the first purpose of medicine, the restoration of health, can no longer be achieved there is still much for a doctor to do, and he is entitled to do all that is proper and necessary to relieve pain and

suffering, even if the measures he takes may incidentally shorten human life.

After 42 minutes' deliberation, the jury returned a 'not guilty' verdict. Thus liability can be avoided if beneficial medication is given, despite the certain knowledge that death will occur as a side effect.

Davies in his *Textbook on Medical Law* (1996) has argued that, although one can sympathize with a judicial reluctance to see competent and highly regarded medical practitioners convicted of murder, the doctrine of dual effect is both illogical and inconsistent with English criminal law. If a doctor injects a severely ill patient with a powerful painkiller in the certain knowledge that the drug will cause death within a matter of minutes, under the ordinary principles of criminal law this doctor intended to kill. English law has traditionally excluded any considerations of motive in determining criminal responsibility.

In practice individuals are rarely convicted following an act of euthanasia. This is because either the jury refuse to convict or the prosecution choose not to proceed. This was the case in March 1996 when the prosecution against the care worker, Rachael Heath, for the attempted murder of a 71-year-old cancer victim was dropped. On 11 May 1999 David Moor, a Newcastle upon Tyne GP, was acquitted of the murder of George Liddell, an elderly and terminally-ill patient. The prosecution had alleged that Dr Moor had injected Mr Liddell with a potentially lethal dose of diamorphine with the intention of causing death. The defence argued that the drug had been provided for purely therapeutic reasons – to relieve Mr Liddell's pain. In interviews he had apparently admitted that he administered diamorphine to hundreds of other terminally-ill patients. The prosecution of David Moor was opposed by members of George Liddell's family. Mr Liddell's daughter, Doreen Ryan, said that Dr Moor was 'a hard-working and dedicated GP who doesn't deserve to be at the centre of a police investigation. The police should concentrate on catching criminals and not prosecuting this marvellous doctor.'

But doctors are still in a very vulnerable position. It should be noted that the defence of diminished responsibility – which is sometimes used by spouses and others who kill loved ones in order to relieve suffering – will seldom be available to medical practitioners. In the case of **R** *v* **Cox** (1992) Dr Cox carried out the wishes of his dying patient and deliberately injected her with strong potassium chloride, a drug which causes death but has no therapeutic value. She died soon afterwards. Her family felt that, by giving her the injection, Dr Cox had released her from her pain and allowed her to die with dignity. The jury convicted though their reluctance to do so could be seen from the fact that many of them wept openly when the verdict was returned.

Many people would like to see the law in this area reformed. Sixty per cent of doctors questioned in the *Sunday Times* survey agreed with the proposition that 'doctors should have the power to assist death without fear of prosecution . . . by prescribing lethal drugs for patients to take themselves'. Hazel Biggs (1996) has suggested that the criminal law should look at the harm caused in each situation. In most instances of homicide, death is the harm caused by the conduct of the killer. With euthanasia, the indignity of a living death in a persistent vegetative state, or the protracted and painful dying process associated with terminal disease, can appear more harmful than death itself.

In the Netherlands, euthanasia has been legalized. Although the Dutch Penal Code recognizes the offences of taking another's life at his or her request (Article 293) and assisting suicide (Article 294) the courts have held that these crimes are subject to the defence of necessity (Article 40). The effect of this is that doctor-assisted suicide is available in the Netherlands, subject to guidelines made by the courts and the Dutch Medical Association. In Germany, euthanasia does not give rise to liability for murder but to a lesser offence with a reduced sentence. Such an approach has, however, been rejected by the Criminal Law Revision Committee in 1980, which decided to reject proposals for a new offence of mercy killing subject to a maximum sentence of two years' imprisonment. Another approach would be to have a defence of mercy killing available. If the ban on the defence of duress for the offence of murder was lifted, then, as the defence of duress of circumstances evolves, it could be applied in this context.

• •
LAWFUL CHASTISEMENT

Under common law, parents are allowed to use a moderate level of physical punishment on their children. The amount of force used must not be excessive. In **R** *v* **Hopley** (1860) it was stated that the force would be unlawful it was:

> administered for the gratification of passion or rage or if it be
> immoderate or excessive in its nature or degree, or if it be
> protracted beyond the child's powers of endurance or with an
> instrument unfitted for the purpose and calculated to produce
> danger to life and limb . . . .

In **A** *v* **United Kingdom** (1998) the applicant was 9 years old and had been beaten regularly by his stepfather. The beatings had been carried out using a stick. The stepfather was charged with causing actual bodily harm and offered the defence of lawful chastisement. He was acquitted and the applicant took his case to European Court of Human Rights arguing that the state had failed to protect the defendant from physical abuse. The European Court held that Article 3 of the European Convention of Human Rights prohibiting torture or inhuman and degrading treatment had been violated. It felt that the defence of lawful chastisement did not provide adequate protection to children who were vulnerable members of society. This is a delicate area of the law as some parents are quite vociferous about their right to smack their children. While the UK Government accepted that there had been a breach of Article 3, it felt that it was difficult to resolve the problem as different juries would come to different conclusions as to whether or not a particular act constituted reasonable chastisement. It pointed out that no one can know for sure why juries acquit. Even if the defendant offers a defence of lawful chastisement, a jury might acquit because the harm alleged had not been made out, or the required *mens rea* not established beyond all reasonable doubt.

Following the Education (No. 2) Act 1986 members of staff in state schools no longer have the right to use corporal punishment on pupils – thus the days of the headmaster equipped with a cane and slipper are over.

• •
ANSWERING QUESTIONS

1 Maggie and Bert are both staying in a hospital. Maggie is expecting her first child and is of low intelligence. She is trying to read a book and Bert starts to taunt her about her inability to read and the fact that her unborn child is illegitimate. In a violent rage Maggie throws a plate at Bert but it strikes Rose, a doctor, who is killed.

Bert is being treated for epilepsy. He walks into the hospital grounds and is approached by a policeman, PC Scott. He mistakes him for an alien from another planet and attacks him, and he dies two weeks later from his injuries.
Consider the criminal liability of
(a) Maggie *(25 marks)*
(b) Bert. *(25 marks)*
Problem questions like this commonly combine the general defences discussed in this chapter with specific defences such as provocation for murder. You need to keep the divisions used in the question, so divide your answer into two parts, (a) and (b). In part (a) consider whether Maggie could be liable for murder. Look first of all at whether she has the *actus reus*, and then the *mens rea* of the offence. On the facts, she would appear to have both. However, she would seek to rely on a defence. The most relevant defence would be provocation. Applying the subjective test first, she seems to have had a sudden and temporary loss of self-control. As regards the objective limb, a court may take into account the fact that she is of low intellect, is pregnant with an illegitimate child and has difficulty reading – **Camplin**, **Luc Thiet Thuan**. Even if this defence should succeed it is only a partial defence and she would still be liable for voluntary manslaughter.

In part (b) you would need to consider Bert's liability for murder. Again, he would appear to have both the *actus reus* and *mens rea* of the offence and the crucial issue would be whether he has any defence. The partial defence of diminished responsibility and the complete defence of insanity would both be relevant here and you would need to look at these in detail. Mention should be made of the case of **Sullivan** on epileptics and insanity. You also ought to discuss the different effect of a successful defence of diminished responsibility and a successful defence of insanity.

2 Critically evaluate the M'Naghten rules. Are they an appropriate test for insanity in the modern world? *Oxford*

This is a fairly easy question to deal with if you are properly prepared. As is so often the case, the question is divided very clearly into parts and so your answer should also be divided in this way. In the first part, you need to state what the rules are, and critically evaluate them – this means highlighting the strengths and weaknesses of the law. You can answer the second part by discussing, among other things, the criticisms made of the rules by medical experts, and the movement in America for the abolition or restriction of a defence of insanity.

3 Should the defence of insanity be abolished?

This question requires similar material to the previous one, but here the emphasis of your argument will be whether the defence should be abolished, rather than whether it is out of date, though the two issues overlap. With a question such as this you will still want to show the examiner that you know what the current law of insanity is, but you should use this material as part of your argument that the defence still has/no longer has a useful function in today's society.

4 K, who is attending a lecture by L, a well-known hypnotist, agrees to be hypnotized. L tells K that he intends to induce a state of aggression in him by means of a keyword 'bananas'. K agrees and is duly hypnotized. When L mentions the keyword 'bananas', K reacts by smashing the microphone on L's head causing bruising. N, a member of the audience, attacks and kills P, who is sitting beside him. P had been calling N 'a stupid loony'. N is in fact severely retarded and lost his self-control when P taunted him. Doctors are prepared to give evidence that N is not insane although he has a mental age of seven. Advise K who is charged with assault occasioning actual bodily harm to L and criminal damage to the microphone *(25 marks)* **and N who is charged with murder.** *(25 marks) Oxford*

You need to divide your answer into two clear parts, the first considering K's liability and the second considering N's liability. Looking first at K, we are told that he has been charged with assault occasioning actual bodily harm and criminal damage. You need to discuss these offences in detail. As regards assault occasioning actual bodily harm, since its *mens rea* is subjective (either intention or subjective recklessness as to an assault or a battery) K could argue that he lacked the *mens rea* at the time. In relation to the offence of criminal damage the *mens rea* includes *Caldwell* recklessness as to the causing of damage or destruction to property and the courts are likely to find that this exists.

K's main defence would appear to be automatism, but this is narrowly interpreted and the courts are reluctant to allow it when the automatist state is self-induced.

Moving to the second part of your answer, you would need to consider first whether N had the *actus reus* and *mens rea* of murder. He would appear to do so. You could then consider whether he had the partial defences of either diminished responsibility or provocation. Because we are told that the doctors will give evidence that he is not insane, you should only look at the issue of insanity very briefly, though you should point out that the legal definition of insanity is not the same as the medical definition.

5 Miranda senses that her husband, Terry, although very possessive, has stopped loving her. She feels a little depressed and consults her doctor who prescribes a daily dose of one tablet of the drug Amzac, saying that it will take several days to work but that 'if it doesn't work after a while we will probably increase the dose'. The doctor does not warn Miranda about taking alcohol with Amzac, but Miranda does read the information sheet supplied with the tablets, which says, 'Take the whole of the prescribed dose every morning. You should not drink alcohol when you take Amzac.'

After four days Miranda is worried that the tablets have not started working. She takes an extra tablet, and the next morning takes three tablets. Within a few hours Miranda, who had never previously had any disposition towards aggressive thoughts, begins to feel that her unhappiness would be lessened if she could take revenge on her husband by setting fire to his new car. That evening Miranda's friend Barbara visits Miranda, and after both women have consumed two glasses of wine Miranda tells Barbara what she wants to do. Barbara has never really liked Terry, and although she is aware that her friend is behaving strangely, thinks it would be fun to watch the car burn.

Terry arrives home just as Miranda has found a can of petrol in the garage. Barbara is a little scared and leaves the house, although she does not tell Terry what is going on as she passes him in the hall. Barbara watches from the other side of the road as Miranda successfully sets fire to the car.

When the police arrive Miranda says she has no recollection of what happened until the moment she found herself standing by the burning car. A psychiatrist gives his opinion that in a very small number of cases Amzac has been associated with unexplained violence, and that alcohol may well increase the risk of unpredictable effects from the drug.

Consider the criminal liability, if any, of both Miranda and Barbara. *NEAB*
Miranda is the principal offender because she is the one who actually sets fire to the car, so it is easier to discuss her liability first. The main offence that she would be liable for is arson, which is when criminal damage is caused by fire. She would appear to have both the *actus reus* and *mens rea* of this offence.

Miranda and Barbara could also be liable for conspiring to commit criminal damage. There is an agreement between two people for the commission of the offence. It does not matter that Barbara intends to play no part in this. All that need be proved is that they intended that one of them would carry out the acts that constituted the offence.

Miranda may claim that she has a defence of intoxication. In order successfully to argue this she must have lacked the *mens rea* for the offence: **Kingston**. The fact that when the police arrive she says she has no recollection of what happened might support this, but on the other hand she seems to know what she is going to do when she explains herself to Barbara. If Miranda consumed the wine to get Dutch courage this also would exclude the defence: **Gallagher**.

If she does lack the *mens rea* then the next consideration is that criminal damage is an offence of basic intent, but she may claim that she is involuntarily intoxicated. This may be arguable in relation to the taking of too much Amzac due to the ambiguous words of the doctor. However, she may have difficulties in relation to her consumption of the wine as she has read the instructions which clearly state: 'You should not drink alcohol when you take Amzac.' She may argue that at the time of drinking the wine she was already under the influence of the overdose of Amzac and was therefore unable to appreciate this warning at the time of her actions. The case of **Hardie** will need to be considered.

Barbara may be liable as a secondary participant. This will depend on whether her conduct prior to the offence or at the time of the offence was felt to be sufficient to constitute encouragement. You could look at the cases on whether mere presence at the scene of the crime can be sufficient to amount to abetting. She has done nothing actually to help Miranda. She may want to argue that she has withdrawn from the offence, and you can analyse the cases in the field to decide whether her conduct is sufficient to constitute a withdrawal.

6 **Give a critical evaluation of the law relating to duress and necessity.** *NEAB*

With a question like this it is important to answer the whole of what you are being asked – an essay purely on either duress or necessity, rather than both of them, will not get you good marks. You do not need to divide your coverage absolutely equally between the two, but you must discuss both. As duress and necessity are being linked in the same question a good point to make is that duress of circumstances may have taken over the gaps left by the defence of necessity. Also remember that in answering this type of question you need to show both an understanding of what the law is and also criticism of that law and how it could be reformed.

7 **Robert is being held by two armed terrorists in his own home. They have threatened to kill him, but have said that they would not harm any of the children in the house. When an opportunity arises Robert grabs Anna, a girl aged seven who had been playing with his daughter in the house when the terrorists arrived. Holding the girl to him as a shield, Robert leaves the house.**

Outside, unknown to Robert, there are two police marksmen. One of them sees Robert, still holding the girl, emerge from the house. Believing Robert to be one of the armed terrorists he shoots at him when he believes he has a clear shot. However, the shot misses Robert and hits Anna, who is very seriously injured. The second police marksman, hearing the shot, believes that he is being fired at and shoots at Robert. He misses and hits Rose, an elderly neighbour, who was watching events from her window. Rose dies. Anna dies in hospital after a delay to her treatment caused when her father, a Jehovah's Witness, refuses to allow her to be given a blood transfusion.

Consider what criminal liability may exist in these circumstances in relation to the deaths of Anna and Rose. *NEAB*

You would need to consider the criminal liability of Robert, the two policemen, the terrorists and Anna's father in turn. Consider first of all the liability of Robert for the death of Anna. On the issue of murder the main problem in finding the *actus reus* will concern the question of causation. There are two possible breaks in the chain of causation. The first is the shot by the first policeman. The case of **Pagett** should be looked at in detail, though some important distinctions on the facts can be made as in **Pagett** the defendant was the person who created the dangerous situation in the first place when he emerged using the victim as a shield. The second possible break in the chain of causation is the refusal by Anna's father to allow a blood transfusion. The case of **Blaue** is relevant here.

On the issue of *mens rea*, Robert does not have the direct intention to kill or to cause grievous bodily harm. Nor does he seem to have indirect intention because we are told that he did not know that there were two police marksmen outside and the terrorists have said that they would not harm the children in the house, therefore he probably does not foresee as a virtual certainty the risk of the child suffering at least grievous bodily harm (**Nedrick**).

If causation was found to exist then he might be liable for some lesser homicide offence, in particular gross negligence manslaughter. He may have a defence, the most relevant ones being the public and private defences.

As regards the liability of the first policeman for the death of Anna, the most serious offence he could be liable for is murder. On the issue of causation the only possible break in the chain of causation is the refusal of a blood transfusion and this is unlikely to be sufficient in the light of **Blaue**. As regards *mens rea* he intends to shoot Robert but hits Anna. His intention as regards Robert can be transferred to Anna according to the principle of transferred malice. His exact intention is not clear from the facts; it is unlikely that he was carrying out a shoot-to-kill policy, but was he intending to cause him grievous bodily harm? If so, then he would have the *mens rea* for murder. If not, then he might be liable for involuntary manslaughter. He could argue that he fell within the public and private defences. You could explore how this case differs from that of **Clegg**. You could also consider duress of circumstances.

As regards the second policeman's liability for Rose's death, again you could look first at his liability for murder. Causation will not be an issue because there is no intervening act between his shot and her death. As regards *mens rea*, the doctrine of transferred malice would be relevant, but again his original intention is not clear. If he is found not to have the *mens rea* of murder then consideration could be given to his liability for involuntary manslaughter. You could also raise the issue of public and private defences.

Looking at the terrorists' liability, the threat to kill would constitute an assault. Their exact plans are unclear but they may have already committed a blackmail if they have issued their demands, and they could be liable for conspiracy to blackmail. If they have not yet issued any demand they could be liable for attempted blackmail. How far they would be found liable for the injuries or deaths will depend on whether there is causation. Close analysis of the decisions in the field will be necessary. If causation exists, whether they will be convicted for murder or manslaughter will depend on what their intentions actually were at the time: they threaten to kill Robert but did they have any real intention of doing so? If they did, then it might be possible to rely on transferred malice again.

Lastly, you could consider whether any criminal liability might be imposed on Anna's father.

Appendix

ANSWERING EXAMINATION QUESTIONS

A t the end of each chapter in this book, you will find detailed guide-lines for answering exam questions on the topics covered. Many of the questions are taken from actual A-Level past papers, but they are equally relevant for candidates of all law examinations, as these questions are typical of the type of questions that examiners ask in the field.

In this section, we aim to give some general guidelines for answering questions on criminal law.

Citation of authorities

One of the most important requirements for answering questions on the law is that you must be able to back the points you make with authority, usually either a case or a statute. It is not good enough to state that the law is such and such, without stating the case or statute which lays down that law.

Some examiners are starting to suggest that the case name is not essential, as long as you can remember and understand the general prin-ciple that the case laid down. However, such examiners remain in the minority and the reality is that even they are likely to give higher marks where the candidate has cited authorities; quite simply, it helps give the impression that you know your material thoroughly, rather than half-remembering something you heard once in class.

This means you must be prepared to learn fairly long lists of cases by heart, which can be a daunting prospect. What you need to memorize is the name of the case, a brief description of the facts, and the legal principle which the case established. Sometimes it is useful to know the court, particularly if it is a House of Lords judgment. Learning the cases is often a slow and dull process, but is necessary in order to perform well in the examination.

Knowing the names of cases makes you look more knowledgeable, and also saves writing time in the exam, but if you do forget a name, referring briefly to the facts will identify it. It is not necessary to learn the dates of cases, though it is useful if you know whether it is a recent or an old case. Dates are usually required for statutes.

You need to know the facts of a case in order to judge whether it applies to the situation in a problem question. However, unless you are making a detailed comparison of the circumstances of a case and the facts of a problem question, in order to argue that the case should or could be distinguished or applied, you should generally make only brief reference to facts, if at all – long descriptions of facts waste time and earn few marks.

When reading the 'Answering questions' sections at the end of each chapter in this book, bear in mind that for reasons of space, we have not highlighted every case which you should cite. The skeleton arguments outlined in those sections *must* be backed up with authority from cases and statute law contained in the relevant chapter.

There is no right answer

In law exams, there is not usually a right or a wrong answer. What matters is that you show you know what type of issues you are being asked about. Essay questions are likely to ask you to 'discuss', 'criticize', or 'evaluate', and you simply need to produce a good range of factual and critical material in order to do this. The answer you produce might look completely different from your friend's but both answers could be worth 'A' grades.

Breadth and depth of content

Where a question seems to raise a number of different issues – as most do – you will achieve better marks by addressing all or most of these issues than by writing at great length on just one or two. By all means spend more time on issues which you know well, but be sure at least to mention other issues which you can see are relevant, even if you can only produce a paragraph or so about them.

The structure of the question

If a question is specifically divided into parts, for example (a), (b) and (c), then stick to those divisions and do not merge your answer into one long piece of writing.

Law examinations tend to contain a mixture of essay questions and what are known as 'problem questions'. Tackling each of these questions involves slightly different skills so we will consider each now in turn.

▶ Essay questions

Answer the question asked

Over and over again, examiners complain that candidates do not answer the question they are asked – so if you can develop this skill, you will stand out from the crowd. You will get very few marks for simply writing all you know about a topic, with no attempt to address the issues raised in the question, but if you can adapt the material that you have learnt on the subject to take into account the particular emphasis given to it by the question, you will do well.

Even if you have memorized an essay which does raise the issues in the question (perhaps because those issues tend to be raised year after year), you must fit your material to the words of the question you are actually being asked. For example, suppose during your course, you wrote an essay on the advantages and disadvantages of strict liability, and then in the exam, you find yourself faced with the question 'Should strict liability offences be abolished?' The material in your coursework essay is ideally suited for the exam question, but if you begin the main part of your answer with the words 'The advantages of strict liability include . . .', or something similar, this is a dead giveaway to the examiner that you are merely writing down an essay you have memorized. It takes very little effort to change the words to 'Abolition of strict liability would ignore certain advantages that the current law has . . .', but it will create a much better impression, especially if you finish with a conclusion which, based on points you have made, states that abolition is a good or bad idea, the choice depending on the arguments you have made during your answer.

In your essay, you should keep referring to the words used in the question – if this seems to become repetitive, use synonyms for those words. This makes it clear to the examiner that you are keeping the question in mind as you work.

Plan your answer

Under pressure of time, it is tempting to start writing immediately, but five minutes spent planning each essay question is well worth spending – it may mean that you write less overall, but the quality of your answer will almost certainly be better. The plan need not be elaborate; just jot down everything you feel is relevant to the answer, including case names, and then organize the material into a logical order appropriate to the question asked. To put it in order, rather than wasting time copying it all out again, simply put a number next to each point according to which ones you intend to make first, second and so forth.

Provide analysis and fact

Very few essay questions require merely factual descriptions of what the law is; you will almost always be required to analyse the factual content in some way, usually highlighting any problems or gaps in the law, and suggesting possible reforms. If a question asks you to 'analyse whether the defence of insanity is satisfactory', you should not write everything you know about the defence of insanity and finish with one sentence saying the defence is or is not satisfactory. Instead you should select your relevant material and your whole answer should be targeted at answering whether the defence is satisfactory, by, for example, pointing out any gaps or problems in it, and highlighting changes which have improved it as a defence.

Where a question uses the word 'critically', as in 'critically describe' or 'critically evaluate', the examiners are merely drawing your attention to the fact that your approach should be analytical and not merely descriptive; you are not obliged to criticize negatively every provision you describe. Having said that, even if you do not agree with particular criticisms which you have read, you should still discuss them and say why you do not think they are valid; there is very little mileage in an essay that simply describes the law and says it is perfectly satisfactory.

Structure

However good your material, you will only gain really good marks if you structure it well. Making a plan for each answer will help in this, and you should also try to learn your material in a logical order – this will make it easier to remember as well. The exact construction of your essay will obviously depend on the question, but you should aim to have an introduction, then the main discussion, and a conclusion. Where a question is divided into two or more parts, you should reflect that structure in your answer.

A word about conclusions: it is not good enough just to repeat the question, turning it into a statement, for the conclusion. So, for example, if the question asks 'Is the law on rape satisfactory?', a conclusion which simply states that the law is or is not satisfactory will gain you very little credit. Your conclusion should summarize your argument, so for example, in the rape question you could say something like: 'The reforms of the law on male rape and the definition of penetration have substantially improved the law on rape, bringing it up to date and addressing some of the gaps in the previous law. However, problems with consent, an overly narrow *actus reus* and the procedural rules mean that it is still far from satisfactory. Further reforms are clearly necessary, but even these will not be entirely successful in protecting women from rape unless social and judicial attitudes change as well' (assuming of course that you have made these points in your essay).

▶ Problem questions

In problem questions, the exam paper will describe an imaginary situation, and then ask what the legal implications of the facts are – usually by asking you to advise one of the parties involved. For example, 'Jane hits Peter who falls back and knocks over Deirdre who hits her head on the pavement and dies. Advise Jane and Peter as to their criminal liability.'

Read the question thoroughly

The first priority is to read the question thoroughly, at least a couple of times. Never start writing until you have done this, as you may well get halfway through and discover that what is said at the end of the question makes half of what you have written irrelevant – or at worst, that the question raises issues you have no knowledge of at all.

Answer the question asked

This includes paying close attention to the words printed immediately after the situation is described. If a question asks you to advise one or other of the parties, make sure you advise the right one – the realization as you discuss the exam with your friends afterwards that you have advised the wrong party and thus rendered most of your answer irrelevant is not an experience you will enjoy. Examiners do sometimes show mercy when they feel a genuine mistake of this kind has been made in the heat of the moment, but you cannot rely on that, and you will certainly not get a good mark for work done in this way. Similarly, if a criminal law question states that you should consider liability for murder, for example, then that is what you should discuss, even if the problem seems to you to raise issues of other offences – part of the skill is sorting out what is and is not relevant. However, where there is no such limitation, you should discuss all the possible options.

Spot the issues

In answering a problem question in an examination you will often be short of time. One of the skills of doing well is spotting which issues are particularly relevant to the facts of the problem and spending most time on those, while skimming over more quickly those matters which are not really an issue on the facts, but which you clearly need to mention.

Apply the law to the facts

What a problem question requires you to do is to spot the issues raised by the situation, and to consider the law as it applies to those facts. It is not enough simply to describe the law without applying it to the facts. Do not start your answer by copying out all the facts, or keep referring to them at great length. This is a complete waste of time, and will gain you no marks.

Unlike essay questions, problem questions are not usually seeking a critical analysis of the law. If you have time, it may be worth making the point that a particular area of the law you are discussing is problematic, and briefly stating why, but if you are addressing all the issues raised in the problem you are unlikely to have much time for this. What the examiner is looking for is essentially an understanding of the law and an ability to apply it to the particular facts given.

Use authority

As always, you must back up your points with authority from case or statute law.

Structure

The introduction and conclusion are much less important for problem questions than for essay questions. Your introduction can be limited to pointing out the issues raised by the question, or, where you are asked to 'advise' a person mentioned in the problem, what outcome that person will be looking for. You can also say in what order you intend to deal with the issues. It is not always necessary to write a conclusion, but you may want to summarize what you have said, highlighting whether, as a result, you think a person is liable or not for a criminal offence.

There is no set order in which the main part of the answer must be discussed. Sometimes it will be appropriate to deal with the problem chronologically, in which case it will usually be a matter of looking at the question line by line; while in other cases it may be appropriate to group particular issues together. A clear way to do this with criminal law questions, for example, is to take the possible offences in descending order of seriousness, or in descending order of relevance to the facts, so that you take the most likely offence first. If you are asked about the liability of more than one person, it is best to consider each one in turn, unless they have done exactly the same things and have the same characteristics.

If the question is broken down into clear parts – (a), (b), (c) and so on – the answer must be broken down into the same parts; whether this is the case varies with different examining boards.

Whichever order you choose, try to deal with one issue at a time – if you choose to consider each person or each offence in turn, for example, finish what you have to say on each before going on to the next. Jumping backwards and forwards gives the impression that you have not thought about your answer. If you work through your material in a structured way, you are also less likely to leave anything out. In criminal law questions, for example, it is a good idea when considering each possible offence to ask first whether the defendant has committed the *actus reus*, then whether he or she had the *mens rea*, and finally whether any defences are available – you should certainly never start considering possible defences before you have explained what the offence is.

No right answer

It is particularly important with problem questions to realize that there is often no single right answer. In the Jane/Peter/Deirdre problem, for example, you are not required to prove beyond doubt that Jane or Peter would or would not be guilty of murder; you are simply required to spot the issues that the courts will take into account in deciding this, and the rules they will use to make that decision, giving authority for all those points.

In most cases, you will need to specify the possible implications of different issues. In the Jane/Peter/Deirdre problem, for example, you might say that the court first needs to discover whether causation can be proved, explaining the rules on causation as they apply to these facts. You then have two possible situations: where causation is proved, and where it is not. Simply discuss them in turn: first state that if causation is proved, the court will need to consider whether Jane had the *mens rea* for murder, and then go on to explain what this entails; then state that if causation is not proved, Jane may be liable for a non-fatal offence, and explain what is required for this liability.

Bibliography

Aldridge, P. (1997) 'The Sexual Offences (Conspiracy and Incitement) Act 1996' *Criminal Law Review* [1997] *Criminal Law Review* 30.

Ashworth, A. (1995) *Principles of Criminal Law*, Oxford: Clarendon Press.

Becker (1974) 'Criminal Attempts and the Law of Crimes', *Philosophy and Public Affairs*, Vol. 3 (Spring 1974).

Biggs, H. (1996) 'Euthanasia and Death with Dignity: Still Posed on the Fulcrum of Homicide' [1996] *Criminal Law Review* 878.

Box, S. (1983) *Power, Crime and Mystification*, London: Tavistock.

Brady, J. (1980) 'Punishing Attempts' 63 *The Monist* 246.

Brereton, D. (1997) 'How Different are Rape Trials? A Comparison of the Cross-Examination of Complainants in Rape and Assault Trials', (1997) 37 *Brit J. Criminol.* 242.

Brownmiller, S. (1976) *Against Our Will: Men, Women and Rape*, London: Penguin.

Buchanan, Alec and Virgo, Graham (1999) 'Duress and Mental Abnormality' [1999] *Criminal Law Review* 517.

Chambliss, W.J. (1984) *Criminal Law in Action*, New York/London: Wiley.

Clarkson, C.M.V. (1998) 'Complicity, Powell and Manslaughter' [1998] *Criminal Law Review* 556.

Clarkson, C. and Keating, M. (1994) *Criminal Law: Text and Materials*, London: Sweet & Maxwell.

Criminal Law Revision Committee, Fourteenth Report (1980) *Offences Against the Person*, London: HMSO.

Eekelaar, J. and Bell, J. (eds) (1987) *Oxford Essays in Jurisprudence*, Oxford: Clarendon.

Ellison, Louise (1998) 'Cross-Examination in Rape Trials' [1998] *Criminal Law Review* 605.

Feldman, D. (1993) *Civil Liberties and Human Rights in England and Wales*, Oxford: Oxford University Press.

Fletcher, George (1978) *Rethinking the Criminal Law*, London: Little Brown.

Grigg-Spall, I. and Ireland, P. (eds) (1992) *The Critical Lawyers Handbook*, London: Pluto Press.

Grubin, Don (1999) *Sex Offending Against Children: Understanding the Risk*, Home Office, Police Research Series, Paper 99.

Hall, 'Negligent Behaviour should be excluded from Penal Liability' 63 *Columbia Law Review* 632.

Hall, R.E. (1985) *Ask Any Woman, a London Enquiry into Rape and Sexual Assault*, Bristol: Falling Wall Press.

Home Office (1998) 'Reforming the Offences Against the Person Act 1861', London.

Jones, T., MacLean, B. and Young, J. (1986) *Islington Crime Survey: Crime, Victimisation and Policing in Inner-City London*, London: Gower.

Kalvin, H. and Zeisel, H. (1996) *The American Jury*, New York: Legal Classics Library.

Keating, H. (1996) 'The Law Commission Report on Involuntary Manslaughter (1) The Restoration of a Serious Crime' [1996] *Criminal Law Review* 535.

Kinsey, R., Lea, J. and Young, J. (1986) *Losing the Fight Against Crime*, Oxford: Basil Blackwell.

Langan, Patrick and Farrington, David (1998) *Crime and Justice in the United States and in England and Wales, 1981–96*, United States Department of Justice.

Law Commission (1996) 'Legislating the Criminal Code: Involuntary Manslaughter' (Law Com: no. 237), London: HMSO.

Lea, J. and Young, J. (1984) *What is to be Done About Law and Order?* London: Penguin Books.

Lees, Sue (1996) *Carnal Knowledge Rape on Trial*, London: Hamish Hamilton.

Levi, Michael and Handley, Jim (1998) *The Prevention of Plastic and Cheque Fraud Revisited*, Home Office Research Study No. 182, London: Home Office.

Matza, D. (1964) *Delinquency and Drift*, London: Wiley.

Norrie, Alan (1999) 'After Woollin' [1999] *Criminal Law Review* 532.

Parish, Stephen (1997) 'Self Defence: the Wrong Direction?' [1997] *Criminal Law Review* 201.

Parrot, A. and Bechhofer, L. (1991) *Acquaintance Rape*, New York: John Wiley & Sons.

Parsons, Simon (1998) 'Criminal Liability for the Act of Another: accessorial liability and the doctrine of joint enterprise,' *Journal of Criminal Law*, August 1998, p. 352.

Rock, Paul (1993) *The Social World of the English Crown Court*, Oxford: Clarendon Press.

Rumney, Philip N.S. and Morgan-Taylor, Martin P. (1998) 'Sentencing in cases of male rape', *Journal of Criminal Law* 263.

Smart, C. (1989) *Feminism and the Power of Law*, London: Routledge.

Smith, Sir J.C. (1996) '**R** *v* **Adomako**' [1996] *Criminal Law Review* 285, 515.

Smith, J.C. (1997) 'Obtaining Cheques by Deception or Theft' [1997] *Criminal Law Review* 396.

Smith, J.C. and Hogan, B. (1992) *Criminal Law*, London: Butterworths.

Temkin, J. (1987) *Rape and the Legal Process*, London: Sweet & Maxwell.

Victim Support (1996) *Women, Rape and the Criminal Justice System*, London: Victim Support.

Walker, Nigel (1999) 'The end of an old song'? *New Law Journal* 15 January 1999 64.

Warshaw, B. (1984) *The Trial Masters: a Handbook of Strategies and Techniques that Win Cases*, Englewood Cliffs N.J.: Prentice Hall.

Watson, Michael (1998) 'Cannabis and the Defence of Necessity', 148 *New Law Journal* 1260.

Watson, Michael (1999) 'A case of medical necessity', *New Law Journal* 4 June 1999 863.

Wells, Celia (1997) 'Stalking: The Criminal Law Response' [1997] *Criminal Law Review* 30.

Williams, G. (1961) *Criminal Law: The General Part*, London: Stevens.

Williams, G. (1983) *Textbook of Criminal Law*, London: Stevens.

Williams, G. (1992) 'Rape is Rape' 142 *New Law Journal* 11.

Wootton, B. (1981) *Crime and the Criminal Law: Reflections of a Magistrate and Social Scientist*, Oxford: Clarendon.

Index